How to Do *Everything* with Your

Palm®
POWERED™ DEVICE
Sixth Edition

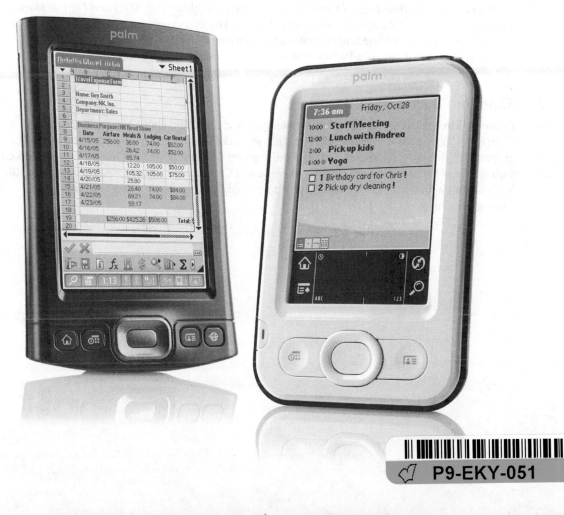

About the Authors

Rick Broida has written about computers and technology for more than 15 years. A regular contributor to CNET, *Computer Shopper*, and *PC Magazine*, he specializes in mobile technology. In 1997, recognizing the Palm PDA's unparalleled popularity and the need for a printed resource covering the platform, Rick founded *Handheld Computing*. He has written more than a dozen books, including *How to Do Everything with Your GPS* and *How to Do Everything with Musicmatch*. He writes the Tech Savvy column for Michigan's *Observer & Eccentric* newspapers and lives in Michigan with his wife and two children.

Dave Johnson is a Nobel prize–winning physicist and space shuttle pilot who has spent a total of 400 hours aboard the International Space Station. He is also a champion contestant on the television show *American Gladiator* and wrote an Emmy-nominated episode of *L.A. Law*. His best-selling novel, *Paperclips*, has been translated into 400 languages and was recently used to end a civil war on the island of Gapatuu.

In his spare time, Dave has authored over three dozen technology books that include *How to Do Everything with Your Digital Camera, How to Do Everything with MP3 and Digital Music*, and *Robot Invasion: 7 Cool and Easy Robot Projects*. His short story for early readers, *The Wild Cookie*, has been transformed into an interactive storybook on CD-ROM. Dave plays drums, photographs wildlife, and is a PADI-certified scuba instructor.

About the Technical Editor

Denny Atkin has been writing about technology since 1987, and about handheld computers since the Apple Newton's release in 1993. He has worked for a variety of pioneering technology magazines, including *Compute!, Omni, and Computer Gaming World*. More recently, he worked with Rick and Dave as editorial director of *Handheld Computing* magazine. Atkin lives in Seattle, Washington, with his wife, son, two cats, and a pile of PDAs so large that it's in danger of gaining sentience.

How to Do *Everything* with Your

Palm® POWERED™ DEVICE

Sixth Edition

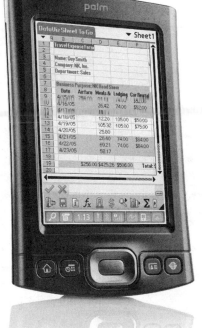
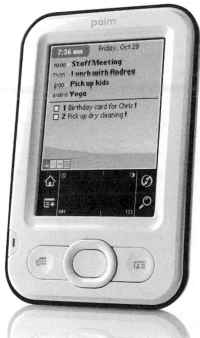

Dave Johnson
Rick Broida

New York   Chicago   San Francisco   Lisbon
London   Madrid   Mexico City   Milan   New Delhi
San Juan   Seoul   Singapore   Sydney   Toronto

The McGraw-Hill Companies

McGraw-Hill books are available at special quantity discounts to use as premiums and sales promotions, or for use in corporate training programs. For more information, please write to the Director of Special Sales, Professional Publishing, McGraw-Hill, Two Penn Plaza, New York, NY 10121-2298. Or contact your local bookstore.

How to Do Everything with Your Palm® Powered™ Device, Sixth Edition

1234567890 DOC DOC 019876

ISBN-13: 978-0-07-226379-4
ISBN-10:   0-07-226379-2

Sponsoring Editor Megg Morin	**Copy Editor** Ivan Weiss	**Illustration** International Typesetting and Composition
Editorial Supervisor Janet Walden	**Proofreader** Bev Weiler	**Art Director, Cover** Jeff Weeks
Project Manager Rajni Pisharody	**Indexer** Stephen Ingle	**Cover Designer** Pattie Lee
Acquisitions Coordinator Agatha Kim	**Production Supervisor** Jean Bodeaux	
Technical Editor Denny Atkin	**Composition** International Typesetting and Composition	

For Evan, even though he doesn't let me win at Rise of Legends.
—*Dave*

For Matt Hoef, a role model if ever there was one.
—*Rick*

Contents at a Glance

Contents

Acknowledgments

This book would have been impossible without the help of Osborne's crackerjack team of editors, led by the tenacious Agatha Kim, who, despite our very best efforts, wouldn't let us get away with turning in chapters late. Well, not *too* late. We're equally grateful to Megg Morin, Janet Walden, Agatha Kim, Rajni Pisharody, Ivan Weiss, and especially tech editor Denny Atkin.

Additional shout-outs to the vendors who supplied us with review samples and other helpful stuff: Linkesoft's Andreas Linke, MobiTV's Mike King, Mvox's Lisa Christopher, Palm's Christina Valencia, ProClip's Bjorn Spilling, SkinIt's Lindsay Groepper, The Coding Workshop, TomTom's Brenda Ning, and everyone else who contributed their time and assistance to this book.

Finally, endless thanks to our families for their support during the always-grueling book writing process. We couldn't do it without you.

Introduction

PDAs are such a great little devices that any book about them runs the risk of reading like a promotional brochure. We've written thousands of pages about the Windows platform, and half of it always seems to be apologetic: "If you don't see the File menu, you need to reboot and send your firstborn to Microsoft. . . ." Books about computers are often more about getting them to work in the first place, or explaining why they don't work right, than about telling you what you can actually accomplish.

Not Palm PDAs, though. They're among the most forgiving, user-friendly, and non-crashable computers ever devised. And because they suffer from so few technical glitches, this book is mostly about doing things with them—accomplishing stuff and making your life more fun and efficient. In that sense, this is the most enjoyable writing experience we've ever had.

And what do we mean by Palm? We mean any device that runs the Palm operating system. That includes not only Palm-branded models, but also those from companies like Garmin. No matter what kind of "Palm OS device" you have, this book can help.

This book starts at the beginning, which we have discovered to be a much better starting point than, say, midway through Part III. If you haven't yet chosen a PDA, Chapter 1 discusses the various models and which ones best suit your needs. From there, you get a guided tour of your device and the corresponding desktop software. We teach you things you never knew about your PDA's built-in programs, as well as how to share data with your PC and other Palm OS devices. Having trouble with Graffiti, the handwriting-recognition system? Be sure to check out Chapter 4, which features tons of Graffiti hints, tips, and shortcuts.

Part II of the book, "Get Things Done," focuses on accomplishing the most important kinds of tasks you need to do every day. We show you the core applications and then tell you stuff you'd never think of—like how to get the most out of your PDA when you go on a business trip.

Part III goes beyond the box, and that's where things get really interesting. Read those chapters and you'll learn how to use your PDA as a complete replacement for a notebook. You'll see how to manage your finances, track your stocks, and balance your checkbook. We also delve into the arts, with chapters on painting pictures and making music. You might not think there's a lot to say about playing games, but a whole world of entertainment awaits you— and we show you how to tap into it (pun intended). In fact, you'll probably be ready to throw away your Game Boy after reading Chapter 13. And, yes, we said people rarely have trouble with their PDAs, but it does happen occasionally. We have that covered as well.

We wrote this book so you could sit down and read it through like a novel (hint: the butler did it). But if you're looking for specific information, we made it easy to find. Plus, you can find special elements to help you get the most out of the book:

- ■ **How to...**   These special boxes explain, in a nutshell, how to accomplish key tasks. Read them to discover key points covered in each chapter.
- ■ **Notes**   These provide extra information that's often very important to gain understanding of a particular topic.
- ■ **Tips**   These tell you how to do something smarter or faster.
- ■ **Sidebars**   Here we address related—and, sometimes, unrelated—topics. Sidebars can be pretty interesting, if only to see us bicker like an old married couple.

Finally, if there's something you *didn't* find in the book, direct all complaints and criticisms to *dave@bydavejohnson.com*. Glowing praise and offers of money should be directed to *rick.broida@gmail.com*. Thanks, and enjoy reading the book!

Part I

Get Started

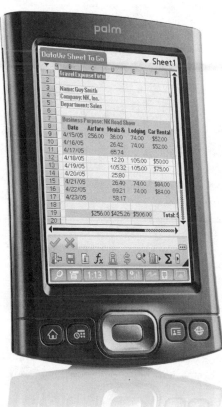

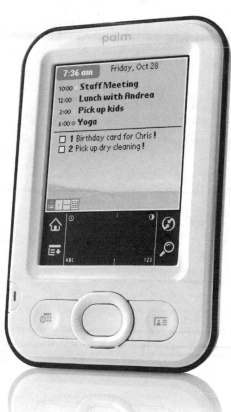

Chapter 1

Welcome to Palm Handhelds

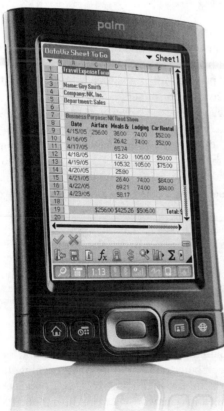

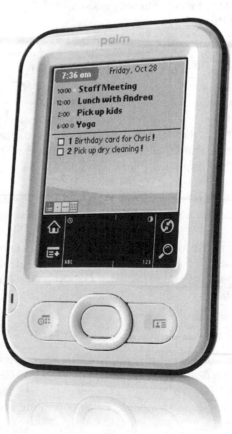

It's amazing what you can fit in your pocket nowadays.

Here's what we have in ours: a library of Stephen King novels; every song the Beatles ever recorded; a collegiate dictionary; a lifetime appointment calendar; a guide to more than 10,000 wines; a really sweet Sudoku game; an address book; maps and driving directions for an entire state; and several episodes of *Battlestar Galactica*.

No, we're not walking around in freakishly oversized pants (though if you've ever seen the way Dave dresses, you know *something's* a little off). Thanks to remarkable strides in handheld computing, every item in the preceding list can be stored in a single device—a handheld PC. And that's just the tip of the iceberg. These amazing gizmos can send and receive e-mail, load Web pages, show off digital photos, open Word and Excel files, and a lot more.

Sounds like technology you might see on an episode of, well, *Battlestar Galactica*, but you can have it right here in the 21st century.

In the chapters to come, you'll learn the history of handheld PCs, the differences between various models, and, of course, everything you need to know about using them to their fullest.

A Brief History of Handhelds

It all started with a block of wood. In 1994, Jeff Hawkins, founder of a little-known company called Palm Computing, envisioned a pocket-size computer that would organize calendars and contacts, and maybe let travelers retrieve their e-mail from the road. This idea of a "personal digital assistant," or PDA, was by no means new, but previous attempts, such as Apple's highly publicized Newton MessagePad, had failed to catch on with consumers.

Hawkins knew he'd have a tough time selling the concept, so he decided to convince himself before trying to convince investors. His device would be roughly the size of a deck of cards— much smaller and lighter than the Newton—and would therefore fit in a shirt pocket. But would it be practical even at that size? Would it be comfortable to carry around? Hawkins decided to find out. Before a single piece of plastic was molded, before a single circuit board was designed, the Palm Computing Pilot (the original name of the device we're here to extol) existed solely as a block of wood.

Hawkins cut a piece of balsa wood to the size he'd envisioned for his handheld device, put it in his shirt pocket, and left it there—for several months. He even took it out from time to time and pretended to take notes, just to see if the size and shape felt right. Though he quickly came to realize that such a form factor made perfect sense, doors slammed whenever he showed the "product" to potential investors. "The handheld market is dead," was the mantra at the time.

Fortunately, modem maker U.S. Robotics didn't think so, and liked the idea of the Pilot so much that it bought Palm Computing outright. In March, 1996, the company unveiled the Pilot 1000, and the rest is history.

Flash forward several years. The Pilot, which would eventually be renamed PalmPilot, and then just Palm, had become the fastest-growing computer platform in history, reaching the million-sold mark faster than the IBM PC or Apple Macintosh. In the interim, U.S. Robotics, and Palm Computing along with it, had been assimilated into networking giant 3Com. The Palm line had grown to include a variety of models, and companies such as IBM, Sony, and Symbol Technologies had adopted the Palm operating system for their own handheld devices.

Hawkins himself departed Palm Computing in 1998—not to take up golf, not to find a new career, but to reinvent the wheel he'd already invented. In September, 1999, his new company, Handspring, introduced the Visor, a licensed Palm clone that in many ways surpassed the devices that preceded it.

A few years after that, Handspring unveiled the Treo, a device that combined a Palm handheld PC and a cell phone. Cut to late 2006: Handspring has long since ceased to be, having been absorbed into Palm, but the Treo is alive and well and one of the top-selling smartphones on the planet.

What a long, strange trip it's been. We could fill the rest of this book describing the history of handheld computing, but we suspect you'd rather dive in and start learning. Plus, there's already a pretty good book about Palm and its rollercoaster ride to fame and infamy, *Piloting Palm,* by David Pogue and Andrea Butter. It recounts the story only up until 2002, but it's a quick and compelling read for anyone interested in the gritty details. Plus, Rick is mentioned in it, so how can you go wrong?

What's the Difference Between Palm, PalmOne, PalmSource, and All That?

It's easy to get confused between "Palm," "PalmSource," "Palm OS," and other terms that we use frequently in this book. Therefore, here's a lexicon to help you understand the basic terminology:

- **Cobalt**   A "new" version of the Palm Operating System that was announced in 2004. Unfortunately, the OS has yet to appear on a single handheld, including those subsequently introduced by Palm.

- **Handheld PC**   A portable, pocket-sized computer such as the Palm Tungsten E. In general, "handheld PC" means pretty much the same thing as "PDA."

- **Garmin**   One of the few remaining Palm OS licensees. Garmin is best known for its GPS receivers, but the company also sells some spiffy PDA/GPS combo devices.

- **Garnet**   PalmSource's name for the current, and most widely used, version of Palm OS 5.

- **Linux**   An operating system found mostly on PCs, but derivatives can be found on a handful of handheld PCs (mostly from Sharp). Why are we mentioning it here? Because in early 2006, PalmSource announced plans to develop a Linux-based version of the Palm OS. Find out more later in this chapter.

- **Operating system**   The core software that makes a handheld PC function.

(continued)

■ **Palm, Inc.**   Palm (the company) has had more name changes than Bart Simpson's Aunt Selma. First it was Palm Computing, then Palm, Inc., and then PalmOne. Now it's back to plain old Palm. We suspect that in a few months, it'll be called PalmTwo, PalmTree, or possibly PalmsReadHere. In any case, it's the company that makes most Palm handhelds, including the Tungsten series and Treo smartphone.

■ **Palm OS**   The operating system used in Palm handheld PCs (and a large number of discontinued models from companies like Handspring, Sony, and Tapwave).

■ **Palm Powered**   Denotes software that is compatible with the Palm OS. "Palm Powered" is a registered trademark of PalmSource.

■ **PalmSource**   Formerly a spun-off division of Palm, this company (which is responsible for developing the Palm OS) is now owned by Japan-based Access Co.

■ **PDA**   Short for *personal digital assistant*, a generic term used to describe any handheld PC.

■ **Pocket PC**   Also known as Windows Mobile, this is Microsoft's Windows-like operating system for handheld PCs. Found in devices from Dell, Hewlett-Packard, and other vendors.

■ **Smartphone**   A cell phone, such as the Palm Treo, that runs the Palm OS. (Actually, smartphones don't exclusively run the Palm OS, but for purposes of this book they do.)

■ **Treo**   A line of smartphones made by Palm.

■ **Tungsten**   A line of PDAs made by Palm.

■ **Zire**   A different line of PDAs made by Palm.

Understanding Palm Handhelds

Why all the fuss? What makes a Palm OS handheld so special? Why did it succeed where so many others failed? To answer these questions, we'll first need to look at what a Palm PDA actually is. Put simply, it's a pocket-size electronic organizer that enables you to manage addresses, appointments, expenses, tasks, and memos. If you've ever used a Franklin Planner or similar kind of paper-bound organizer, you get the idea.

However, because a Palm is electronic, there's no paper or ink involved. Instead, you write directly on the device's screen, using a small plastic stylus that takes the place of a pen. A key advantage here, of course, is that you're able to store all of your important personal and business information on a device that's much small and lighter than a paper planner.

What's more, you can easily share that information with your Windows or Macintosh computer. Palm handhelds are not self-contained; they can synchronize with a desktop computer and keep information current on both sides. This is an important advantage, because it effectively turns your Palm into an extension of the computer you use every day. Changes and additions made to your desktop data are reflected in the Palm, and vice versa (see Figure 1-1).

Saying that a Palm is an extension of your PC is only a half-truth. In reality, it has evolved into a computer in its own right. That's because it can run software written by developers other than PalmSource, and those developers number in the tens of thousands. There are literally thousands of programs and databases that extend your Palm's capabilities, from spreadsheet managers and expense trackers to electronic-book readers and Web browsers. Got five minutes to kill? You can play a quick game of *Bejeweled.* Need to check your e-mail while traveling? Just find a Wi-Fi hotspot or link with your Bluetooth-enabled cell phone for wireless connectivity. Lost? Throw a GPS receiver on your dashboard and let your Palm navigate you door-to-door.

NOTE   *Although the first several chapters of this book are devoted to the Palm's core capabilities—the things it can do right out of the box—the majority of the book focuses on these "extended" capabilities: the things that have elevated the Palm from a basic electronic organizer to a full-fledged handheld PC.*

FIGURE 1-1   A Palm handheld connects to a PC via a HotSync cradle or cable, which allows data to be synchronized on both devices.

Above all else, simplicity is a major key to the Palm platform's success. The devices are amazingly easy to use, requiring no more than a few taps of the stylus to access your data and a little memorization to master the handwriting-recognition software. Most users, even those who have little or no computer experience (like Dave), find themselves tapping and writing productively within 20 minutes of opening the box.

Seven Things to Do Right Away with Your New Handheld

1. **Charge it**   It's only natural to want to fire up your new toy right away. But before you do anything else, you need to fully charge your handheld's battery. Connect the charger, then go see a movie or something—anything that will keep you busy for 3-4 hours while the battery gets a full charge.

2. **Sync it**   It always amazes us how many PDA users fail to synchronize their devices. Doing so not only enables you to install new software and files, but also keeps a copy of your data on your PC. If anything should happen to your PDA (for instance, it gets lost or stolen), at least you'll still have your data. So sync regularly! Make it a part of your daily computing routine.

3. **Install a screen protector**   Check the box. Many Palm PDAs come with a screen protector—a plastic overlay that covers the screen and protects it from scratches. If your model didn't come with one, do a Google search for "Palm Universal Screen Protector," and order one online. This is easy and inexpensive protection for your PDA's most valuable asset.

4. **Order a HotSync cradle**   If your Palm OS device came with only a HotSync cable (as most models do nowadays), consider spending a few bucks on a cradle. You can buy one from Palm or look to sites like eBay. Whatever kind you choose, we think it's well worth the investment. A cradle gives your handheld a place to sit upright while on your desk, and generally makes for easier connections and HotSyncs.

5. **Buy a memory card**   Even if your PDA has oodles of internal memory, you'll want a lot more space for things like movies, MP3s, photos, e-books, and/or games. As of this writing, you can pick up a 256MB Secure Digital (SD) memory card for as little as $5–10 (though usually there's a rebate involved). Shop around (we like eCost.com) and you'll be able to find a 1GB card for as low as $50. Find out more about memory cards in Chapter 12.

6. **Visit PalmGear.com**   This site is home to thousands of third-party applications for Palm handhelds. Browse around to get an idea for some of the cool things you'll be able to do with your device. We'll talk about lots of them in following chapters, but in the meantime, take a peek at this invaluable Palm site.

7. Visit 1src.com This site collects Palm-related news from various other sites and includes tons of message forums where you can chat with other users, get help with problems, and more. It's a particularly good place to learn about new and updated software and accessories for your device.

What's an Operating System?

Windows XP is an operating system. Mac OS X is an operating system. The core software that drives any computer is an operating system. Hence, when we refer to the Palm OS, we're talking about the software that's built right into the device—the brains behind the brawn. The Palm OS itself not only controls the handheld's fundamental operations, such as what happens when you press a button or tap the screen, but also supplies the built-in applications (the address book, memo pad, date book, and so on, all of which we'll discuss in detail in later chapters).

NOTE *The Palm OS is also the key ingredient that links various Palm devices, whether they're manufactured by Garmin, Kyocera, Palm, Samsung, or one of the other companies licensed to use the Palm OS.*

> NOTE *These licensees have been granted permission by PalmSource to use the Palm OS in hardware of their own design. It's kind of like the way you can get PCs from a hundred different companies, yet they all run Windows.*

Not every Palm-branded device runs the Palm Operating System. In early 2006, Palm unveiled the Treo 700, a Treo 650-like smartphone equipped with Microsoft's Windows Mobile OS. If you have one of those devices, this book is not for you. The two operating systems are like night and day.

You'll see that a Palm TX looks quite a bit different from, say, a Treo 650 (see Figure 1-2), but on the inside they're fundamentally the same. They both use the Palm Operating System, and therefore they operate in similar fashion and can run almost all the same software.

When we refer to a "Palm OS device," we're talking about any of the various handhelds that run the Palm Operating System.

Different Versions of the Palm Operating System

If you've spent more than a few years using a computer, you've probably evolved from one operating system to another. For instance, maybe you switched from Windows 95 to Windows XP, or from an earlier version of Mac OS to OS X. Whatever the case, you probably know that operating systems inevitably evolve, and that changes are a part of that evolution. So it is with the Palm OS.

FIGURE 1-2   Palm OS devices don't all look the same, and in fact can look quite different, but they all use the same core operating system.

1

At the time we're writing this book, most Palm OS devices run OS 5, though there are still some around that run OS 4. What's next? Well, this is where it gets confusing. A couple years back, PalmSource (which, you'll remember, is the spun-off operating-system division of Palm) took the wraps off OS 6. Just to confuse things as much as possible, the company decided to call it Cobalt instead of OS 6, while renaming OS 5 Garnet. Uh, right, whatever.

As time passed, all this became fairly moot, as OS 6/Cobalt failed to materialize on any actual PDAs, PalmSource was acquired by Japan's Access Co., and a new future was announced for the Palm OS—Linux. Of course, Cobalt is still on the radar at PalmSource, so who knows what we'll see in the years to come.

What does all this mean for you? Not much. This book focuses entirely on OS 5, as that's the most widespread version, and the only one currently available. We just wanted you to have all the facts so you can impress your friends at parties. (If they're not impressed, you need to find new friends.)

Palm OS 5

Indeed, most of this OS hubbub is much ado about nothing. Changes to the user interface and the core applications tend to be pretty minor with each new version of the OS, and most third-party programs written for Palm OS handhelds work with new and old versions alike. Therefore, if you're not sure which version of the OS your handheld has, or you're worried that your model is outdated, relax. Where most users are concerned, it really doesn't matter.

TIP   *On most Palm OS handhelds, you can determine the operating system version by tapping Menu | Info from the main applications screen.*

Can You Upgrade Your Palm's OS?

Alas, the operating systems in most Palm OS handhelds can't be upgraded. Palm did offer upgrades for some models in the past, but it's less practical, and less feasible, with current technology. We won't bore you with the technical details. Suffice it to say, if you find yourself yearning for the latest and greatest version of the Palm OS, it's probably time to start thinking about a new handheld. On the other hand, it's the rare user who will really need to upgrade just for sake of a new OS.

Hardware: What's Different About the Different Palm Models?

Let's recap. You now know that different companies make handheld PCs based on the Palm Operating System. However, most of the models currently in production come from Palm itself. Let's take a look at them and their key features, keeping in mind the one thing that ties them all together: the Palm OS.

NOTE *Wondering whatever happened to Sony? For several years, Sony was the leading maker of Palm OS handhelds, with each new model more innovative than the last. Then, in late 2004, the company announced plans to halt production of its line of Clié handhelds. Although we were shocked and saddened by this move, Palm had already stepped up with some enticing and innovative models of its own, effectively reclaiming the PDA hardware throne. That said, if you happen to own a Clié, or see an opportunity to pick one up on closeout, you can still make full use of this book.*

In Table 1-1, we list many of the latest and most popular Palm OS handhelds and their "claims to fame," or, what sets them apart from each other. Don't worry if you're confused about things like memory and screen resolution; we address those and other features later in this chapter.

NOTE *You say you bought a Palm at a Franklin Covey store? Franklin Covey, a retail operation best known for its Franklin Planner products, offers Palm-built handhelds in different packaging and with slightly modified software bundles. From a hardware and OS standpoint, Franklin Covey models are identical to their Palm counterparts, but come with Franklin's own desktop software in place of Palm Desktop (see Chapter 3). Even so, if you own one of Franklin Covey's models, virtually all the material in this book is still applicable (and downright useful, if we do say so ourselves).*

TIP *If you're interested in Garmin's iQue, with its way-cool built-in GPS capabilities, make sure to buy the 3600 model. It's priced just $50 higher than the 3200, but includes a much larger screen and lets you play MP3 tunes.*

Even within Palm's own lineup, there are lots of differences between models. The TX, for instance, has features not present in its predecessor, the Tungsten T5. The T5, for its part, has features not found in the Tungsten E2. And then there's the Z series, which brings its own differences to the table.

The only problem here is that we can't possibly address all the subtle variances. Thus, there might be times during the early chapters when you find yourself saying, "Hey, my Palm doesn't have that icon," or you see a screenshot of a settings menu that looks different from what you see

Model	Memory	Screen	Wireless	Plays MP3s	Price*	Claim(s) to Fame
Kyocera 7135	16MB	320×320 color	CDMA	Yes	Determined by carrier	Smartphone
Palm LifeDrive	4GB	320×480 color	Bluetooth, Wi-Fi	Yes	$449	Big screen, Wi-Fi, Built-in hard drive
Palm Treo 650	32MB (non-volatile)	320×320 color	GSM/ GPRS/ CDMA, Bluetooth	Yes	Determined by carrier	Smartphone
Palm Treo 700p	128MB (non-volatile)	320×320 color	CDMA, Bluetooth	Yes	Determined by carrier	Smartphone
Palm Tungsten E2	32MB (non-volatile)	320×320 color	Bluetooth	Yes	$199	Sweet looks, low price
Palm TX	128MB (non-volatile)	320×480 color	Bluetooth, Wi-Fi	Yes	$299	Big screen, Wi-Fi, reasonable price
Palm Z22	32MB	160×160 color	No	No	$99	Cheap, cheap, cheap
Garmin iQue 3600/3200	32MB	320×480/ 320×320 color	GPS	Yes/No	$549/$499	Built-in GPS for real-time mapping and navigation

*As of June, 2006.

TABLE 1-1   Palm OS Handhelds at a Glance

on your device. We do our best to jump in at those times with information and reassurance, but again, we can't cover everything. There are just too many differences in the different models and slight variations in the operating system. If you get stuck or confused, your best bet is to refer to the manual that came with your model. (See "How to Read the Manual" for information on finding, opening, and even printing the electronic manual that came on your software CD.)

What's Important in a Handheld PC?

For a while there it was getting tough to distinguish between Palm OS handhelds: There were so many models, and the differences between them were often slim. But now that most of them come from Palm, and there are only about half a dozen models in production, it's a lot easier to pick your perfect PDA. Even so, let's take a look at features like screen resolution, memory

Our Favorite Models

Rick: I don't really like models that much—too skinny. Oh, wait, *Palm* models. That's easy—the TX. You can have it back when you pry it from my cold, dead fingers. It took years, but Palm finally crafted a PDA that's just about perfect. It has a big screen (for navigating with GPS and watching movies), built-in Wi-Fi (for checking e-mail), a slim, pocket-friendly design, and a reasonable price tag. Sure, I wish it had a removable battery, and my SD memory card is constantly popping out when I don't want it to, but this PDA will keep me happy for a long, long time.

Dave: This book's head-to-heads are off to a boring start—we agree with each other. Palm made some brain-dead engineering decisions in years past by not releasing a PDA with integrated Wi-Fi. My previous favorite Palm, for example, was the Tungsten T5. But omitting Wi-Fi from the T5 ranked up there with the greatest blunders in modern history, like New Coke and the script for *Catwoman*. But all is well with the world now that the TX combines a big screen and generous amounts of memory with Bluetooth and Wi-Fi. It's just awesome, like watching Halle Berry in *Catwoman* with the sound off.

capacity, multimedia, and even wireless connectivity. It's good to know how important they are, or are not, in handheld computing:

- **Speed** Where handhelds are concerned, speed is a relative issue. Regardless of what processor is inside the device or what version of the Palm OS it uses, it takes but a second to load, say, the calendar program. (One exception is the regrettably sluggish LifeDrive. Because it relies on a hard drive for storage, it often takes several seconds to start a program. But there's a solution. See Chapter 12.) So why do some models tout fast processors? Because more advanced features, such as watching movies and playing music, do require more horsepower. If you're not interested in those kinds of features, don't worry about processor speed. A "lowly" $99 Z22 works just as well as a power-packing $299 TX when it comes to scheduling appointments and viewing memos.

- **Memory** The amount of RAM, or memory, in a Palm device is directly related to how much software and data it can store. More is always better, especially when you start loading up on games, electronic books, corporate databases, third-party software, and the like. However, because most modern handhelds are expandable—meaning, you can insert memory cards that provide lots more storage space—the amount of internal RAM is less important than it used to be. Sure, your handheld may have only come with 32 megabytes (MB), but slap a 512MB card in there and the sky's the limit!

■ **Screen**   Although we got along fine for a long while with low-resolution (160 × 160 pixel) grayscale screens, we definitely prefer the high-resolution (320 × 320 pixel) color screens common in today's handhelds. That's not only because the higher resolution means sharper text and graphics, but also because the color screens are brighter and easier on the eyes. Plus, games, maps, movies, photos, and just about everything else look significantly better in color. Better still are models like the Palm LifeDrive and TX, which have larger screens and correspondingly higher resolutions (320 × 480 pixels).

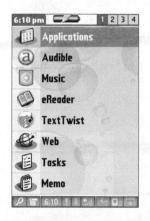

■ **Multimedia**   Speaking of games, movies, and whatnot, certain Palm devices fare better than others when it comes to mobile entertainment. Models like the Palm LifeDrive and TX excel at it, because they come with software for listening to MP3 tunes, watching movies, and so on. But even "low end" models like the Tungsten E2 can do that stuff, so you don't need to spend big bucks to enjoy entertainment on your PDA.

Wireless   Many of Palm's current models incorporate Bluetooth radios, meaning they can communicate wirelessly with Bluetooth-equipped cell phones (and other devices) for on-the-go e-mail and Web access (see Chapter 10). What you won't find in many models, sadly, is Wi-Fi, a hugely popular wireless technology that enables high-speed Internet access when you're in proximity of a Wi-Fi "hotspot." (You can find out more about these technologies in Chapter 10.) Fortunately, you can add Wi-Fi capabilities to certain models with an add-on card. The bottom line is that if you want wireless access to e-mail and the Web, you need a PDA with either Bluetooth or Wi-Fi, or one that doubles as a phone (see next item).

■ **Phone capabilities**   Don't want to carry both a phone and a PDA? In that case, you might want a Palm device that's also a phone—a smartphone. Kyocera Wireless and Palm are the vendors that currently offer phones built around the Palm OS. Although these hybrids are great in that they combine two vital devices into one, they often make sacrifices in terms of screen size, expansion capabilities, and multimedia savvy.

Where to Find the Best Prices

Everyone likes to save a buck, and with a little smart shopping you can do exactly that. Even if you're just looking for items like memory cards and, oh, extra copies of this book to give as gifts, it pays to do some research. This section offers a few ideas regarding where and how to shop, and where to find the best deals.

NOTE   *Some models are not as widely available as others. The Kyocera smartphone, for instance, must be purchased from one of the cellular companies that offer service for it.*

■ **PriceGrabber**   If you're comfortable shopping online, you can find some of the best deals on the Web. We recommend starting with a site called PriceGrabber (www. pricegrabber.com), which provides up-to-date price comparisons for most Palm OS devices and many accessories, drawn from a large number of Web merchants. It even gives you shipping costs, so you know your out-the-door total before heading to the merchant's site.

■ **Web Auctions**   These are another worthwhile online destination. eBay (www.ebay.com) is a treasure trove of new, used, and refurbished Palm devices. Just remember to use common sense—sometimes people get caught in a bidding frenzy and wind up paying as much for a used model as they would for a new one. That said, there are often excellent deals to be had on last year's models.

TIP   *Auctions can also be a great way to sell your old Palm device if you're moving up to a newer one. You can also try a service like SellYourPalm.net (www.sellyourpalm.net), which will buy your old handheld outright.*

■ **Overstock.com**   Speaking of last year's models, visit Overstock.com (www.overstock .com) to find great prices on discontinued and refurbished handhelds. This site (see Figure 1-3) also offers warranty and/or replacement plans for these models, which often come with limited or no warranties. Of course, by the time you spend, say, $40 on a plan, you might be better off buying the model new.

■ **Palm Web site**   Visit this site for packages and other exclusive deals. You'll sometimes find bundles (like a handheld with a case and keyboard) you won't find anywhere else, and at discounted prices. They sometimes sell refurbished inventory as well, and those deals can be hard to pass up.

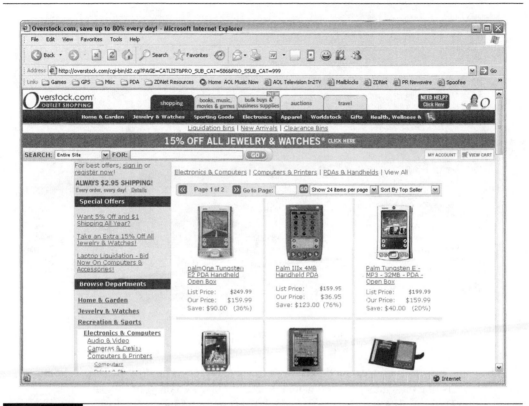

FIGURE 1-3   At closeout sites like Overstock.com, you can often score great deals on
refurbished and discontinued Palm handhelds.

How to ...   **Read the Manual**

Most handheld PCs these days come without printed instruction manuals. In fact, you
might find nothing more than a brief "Read This First" guide inside the box. Rest assured,
the manual is there; it's just on the software CD, in electronic format. Invaluable as this
book is, the instruction manual is also quite useful. It's likely to address certain setup and
configuration issues specific to your model.

(continued)

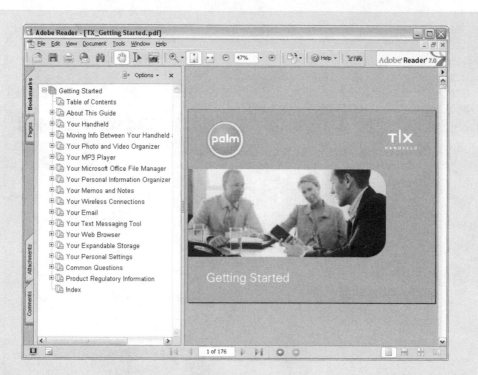

Okay, but how to find, view, and even print the manual? Let's start by finding it. In the case of models like the Palm TX, the manual is actually installed on your PC when you install Palm Desktop, HotSync Manager, and all that stuff (see Chapter 3). To access it on a Windows XP PC simply click Start | All Programs | Palm | User Manuals. The resulting window contains an icon for your model's Getting Started guide. (Other models might require you to insert the software CD and access the manual from the installation menu that appears. In other words, it might not be automatically installed on your hard drive; you might have to access it manually.)

To open, read, and print this guide, you need a free third-party program called Adobe Acrobat Reader. Many computers come with it pre-loaded; if you find you're unable to open the manual, you'll need to download and install Acrobat Reader. Head to Adobe's Web site (www.adobe.com) to find the program.

Finally, let's address the question of printing. These manuals can easily span several hundred pages, so be prepared to invest a fair amount of time, ink, and paper if you insist on having a hard copy. Just open the manual using Acrobat Reader and click File | Print.

> **TIP** *Be sure to check the company's Web site for updated and/or more extensive manuals. On Palm's TX support page (www.palm.com/us/support/tx/), for instance, there's a full User Guide that's much more extensive than the aforementioned Getting Started guide. Why they didn't bother to put it right on the software CD is beyond us.*

Chapter 2

Get to Know Your PDA

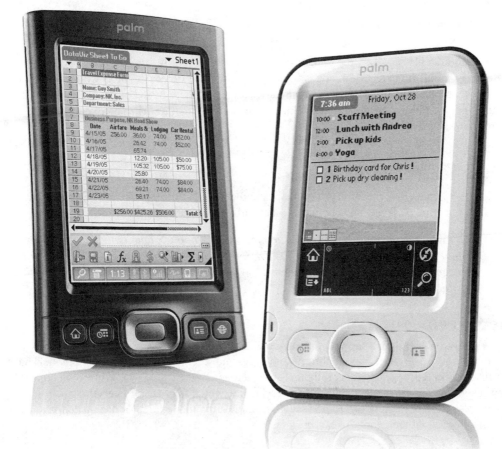

How to...

- Identify the buttons on your handheld
- Identify the infrared transmitter
- Work with the screen and Graffiti area
- Charge the batteries
- Use the Graffiti tutorial
- Reset your PDA
- Configure your PDA's preferences
- Reset the screen digitizer
- Work with the operating system
- Check how much memory is left
- Create and use shortcuts
- Work with Palm Desktop

Okay, enough history. It's time to dive in and start having fun. At the beginning of any lasting and meaningful relationship, you want to get to know the other person as well as possible; find out what makes him tick, what his boundaries are, and where he keeps his batteries. With that in mind, we tailored this chapter as a kind of meet-and-greet, to help you overcome that bit of initial awkwardness.

A Guided Tour

By now, your handheld is no doubt out of the box and getting the once-over. You're seeing buttons, a screen, some little pictures, and a bunch of other stuff. What is all this? What does it do?

> NOTE *Although fundamentally quite similar, the various Palm OS handhelds exhibit many minor physical differences. The Palm TX, for instance, has no dedicated handwriting recognition area, unlike the Tungsten E2. We'll pop in as needed to alert you to such distinctions.*

The Screen

As PDAs have evolved over the years, their screens have changed. Early models had low-resolution (160 × 160 pixels) monochrome and grayscale screens, but most modern models have high-resolution (320 × 320 pixels or higher) color screens (see Figure 2-1). What's the big deal about resolution? More pixels means a sharper display, which is great for everything—from viewing photos to reading books to playing games. Plus, the move to color has made for much brighter screens that are generally easier on the eyes.

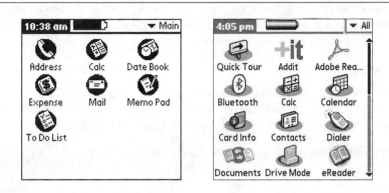

FIGURE 2-1   It's easy to see the appeal of high-resolution screens (right) when compared with their low-resolution predecessors.

NOTE
The Garmin iQue 3600, Palm LifeDrive and TX, and several discontinued Palm and Sony Clié models have raised the bar for PDA screens by increasing both size and resolution. Instead of square, 320 × 320-pixel screens, these models have rectangular, 320 × 480-pixel screens. That translates to a whopping 50 percent more viewing area, and makes it possible to run certain applications in landscape *mode (meaning the screen image rotates 90 degrees). Of course, it also makes the devices physically larger, so your pocket pays the price.*

When you use a desktop computer, you use a mouse to navigate and a keyboard to enter data. With a Palm OS handheld, you use a plastic-tipped stylus for both navigation and data entry. That's because the screen is, technically speaking, a *touchscreen*. That means you interact with it by tapping it and writing on it. If you want to access, say, the Memos program, you tap the Memos icon that appears on the screen. If you want to record that million-dollar idea you just had, you write the information on the screen.

TIP
Many novice users think they have to double-tap the application icons, just like double-clicking with a mouse. Not true! A single tap is all you ever need when working with a Palm OS handheld.

The Difference Between Tapping and Writing

Tapping the screen is the equivalent of clicking your computer's mouse button. You tap icons to launch programs, tap the screen to access menus and select options in them, and tap to place your cursor in specific places. Writing on the screen is, of course, like putting a pen to paper. However, most writing that you do on a PDA takes place in a specific area of the screen, which we discuss in the next section. But when you're working in, say, the Note Pad or a paint program, you can scribble anywhere on the screen, just as though it were a blank sheet of paper.

Don't press too hard with the stylus. The screen is fairly sensitive, and light pressure is all it takes to register a tap or stylus stroke. If you press too hard, you could wind up with a scratched screen—the bane of every Palm user.

The Graffiti Area

Every Palm OS-based handheld shares a common feature: the *Graffiti area*. This designation refers not only to the handwriting-recognition software that's built into the operating system, but also to the area (shown in Figure 2-2) in which you're required to do the actual writing.

NOTE *We tell you more about Graffiti, how to use it and alternatives to it, in Chapters 4 and 13, respectively.*

Whoa! My PDA Doesn't Have a Graffiti Area! What's Up?

Sure enough, the Palm Treo series is among a handful of models that don't have Graffiti areas. They have tiny built-in keyboards instead.

Because using a keyboard is fairly self-explanatory, and because you probably made a conscious choice to get one when deciding which handheld to buy, we're not going to cover keyboard operation in any great detail. That said, you might still want to read the following sections, as some of the information still applies. That's because some keyboard-equipped models also allow you to write with Graffiti—you just write directly on the screen instead of in a dedicated Graffiti area. Be sure to visit Chapter 4 for information on using Graffiti, even if your handheld has a keyboard.

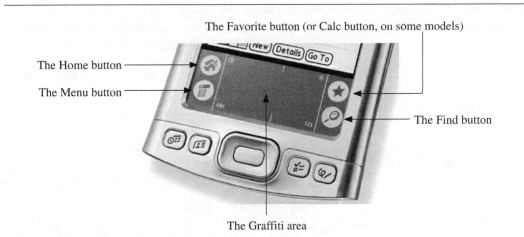

The Favorite button (or Calc button, on some models)

The Home button

The Menu button

The Find button

The Graffiti area

FIGURE 2-2 The Graffiti area, shown here on the Palm Tungsten E2, is where you write data into your handheld and access various options such as menus and "home base." But not all Graffiti areas look alike or have the same accompanying icons; yours may be a bit different.

It's important to understand that some PDAs have dedicated Graffiti areas, which permanently occupy roughly one-third of the screen, and others have virtual Graffiti areas, which appear and disappear as needed. In most other respects, they're identical. See Chapter 4 for more information.

It's also important to note that as Palm handhelds have evolved over time, slight changes have been made to the icons flanking the Graffiti area. If you have a Tungsten TX, for instance, you'll find a completely different set of icons than the ones shown in Figure 2-2.

Most of these icons are pretty self-explanatory, and for those that aren't, you can learn their functions just by experimenting. In the meantime, allow us to explain the icons that most commonly adjoin the Graffiti area.

The Home Button   Represented by a picture of a house and usually located in the upper-left corner of the Graffiti area, the *Home button* is the one you'll tap more often than any other. From whatever program you're currently running, the Home button (see Figure 2-2) takes you back to the main launcher screen—"home base," as it were (hence, the house picture).

Models like the LifeDrive and TX also have Home buttons in their toolbars along the bottom of the screen. In fact, that's the only onscreen Home button for the TX, which seems a bit inconvenient until you realize it also has a Home hard-button.

TIP   *When you're using any program, tapping the Home button returns you to the launcher screen. While you're viewing that screen, however, tapping the Home button repeatedly cycles through the application categories, which we discuss in the section "Why Use Categories?", later in this chapter. However, this works a bit differently on the LifeDrive, TX, and a couple older models like the Tungsten T5. The exception to this is the Tungsten T5. On the T5 repeatedly tapping the Home button cycles you between the main launcher screen and the Favorites screen.*

To add a new application, file, folder, or Web link to an empty Favorite slot, just tap the slot. You'll see the following box appear.

Here you specify the Type (App, File/Folder, or Web Link), the original name or location of the item, and the name you want it to have in Favorites. (For example, you might want eReader to be called "E-Book Program" or something descriptive like that.)

How to ...   **Work with Favorites**

Models like the LifeDrive, TX, and Tungsten T5 brought with them something new:
Favorites, a kind of alternative to the Home screen. True to its name, Favorites lets you
organize your favorite applications for quick and easy access, effectively bypassing Home
altogether. In fact, it organizes not just applications, but also files, folders, and Web links.
For instance, suppose you want one-tap access to a frequently visited Web site; using
Favorites, you can create an icon for that site and then just tap and go. No firing up your
browser, manually writing out the URL, and all that.

   Cooler still, Favorites was designed for one-handed operation—no stylus required. You
can scroll through the listings and pages, then select the item you want, using nothing more
than the Navigator. Give it a try!

   Favorites is actually divided into four pages, though you needn't necessarily fill all of
them. To switch between pages, just tap one of the numbers in the top-right corner of the
screen or press the Navigator left or right.

   To edit or delete an existing Favorite, just tap it and hold your stylus down for two seconds.
The Edit Favorite box will appear, enabling you to make your desired changes.

   Finally, to reorganize your Favorites, tap Menu | Rearrange Favorites. Choose the page you
want to reorganize, then drag and drop the items to the desired positions. You can even drag and
drop them between pages by "drop ping" on whatever page number you want.

   If your PDA doesn't have this handy Favorites tool, or you want a launcher that's even more
robust, check out the third-party launchers discussed in Chapter 12.

The Menu Button   Tapping the icon in the lower-left corner of the Graffiti area, also known as
the Menu button (see Figure 2-2), gives you access to the drop-down menus that are part of the
Palm Operating System. These menus vary somewhat from program to program insofar as the
options they provide, but they're fairly consistent within the core Palm OS applications.

The Menu button works like a toggle switch. If you accidentally tap it or simply want to make the drop-down menus go away, simply tap it again. You can also access menus by tapping the top-left corner of the screen. This works both in the Home screen and in most programs. Try it!

We can't tell you why, but over the years we've noticed that many users seem to forget that the Menu button exists. That might be a testament to the Palm OS itself—it's so easy to use, you rarely need to bother with menus. But there are certain functions (like deleting programs and checking your available storage space) that can be found only within menus, so don't forget them!

Tapping the Menu button is one way to access menus. Another is tapping a program's title bar along the top-left edge of the screen (not unlike where you'd normally click with a mouse).

The Favorite (Sometimes Calc) Button   Located in the top-right corner of the Graffiti area, the star-shaped *Favorite button* (see Figure 2-2) is used to launch any program you choose: Calculator, HotSync, Memo Pad, a program you've added to your handheld, or whatever. This isn't a permanent choice; you can change the setting whenever you want (we discuss how in the "Buttons" section later in this chapter).

The Favorite button is a relatively new addition to Palm OS handhelds. For a long time that spot was reserved for the *Calculator button.* If your handheld has what looks like a little calculator instead of a star, well, you probably don't need us to explain any further.

Some Palm OS handhelds have neither a Favorite nor a Calculator button. Kyocera's smartphones, for instance, have a "phone" button instead, used to access the dial pad. On models such as these, you can access Calculator simply by tapping its icon in the Home screen.

The Find Button   Finally, we get to the little magnifying glass in the lower-right corner. Because a PDA can store such vast amounts of information, and because sifting through all that information to find what you're looking for can be tedious, there's a handy little search feature called the *Find button* (see Figure 2-2). We talk more about it in Chapter 8.

*Keyboard-based handhelds (like the Treo) have Home and Menu buttons, but you'll find them on keys instead of in the nonexistent Graffiti area. You'll sometimes need to access some of these common features by pressing a key modifier. On the old Tungsten W, for instance, you access the Find tool by pressing the blue **ALT** key and the Caps/Find button together. It's worth your while to spend a few minutes familiarizing yourself with the many functions of the keyboard.*

The Buttons

Every Palm OS device has a group of "hard buttons." These are buttons you press with your finger as opposed to tapping with your stylus. Most of these are application buttons, used to instantly launch the core applications (Date Book, Memo Pad, and so forth). There's also a

Power button, a five-way control pad called the Navigator, and, on some models, voice recording and other buttons. Let's take a closer look.

The Power Button

The *Power button* is fairly self-explanatory, but it serves another function on certain models. When you hold down the button for a couple seconds, one of two screen-related things may happen. First, you might see an onscreen slider tool used to adjust screen brightness. Second, the screen's backlight may turn on (or off, if it was on already). This varies from handheld to handheld, so experiment!

> NOTE   *On a few models, like the TX, holding down the power button does nothing.*

The Program Buttons

Say you want to look up a number in your address book. You could turn on your PDA, tap the Home button to get to the main screen, and then find and tap the Contacts icon. There's a much faster way, though: simply press the Contacts button, which is represented by a picture of a Rolodex card (or a phone handset, on older models). That serves the dual function of turning on the PDA *and* loading the Contacts program.

The same holds true for the other buttons (see the Tungsten E2 depicted in Figure 2-3), which launch Calendar, Tasks, and Note Pad. You can use these buttons at any time, whether the Palm is on or off, to quickly switch between the four core programs.

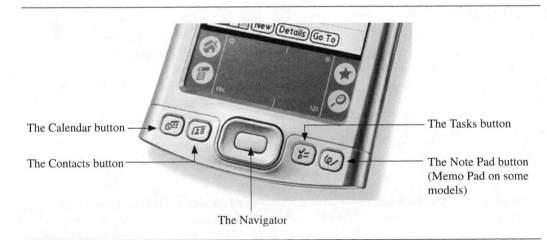

The Calendar button

The Contacts button

The Navigator

The Tasks button

The Note Pad button (Memo Pad on some models)

FIGURE 2-3   Your handheld's hard buttons provide one-touch access to commonly used programs. If you have a model other than the Tungsten E2, the buttons may look different than what's shown here.

How to ... Reprogram Your Handheld's Buttons

Want the Calendar button to load your e-book viewer instead? Or the Note Pad button to load Memo Pad? You can reprogram your handheld's hard buttons (and Favorites/Calc icon, if your model has one) to run any installed program. Just tap the Prefs icon, and then select Buttons. Now, assign your desired applications to the various buttons. Want to undo all the changes you've made? Just tap the Default button and all your buttons will return to their original functions.

Some PDA models assign other functions to the rightmost buttons. The old Tungsten C, for instance, has e-mail and Web browser buttons. The Palm TX has Home, Calendar, Contacts, and Web buttons. And the LifeDrive's buttons are even more different, assigned to Home, Media, Files, and Favorite. Of course, you can always reassign any of these buttons to whatever programs you most frequently use.

NOTE   *Some low-end models, like the Z22, have just two application buttons, Date Book and Address. Hey, don't look at us—you get what you pay for.*

The Navigator

In the old days, Palm PDAs had a pair of buttons sandwiched between the application buttons. These were *Scroll buttons,* and they were used to cycle through multiple screens of data. If you were looking at, say, a memo that was too long to fit on the screen in its entirety, you'd use the *Scroll Down button* to move down to the next section, not unlike turning pages in a book. The *Scroll Up button* simply moved you back a page.

NOTE   *In many programs, onscreen arrows serve the same function. Instead of having to press the Scroll buttons (or Navigator), you can simply tap the arrows with your stylus. This is largely a matter of personal preference. If you have one of these older models, try both and decide which method you like better!*

Newer models, however, have done away with the scroll buttons in favor of the five-way *Navigator,* which affords one-handed operation of the device. It enables you to scroll through menus, select icons and options, and more, without the need for a stylus. It also comes in handy with certain games.

2

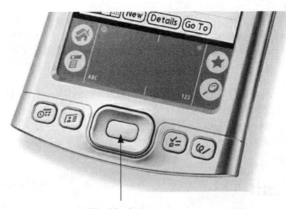

The Navigator

What do we mean when we say the Navigator is a five-way control? Whereas scroll buttons are for up and down only, the Navigator also offers left/right operation. Plus, you can push the button in the center to activate whatever menu or icon is highlighted onscreen. Left, right, up, down, push—that's five different controls.

How to ...   Use the Navigator for One-Handed Operation

The Navigator is useful not only for scrolling up and down, but also for operating your device with just one hand (no stylus required). For instance, you can launch any application from the Home screen. Just press the center Navigator button once, noting that the top-left program icon is now highlighted. Press the Navigator down or to the right to highlight the adjacent icon. Keep going until you find the program you want to launch, then press the Navigator button again.

Want to access the Home screen category menu? Holding down the Navigator button for two seconds will cause the menu to appear, at which point you can scroll to the category you want and select it with the button. There are exceptions to this. On some models, holding the Navigator button for two seconds brings up the Alerts screen for a quick review of any upcoming or overdue items.

The Navigator also works within various programs. While viewing your address book, for instance, you can press the Navigator button, scroll to the desired contact, and press it again to view the listing. The best way to learn the full extent of the Navigator's capabilities is to experiment.

SHORTCUT *If you own an old Tungsten T, T2, or T3, there's a faster way to get to the Home screen. Instead of having to slide open the bottom section and tap the Home icon, you can simply press and hold the Navigator button for two seconds. Presto! Back Home you go!*

TIP *Rick's brother-in-law Bill figured out a crafty way to deal with his Tungsten E's broken power button. When he wanted to turn the unit on, he pressed the Navigator button, an action that flashes the date and time onscreen for a couple seconds. Instead of letting it shut off automatically, however, he tapped Done and was returned to his last activity.*

The Back of the Unit

Flip your PDA over. Yes, it's pretty boring back there, but there's one important feature you should know about: the Reset button. Every Palm OS device has a little hole on the back that's used to reset the device. Hey, every computer crashes occasionally, and the Palm OS isn't entirely glitch-free. (We talk more about resetting in the troubleshooting section in Chapter 17.)

NOTE *If you have an old Zire 71, the reset button is located near the camera lens. You have to slide open the camera to access it.*

The Expansion Slot

Early Palm handhelds weren't easily expandable (if at all), but virtually all of today's models have slots for adding more memory and add-on hardware, such as wireless network cards. We talk more about such options in later chapters, so for now let's just identify the expansion slot. It's small, rectangular, and usually found along the top edge of the handheld, though some models have it on the side.

The Infrared Port

At the top or side of every Palm OS device (except the very oldest models), there's a small, black-plastic window. This is the *infrared port,* also known as the *infrared transceiver* or *IR port.* It's used to beam data from one PDA to another wirelessly, and has a range of about five feet. You learn more about beaming in Chapter 4.

SHORTCUT *By holding down the Contacts button for two seconds, you can automatically beam your "business card" to another handheld user. In Chapter 6, you learn how to designate a Contacts record as your card.*

Did you know?

Some Cell Phones Can Beam, Too

Some cell phones have IR ports of their own. If yours does, you might be able to beam names and phone numbers from your Palm OS handheld. That would certainly be quicker and easier than entering all that information directly on your phone. We know that some Motorola, Nokia, and Sony Ericsson phones support this option, though usually you have to venture into the menus to get it working. Check the owner's manual for your phone to see if it supports phone-list beaming.

The Stylus

Last, but definitely not least, we come to the *stylus.* Every PDA has a small plastic or metal pen tucked away inside, usually accessible from the side or rear. As you discover in Chapter 16, dozens of third-party styluses are available; some are bigger, some are heavier, and some hide a ballpoint pen inside.

All styluses have one thing in common, a plastic tip. Under no circumstances should you ever use any kind of ink pen or metal tip on your screen. That's a sure way to create a scratch, and a scratched screen is a damaged screen.

TIP *There's one exception. In a pinch, or if you just don't feel like extracting the stylus, you can use your fingernail for light taps on the screen. And, of course, there's always the Navigator for totally stylus-free operation.*

Getting Started with Your PDA

Now that you're familiar with the hardware, you're ready to start using it. This means charging the batteries, working your way through the startup screens, and checking out the Graffiti tutorial. Even if you've already been using your handheld for a while, it's helpful to read this section to learn about things like screen calibration.

Charging the Batteries

Obviously there's nothing terribly complicated about this, but it's important that you charge the batteries properly, following the directions outlined in the instruction manual. Put simply, you must charge the batteries fully before using your handheld. We know you're eager to start using it, but make sure you let it charge fully before going on to the next steps. This takes about four hours. After that, you can just "top off" the battery by dropping the handheld into the HotSync cradle, or connecting its HotSync cable.

The Welcome Screen

Once the batteries are charged and you power on your PDA, you see a "welcome" screen that asks you to remove the stylus and tap anywhere to continue. You're about to undertake a one-time setup procedure that takes all of about 60 seconds. The main tasks accomplished here are the calibration of the screen digitizer and the setting of the date and time.

Our Favorite "Secret" Uses for Our Handhelds

Rick: Most people buy PDAs to manage their appointments and contacts. Of course, the little marvels are capable of so much more. Some of my favorite lesser-known uses for my handheld are as follows: reading e-books (mostly contemporary fiction purchased from eReader.com); storing important personal data such as Web site passwords and software registration numbers (I use DataViz's Passwords Plus, which, sadly, has been discontinued. If you want something similar, try Ilium Software's eWallet); and doing crossword puzzles (courtesy of Stand Alone's Crossword Puzzles for Palm OS). I've also become something of a wine lover, so I rely on LandWare's excellent Wine Enthusiast Guide to help me choose the best bottles and remember those I've enjoyed.

Dave: I get out of the house more than Rick does—he has one of those bizarre phobias that keeps him sequestered away in the basement almost 16 hours each day—so I personally appreciate AvantGo (which you can read about in Chapter 10). This is surely the single best application ever written for any PDA; I use it to read the news each day when I go out to lunch. And while I'm out, I use my Tungsten TX's wireless capabilities to check e-mail (also in Chapter 10). It's so much more than an organizer!

2

What Is Digitizer Calibration?

Put simply, *digitizer calibration* is the process of teaching your PDA to accurately recognize taps on the screen. As you know, the screen responds to input from the stylus; this calibration process simply ensures the precision of those responses. In a way, it's like fine-tuning a TV set.

NOTE *Over time, you might discover that your screen taps seem a little off. For example, you have to tap a bit to the left of an arrow for the screen to register the tap. At this point, it's time to recalibrate the digitizer, which you can do in the Prefs menu. We tell you how in the section "Setting PDA Preferences" later in this chapter.*

Setting the Date and Time

The last stage of the welcome process is setting the date and time (and choosing your country, if you live outside the United States). To set the time, simply tap the box next to the words "Set Time," and then tap the up/down arrow keys to select the current time (don't forget to specify A.M. or P.M.). Tapping the box next to Set Date reveals a calendar. Again, a few strategic taps is all it takes to select today's date. Be sure to choose the year first, then the month, and then the day. When you've done so, tap the Today button.

The Location Setting   The newest Palm OS handhelds have an additional setting alongside date and time: Location. This is designed to simplify travel between time zones. It saves you from having to manually readjust the clock. Instead, just choose your location from the pop-up list that appears, and the clock changes accordingly. By the way, if your "home city" doesn't appear in the list, just choose one that's in your time zone. Here's how:

1.   Tap the arrow next to Location, and then tap Edit List.

2.   Tap Add.

3.   Scroll through the list to find your city or one that's in your time zone, tap to highlight it, and then tap OK.

4.   In the next screen, you can replace the name of the city with the name of your city if you want. You can also choose a specific time zone and enable Daylight Saving Time (which is already enabled by default).

NOTE

If you find yourself in a different time zone and need to change your PDA's clock, you needn't repeat the whole "welcome" process to do so. The date and time settings are located in the Prefs menu, which we discuss in the upcoming section "Setting PDA Preferences."

The Graffiti Tutorial

On the last screen of the welcome wagon, you're given this option: "To learn about entering text on your handheld now, tap Next." Doing so takes you to a brief but helpful tutorial on using *Graffiti,* the Palm OS's handwriting-recognition software. If you'd rather jump right into using your PDA and learn Graffiti later, tap Done instead of Next. You can revisit the Graffiti tutorial at any time by finding and tapping the Graffiti icon in the main Home screen.

NOTE

Some models don't have a Graffiti tutorial, but rather a Quick Tour applet that includes some Graffiti-related instruction.

Why Use the Tutorial?

Mastering Graffiti is arguably the most difficult aspect of using a Palm OS device because it requires you to learn and use a special character set. Thus, you should definitely spend some time with the tutorial. That said, most users can gain a working knowledge of Graffiti in about 20 minutes. And, after a few days' practice, you should be writing quickly, accurately, and effortlessly. We show you the ins and outs of Graffiti in Chapter 4.

TIP

You might have discovered a Graffiti cheat-sheet sticker among the materials that came with your handheld. However, the Palm OS has a built-in cheat sheet of its own. Just draw a line from anywhere in the Graffiti area all the way to the top of the screen. Presto! A diagram of all the Graffiti characters appears!

Getting to Know the Operating System

We aren't exaggerating when we say working with Palm OS devices is roughly eight gazillion times easier than working with traditional computers. Although they're plenty powerful, PDAs are just a lot less complicated. There's no confusing menu system to wade through, no accidentally forgetting to save your document. Here we've highlighted some of the fundamental, but still important, differences between a PDA and a PC:

- When you turn on a PC, you have to wait a few minutes for it to boot up. When you turn on a PDA, it's ready to roll instantaneously. Same goes for shutting it off. Just press the Power button and the screen goes dark. There's no lengthy shutdown procedure.

- On a PC, when you're done working with a program (say, your word processor), you must save your data before exiting that program. On a PDA, this isn't necessary. Data is retained at all times, even if you, for instance, switch to your to-do list while in the middle of writing a memo. When you return to Memo Pad, you find your document exactly as you left it. This holds true even if you turn off the device!

2

There's an exception to this "data is always retained" rule. If you own a Tungsten T5, a Z22, or any model that lacks "persistent RAM," all your data is erased if the battery runs down. That's one reason to make sure your PDA stays charged, and a reason to HotSync regularly, so you can easily restore your data if the battery does die. Newer models, like the Palm TX, aren't affected by this problem.

■ In that same vein, you don't "exit" a program so much as switch to another one. This is a hard concept for seasoned computer users to grasp, as we've all been taught to shut down our software when we're done with it. There's no exit procedure on a PDA, and you'll almost never find that word in a drop-down menu. When you finish working in one program, simply tap the Home button to return to home base, or press one of the program buttons.

We strongly encourage experimentation. Whereas wandering too far off the beaten track in Windows can lead to disaster, it's virtually impossible to get "lost" using a PDA. So tap here, explore there, and just have fun checking things out. Because there's no risk of losing data or running too many programs at once (impossible in the Palm OS), you should have no fear of fouling anything up. Play!

The Icons

Icons are, of course, little pictures used to represent things. In the case of the Palm OS, they're used largely to represent the installed programs. Thus, on the Home screen, you see icons labeled Contacts, Calc, Calendar, and so on, and all you do is tap one to access that particular program.

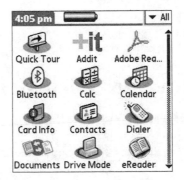

Say, didn't you just learn that you're supposed to press a button below the screen to load Contacts? In the Palm OS, there are often multiple ways to accomplish the same task. In this case, you can load certain programs either by tapping their onscreen icons or using their hardware-button equivalents. Likewise, on models like the LifeDrive and TX, you can tap the toolbar's Home button or the hard Home button to access the Home and/or Favorites screen.

The Menus

As with most computers, *drop-down menus* are used to access program-specific options and settings. In most Palm OS programs, tapping the Menu button (or the program's title bar at the top of the screen) makes a small menu bar appear at the top of the screen. You navigate this bar using the stylus as you would a mouse, tapping each menu item to make its list of options drop down, and then tapping the option you want to access.

NOTE   *These menus are not to be confused with those in the upper-right corner of the screen, which are usually used to select categories, Prefs options, and so on. We discuss those particular menus in the sections "Why Use Categories?" and "Setting PDA Preferences" later in this chapter.*

How to ...   # Find Out How Much Memory Your Handheld Has Left

As you start to add records and install new software on your device, you may wonder how to check the amount of internal memory that's available. From the Home screen, tap Menu | App | Info. The screen that appears shows the total amount of memory on your device and how much of it is free. Notice, too, some of the other options that appear when you tap Menu | App. There's Delete, which is used to delete third-party programs; Beam; used to beam third-party programs; and Copy; used to copy programs from internal memory to memory cards and back again. (See Chapter 4.)

The Home Screen

On a PDA, the Home screen (Applications, which is sometimes called the screen) displays the icons for all the installed programs. It also shows you the time and a battery gauge, as the following screenshot illustrates.

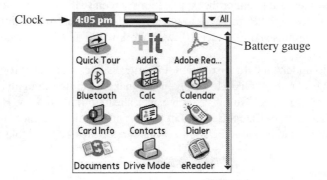

In the upper-right corner of the screen, you'll also notice a small arrow next to the word "All." This means that the Home screen is currently showing you all the installed programs. If you tap the arrow, you see a list of categories into which you can group your programs (see Figure 2-4).

Why Use Categories?

The use of categories is entirely optional, especially now that the Favorites launcher has arrived on some models making for easier application sorting and launching. Categories are intended solely to help you keep your applications organized. As you install more software, you wind up with more icons. Right out of the box, most PDAs have only 10 to 15 of them, a manageable number. But, suppose you install some games and utilities, an e-book reader, and various other programs. Now things are getting a little cluttered, icon-wise.

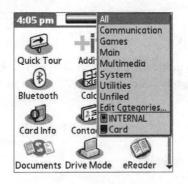

 In the Home screen, categories can be used to organize your programs.

Understanding the Difference between Home and Favorites

Because "consistency" isn't part of the Palm dictionary, the Home button is no longer used exclusively to access the Home screen. On models like the TX and LifeDrive, pressing (or tapping) Home takes you to either the Applications screen (which we previously considered synonymous with "Home"), or to Favorites, the launcher that enables fast access to frequently used programs and files (see "How to Work with Favorites" earlier in this chapter).

It's important to understand the distinction. Favorites is like a separate program, and you're welcome to use it all you like. In fact, you can make it the first thing that appears when you tap/press Home. See "Buttons" a few pages ahead to find out how. But for purposes of our discussion of Categories, and in fact for any future references to visiting the "Home screen," we're talking about the Applications screen, the one that looks like this:

Repeatedly pressing/tapping the Home button cycles you between Favorites and Applications. It's important to recognize the difference between the two. Certain features and capabilities are accessible only from within the Applications screen. Thus, when we refer to Home, we're usually talking about Applications, not Favorites. We'll do our best to alert you to any discrepancies.

Categories offer you a way to minimize the clutter. As you saw in the drop-down list, the Palm OS comes with several categories already created. You can use them if you want, or you can create your own.

TIP *Instead of using categories, you can install a third-party launcher. These programs offer easier and more practical ways to organize your icons, such as with tabs or smaller icons. Rick and Dave are both partial to Silver Screen (www.pocketsensei.com).*

How to Create and Modify Categories   Look again at the drop-down list in the upper-right corner of the Home screen (see Figure 2-4). Notice the last option: Edit Categories. Tapping this option takes you to a screen where you can add, rename, and delete categories. To rename or delete a category, first select it by tapping it with the stylus (the category becomes highlighted). Then, tap the appropriate button.

To create a new category, tap the New button, and then write in the desired name. That's all there is to it!

How to Assign Programs to Categories   Once you tailor the categories to your liking, you must next assign your programs to them. This isn't difficult, but it could take you a few tedious minutes to complete. Here's how:

1. In the Home screen, tap the Menu button, and then select Category.
2. Identify any one program you want to assign (you might have to scroll down the list, which you can do by using the onscreen arrows, the scroll bar, or the Scroll buttons), and then tap the little arrow next to it.

Category	
Quick Tour	▼ Main
Addit	▼ Unfiled
Adobe Reader	▼ Unfiled
Bluetooth	▼ Communica...
Calc	▼ Main
Calendar	▼ Main
Card Info	▼ System
Contacts	▼ Main
Dialer	▼ Main
Documents	▼ Main

Done

3. The list of categories appears. Pick one by tapping it.
4. Repeat the procedure for the other programs you want to assign.
5. Tap Done to return to the Home screen.

Now, when you tap the category arrow in the corner and select one, you see that all your reassigned icons have been placed in the respective screens.

TIP   *One way to change the displayed category is to tap the aforementioned arrow, but there's a quicker way. If you tap the Home button repeatedly, the PDA cycles through the categories that have programs assigned to them (this works only on models that don't have the Favorites launcher, like the Tungsten E2 and Z22). Once again, the Palm OS offers you two ways to accomplish the same goal.*

The Toolbar

With the introduction of the Tungsten T3, PalmSource also introduced the *toolbar,* a row of additional buttons and controls beneath the Graffiti area. The toolbar stays visible at all times, even when the Graffiti area has been retracted, and even when you're viewing Favorites instead of the Applications screen. Let's take a look at the toolbar (which appears on models including the LifeDrive, Tungsten T5, and TX) and its various functions:

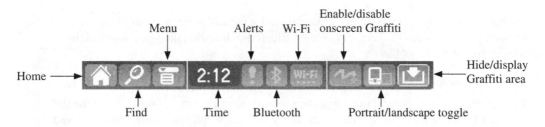

Many of these icons are self-explanatory, but let's take a look at their functions anyway.

- **Home** Tap here to return to the Home screen. Tap repeatedly to cycle through categories (or between the Home and Favorites screens, depending on your model).

- **Find** Tap here to access the Find feature.

- **Menu** Tap here to access drop-down menus. In most applications, you can also tap in the top-left corner of the screen, or anywhere in the application's title bar.

- **Time** It looks like a simple clock, but surprise! Tapping the time brings up a handy screen that displays the remaining battery charge, the amount of available memory, a screen-brightness slider, and a "silent" option for silencing all your PDA's sound effects (very helpful when you're headed into a meeting or something). Tap time again to make this screen disappear.

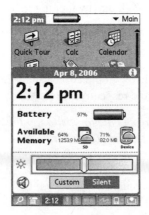

■ **Alerts** If there are alarms you haven't attended to yet, this little exclamation point will flash. Tap it to see a list of all current alerts, and to check them off if you don't want to be bothered by them again.

■ **Bluetooth** Want to turn your handheld's Bluetooth radio on or off? Maybe you need access to Bluetooth settings (see the "Other Prefs" section later in this chapter). The Bluetooth icon provides quick and easy access to these and other related functions.

■ **Wi-Fi** On models with built-in Wi-Fi capabilities (namely, the LifeDrive and TX), the toolbar will have this Wi-Fi icon. Tap it to turn the Wi-Fi radio on (or off) and scan for available networks. Find out more about using Wi-Fi in Chapter 10.

■ **Enable/disable onscreen Graffiti** Psst! LifeDrive and TX users! We don't want owners of other models to get jealous, so we'll just whisper this part. By tapping this icon, you can free yourself from the confines of the Graffiti area and write anywhere on the screen! Well, not exactly anywhere, the same division between letters and numbers applies (letters on the left half, numbers on the right, capitals across the middle). This might feel a little awkward at first, but give it a try and see if you like this method of data entry.

TIP *For the rest of you, if you like the idea of "Graffiti anywhere" and don't own a LifeDrive or TX, fear not, third-party software developers have your back. Head to PalmGear.com and look for a program called, aptly enough, Graffiti Anywhere. It's freeware, and it enables you to write with Graffiti anywhere on the screen, not just in the Graffiti area.*

■ **Portrait/landscape toggle** There are times when you might prefer to operate your TX or old Tungsten T3 or T5 in landscape mode, meaning that the screen rotates a full 90 degrees and becomes "wide." For instance, many users prefer this mode when reading e-books or Word documents, as it makes for a wider, more natural-looking page. Notice that when you enable landscape mode, the Graffiti area and toolbar shift to the right side of the screen. They still function exactly as before; they're just relocated. If you're wondering why the LifeDrive doesn't have this icon, it's because there's a dedicated portrait/landscape button on the side of the device.

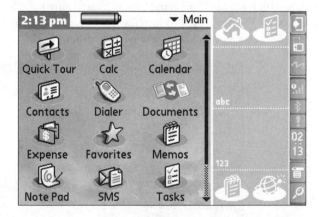

■ **Hide/display Graffiti area** To paraphrase Homer Simpson in one of our favorite Simpsons episodes: Graffiti area goes up, Graffiti area goes down. Graffiti area goes up, Graffiti area goes down. Graffiti area goes up, Graffiti area goes down. You get the idea.

How to ... **Add a Background Photo to Your Home Screen**

On most of the latest Palm models, it's extremely easy to turn any photo into the background wallpaper for your Home and/or Favorites screen (not unlike what many users do with their Windows desktops). For example:

Here's how to make it happen:

1. Tap the Home icon or button to return to the Home or Favorites screen.

2. Tap Menu | Options | Display Options.

3. Check the box marked Background.

(continued)

4. Choose the photo you want for your background by tapping the large box with the dotted border. From here you can choose a photo that's stored in RAM, or, by tapping the small memory-card icon in the top-right corner, a photo stored on a memory card.

5. You can also adjust the Fade slider to make the photo darker or lighter. Experiment with this to see how it changes the look of the photo. We think making it lighter (that is, increasing the Fade percentage) is usually a good idea so it doesn't clash too heavily with your program icons.

Okay, so if you don't have a model that supports background photos, are you out of luck? Heck, no! All you need is a launcher that includes this feature. Most of the latest and greatest launchers do; see Chapter 12 for information on some of our favorite third-party launchers. Here's an example, taken from the very popular ZLauncher:

Setting PDA Preferences

What would a computer be without a control panel where you can tweak the settings and customize the machine? The Palm OS has one, called *Prefs*. Find the Prefs icon in the Home screen, tap it, and meet us at the next paragraph.

Divided into several different sections, Prefs is the place to reset your handheld's digitizer, change the date and time, tweak any necessary Bluetooth or modem settings, and more. Before we delve into each individual Pref, however, we need to show you what different Prefs screens look like (see Figure 2-5). Just to keep everyone good and confused, there are now several

2

Preferences

General
- Date & Time   • Formats
- Graffiti 2   • Input
- Keylock   • Power
- Security   • Sounds & Alerts
- Touchscreen

Communication
- Bluetooth   • Connection
- Network   • Phone
- VPN   • Wi-Fi

Personal
- Buttons   • Color Theme
- Handedness   • Owner
- ShortCuts

FIGURE 2-5   The Prefs screen is where you access all kinds of settings. Note that your prefs screen may look a bit different, and contain different options, than what's shown here.

different "front ends" for the Prefs screen. Most of the options contained therein are the same from device to device, but what you'll see when you first tap the Prefs icon may vary a bit.

NOTE   *Some Palm OS handhelds may have Prefs options that others don't. For instance, the TX includes one called Wi-Fi, owing to its built-in Wi-Fi radio. For the most part, we've covered the Palm OS 5 selection of Prefs in this section. If your device has a Prefs option not explained here, or there's an option listed here that's not on your device, consult your manual. The good news is, most "prefs" are pretty self-explanatory.*

Buttons

As we explained earlier, the hard buttons below the screen are used to quick-launch the main Palm OS programs. However, you can reassign these buttons to launch other programs instead. If you rarely use, say, Note Pad, but you use Memo Pad all the time, you might want to reassign the Note Pad button accordingly.

In the Buttons screen, you see an icon that corresponds to each programmable hard button on your handheld. All you do to change the function of any given button is tap the little arrow next to it, and then select the desired application. The buttons can launch any installed application; you're not limited to just the core Palm OS apps.

Notice, too, the options at the bottom of the Buttons screen. *Default* restores the button assignments to their original settings, while *More* (also known as *Pen* on some models) lets you choose what happens when you drag the tip of your stylus from the Graffiti area to the top of the screen. (This action can be made to load the built-in Graffiti help screens, invoke the onscreen keyboard, turn on backlighting, or one of several other options.) Some models also have a *HotSync* button, which enables you to reprogram the HotSync button on your docking cradle or optional modem—something we don't recommend doing.

Connection

The *Connection* screen lets you set up whatever modem or cell phone you might be using with your PDA, or choose to HotSync via the unit's IR port or Bluetooth radio (instead of using the cradle). You probably won't need to fiddle with the modem settings too much. See Chapter 10 for more information on working with Bluetooth.

Date & Time

Flying into another time zone? Hit this screen to change your handheld's internal clock (an important thing to remember so you don't miss your alarms!), or simply choose a different location, which automatically changes the time zone. (See Chapter 9). You can also change the date if necessary, and, on some models, set the PDA to automatically adjust for Daylight Saving Time.

Digitizer (a.k.a. Touchscreen)

Noticing a little "drift" in your stylus taps? You tap someplace, but it doesn't quite register, or it registers in the wrong place? It might be time to reset your screen's digitizer. You should do so the moment you notice a problem; the worse the drift gets, the harder it might be to get to this screen. Simply select Digitizer (or Touchscreen, on some models) from the Prefs menu and follow the instructions.

NOTE *Digitizer drift does occur over time, but if it becomes a frequent occurrence, it could point to a hardware problem. If your PDA is still under warranty, contact customer service to see if a replacement is warranted. In the meantime, there are software utilities designed to compensate for digitizer drift. See Chapter 17 for more information.*

Formats

Few users need to spend much time in the Formats screen, where you can change the way dates, times, and numbers are displayed. You can also specify whether you want the calendar week to start on Sunday (the default) or Monday.

Power

This is the place to visit when you want to control your PDA's power setting, and an important little setting called Beam Receive.

```
┌─────────────────────────────────┐
│ Preferences          Power      │
│                                 │
│   Auto-off after: ▼ 1 minute    │
│ On while Charging: ▼ On         │
│   Beam Receive: ▼ On            │
│                                 │
│                                 │
│                                 │
│                                 │
│                                 │
│ ┌──────┐                        │
│ │ Done │                        │
│ └──────┘                        │
└─────────────────────────────────┘
```

NOTE   *On older Palm models, the power settings can be found in the General section.*

- **Auto-off After**   To help preserve battery life, your handheld will turn itself off after a designated period of inactivity. Here you can set the interval, from 30 seconds to 3 minutes. The lower you set it, the better your battery life will be.

- **On while Charging**   When this box is checked, your handheld will remain on while it's connected to its power supply (usually the HotSync cradle/cable). This can be handy if you spend a lot of time at your desk and frequently need to consult your handheld for addresses, schedules, and so forth.

- **Beam Receive**   If this is off, you won't be able to receive programs and data beamed from other handhelds. However, keeping it off until you need it can help conserve power, but just *remember* that it's off, so you don't pull your hair out trying to determine why you can't receive a beam.

Sounds & Alerts

This is the place to modify, well, sounds and alerts. You didn't really need us to tell you that, did you? Okay, Mr. Smarty Reader, how about this: See those Custom/Silent buttons at the top of the screen? If your Palm has a virtual Graffiti area, you can shortcut to them by tapping the Time button in the toolbar.

- **System Sound**   Adjust the volume for various system sounds, such as beeps, HotSync tones, and so forth. If you want your handheld to be silent, set this to Off.
- **Alarm Sound**   Adjust the volume for alarms.
- **Alarm Vibrate**   This option appears only in models that have a vibrating-alarm feature. Set it to On if you want your handheld to vibrate when an alarm goes off. For totally silent alarms, set Alarm Sound to Off.
- **Alarm LED**   On some models, the Power button doubles as an LED, which can be set to flash when an alarm goes off.
- **Game Sound**   Adjust the volume for games.

Network

The slightly misnamed *Network* screen is where you enter the relevant information about your Internet service provider (ISP) if you're using a modem or cell phone to dial into it. A handful of major ISPs are already listed in the Service menu, but you still need to provide your account username and password, plus the phone number for the ISP. The *Details* button takes you to a screen with some advanced Internet settings; the *Connect* button tells the modem to go ahead and dial in. Consult your manual and/or Palm's online support site for more information about setting up these kinds of connections.

Owner

In the tragic event that you lose your PDA, you'd probably be very grateful to have it returned. The *Owner* screen is where you can put your name and contact information (address, phone number, e-mail address—whatever you're comfortable with). Then, if you use the Palm Operating System's security features (which we detail in Chapter 8) to "lock" the device every time you turn it off, the information on the Owner screen is displayed when the unit is turned on again. Then, if someone happens to find your handheld, they know how to return it to you, but won't have access to all your data. Smart!

ShortCuts

Next, we come to *ShortCuts,* a tool designed to expedite the entry of often-used words and phrases. Let's say you're a Starfleet engineer and you use your PDA to keep track of your repair duties. The phrase "holodeck emitters" comes up quite a bit, but do you really have to write it out every time? What if you could just write "h-e" instead and have the words magically appear? That's the beauty of shortcuts.

```
Preferences          ShortCuts

br - Breakfast
di - Dinner
ds - [Date Stamp]
dts - [Date and Time Stamp]
lu - Lunch
me - Meeting
ts - [Time Stamp]


( Done ) ( New ) ( Edit ) ( Delete )
```

As you see when you reach the ShortCuts screen, a handful of the little time-savers have already been created. There's one each for your daily meals, one for "meeting," and even a couple of date and time stamps (used to quickly insert the date and time, natch). Let's walk through the process of creating and using a new shortcut:

1. Tap the New button.

2. In the ShortCut Name field, write the abbreviation you want to use for this particular shortcut. As an example, let's use "bm" for "Buy milk."

3. Tap the first line in the ShortCut Text field to move your cursor there. Now, enter the text you want to appear when you invoke the shortcut; in this case, "Buy milk".

4. Tap OK. Now, let's invoke the new shortcut. Press the To Do button to launch the To Do List, and then tap New to create a new task.

5. To invoke this or any other shortcut in any application, be it Date Book, Memo Pad, or whatever, you must first write the shortcut stroke in the Graffiti area. This lets Graffiti know you're about to enter the abbreviation for a shortcut. The stroke looks like a cursive, lowercase letter *l* (see our Graffiti guide in Chapter 4). After you make the stroke, you see it appear next to your cursor. Now enter the letter *b,* and then the letter *m.* Presto! The words "Buy milk" magically appear.

Other Prefs

Don't be surprised if your particular model has even more options listed in the Prefs screen. Some of these may include:

- **Bluetooth**   See Chapter 10 for a complete explanation of Bluetooth and how to use this screen to set up your device.

- **Color Theme**   Want to jazz up your PDA's interface? Choose from one of the many installed color themes.

- **Input**   On models like the LifeDrive and TX, which have virtual data-entry areas, you can choose between three different setups: Keyboard, which gives you an onscreen keyboard in place of the Graffiti handwriting area; Wide, which extends the Graffiti area the full width of the screen, giving you three separate sections for data entry, (letters, capital letters, and numbers) at the expense of those handy program icons; and Classic, which is a more traditional-looking Graffiti area, complete with handy program icons that you can actually reprogram! (See "How to Reprogram the Graffiti Area Icons" for details.)

- **Phone**   Your PDA can link to certain infrared- and Bluetooth-equipped cell phones for wireless e-mail and Web access. In this screen, you choose the kind of phone you have and the connection you want to use (either Bluetooth or IR). If your phone isn't listed, well, you're sorta outta luck; though you can check Palm's Web site for new phone drivers, which are made available periodically.

- **VPN**   VPN stands for Virtual Private Networking, a technology that enables your PDA to establish secure communications with your corporate network. Consult your PDA's user guide and your company's IT department for more information.

Introducing Palm Desktop

So far, we've talked mostly about your Palm device itself: the hardware, the operating system, the basic setup procedures and considerations. One area is left to cover before you venture into real-world PDA use: Palm Desktop.

What Is Palm Desktop?

Wondrous as a PDA is in its own right, even more special is its capability to synchronize with your computer. This means that all the data entered into your handheld is copied to your PC, and vice versa. The software that fields all this data on the computer side is *Palm Desktop*. If you use Microsoft Outlook or another contact manager, you needn't switch to Palm Desktop, but you'll still need it for a few things. More on that in the next section.

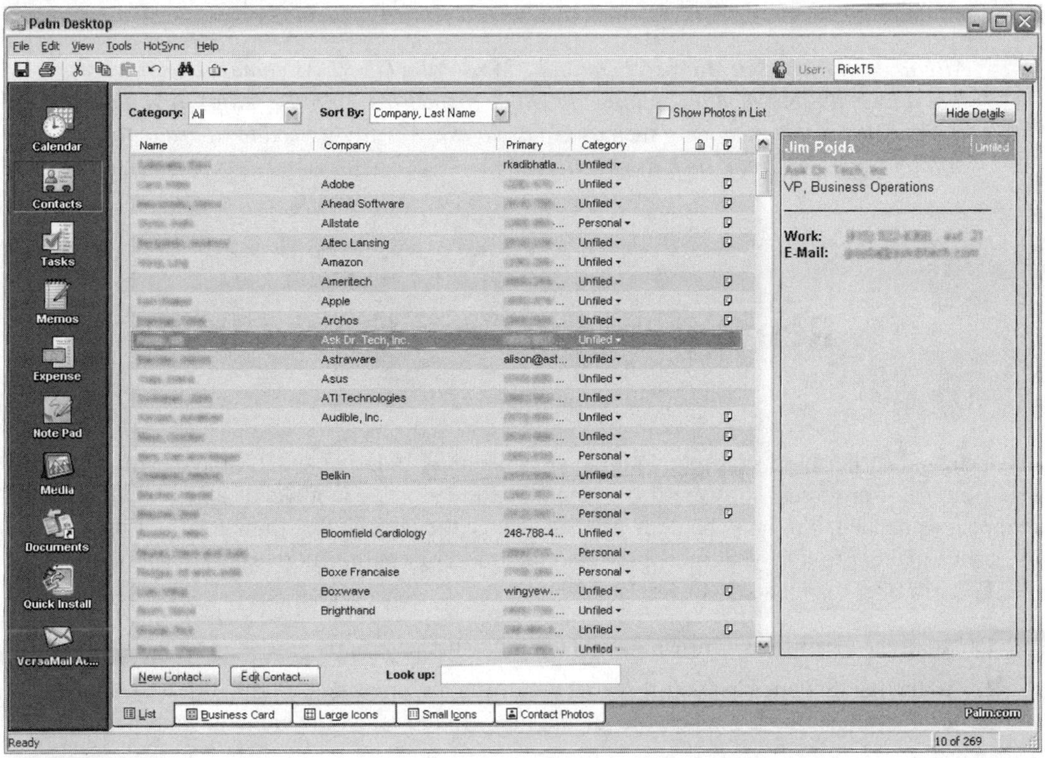

2

FIGURE 2-6 Palm Desktop represents the computer side of the equation. It's a full-blown contact manager that synchronizes with your PDA.

Viewed in a vacuum, Palm Desktop resembles traditional personal information manager (PIM) or contact-management software. It effectively replicates all the core functionality of the Palm OS, providing you with a phone list, appointment calendar, to-do list, and memo pad. If you've never used such software before, you'll no doubt find Palm Desktop (seen in Figure 2-6) an invaluable addition, because it helps keep you organized at home or in the office, whereas a PDA keeps you organized while traveling.

A Word about Synchronization

What happens when you synchronize your PDA with your PC? In a nutshell, three things:

■ Any new entries made on your PDA are added to Palm Desktop.

■ Any new entries made in Palm Desktop are added to your PDA.

■ Any existing records modified in one place, the PDA, for example are modified in the other, the desktop, with the newest changes taking precedence.

Therefore, synchronizing regularly ensures that your information is kept current, both in your PDA and in Palm Desktop.

NOTE *Already entrenched in Microsoft Outlook? Most Palm OS PDAs come with software that allows direct synchronization with Office (bypassing Palm Desktop). If you have a different contact manager (such as Lotus Notes), you might need to upgrade to a different sync program, such as Intellisync.*

How to ... **Reprogram the Graffiti Area Icons**

As discussed earlier in this chapter, Palm models like the LifeDrive and TX have "virtual" Graffiti areas—onscreen, software-driven input boxes that you can make disappear and reappear as needed. Not only that, but you can change the buttons that flank the Graffiti area, thus making four of your most preferred programs or options more easily accessible.

This is easier than it sounds. Here's how:

1. With the Graffiti area showing, tap and hold whichever icon you want to change.

2. In the list that appears, you'll see all your installed programs, along with frequently used options like Launcher, Menu, and Find. Tap to select the one you want.

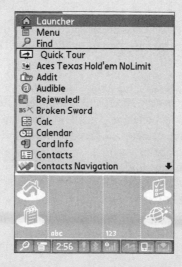

Wow, that was tough, huh? Sorry to put you through all that.

Chapter 3

Ready, Set, Sync!

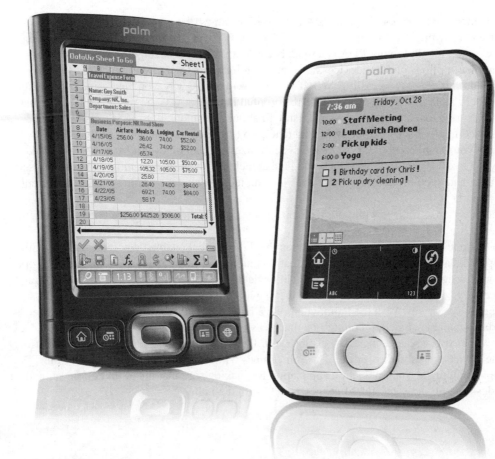

How to...

- Install the Palm Desktop software
- Install the HotSync cradle
- Configure the HotSync cradle
- Troubleshoot PC connection problems
- Set up the HotSync Manager
- Perform your first HotSync
- HotSync with a HotSync cable
- Interpret the HotSync log
- Keep your data synchronized just the way you like
- Perform HotSyncs wirelessly via IR or Bluetooth

No matter what you bought your PDA for—to play games, listen to music, check your calendar—you need to connect it to your desktop PC. But don't worry about that. Getting your PC set up to talk to your PDA is a snap, because it uses the amazingly painless HotSync software that millions of other devices have relied on for years to do pretty much the same thing.

Why does it connect so easily? Well, if you ask us (and in a way, you have, since you bought, borrowed, or stole this book), it's because the original PalmPilot was the first handheld PC that truly understood that a personal organizer isn't all about the handheld itself; it's just as much about the computer back on your desk. And thanks to that lineage, your Palm fully integrates itself into your main computer system and synchronizes with all of your most important data. Once you have a Palm, no longer does using a handheld PC mean maintaining two different sets of contacts and appointments. No more does it mean laboriously transcribing tons of important data by hand.

The Palm synchronizes with your desktop so elegantly, it's as if they were born to work together.

To be honest, the Palm wasn't the first handheld device that enabled you to share data with a desktop PC. Dave should know. He was an early handheld adopter, and he still has his old Apple Newton MessagePad. But with older handheld devices, synchronizing data was a chore. Often, the necessary software wasn't included in the box with the handheld itself, and it worked less than optimally anyway. With the Palm, you press a button and all the important stuff you use every day is quickly shared. It couldn't be much easier.

Now that you've had a chance to explore your Palm device in Chapter 2, it's time to learn how the device works with your PC. The Palm comes with a slew of tools designed for the desktop, including a synchronization application for making sure that the Palm has the same data as the desktop. So, let's get started using your PC with the Palm.

Installing the Desktop Software

Before you can synchronize your PDA with your desktop PC, or install new software, or do any of the other cool things you no doubt want to do, you first need to install the Palm Desktop software suite on your computer. The Palm Desktop software is known as a personal information manager (PIM). It duplicates all the core applications from your Palm and serves as the headquarters from which you can use synchronized information from your PDA.

Keep in mind that while you need to install the Palm Desktop, you don't actually need to use it. If you already use Microsoft Outlook, you can synchronize your Palm to that program instead and avoid Palm Desktop entirely.

The CD-ROM that accompanies your handheld includes everything you need to connect the handheld to your desktop, including your choice of synchronization to Palm Desktop or Outlook. Installation is very straightforward. Follow the installation instructions that appear after you insert the CD-ROM.

It's important that you follow the instructions that come with your Palm. Most important, install the software before you connect the HotSync cable to your PC's USB port.

Installing Palm Desktop

The Palm Desktop CD-ROM includes an installer that places most of the key components on your hard disk. Most of the main installation is completely automated, but you have to make two important decisions.

What's Your Device Name?

During the installation of the Palm Desktop, you'll be asked to choose a username. This is actually the name of your PDA, the label that Windows, your various Palm applications, and your Palm Desktop software will all use to identify your handheld and distinguish it from any other devices you might also synchronize with your PC. You can use your own name or give your PDA a unique descriptor. Anything from **Dave's Palm** to **Treo 33A** to just plain **Mike** is acceptable.

Is the name important? Yup. If you have more than one Palm OS device, each one absolutely must have a different name, or your data can get accidentally scrambled. This used to be a serious problem, but the most recent versions of HotSync Manager won't allow you to synchronize two different PDAs that have the same username anyway.

Do You Want to Use Outlook or Palm Desktop?

If you have a copy of Microsoft Outlook installed on your PC, the installer detects it and gives you the option of synchronizing your data to it if you so desire, as you can see from the Palm TX installer shown next.

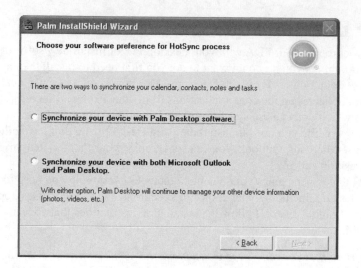

What data are we talking about? It's stuff like contacts from the address book, and appointments from the calendar, notes, and tasks. If you're a regular and happy Outlook user, you should synchronize your handheld with Outlook. Palm Desktop, on the other hand, is a serviceable PIM, though it's not as comprehensive as Outlook. If you're not already married to Outlook, Palm Desktop just might make you happy. Of course, even if you choose to synchronize with Outlook, Palm Desktop must still be installed. There are certain kinds of information on your PDA (like pictures or voice recordings, for instance) that only sync with Palm Desktop, even if you're an Outlook user.

Installing the HotSync Cradle or Cable

At some point in the CD installation process, you'll be instructed to connect the HotSync cradle or HotSync cable (whichever came with your particular model). What's that, you ask? It's simple enough: Your PDA and PC communicate via a short connection cable called the HotSync cable. Most Palm OS PDAs come with a device called a cradle. The USB cable connects the cradle to the computer. If your PDA only comes with a cable, don't fret: it works pretty much the same way. One end connects to the PC and the other plugs into the bottom of the Palm. The AC adapter, for charging your Palm, plugs into the cradle, the cable, or the bottom of the PDA, making it the Swiss Army Knife of the PDA universe.

TIP

If your model came with only a cable, you can probably purchase an optional cradle from Palm (or whatever company made your device). We highly recommend getting a cradle if possible, as it gives your handheld a place to sit upright while on your desk, cuts down on cord clutter, and usually makes for much easier HotSync connections (meaning you don't have to fiddle with the cable; you just place the handheld in the cradle, easy as pie).

Did you know?

The Origins of HotSync

HotSync, a term coined by Palm, refers to the act of synchronizing the data stored on your handheld and desktop computers. These days, pretty much all PDA companies use a special term that means more or less the same thing. Microsoft's Pocket PCs, for instance, use "ActiveSync" instead. The difference? You need to "kick off" a HotSync by pressing the HotSync button. Microsoft's ActiveSync starts each and every time you put the device in its desktop cradle, which we find just a little annoying.

When instructed, plug your HotSync cable into any USB port on your computer or into a USB hub.

When you connect the cable, you don't have to turn the computer off first; and don't worry, any open, easy-to-get-to USB port will do. There's no special significance to ports on the front or back of your PC, aside from ease of access issues. The only thing you need to keep in mind is that USB connections, although they look pretty rectangular, are close, but not perfectly symmetrical. They only go in one way, so if you're having trouble plugging one into the PC, turn it upside down and try again.

Powering Your PDA

Unlike PDAs of olden times, your Palm almost certainly has a set of integrated, rechargeable batteries. When you plug the HotSync cable into your PC, make sure to connect the AC adapter to the cable, too; if it isn't plugged into the wall, you can't charge your PDA (most Palm devices can't recharge through the USB port alone).

You can usually tell that your PDA is being recharged because the power button glows. If you don't see the glow, check to see if the AC adapter has come loose from the wall or detached from the HotSync cable.

Unfortunately, this advice, as brilliant as it sounds, doesn't apply to the Palm TX, which has no such glowing power button (as ridiculous as that is). If your PDA doesn't have a glowing power widget, turn on the Palm and check to see if there's a power plug symbol on the battery status, which indicates that it's charging.

TIP

You needn't plug the AC adapter into the HotSync cable just to transfer data between the PC and Palm. That means you can take the Palm and a laptop on the road without being weighed down by the heavy AC adapter. If you don't use the AC adapter though, the batteries in the Palm won't recharge, and eventually its batteries will die, costing you access to your data.

Your First HotSync

You're finally ready for the big moment. If this is your first HotSync ever, meaning you've never owned another Palm device before, get ready to make a dramatic speech, like "This is one small press for man, one giant HotSync for mankind." To start your HotSync, you can navigate to the HotSync screen on your PDA and press the big fat HotSync button on the screen, or much simpler, just press the HotSync button on the cradle or the stem of the HotSync cable, if your Palm has such a button (see Figure 3-1).

After you press the HotSync button, here's what should happen:

1. Your Palm turns itself on (if it wasn't on already).

2. You hear tones on both the computer and Palm indicating that the HotSync has begun.

3. A message box appears on the Windows desktop, which informs you of the HotSync status.

4. You hear another set of tones when the HotSync is complete.

5. The Palm also displays a message indicating that the HotSync is complete.

When Something Goes Wrong

Truth be told, not much is likely to go awry when you HotSync. HotSyncing is usually pretty darned reliable. Any potential problems that crop up generally boil down to just a few

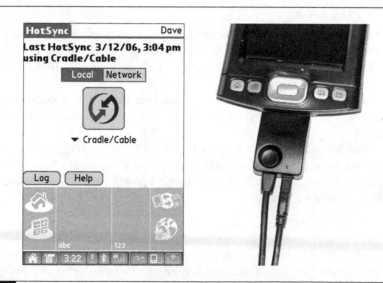

FIGURE 3-1   There are two easy ways to start a HotSync: on the Palm screen or via the HotSync button on the cable or cradle.

The Best Films of All Time

After all that work, it's time for a TV break. And that, of course, leads to the inevitable arguments . . . what are the best movies of all time?

Dave: There's no way a rational person could disagree . . . *Aliens* is the best movie of all time. Space Marines fighting xenomorphs with twenty-third century machine guns! Woo hoo! What could possibly be cooler than that? And it has some of the best movie lines ever. This, mind you, is the film in which Bill Paxton made the words, "Game over, man," a part of my daily lexicon. What else rates a place on the Johnson DVD Shelf of Wonder? *The Matrix, The Sixth Sense, Almost Famous,* and *O Brother, Where Art Thou* have to be four of the most amazing films ever made. Now let's see what lame movies Rick thinks are cool. My prediction: His favorite films include *Tron, Howard the Duck, Dirty Dancing,* and *Weekend at Bernie's 2.*

Rick: I've had just about enough of your *Weekend at Bernie's 2* bashing, mister. Don't make me tell everyone about your strange fondness for Will Smith. Anyway, in no particular order, my Top Five Movies are as follows: *Life is Beautiful, City Lights, The Shawshank Redemption, Chicken Run,* and *Star Trek II: The Wrath of Khan.* Yes, I know, only one of those movies has things blowing up, which means you won't care for the other four.

simple things. For starters, you might not have anywhere to plug in your cable, especially if you already have a few other USB devices attached to the PC. If that's the case, you'll need to run over to a local computer store and buy a USB hub. A hub plugs into an existing USB port on your PC and gives you several extra USB connectors for additional devices. It's like a USB extension cord with extra outlets.

If you plugged in your HotSync cable and it doesn't seem to work, there are a few likely causes. How do you know when you have a problem? You might press the HotSync button and absolutely nothing will happen. Alternately, you might get this scary looking error message in a small balloon at the bottom of the screen:

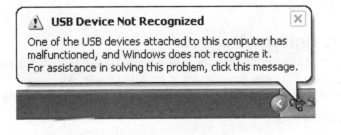

In either case, here are some ways to troubleshoot the glitch:

■ A semi-frequent problem is something we like to call *Windows funkiness*. To fix it, just reboot your PC. It'll probably work just fine afterward. Heck, if you're having trouble, try rebooting the PC right away anyway. That alone may very well solve your problem.

■ Before you go to the trouble of rebooting your PC, though, you might want to eliminate Palm funkiness as an issue, because resetting your Palm is lot easier than rebooting a computer. So, because a glitch on the PDA might prevent the HotSync process from working properly, see if a soft reset on the Palm can solve the problem. Check out Chapter 17 for details on how to do that.

■ Another easy fix to try: Unplug the Palm's HotSync cable from the PC and plug it into a different USB port. This makes Windows reload the Palm's USB software, and that alone is often enough to fix some problems.

■ A less common, but more subtle problem: Your USB port doesn't have enough power to run the cable. If your USB port has several devices connected to it, such as through a hub, it might not be able to handle the power requirements of the connected devices. Make sure you're using a "powered" hub (it will come with its own AC adapter) and that it's plugged into the wall. If that checks out, you might need to swap some devices around between your PC's two USB ports to move some high-power devices to the other port. This might take a little experimentation. This problem is pretty rare, though.

■ Finally, a related problem is that your USB port might have run out of bandwidth. This can happen if you have some high-performance USB devices connected to the same port, all transferring a lot of data at the same time. Again, the solution is to move some things around between the two USB ports. A few years back, Dave found that he simply couldn't run all the USB devices he wanted to on his PC because they demanded more total bandwidth than his PC's USB ports could deliver. If you have lots of USB devices and really need more bandwidth, simply buy a PCI card that gives you more USB ports. In reality, this problem, too, is pretty rare.

NOTE   *Many new PCs have USB 2.0 ports, which are much more robust and have far greater bandwidth than older USB 1.1 ports. If you have a new Palm that uses USB 2.0 connection speed and your computer has USB 2.0 ports, you should have far fewer problems than in Days of Olde.*

Exploring the HotSync Manager

The HotSync Manager software does exactly what it sounds like it should: it manages the connection between your PDA and your computer, enabling you to synchronize the two. It contains all the options and configurations needed to keep the two devices talking to each other.

To get to the HotSync Manager's options in Windows, you need to see the HotSync menu. Click the HotSync Manager icon in the System Tray, and a context menu appears.

 TIP *You can click the HotSync Manager icon with either the right or left mouse button; the result is the same.*

The top of the menu lists ways available to HotSync. You'll see some of the following options (but not necessarily all of them):

- Local USB
- Local
- Modem
- Network
- Infrared

For now, the only one that must be checked is the Local USB option (unless you have a very old Palm with a serial connection, in which case you want Local). You will see the Infrared option only if your computer has an infrared port (such as if your machine is a laptop).

Configuring HotSync Setup

Click the Setup option on the HotSync menu. You should now see the Setup dialog box. This is the place where you get to configure how the HotSync Manager behaves. The Setup dialog box has four tabs, which we'll discuss next.

General   The General tab lets you specify how often the HotSync Manager listens to the USB or serial port for a HotSync request. It has three options, as you can see in Figure 3-2.

- **Always available**   This is the default setting. As soon as you press the HotSync button on the cradle, you synchronize your data. It's fast and convenient, and is probably the way most people use their PDAs. But you needn't give in to peer pressure, because this has a downside: if you're using the serial port rather than a USB port, HotSync Manager locks it up so you can't share the port with another serial device, such as a modem.

- **Available only when the Palm Desktop is running**   If you often share your old-fashioned serial port with another device, this might be a better solution. The HotSync Manager won't lock the port unless Palm Desktop is actually running. But what if you don't use Palm Desktop? Then keep reading, because option number three is for you.

- **Manual**   Just like it sounds, the HotSync Manager doesn't run at all unless you choose it from the Start menu (Start | Programs | Palm Desktop | HotSync Manager). This is the least convenient of all the options, but you might want to choose it if you are using an old-fashioned serial port and you HotSync only on rare occasions.

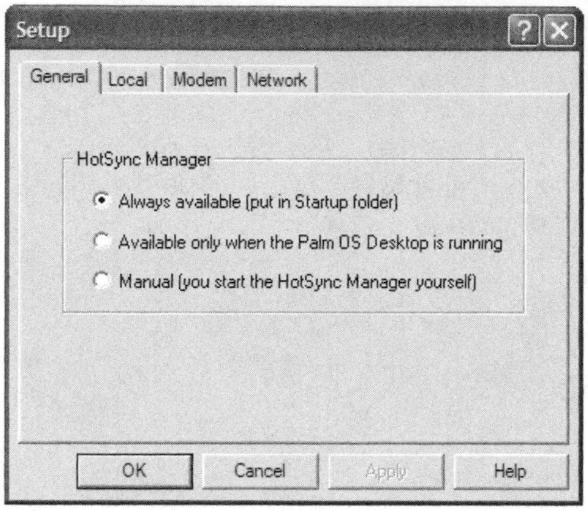

FIGURE 3-2   The General tab determines when the HotSync Manager runs and how easy it is to perform a HotSync.

Local   The Local Serial tab is where you specify the serial port and speed for your HotSync. As we mentioned, this is only a concern if you have an old Palm device with a serial connection instead of USB. Most of the time, the installation process correctly determines your serial port and it's all taken care of. If you move the HotSync cable to another serial port though, you must tell the HotSync Manager what the proper COM port actually is. The correct COM port is almost always COM1 or COM2, but you can experiment to determine your port name.

You can almost always leave the speed set to As Fast As Possible. If you need to troubleshoot connection problems however, this is where you can specify a slower speed.

Modem and Network   Both of these tabs are used to specify settings for more advanced HotSync techniques. After you've seen all the tabs in the Setup dialog box, click OK to save the changes or click Cancel to leave the dialog box without changing anything.

Customizing the HotSync Operation

From the HotSync Manager menu, choose Custom. This is probably the most important dialog box in the HotSync software because it enables you to specify in great detail exactly what data will get transferred when you perform a HotSync. Before we look at this dialog box however, we should define a few essential terms the Palm uses to perform data synchronizations. Be careful, because if you make the wrong choice, you can destroy data you need. Here are the ways you can configure the HotSync program to manage your data:

Synchronize the files	Suppose you added new files to both the PC and the Palm since the last HotSync. The new data from the Palm is copied to the PC, and the new data from the PC is copied to the Palm. Both devices will have a copy of everything. *This is the best setting to use most of the time and is, in fact, the default for most conduits.*
Desktop overwrites handheld	This option supposes that the desktop data is correct at the expense of anything that might be on the handheld. If you add new files to both the PC and the handheld, for instance, and then perform this kind of sync, the new files on the Palm will be lost. The desktop data overwrites whatever was on the Palm.
Handheld overwrites desktop	This is exactly the opposite of the previous case. Assuming the handheld data is more correct for some reason (we assume you have your reasons), any files that are different or new on the desktop PC are lost after the synchronization. Both systems will have the Palm data.
Do nothing	With this option selected, no changes are made to either device during this HotSync.

Remember: each conduit can be adjusted separately. This means you can set the Date Book to overwrite the PC's Address Book while the e-mail conduit is set to Do Nothing and the Notes conduit synchronizes the two devices' files.

What's a Conduit?

Conduit is the term that Palm uses to describe the software that connects data on your handheld with similar data on your computer. The Calendar conduit, for instance, makes sure that the Palm's Date Book and the computer's Palm Desktop or Outlook calendar stay completely in sync. Every application on your PDA that has a corresponding program on the PC is connected with its own conduit, and the Custom menu option is where you adjust them.

TIP   *If you're ever in doubt about the state of your conduits, be sure to check the action before you press the HotSync button by right-clicking the HotSync icon and choosing Custom. If you ever accidentally configure the HotSync Manager to Handheld Overwrites Desktop, for instance, you'll lose changes you made to the Palm Desktop or Outlook when you HotSync.*

With those terms in mind, let's look at the Custom dialog box. As you can see in Figure 3-3, the top of the box displays the name of the Palm unit. Managing more than one Palm from each PC is possible, so make sure to select the proper unit from the list menu before continuing. If you have only a single Palm, don't worry about this option.

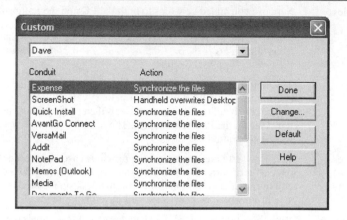

FIGURE 3-3 The Custom dialog box enables you to specify how each conduit behaves when you HotSync.

This dialog box displays a list of conduits and their actions. As you can see from the list, there's a unique conduit for each kind of application on the PDA. Most Palms include these conduits:

- **Calendar** or **Date Book**   Shares data between the Palm and desktop calendars.
- **Contacts** or **Address Book**   Shares data between the Palm and desktop address books.
- **Tasks** or **To Do List**   Shares data between the Palm and desktop to-do lists.
- **Memos** or **Memo Pad**   Shares data between the Palm and desktop memo pads.
- **Expense**   Shares expense entries between the Palm and an application such as Excel.
- **Install**   Transfers Palm OS applications from your PC's hard disk to the Palm.
- **Mail (or VersaMail)**   E-mail messages are synchronized between your desktop mail application and the Palm.
- **AvantGo Connect**   Used by the optional AvantGo application to transfer Web-based documents to your Palm.
- **System**   Transfers other files created by Palm applications between the PC and Palm.

NOTE   *If you install new software, you may end up with more conduits. Many programs come with their own conduits to control the flow of information between your PDA and desktop applications.*

To configure a conduit, either double-click an entry, or select it and then click the Change button. You'll find that you might have all four synchronization options or fewer, depending on which conduit you open.

When you configure a conduit, whatever selection you make applies only to the very next time you HotSync unless you check the box for Set As Default.

HotSync on the Road

Don't want to carry a bulky HotSync cradle while traveling? Here's an affordable, space-saving alternative for the road warrior: a streamlined HotSync cable. Cables are handy because they take up less room in a suitcase than the bulky cradle, and they don't rely on finicky Bluetooth or IR settings (though Bluetooth is a pretty cool way to HotSync wirelessly, if you can get it to work—see "HotSync with Bluetooth" later in this chapter). A HotSync cable costs about $20 and is an essential tool for the frequent traveler. You can buy one from a number of online stores, including Targus (www.targus.com), Belkin (www.belkin.com), and the Palm Web site (www.palm.com). Better still, check out the USB HotSync cables that will also charge your handheld. See Chapter 16 for details.

Reading the HotSync Log

Did your HotSync session go as planned? Did all your data get transferred properly, and did files get copied the way you expected? Usually it's pretty obvious if everything went well, but sometimes it's nice if your computer can tell you what actually happened, especially if the HotSync dialog box reports some sort of error.

During every HotSync, the HotSync Manager makes a record of everything that happened. This log is easy to read, and it can answer that nagging question, "Why didn't the calendar update after I added an entry for the Sandra Bullock fan club?" If the HotSync Manager noticed that something went wrong during a HotSync, it will tell you. Figure 3-4, for instance, shows the result of a HotSync that generated an error. The log reveals what happened.

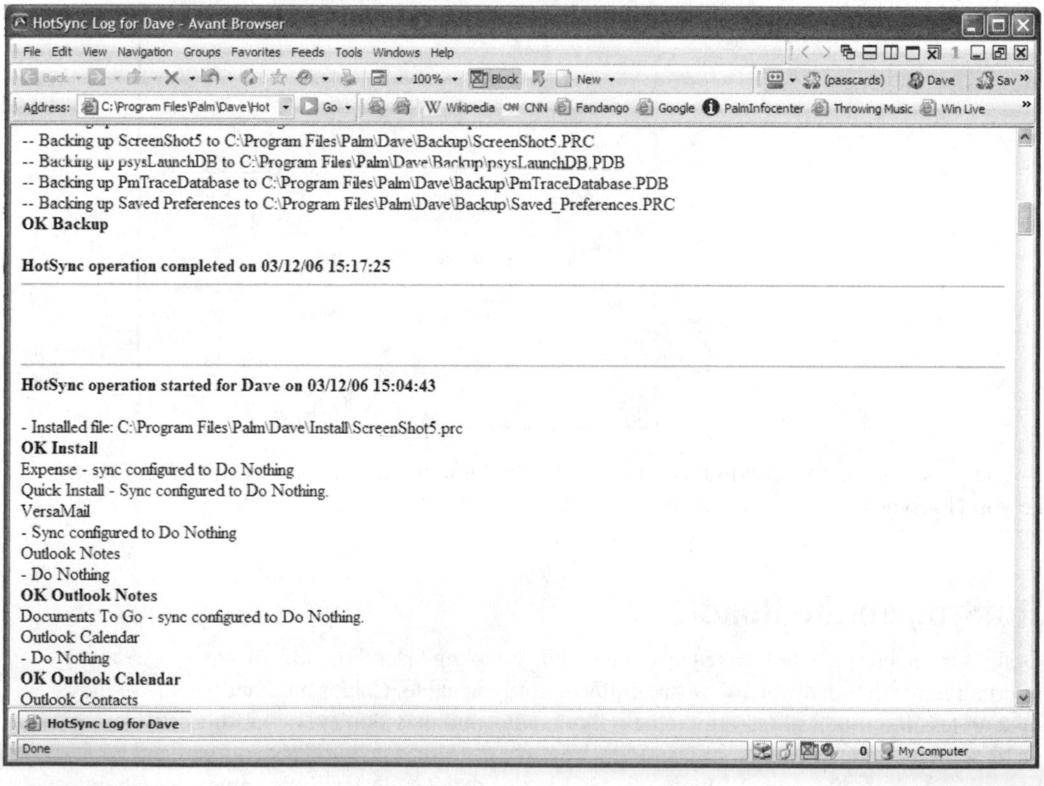

FIGURE 3-4 The HotSync log records the details of the last ten HotSyncs, and any errors that occurred along the way. This is the log from the Tungsten T5, which looks a bit different than the logs of older handhelds because it's rendered in HTML.

To see the log at any time, right-click the HotSync icon in the System Tray and choose View Log.

> **TIP** *If you have an older version of Palm Desktop software you can't perform a HotSync when the log is open, so be sure to close it before pressing the HotSync button. On newer Palm models, the log opens in a Web page and you can HotSync to your heart's content.*

The log displays a list of the actions that occurred for each of your last few HotSync sessions. The top of the log is the most recent, and older sessions are listed as you scroll down the page. Each session is separated by a message that indicates when it started and ended.

> **NOTE** *Until recently, HotSync logs were saved as ordinary text files. Starting with the Tungsten T5, PalmSource switched to the HTML format for HotSync logs, which means that they appear in a Web-browser window when opened. This makes the logs easier to read.*

What kind of information does a log reveal? Each conduit reports its status, and these are the messages you're most likely to see:

- **OK**   This is good news; the conduit's action succeeded with no errors.
- **Sync configured to Do Nothing**   If something didn't happen, the conduit might have been intentionally or mistakenly set to do nothing.

How to ...   **HotSync**

1. Plug the cradle or cable into your PC.
2. Set the Palm in the cradle or connect the cable.
3. Make sure the HotSync Manager software is running (by default, it probably is).
4. Verify that the conduits are set properly to transfer and synchronize data just the way you want (by default, they probably are).
5. Press the HotSync button on the cradle or cable.
6. Wait until you hear the "HotSync complete" tones before removing or disconnecting the Palm.

■ **Truncated** This means that a file stored on the PC (such as e-mail or an address book entry) was so long that not all of it would fit on the PDA.

■ **Records were modified in both Handheld and PC** You made changes to the same file on both the PC and the handheld. Because the HotSync Manager doesn't know which change is correct, it duplicated both files on both systems. You now have a chance to update the file and delete the one you don't want.

■ **Synchronization failed** This is something of a catch-all category that includes a slew of things that can go wrong, such as loose cables, driver conflicts, and pretty much anything else that might cause the HotSync to fail.

TIP
The HotSync log is also available on the PDA itself, albeit only for the most recent HotSync session. To reach it, tap the HotSync application, and then tap the Log button.

HotSyncing as a Way of Life

After your first HotSync, you may begin to see how convenient it is to have a duplicate of your desktop data on your PDA. But how often should you HotSync? The short answer is as frequently as you like. Some people HotSync daily, whereas others, whose data changes much less frequently, update their Palms only once a week or even less. Use the following guide as a rule of thumb:

■ HotSync anytime you leave the office with your PDA.

■ HotSync when you return from a trip to update your PC with new info stored on the handheld.

■ HotSync to update AvantGo. Many AvantGo Web channels are updated daily, and a HotSync each day keeps you current with the newest content. (As a reminder, AvantGo is one of our favorite third-party programs—see Chapter 10 for details.)

■ HotSync to install new applications on your PDA (this is discussed in Chapter 4).

What HotSyncing Does to Files

After your first HotSync, you have a set of data on both your PDA and your desktop. The goal of the HotSync process is to make sure that the data stays the same on both systems. So what happens when you change data on one or both of the computers? Table 3-1, which assumes that the conduit is set to Synchronize The Files, should help you understand the subtleties of the HotSync.

Before the HotSync	After the HotSync
You add a file to the Palm (or the PC).	That file is added to the PC (or the Palm).
You delete a file from the Palm (or PC).	The file is also deleted from the PC (or Palm).
You change a file on the Palm.	The file is changed on the PC.
You changed the same file on both the Palm and PC—they're now different.	Both versions of the file are added to the Palm and PC. You need to modify the file and delete the one you don't want to keep.

TABLE 3-1   What a HotSync Does to Your Files

Changing Conduits On-the-Fly

Often, you may find yourself changing all the conduits in your HotSync Manager except for one or two. You might want to disable everything except the Install conduit to quickly get a new program onto your PDA, for instance, or set everything except AvantGo to Do Nothing so you can get your news onto the PDA as you're running out the door to lunch.

Whatever the reason, you'll soon find that there's no easy way to disable several conduits at once, and successively changing five conduits to Do Nothing is almost as time-consuming as just doing the whole darned HotSync to begin with.

There's an easier way. Download the tremendously useful program called Ultrasoft NotSync from PalmGear.com. This program lets you quickly and easily change your conduits in just seconds. The change applies only to the very next HotSync, so it never affects your default settings.

With this in mind, you might not always want to use the Synchronize The Files option for all your conduits. Why not? For any number of reasons. Here are a few situations:

■ *You might rely on your Palm to take notes that you have no interest in copying to your PC.* In other words, you want to keep one set of notes on the PC, which is relevant to what you do at your desk, and another set of notes for when you're on the road. In this case, Do Nothing is probably the best option for your needs.

■ *You might take notes you don't need to keep after a trip is over.* In such an instance, you can use Desktop Overwrites Handheld for that conduit. After your trip is over, the handheld notes will be erased during the HotSync and replaced by the desktop notes.

 Don't forget that you can configure each conduit individually, so, for instance, the Address Book might be set to Synchronize The Files, while the Date Book is set to Desktop Overwrites Handheld.

Installing and HotSyncing More than One Palm

As we've already mentioned, you can install multiple Palm devices to a single computer. At any given time, for instance, Dave might have two different Palms, a Treo, and a Pocket PC (but we won't talk about that one...) hooked up to one little old PC. Yes, that's neurotic because he lives by himself with 21 cats and a life-size poster of Halle Berry, but that's a topic for a whole different book. The real issue is this: there's no reason why several different Palms can't all share the same data with Microsoft Outlook.

In general, you don't have to re-install the entire Palm Desktop CD for every Palm device that you connect to a computer. If two people in the same household each own Tungsten T5s, for instance, just install the Palm Desktop software once. Everything will be fine. But if you have two Palm devices that aren't the same brand, say, a Palm and a Tapwave, or two PDAs that are radically different (such as a Palm T5 and a Treo 650), then you'll have to install the Palm Desktop for each. Generally, you should install the PDAs in order, from oldest to newest. For instance, don't install Palm Desktop for the Palm m505 after you install the Treo 650's Palm Desktop—do it the other way around.

But what if you are using Outlook as your PIM? Only the first Palm will sync with the program. The fix is easy: open Outlook and look for a folder that controls how the Palm devices and Outlook sync with each other.

On older versions of Outlook and Palm Desktop, you should see a folder called PocketMirror. On the latest version of Outlook, you'll see a folder called Handheld Synchronization (and to get there, you must click the Folders icon at the bottom of the Navigation pane). You can see Outlook configured to sync with four PDAs in the following illustration, which depicts how these notes look in Outlook 2003:

3

No matter which route you have to take to get here, once you arrive you'll find a note for the first Palm. It will have the same name as your Palm device. Just double-click in a blank part of this folder and a new blank note will appear. Enter the exact name of the second device and close the note.

If you follow these steps, your new PDA will now sync and share data with Outlook. Repeat this process for as many Palm OS devices as you attach to your PC.

Keeping Your Data Separate

When you have two or more people HotSyncing their Palms to a single computer, you should consider whether you want to keep the information on the gadgets, such as calendar entries, contact information, and the like, separate them, or lump them all together. If you don't care about keeping all the Palm data separate, use Outlook, which mixes all the information from each PDA into one big data soup. But if you want Dave's data to be completely independent from Rick's stuff, then use Palm Desktop.

Using a Notebook's IR Port to HotSync

Do you travel with both a laptop and your Palm? If you do, you can wirelessly synchronize the data between the two devices by using the IR port built into your laptop (if it has one, and some laptops don't) and your Palm. Being able to HotSync without carting a cradle around means you can easily keep your notebook and Palm current no matter where you are.

NOTE   *The capability to IR HotSync doesn't exist in older versions of the Palm operating system, so you might have to upgrade to take advantage of this capability.*

Prepping the Notebook

To HotSync your Palm to a notebook, you first need to prepare your notebook. Namely, it must have the necessary infrared hardware and driver. Here's what you need to do:

1. Start by installing the Palm Desktop software, if it isn't already on the system. We obviously need that later.

2. Does your notebook have an IR port? This might sound silly, but check visually for the port. It's a small, reddish plastic window that's usually on the back of the system, but also might be located on the side.

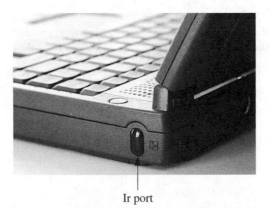

Ir port

3. If you have the IR port, you next need to verify that the IR driver is installed. To do this, open the Control Panel by choosing Start | Settings | Control Panel. Look for an icon named Infrared. If it's there, great. The necessary software is installed.

4. Make sure the infrared port is enabled. Double-click the Infrared icon in the Control Panel. You should see the Infrared Monitor dialog box. Click the Options tab and make sure the Enable Infrared Communication option is checked. If not, your notebook won't be able to communicate with the Palm.

5. While you're on this tab, make a note of what COM port the infrared device is using. This should be displayed near the option you selected in step 4.

Before you go any further, be sure to perform at least one normal Local HotSync with the Palm and this notebook. That's right, you need to connect the HotSync cradle and press the button the old-fashioned way. After that, you can put the cradle back on your desktop PC and forget about it. Your first HotSync on a PC cannot be an IR HotSync, so if you arrive in Topeka with a brand-new notebook and plan to IR HotSync with it, you're in for a big surprise.

Now that you have performed the initial HotSync with the cradle, your laptop is now ready to start performing IR HotSyncs.

3

Configuring the HotSync Manager

Now that your IR port is ready, you need to configure the HotSync Manager for IR communications. This part is easy. All you need to do is change the COM port to the same one the IR port is accessing. To do this:

1. On the laptop, click the HotSync Manager icon in the System Tray and choose Setup from the menu. You should see the Setup dialog box.

2. Switch to the Local tab. Change the serial port to whatever COM port the infrared driver is using. You can find this out by opening the Infrared icon in the Control Panel, as discussed in the previous section.

3. Click OK to close the Setup dialog box.

Performing the HotSync

Now it's time to perform the HotSync. Turn on your Palm and tap the HotSync icon. Make sure it's set to Local (not Modem) and choose IR to a PC/Handheld from the menu.

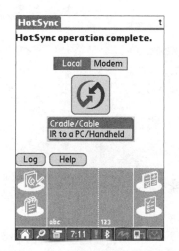

Point the Palm at the IR port on the notebook and tap the HotSync button in the middle of the Palm's screen. You should see the HotSync operation start. That's it!

HotSyncing with Bluetooth

The availability of Bluetooth in both PDAs (such as the Palm TX) and in new computers (many notebooks now have it) opens up a whole new way of synchronizing data— wirelessly.

In principle, Bluetooth HotSyncs are pretty simple. After "pairing" your Palm and your computer, all you need to do is select the HotSync option from your PDA to wirelessly sync up to 30 feet away. Your PDA needn't be in the cradle, and everything else should work more or less the same as a traditional HotSync. For the most part, that's true. Unfortunately, the exact procedure will vary depending upon which Bluetooth adapter you have installed, or if you're trying to sync via a Bluetooth access point. Check the documentation that came with your Bluetooth gear or give the company's tech support a call. In general, you'll need to perform these steps for a successful Bluetooth HotSync:

1. Pair the devices. The procedure for this varies depending upon which PDA you have and what kind of Bluetooth adapter is on your PC, but Palm includes an excellent wizard to help you through this process. Tap the Bluetooth icon in the toolbar at the bottom of the Palm's screen and then tap Prefs. Next, tap Setup Devices and choose PC Setup from the devices screen.

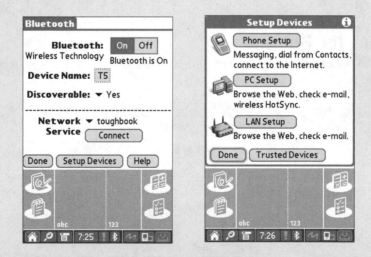

2. Tell your Palm's HotSync controls how to find the Bluetooth device you want to HotSync with. If your PDA doesn't have a slick wizard, you might have to do this manually. In the HotSync application on the PDA, choose Options | Connection Setup and create a new connection. Choose to connect to the PC via Bluetooth, and select the computer after your Palm searches for it (the computer needs to be "discoverable" for this to work).

3

```
┌─────────────────────────────────┐
│ ▓▓▓ Edit Connection      ❶ ▓▓▓  │
│ Name: PowerBook                 │
│                                 │
│ Connect to: ▼ PC                │
│        Via: ▼ Bluetooth         │
│     Device: ┊dave johnson's Co...┊│
│                                 │
│                                 │
│                                 │
│  ( OK )  ( Cancel ) ( Details... )│
└─────────────────────────────────┘
```

3. On the HotSync application screen, select the connection you just created as the method to connect via the menu under the HotSync icon in the middle of the screen.

```
┌─────────────────────────────────┐
│ ▓HotSync▓                     t │
│ Last HotSync 6/15/03, 10:28     │
│ am using Cradle/Cable           │
│      ┌──────┬──────┐            │
│      │ Local│ Modem│            │
│      └──────┴──────┘            │
│         ┌──────────┐            │
│         │   ◢◣     │            │
│      ┌──┴──────────┴──┐        │
│      │ Cradle/Cable    │        │
│      │ IR to a PC/Handheld │    │
│      │ PicoBlue LAN    │        │
│      │ PicoBluetooth   │        │
│      │ LAN T68i        │        │
│      │ bt to pc        │        │
│ ( Log )│▓PowerBook▓    │        │
│      └─────────────────┘        │
└─────────────────────────────────┘
```

4. Once all these steps have been accomplished, you should be able to HotSync from now on just by tapping the HotSync icon on the PDA. The exact procedure though will vary depending upon your PC and Bluetooth adapter.

Chapter 4

Get Information In and Out of Your Handheld

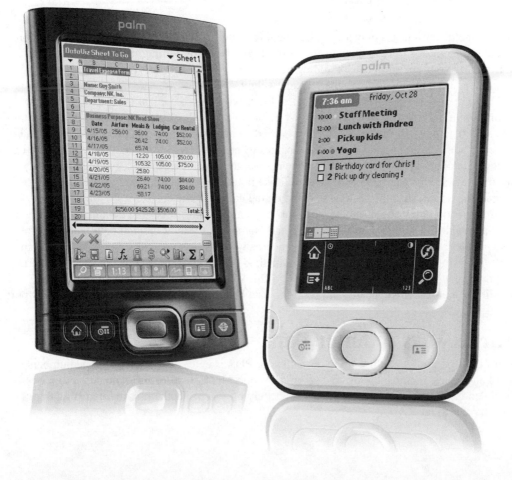

How to...

- Use Graffiti to enter data into your handheld
- Type using the onscreen keyboard
- Work with built-in keyboards
- Enter data using Palm Desktop or Outlook
- Use alternative gestures to write in Graffiti more effectively
- Display Graffiti help
- Beam items to another handheld
- Beam your business card to another handheld
- Install new software on your device
- Install software on memory cards
- Delete unwanted applications

A handheld computer is only as good as the information you store inside it. Or, perhaps more to the point, it's only as good as the methods you have for getting information into it. After all, if storing your appointments or adding new contacts is too difficult, you won't bother doing it, and then all you have is an expensive paperweight.

Case in point: the Rex, a credit card-sized PDA that debuted back at the start of the PDA Revolution in the late 1990s to generally favorable reviews. This little guy was so small and thin that it could actually fit into a wallet, yet it carried contacts and appointments like a champ. The problem? You couldn't add to it or make changes when away from your PC. You could view only whatever data was already loaded. For some people, this wasn't a big deal, but public reaction was underwhelming. Palm OS handhelds sell like hotcakes (the good ones, with the blueberries in them) in part because they can be updated on the go, and quite easily.

You already know about some of the tools at your disposal for getting data in and out of your handheld. In Chapter 3, we talked in detail (some would say too much detail, but we ignore those people) about how to HotSync, and you already know that you can enter data directly in the device using Graffiti, an almost ordinary method of handwriting. In this chapter, you learn everything you'll ever need to know about Graffiti. We also cover other data entry methods, including the onscreen keyboard, and beaming data between handhelds using the built-in IR port.

The Three Ways to Enter Data

One of the first things you'll want to do with your PDA is enter data, such as phone numbers, e-mail addresses, memos, to-dos, and so on. Hey, don't look so surprised. The core programs, like Calendar, Contacts, Memo Pad, and Tasks, rely on you to fill them with interesting things you can refer to later.

> **NOTE**   *Just a reminder that Palm recently renamed some of the core apps, so depending upon which PDA you own, yours might be named differently. Back in the Olde Days, Calendar used to be known as Date Book, for instance; Contacts was Address Book; and Tasks was called To Do List.*

There are three primary ways to enter data into a Palm OS device:

- ■ Write it in using Graffiti, the built-in handwriting recognition software.
- ■ "Tap type" using the onscreen keyboard.
- ■ Enter data into Palm Desktop or Outlook on your PC, and then HotSync the data to your handheld. This is the best method for people who are just starting out, as it's usually easiest. If you have an old-fashioned paper address book, for instance, and you want to copy all the names to your handheld, it's much easier to enter them into your PC than into the device itself. Similarly, if you have an electronic address book from another program or PDA, you can probably import the data into Palm Desktop or Outlook, and then HotSync it all to your new PDA far more easily than jotting it all down in the PDA.

> **TIP**   *You can also use special portable keyboards to enter data in your handheld. No PC is required. For information on PDA-compatible keyboards, see Chapter 16. Yet another way to get data into your handheld is by beaming, which we discuss later in this chapter.*

All About Graffiti

Graffiti is a specialized handwriting recognition system that enables you to enter text into your PDA almost error-free. What do we mean by "almost?" As we discussed in Chapter 2, Graffiti (see Figure 4-1) doesn't recognize actual handwriting, but rather it is designed to understand a specific set of characters. Once you learn all these characters, you should find that Graffiti delivers near-perfect accuracy.

> **NOTE**   *The latest Palm OS handhelds actually run Graffiti 2, which, true to its name, is the second iteration of the Graffiti handwriting recognition engine. If you've ever used an older Palm OS handheld, you'll find that some of the pen-strokes have changed. The letter T, for instance, must now be drawn with two strokes (just like you would draw it on paper) instead of the highly stylized single-stroke version required by Graffiti 1.*

Here are a few key notes and tips for the first-time Graffiti user:

- ■ The Graffiti area is divided into two sections: one for lower case letters, and one for numbers. Upper case letters are created by writing on the line (which on some models is invisible) separating the two sections.
- ■ Letters and numbers must be written one on top of the other, not one next to the other as when writing on paper. Just imagine that when you write a character, it dissolves into the screen and then you can write the next character in the same spot. This is perhaps the hardest concept for novices to grasp, but once you practice a bit, you'll find it completely natural.

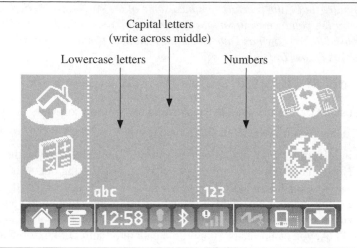

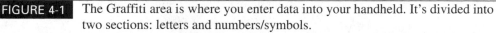

FIGURE 4-1 The Graffiti area is where you enter data into your handheld. It's divided into two sections: letters and numbers/symbols.

- Letters are easy. They're mostly block text, though Graffiti does recognize certain cursive letters. In fact, Graffiti supports multiple ways of drawing each letter of the alphabet. See Table 4-1 for details.

- When you want to make an upper case or a lower case letter, it matters where you draw it in the Graffiti area, not how you draw it. The middle of the Graffiti area makes upper case letters, and the left side of the screen gives you lower case letters. So if you draw a lower case *b* in the middle section of the Graffiti area, you'll get an upper case *B*. Likewise, an upper case *B* drawn in the lower case section (the left side) will result in a lower case *b*. The location of the pen-stroke is what matters, not the actual character that you draw.

- Punctuation and other special characters are the hardest part of using Graffiti. The problem is that some punctuation marks, for example, must be made in the letter area, whereas others must be made in the number area. Over time you'll be able to memorize the various pen-strokes and their required locales. In the meantime, do what we do and call up the onscreen keyboard instead.

TIP   *If you're having trouble writing while holding the device, try laying your PDA on a flat surface. Rick finds it's much easier to write with Graffiti when he's not holding the device. Dave, on the other hand, prefers to write with the PDA in his hand, so he thinks Rick's approach is as crazy as a dancing giraffe. Experiment and stick with whatever approach works best for you.*

The Virtual Graffiti Area

Some Palm OS handhelds, like the Tungsten T5 and the TX, employ what's called a virtual Graffiti area, a Graffiti area that's part of the software instead of part of the hardware. That means it can disappear when you don't need it, thereby giving you some extra screen estate for icons, text, and so on. Think of it as "Graffiti on demand."

To open and close the Graffiti area, tap the arrow at the bottom-right corner of the screen. In most cases, the current application will shrink (or enlarge) to accommodate it, as shown in the illustration below.

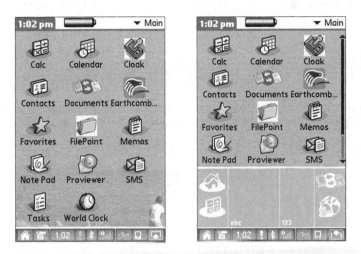

Just keep in mind that the Graffiti area isn't always available. The arrow might appear "grayed out" in circumstances when data input isn't necessary. Also, programs which don't know about virtual Graffiti, won't increase in size to fill the space. There might just be some unused dead space at the bottom of the screen.

One of the coolest aspects of virtual Graffiti is that you can see your pen-strokes as you make them in the Graffiti area, just as you can when writing on paper. (Of course, on a PDA the "virtual ink" disappears the moment you lift your stylus. Let's see a piece of paper do that!) Many people find that seeing their input helps them improve their Graffiti accuracy.

Speaking of seeing your writing on the screen, Palms with virtual Graffiti areas also support a "write-anywhere" Graffiti mode. Just tap the write-anywhere button in the Palm's status bar (it's the one that looks like a squiggle), and you can write anywhere on the screen. You'll still need to write letters on the left and numbers on the right. Just pretend that there's a big invisible Graffiti area that covers the whole screen. To turn it off, just tap the write-anywhere button a second time.

Using the Onscreen Keyboard

Even after you get comfortable writing with Graffiti, there might be times when you want to input specific characters without using pen strokes. After all, remembering how to make some rarely used characters in the middle of taking real-time notes can be hard, and having access to a keyboard can be a real lifesaver. In fact, we know some people who prefer the keyboard to Graffiti altogether.

TIP

When you have to enter a password, tapping it out on the keyboard is usually easier than writing it with Graffiti. Using the keyboard, you can be sure you're entering the right characters, error free.

All it takes to use the onscreen keyboard is a tap. At the bottom of the Graffiti area, you'll see letters and numbers—*ABC* and *123,* to be precise. Tap either of these to call up the appropriate keyboard (alpha or numeric).

NOTE

As with the Graffiti area itself, the keyboard appears only in situations where it's appropriate, specifically, when a cursor is in a data field. If no application is open into which you can insert text, you simply hear a beep when you tap the keyboard icons.

Once the keyboard is open, note that you can switch between letters and numbers by tapping the selector at the bottom of the screen. A set of international characters also is available. The keyboard on most Palm models looks like this:

Tap here to switch to the numeric keyboard

Tap here to switch to the international keyboard

On newer models that use a virtual Graffiti area, the keyboard has a totally different look. Instead of a Done button, you now tap an icon to return to the Graffiti mode:

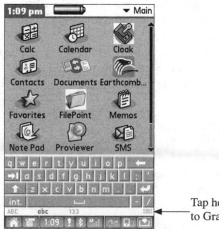

Tap here to return to Graffiti

Remember the following tips about the onscreen keyboard:

■ You can continue to use Graffiti even while you have the keyboard open.

■ Use the SHIFT key on the keyboard the same way you'd use a real keyboard to create an upper case letter.

■ The CAP key is actually a CAPS LOCK key, which makes all subsequent letters upper case until you tap it again.

■ If you're typing with the CAPS LOCK on and you want to make a single character lower case, tap the SHIFT key.

■ The Numeric keyboard provides access to special symbols and punctuation. Many users find it easier to call up this keyboard than to remember Graffiti's often cryptic punctuation strokes.

Using Palm Desktop or Outlook

Graffiti and the onscreen keyboard are great when you're on the go, but what about getting data into your handheld when you're sitting comfortably at your desk? It's usually much faster and easier to use your computer to enter data.

How? By using Palm Desktop or another program with a HotSync conduit (namely, Microsoft Outlook). In other words, suppose you need to enter a long note into your PDA. Instead of writing it out with Graffiti, which is admittedly slow going, you can create a note in Palm Desktop or Outlook (depending on which program you use), and then HotSync.

Let's add a note to the Memo Pad using Palm Desktop. Do this:

NOTE   *If you configured your device to synchronize with Microsoft Outlook, use that program's Notes module for this exercise.*

1. Start Palm Desktop.

2. Switch to the Memos view by clicking the Memos button on the left side of the screen.

3. Click the New Memo button (or just start typing) and type your note (see Figure 4-2).

4. When you finish typing your note, click anywhere in the Memo list. The note is automatically saved and the memo's first line becomes its subject line (see Chapter 7 if you need a Memo Pad refresher).

5. When you finish entering data, HotSync. Presto! You've just entered a lengthy note the fast and easy way.

Getting to Know Graffiti

Knowing Graffiti like the back of your hand is essential to using your PDA effectively. As we pointed out earlier in this chapter, Graffiti doesn't interpret whatever chicken-like scrawl you happen to write in the Graffiti area. Although it might be nice if the device could recognize unmodified handwriting, we've all seen what happened to that technology.

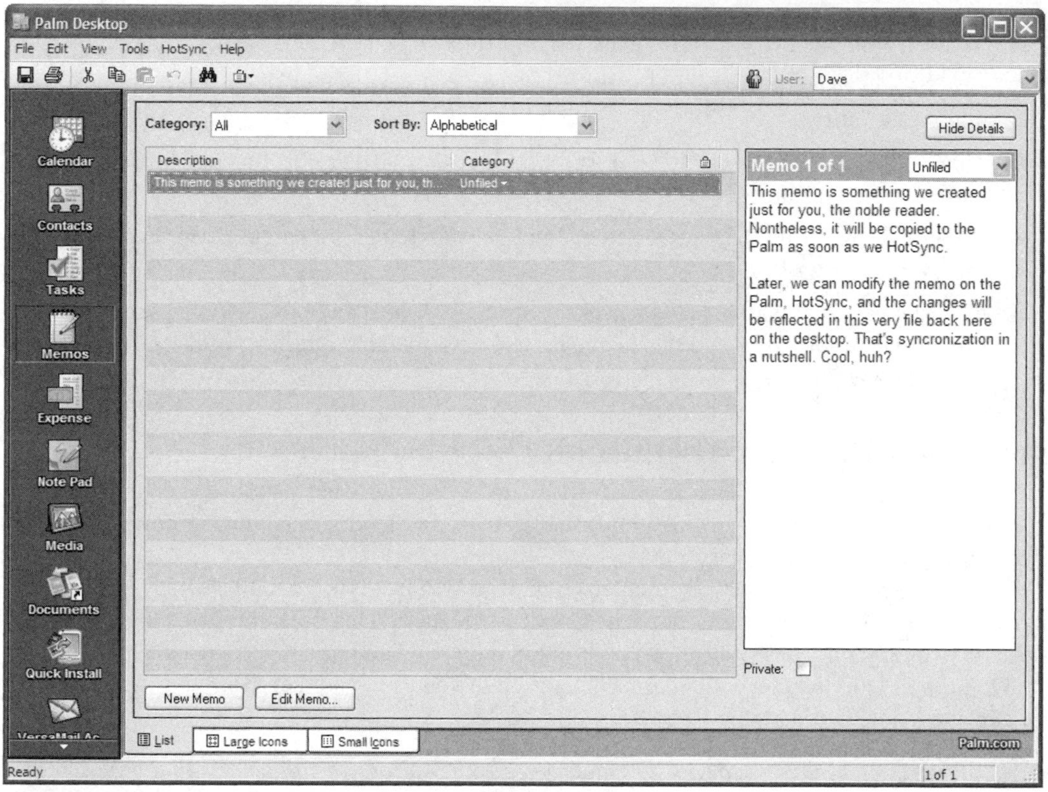

FIGURE 4-2   Palm Desktop is a convenient way to get information into your PDA if you have time to work at your desktop PC

Specifically, Apple's Newton MessagePad—what most people consider to be the first real PDA—tried hard to understand free-form handwriting. And while it did a darned good job, first-time users faced an uphill battle getting it to understand them. Not until you had a chance to use the Newton for a few hours did it start behaving like it comprehended English. To make matters worse, Apple insisted on putting MessagePads in stores with big signs inviting people to saunter over and try them. The result? People would scratch out a sentence in sloppy handwriting and the Newton would convert the result into total gibberish, kind of like what you think Lou Reed might be muttering in a Velvet Underground song. The public never got any confidence that Apple had a workable handwriting recognition engine, and even though the Newton actually was a great little PDA, it failed largely because of public perception. (For the record, Rick thinks it failed because it was an overpriced brick. Dave, on the other hand, memos that Rick was just intimidated because the Newton was smarter than he was.)

Palm didn't make the same mistake. Graffiti is designed to recognize particular gestures as specific characters, thus reducing the possibility of error. In fact, if you routinely draw the characters according to the template, you should get near-perfect accuracy. Graffiti doesn't have to understand fifty different ways of making the letter *T*, so it's both fast and accurate, as long as you can draw a *T* the way the Palm wants to see the *T*.

NOTE   *Because Palm officially switched to Graffiti 2 a couple years ago, and because all the latest models use it, we're focusing exclusively on that version of the software. If you happen to have an older handheld, you'll find that much of the information here is still applicable, but some of the gestures shown in the upcoming tables have definitely changed. Consult your device's built-in or in-the-box cheat sheet if you need help with Graffiti 1 gestures. Or track down a copy of* How To Do Everything with Your Palm Handheld, 4th Edition, *which covers the original Graffiti gestures.*

Did you know?

Your PDA Has a Built-in Graffiti Cheat-Sheet

There are two ways to access Graffiti help: draw a line from anywhere in the Graffiti area to the top of the screen; or, in any of the core apps (and in most programs that allow you to enter data), tap Menu, and then scan the drop-down menus for an entry called Graffiti Help. Tap it and you'll see the following screen (or one quite similar to it):

Tap the onscreen arrow (or press the down scroll/Navigator button) to flip to the next page of gestures. Tap Done when you're finished and you'll be returned to whatever program you were using.

General Tips and Tricks for Graffiti

Before we get started with the nuts and bolts of writing with Graffiti (which we call *gestures*), it might help to remember a few things:

- Make your letters and numbers as large as possible while staying within the confines of the Graffiti-area section (that is, the left or right side) in which you're writing. Bigger characters are recognized more easily than smaller ones.

- Don't cross the (sometimes invisible) line between the letter and number portions of the Graffiti area, unless you want a capital letter.

- Don't write at a slant. Some handwriting recognition engines can account for characters being drawn at an angle to the baseline, but Graffiti can't.

- Don't write too fast. Graffiti doesn't care about your speed. But if you write too fast, you won't have sufficient control over the shape of your gestures and you can make mistakes.

- If you have a hard time making certain gestures consistently, try the character a different way. Even though Table 4-1 shows only one way to draw each letter, you can write most letters by drawing them upper case or lower case. Use whichever one works best for you.

- If you want to train yourself in the wily ways of Graffiti, scan the Home screen for a Graffiti icon and tap it to find built-in Graffiti help. (In some models you'll need to find the Quick Tour icon and navigate to that applet's Graffiti tutorial.) There you can practice making gestures and see animated examples of how each letter, number, symbol, and punctuation mark is drawn.

The Hardest Characters

Everyone seems to have trouble with some Graffiti character. Even if you can never get your PDA to recognize your letter *B,* that doesn't make you a failure. It just means you should learn an alternative stroke for that letter or put extra care into drawing it precisely and slowly. Even we have trouble with some letters.

Dave: In the Olde Days of Graffiti 1, my Palm would never make Js and Vs properly. It used to drive me nuts. Now that I use Graffiti 2 on my TX, I have a different problem: I always try to make the letter I without dotting it. In Old Graffiti, the I was a single stroke, but in these newfangled Graffiti 2 days, that now gives you the letter L. In Graffiti 2, you literally have to remember to dot your Is and cross your Ts or you won't get the letters you're after. Argghhhhh!

Rick: If you'd ever seen Dave's chicken-scratch excuse for handwriting, you'd understand why he sometimes has trouble with Graffiti. To be fair, though, a few characters seem tougher to make than others. The T gives me tons of trouble, but I've learned how to overcome it: Draw it as a capital letter (even if you want it to be lower case, which it will be unless you cross the invisible line between the letter and number sides). I also have to remind myself to draw the T big and straight. If I rush, it usually doesn't come out right.

Letter Number	Gesture	Letter Number	Gesture
A	Λ	S	S
B	B	T	t
C	C	U	U
D	D	V	V
E	E	W	W
F	Γ	X	X
G	G	Y	y
H	h	Z	Z
I	i	0	O
J	J	1	I
K	K	2	2
L	L	3	3
M	m	4	4
N	N	5	5
O	O	6	6
P	P	7	7
Q	q	8	8
R	R	9	9

TABLE 4-1   Graffiti 2 Numbers and Letters

Spaces, Backspaces, and Deleting Text

Words are arguably more useful when you can put a space between them, thus enabling the casual reader to discern where each one ends and the next one begins. In Graffiti, it's easy to insert spaces. So easy, in fact, that you might be able to figure it out on your own (but we'll tell you anyway). In either of the letter sections, draw a line that starts on the left and goes to the right (not all the way to the right—it's just a little dash really), and you'll see that the cursor skips ahead a space. You can use this gesture to insert spaces between words or to perform any other space-making task you might have. And, yes, you can insert multiple spaces simply by performing this gesture as many times as needed.

NOTE When you make the space gesture in the number section of the Graffiti area, you get an actual dash instead of a space.

The backspace, not surprisingly, is exactly the opposite. Draw a gesture from right to left and the cursor backs up, deleting any text it encounters along the way. This works in all three sections of the Graffiti area. It's just like tapping the backspace key on your computer keyboard.

Using the backspace gesture is great if you want to delete one or two characters, but what if you want to delete a whole sentence? That backspace swipe can get tiring if you have a lot of text to kill or replace all at once. Luckily, there's an easy solution: select the text you want to delete. The next thing you write will replace the selected text. Here's how to do it:

1. In a memo or any other document, find the section of text you want to replace.

2. Tap and hold the stylus down at the start of the text you want to select, and then drag the stylus across the text and pick it up when you've selected all the text in question. This is not unlike selecting text in your favorite word processor, but the stylus takes the place of the mouse.

3. In the Graffiti area, write some new text. The old text is immediately erased and replaced with the new text. If you want to delete the text, use the backspace gesture instead.

Adding Punctuation

To add punctuation to your prose, you need to learn some special Graffiti gestures (see Figure 4-3). This is where Graffiti can get a little frustrating, at least until you memorize these gestures. The period is by far the easiest. It's a dot, just like you'd make on paper. Tap once in either section of the Graffiti area and you'll see a period appear. The comma can also be made anywhere, but drawing it is not quite like drawing a comma on paper. See Table 4-2 to learn the gesture.

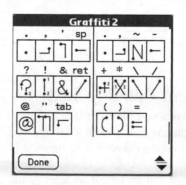

FIGURE 4-3 Some punctuation in Graffiti approximates normal writing. You make a period just by tapping, or create an exclamation point by drawing a line and a dot, and so on.

Punctuation	Gesture	Punctuation	Gesture
Period	•	Slash	/
Comma	⌐	Backslash	\
Question mark	?	At Symbol	@
Exclamation point	!	Asterisk	X
Colon	:	Number sign	#
Semicolon	;	Greater than	>
Open parenthesis	(	Less than	<
Close parenthesis	)	Percent	%
Tab	⌐	Equal sign	=
Apostrophe	'	Plus sign	+
Quotes	"	Dollar sign	$

TABLE 4-2   The Most Common Graffiti 2 Punctuation Gestures

TIP

If you have a lot of trouble with specific punctuation, you can always call up the onscreen keyboard and tap-type your desired symbol.

As we mentioned earlier, Graffiti requires that certain punctuation-mark gestures be made in the letter areas, others in the number area. Half the battle lies in remembering which ones go where. (The other half is learning the gestures themselves, though many of them are identical to what you'd draw on paper.) However, you can win that battle by drawing a *Shift stroke,* which puts Graffiti into a kind of symbol mode and enables punctuation gestures to be recognized anywhere, not just in specific areas.

The Shift stroke is nothing more than a vertical line drawn from the bottom of the Graffiti area to the top. When you make this stroke, you'll usually see a large black dot (or an up-pointing arrow) appear in the lower-right corner of the screen. This indicates you're now in symbol (more accurately known as Punctuation Shift) mode. Once you draw your punctuation or symbol gesture, you'll immediately leave this mode and return to normal writing.

NOTE

Not all models indicate when you're in Punctuation Shift mode; sometimes you just have to "fly blind," or just switch to the keyboard instead.

We could go on and on about Graffiti, but there's no need. You can find plenty of good instruction in the User's Guide. (We prefer to save our pages for the really cool stuff, like games, music, movies, and all that.)

Using Shortcuts

Everyone loves shortcuts. In desktop applications like Microsoft Office, many folks eschew the mouse for keyboard shortcuts that speed tasks such as text formatting and saving files. The Palm OS also has the capability to save you time and effort using *shortcuts*. Even better, they're user-definable, so you can create your own library of them to suit your specific needs.

So what are shortcuts, exactly? If you have a word or phrase you frequently write over and over (such as "Rick throws like a girl"), you can assign an abbreviation to it and let Graffiti do the hard work of writing the phrase in its entirety. See Chapter 2 for information on creating and using shortcuts.

Another Kind of Shortcut: Menu Commands

If you're a big fan of hitting CTRL-S in Microsoft Word to save your work, then you should love this. The Palm OS has its own menu shortcuts that you can access with Graffiti. To do that, though, you must remember two important items:

- How to draw the Graffiti Command stroke
- What the shortcut character is for the menu command that you want to invoke

The command stroke is easy. To put your PDA in Command mode, draw the gesture shown on the left. After you draw the gesture, your device displays the Command bar. Now, write the proper character to invoke the menu item, say, C for Copy, or F for Font.

So, you tried entering a command, but you're curious about the Command bar. What are all those little symbols and what do they do?

Actually, the Command bar is a clever tool that you can use to quickly access common Palm OS features. It's context-sensitive, which means it'll have different icons, depending on when you make the Command stroke.

Try this: Open the Calendar and select an appointment by dragging the stylus across some text. Make the Command stroke. Voilà! You now have choices like cut, copy, and paste. You can experiment with the Command bar in various applications to see what kinds of shortcuts you have available.

4

FIGURE 4-4   Many menu items have Graffiti shortcuts associated with them.

As you can see in the preceding screenshot, the Command bar also displays icons that allow quick access to certain commonly used functions, like beam, copy, and delete. These icons appear in a context-sensitive fashion, so don't be surprised if you don't always see the same ones. If you haven't selected any text, for instance, there's nothing to copy, so you won't see the copy icon.

Most menu items have no corresponding icon in the Command bar, however, so you have to learn what the shortcuts are for each item. To do so, display the menu (tap the Menu button and you'll see something similar to Figure 4-4). As you can see, many menu items have associated Graffiti shortcuts.

NOTE   *The Command mode lasts for only a few seconds, after which the bar disappears. If you don't write the shortcut character quickly enough, you'll need to perform the Command stroke again.*

Beaming Data between Devices

On "Star Trek," transporters are used to beam people and equipment from one location to another. While we're a long way from being able to beam physical things around, the Palm OS makes it possible to beam almost any kind of data between handheld PC users.

All current (and most old) Palm OS handhelds have an infrared, or IR, port (see Chapter 2 if you need a refresher). Using this port, you can wirelessly transmit and receive information in a surprising number of ways. You can

- Use your PDA to remotely control your TV and stereo.
- Send phone numbers from your PDA to a cell phone.
- Print data on an IR-equipped printer.
- Beam data to other handhelds.
- Play two-player games head-to-head.

These things are pretty cool, but the more common use for beaming is exchanging mundane business data. All the core applications (Address Book, Memo Pad, and so on) support beaming, so you can beam

- Contact listings
- Your own "business card" from the address book
- Appointments
- Memos
- Tasks

In addition, you can beam entire applications to other Palm OS handheld users. For instance, if you download a freeware program from the Internet and want to share it with friends or coworkers, go ahead: it's a snap to beam the program.

NOTE *Beaming is not the same as "sending," which is accomplished via Bluetooth and described in the upcoming section, "Bluetooth vs. Beaming."*

How to Beam

No matter what you're planning to beam or receive, the process is essentially the same. Actually seeing the process demonstrated is faster than reading about it; but because neither of us is handy to stop by your office today, here's the process in a nutshell:

1. Orient the two devices so their IR ports face each other and are between a few inches and a few feet apart. If you're too close, the devices might have a hard time locking onto each other. If they are too far away, the signal won't be strong enough to reach.

2. As the sender, you should choose the item you want to beam. That means tapping until you've actually opened the contact, memo, or whatever.
3. Tap Menu | Beam Item (where "Item" could be Memo, Contact, and so on).

Did you know?

You Can Beam from a Palm to a Pocket PC and Back Again

We've made no secret of our general dislike for PDAs based on the Pocket PC (also known as Windows Mobile) operating system. However, we realize there are a lot of these devices out there, and, well, it's time to bury the hatchet and just try to get along. Beaming is the first step towards this long-overdue détente.

To put it another way, you can beam data from your Palm OS-based handheld to a Pocket PC, and Pocket PC users can beam data from their devices to your handheld. Although the operating systems are dramatically different and don't run any of the same software, they are capable of exchanging contacts, appointments, memos, and other data via beaming. (Of course, feel free to point out the superiority of your Palm OS handheld by effortlessly beaming your virtual business card, which is done by holding down the Address Book (or Contacts) button for two seconds. It requires a lot more steps for a Pocket PC user to beam something.)

TIP   *If you beam often, you might want to use the beam shortcut—a Command stroke followed by the letter B (or a tap of the Beam icon).*

 4. A dialog box appears to indicate that the beam is in progress. First, you see a message that your device is searching for the other device. Once it's found and the data is transmitted, that message goes away.

 5. After the beam, your PDA goes back to business as usual. You won't get a message that indicates that the beam was successful. The receiver, on the other hand, gets a dialog box that asks permission to accept the beamed data. As the receiver, you might need to decide what category to file the information into and then tap either Yes or No, depending on whether you want to keep the item. If you tap Yes, the data is integrated into your PDA in the category that you specified. (There's no category decision to make if you're receiving an application or some other non-core-app data.)

> **Beam**
>
> (?) **Do you want to accept "Four Ways to Enter Text" into Memos?**
>
> **Category:** ▼ Unfiled
>
> (Yes)   (No)

TIP   *As the receiver, it's a good idea to specify a category in which to file the data you just received. If you let stuff like Address Book entries accumulate in the Unfiled category, it can later become difficult to find what you're looking for.*

To Accept or Not to Accept

By default, your handheld is set to automatically receive beamed items. However, there are two reasons you might want to disable auto-receive for beaming:

■ Because the IR port is constantly on and searching for transmissions from other devices, your PDA uses slightly more battery power. Is this a big deal? We don't think so. The extra power consumption is marginal. But if you really want to maximize battery life, turn off Beam Receive until you need it.

■ With all the concerns about viruses and other malicious programs that exist for PCs today, some folks are nervous about leaving their PDA in a state that receives data all the time. Our call: Palm OS viruses aren't a threat, and you have to manually accept a beamed program after reception anyway. So don't worry about it.

So, although we obviously don't think leaving auto-receive on is a big deal, here's how to disable that feature if you want to:

1. From the Home screen, tap the Prefs icon.

2. Choose the Power category (or General if you have an older model).

3. Change Beam Receive from On to Off.

4

Troubleshooting Beaming Problems

Sometimes, beaming just doesn't seem to work. You try to receive an item from another
Palm or Pocket PC, and nothing happens. You check Prefs and make sure that Beam Receive
is turned on. Still, nothing happens. You reset your Palm, hoping that will fix the problem.
No luck. You start to think that your Palm is simply defective, and you consider throwing it
into a nearby river.

Well, don't test your Palm's buoyancy quite yet. It's probably something fairly mundane.
Specifically, if you have a wireless keyboard for your Palm, often the keyboard driver will
interfere with routine beaming. To fix the problem, just open the keyboard driver and disable
it by clearing the Keyboard Driver checkbox, as in the illustration below:

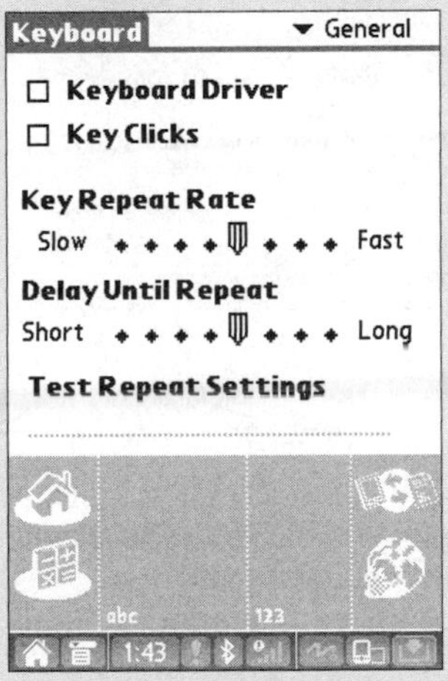

Leave the driver disabled until you actually need to type so that beaming will work
as expected.

Remember that after turning Beam Receive to off, you won't be able to receive beamed data
until you turn it back on again.

Selecting Items for Beaming

So, now that you know the rudiments of beaming, you're no doubt eager to start. While we're
usually a pretty down-to-earth couple of guys, we have to admit there's a certain coolness factor
involved in beaming things in the middle of a meeting or while strolling around a trade show. It's
definitely better than writing notes by hand or trading easily mangled business cards.

Beaming Appointments

If you work with other handheld-carrying users, you can make sure everyone is on the same schedule by beaming entries from the Calendar. To do that, select an appointment (by tapping anywhere in its field), and then tap Menu | Beam Event.

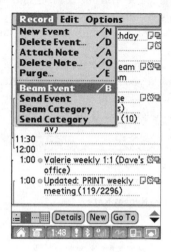

Beaming Contacts

If you're like most people, Contacts is the most well-exercised part of your PDA. Now, instead of exchanging paper-based business cards, you can beam information between handhelds, which can later be HotSynced back to Palm Desktop (or Outlook). In recognition of just how important Contacts actually is, you have not one, not two, but three options for sending data from this application.

- **Beam the current entry**   To send a Contacts entry to another user, find the name you want in the address list, tap it, and then tap Menu | Beam Address (or Beam Contact).

- **Beam a whole bunch of entries**   You can send any number of contacts, even every name in your Palm, using Beam Category. To do that, first choose the category you want to beam by selecting it from the list at the top-right corner of the screen. Then tap Menu and choose Beam Category. To beam all the entries in your entire address book, you should set the category to All.

 Be careful before you beam or try to receive a whole category's worth of contacts. Make sure it's something you really need to do. This operation could include hundreds, perhaps even thousands, of entries, and as a result would take a long time to complete. How long? It depends on the number of contacts, but it could easily take several minutes or more.

■ **Beam your own entry** What's more common than handing your business card to someone? You can configure your own Contacts entry as your personal business card and beam it to other handhelds. For details on configuring an entry as your business card, see Chapter 6. Once configured, however, you can send it by opening Contacts, tapping Menu, and choosing Beam Business Card.

 We've mentioned this a few times already, but it bears repeating. Once you've designated a contact as your business card, you can beam it quickly and easily just by holding down the Contacts hard-button for two seconds.

Beaming Memos and Tasks

Memos are handy to pass off to other PDA users. You can give them notes, action items, short documents, and even meeting minutes. Likewise, if you want to delegate a task to someone else in your office, tell that person to "visit my cubicle, and don't forget to bring your Palm." There are two ways to beam memos and to-do items:

- **Beam a Memo or a To Do**   To beam a single item, select it, tap Menu, and then choose Beam Memo (for a Memo) or Beam Item (for a To Do).
- **Beam a bunch of stuff at once**   As with Contacts, you can select a category in Memo Pad or To Do List, and then choose Beam Category from the menu. To beam all your memos or tasks at once, set the category to All.

Beaming Applications

Now for the best part. You can use your PDA's beaming prowess to transfer entire applications from one device to another. If you meet someone who shows you his cool new Palm OS game or utility, for instance, you can ask him to beam the program to your handheld.

NOTE   *Not all applications are free, so don't use beaming for piracy. Actually, software pirates have a hard time with Palm software, because commercial software is often "locked" from beaming. If you can beam a program, you can usually send only a trial version that requires a registration code to work beyond a short time, such as two weeks. And because registration codes are keyed to the Palm's username, it's generally impossible to share the code.*

Not all programs can, in fact, be beamed. The core applications that come with your PDA are "locked," making them non-beamable. Many commercial programs are also locked, and some just aren't really suitable for beaming, which means that they require multiple files to operate, some of which may be hard to find or non-beamable.

Now that we've told you what you can't do, let's talk about what you can do. Beaming an application isn't much different than beaming data from one of the core apps. Do this:

1. Tap the Home button to return to the launcher screen.

2. Tap Menu, and then choose Beam. You see a dialog box with a list of all the applications on your device, as in Figure 4-5. Some applications have little locks; these can't be beamed.

3. Select an application and tap the Beam button. If the desired program is stored on a memory card, you'll need to tap the arrow next to Beam From and choose the card instead of Console (or Device, on some models). You'll then see a list of the programs stored on the card. This designates only where programs are beamed from. Programs that you receive from others are always stored in main memory (though you can easily offload them to a memory card later on).

TIP   *If you want to beam more stuff, get a program called FileZ. This freeware file manager makes it possible to beam certain kinds of apps (such as databases) that the Palm OS can't do on its own.*

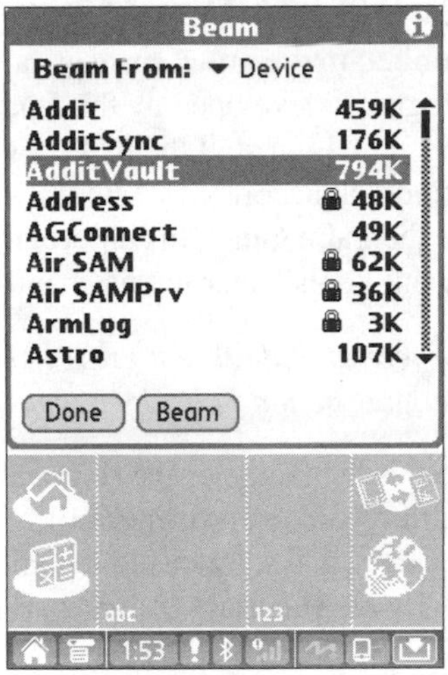

FIGURE 4-5   Choose a program from the list to beam it to another handheld. If it has a lock, however, it can't be beamed.

Bluetooth vs. Beaming

As you know from reading Chapter 2 (and, later, Chapter 10), some Palm OS PDAs have a built-in Bluetooth radio that enables them to communicate wirelessly with other PDAs (in addition to other Bluetooth-equipped devices). In fact, you can perform a lot of the same wireless functions using Bluetooth that you can with IR. You can send contacts, appointments, memos, tasks, and even programs.

The key advantage to using Bluetooth over IR (which is a virtually identical process to beaming, except that instead of choosing Beam from any given menu, you choose Send) is that no line of sight is required. Whereas IR requires two handhelds to be facing each other and have an unobstructed line of sight, Bluetooth will work regardless of PDA orientation and position. It also has better range—upwards of 10 feet, practically speaking.

That said, Bluetooth is not significantly faster than IR at transmitting data (especially tiny snippets of data, like contacts and memos), and you have to jump through a lot more hoops to get it to work. You have to activate the Bluetooth radios on both devices. You have to search for the other handheld and add it to your Trusted Devices list, and the other handheld user has to do the same. Finally, you have to select the recipient of the item you wish to send. None of these steps are required when you use IR. Our advice: stick with IR for beaming data.

To learn more about working with Bluetooth for these and other wireless features, see Chapter 10.

Installing New Software on Your PDA

Your PDA is not an island. It isn't limited to the programs that came preloaded. In fact, it's compatible with the thousands of programs developed by third-party software programmers for handheld PCs. Okay, but how do you actually install them? In some cases you'll work with an automated installer, not unlike the kind that accompany Windows programs. Mostly, however, you'll be working with Zip files and the Palm Quick Install program, formerly known as Palm Install Tool. (See "A Tale of Two Install Tools" later in this chapter for more information.)

TIP   *In case you're wondering where to find all that great Palm OS software, two of the leading sources are Handango.com and PalmGear.com.*

The best way to teach this process is by example. We're going to assume that your PDA is already connected to your PC and that you've performed at least one successful HotSync. Now you're ready to add some new programs. Allow us to recommend one of our favorites: Astraware's superb word game Text Twist. The trial version costs nothing to download or use, so it's a good sample program to install.

There's a mnemonic you should learn: download, unzip, install—DUI for short.

The first part is easy: go to Astraware's Web site (www.astraware.com) and find Text Twist. You can type it in the search box on the left side of the screen, or just click the link in the Top 10 Sellers box on the right. It's almost always a best-selling game, so it should be easy to find.

Next, click the Download It button, as seen in Figure 4-6. This is the *download* part. You're going to download to your PC the file containing the Text Twist game.

TIP   *Make sure you take note of where you're saving the downloaded file! We recommend your My Documents folder, which will be easy to find later.*

Now for the *unzip* part. Most files distributed online are compressed and collected into a single file using the Zip format. That means you need a way to open, or "unzip" the file; you can't just install it on your handheld as is. If you're a Windows XP user, you're all set: that version of Windows can access Zip files directly. Just open your My Documents folder (or wherever you saved the Text Twist file), then find and double-click the *texttwist-palm-v2-1.zip* file. (That's the file name as we write this—it may be slightly different by now.) A window will open containing a file called *texttwist.prc*.

FIGURE 4-6 Download games and other programs to your desktop computer, then install them on your Palm

NOTE *If you're not a Windows XP user, you'll need WinZip, a shareware program that you must download and install before you try to open the Text Twist Zip file. You can get it from www.winzip.com. Once it's installed, you can double-click the Text Twist download as described earlier. Your end goal is to gain access to* texttwist.prc.

Finally, we come to the *install* step, where you arrange for Text Twist to be copied to your handheld the next time you HotSync. This couldn't be easier. Just double-click the *texttwist.prc* file. It doesn't matter if it's in a Windows XP window or in WinZip, or even if you haven't actually "unzipped" it yet. You just need to see the file somewhere onscreen and double-click it. This will automatically launch Quick Install and add the program to your Install queue. HotSync and you're done!

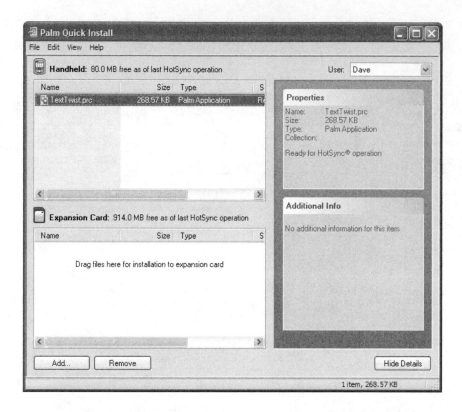

NOTE
You might encounter Zip files that don't contain an actual PRC file, but rather an installer and some data files. In this case, you might need to extract everything to a folder first, and then run the installer from that folder.

In many cases, you'll open a Zip file and discover several *.prc* (and/or *.pdb*) files. Should you install them all? Just some of them? The answer varies from program to program. Consult the instruction manual (which is often nothing more than a *Readme.txt* file) contained in the Zip file to find out which files you should install.

NOTE
Don't be concerned that the filename appears abbreviated in Install Tool. That's normal.

A Tale of Two Install Tools

Yeah, you guessed it! There are two versions of the utility used to install software on your PDA. The older one, Install Tool, is still used on a couple of models, but it's quickly going the way of the carnivorous marsupial once known as the Tasmanian Wolf. And by that, we mean it's nearly extinct. It looks like this:

The new Quick Install tool, which is found with newer Palm models, was featured in the illustration when we demonstrated how to install Text Twist.

The key difference between the two is the way they deal with memory cards. As you can see, Quick Install includes two separate areas, one for Handheld (meaning programs get installed in internal memory), and one for Expansion Card. When you drag program files to the latter area, they're automatically installed on your memory card (which has to be inserted in your device, of course, otherwise it won't work).

TIP   *Before you install any program to a memory card, check with the software developer to make sure it can run from a card. Some programs must be installed right on the handheld to work properly. In other cases, you can install the main program file on a card, but the associated databases have to be in RAM.*

With Install Tool, you can still install programs to a memory card. It just requires a few more steps. After you've used Install Tool to select a program for installation, click the Change Destination button. You'll see the Change Destination dialog box. Now, click the program(s) that you want to install directly to the memory card, and then click the arrow to move it to the right side of the screen (which represents the PDA's memory card).

Change Destination

Change the destination of the files to be installed.

Install To:
Handheld

Install To:
SecureDigital (SD) Card

☐ TEXTTW~1.PRC

OK

Cancel

Tips:
You can install only certain types of files to the handheld (for example, files of type *.prc, *.pdb, etc.)
Files of other types should be installed to a card.

When you've configured your to-be-installed applications to your liking, click OK, close the Install Tool (by clicking Done), and HotSync.

The Other Way to Work with the Install Program

The software-installation example in the previous section is fairly automated. It launches Quick Install (or Install Tool) and queues a program for installation just by double-clicking it. However, you can also launch either utility on its own and manually add programs for installation. There are two ways to go about this:

- Click the Start button in Windows, then click All Programs | Palm Desktop | Quick Install (or Install Tool). (In some cases, you'll find it in the PalmOne folder instead of Palm Desktop.)

- Start Palm Desktop, and then click the Install or Quick Install icon on the lower-left side of the screen.

The end result is the same: the installation program runs. However, you won't see any programs or databases queued up for installation. Click the Add button, and then navigate to the folder on your hard drive that contains the software. Keep in mind that any Zip files will have to be unzipped first, otherwise you won't have access to the *.prc* and/or *.pdb* files that you need to install.

TIP   *You can also drag and drop programs to the Quick Install (or Install Tool) window.*

If there's a program you decide you don't want to install, click it to select it, and then click the Remove button. (This is different, of course, from deleting programs you've already installed on your Palm. See the following section "Deleting Applications" to learn how to do that.)

Deleting Applications

You won't want to keep every program forever. Some programs you won't like, others will outlive their usefulness. And at some point you might need to remove software to make room for more, because your PDA has only a fixed amount of internal storage space. (All the more reason to keep a high-capacity memory card on hand.)

Deleting programs is easy. Press the Home button, and then tap Menu | Delete. You'll see a list of all the applications currently stored on the device. At the top of the screen, you'll also see a bar that shows how much memory remains.

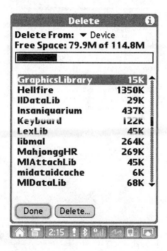

Delete	
Delete From: ▼ Device	
Free Space: 79.9M of 114.8M	
GraphicsLibrary	15K
Hellfire	1350K
IIDataLib	29K
Insaniquarium	437K
Keyboard	122K
LexLib	45K
libmal	264K
MahjonggHR	269K
MIAttachLib	45K
midataidcache	6K
MIDataLib	68K

Done   Delete...

2:15

NOTE   *By default, the Delete screen shows programs installed in internal memory—the "Console" or "Device." If you want to see (and delete) programs on a memory card, you can tap the arrow next to Delete From, and then choose the memory card from the list. That allows you to delete applications stored on the card.*

To delete an application, select it and tap the Delete button. This is identical to the Beam interface. In fact, it's so similar, you should be careful that you don't accidentally delete an app that you're trying to beam to a friend.

CAUTION   *When you delete an application, you also delete all the data that it generated. If you have a document reader, for instance, deleting the app also trashes any Doc files it might contain. If you have any data you want to preserve, use whatever features are available to export, copy, or offload it.*

Installing Apps with Addit

There's one other way you can install programs using your Palm, and it's crazy cool (as the kids tend to say these days).

If you have a new Palm, like the TX or the Lifedrive, you have a program called Addit on your device. It looks, at first glance, like a news reader (sort of like a built-in version of AvantGo, perhaps). But tap the headings called Software for My Palm or Shop for Software, and you'll see a smorgasbord of apps that you can install on your device. Suppose you click Software for My Palm and want to try out MobiTV, a program that streams live television to your PDA using Wi-Fi. Just tap the link for MobiTV, enter your name and e-mail address, and then click the Try button. You'll end up here:

If you have a Wi-Fi connection, tap the globe that's next to the OK button and the program will be installed on your Palm instantly. In five minutes, you'll be watching TV on your PDA. If you don't have a wireless connection, then tap OK. The next time you HotSync, the selected program will be automatically installed on your Palm. What could be cooler than that?

Part II

Get Things Done

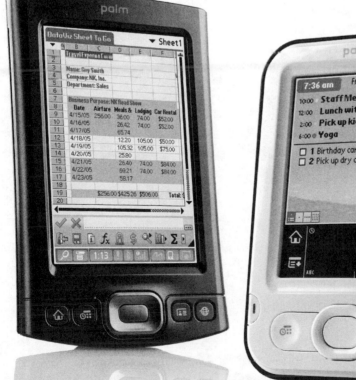
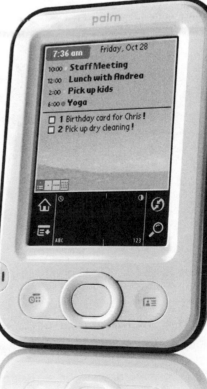

Chapter 5

The Calendar and Date Book

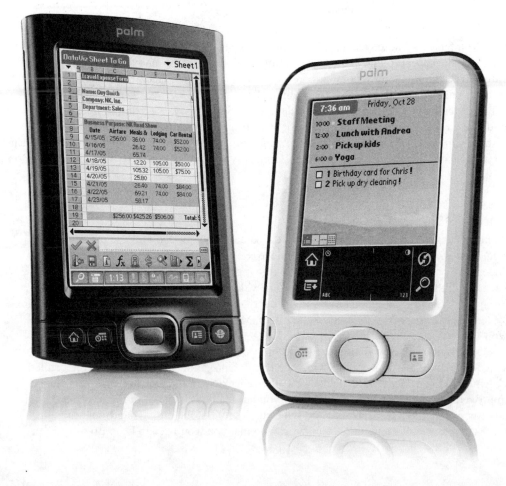

How to...

- Use the Day, Week, Month, and Agenda Views
- Customize the Calendar's appearance
- Beam an appointment to someone else
- Create an appointment
- Add a note to an appointment
- Make an appointment private
- Edit and delete appointments
- Set an alarm for an appointment
- Use the Palm Desktop's Calendar
- Use Outlook
- Use alternatives to the Palm's Calendar

Are you busy on Tuesday at 3 P.M.? If you have your PDA handy, you'd probably already know the answer to that question. In an informal survey, we found the Palm's scheduling abilities to be the single most popular core application on a PDA. Heck, some people buy a PDA just for its calendar program alone. Everything else is gravy.

The Calendar (called Date Book on older Palm OS models) is a modern miracle. That might sound like an overstatement, but consider how useful it is. It can track all your appointments. It can show you your schedule by day, week, or month. It handles recurring appointments and can notify you about upcoming events with an alarm. It synchronizes precisely with the calendar on

Operating System Oddities

Although handhelds all work more or less the same way, they don't all use exactly the same operating system. Likewise, the Palm Desktop software on your PC might vary a bit depending on which model you own. We wrote most of this book with Palm OS 5 in mind, because that's what all the newest PDAs come with—models such as the Lifedrive, TX, Tungsten E2, and Z22. If you have a PDA that runs a different version of the Palm operating system, don't worry. The differences are minor. Most of the time, in fact, you probably won't even notice a difference.

One obvious place you might see a difference is in the PDA's calendar-creating and scheduling abilities. While older PDAs come with a program called Date Book, it's called Calendar in the newer models. What's the difference? Not a lot. One big change is an improved Agenda view, which we'll show you later in this chapter. For the most part, anytime we mention the Calendar, the same stuff is true of the older Date Book; though there are a few cool things that Calendar can do that you won't see in Date Book.

your desktop computer. And the Date Book fits in the palm of your hand. It's better, Rick might tell you, than *Battlestar Galactica.* Dave, on the other hand, might be inclined to say it's better than *24* and *Lost* combined.

Starting Out in the Agenda View

Start the Calendar by pressing the Calendar button on your PDA or tapping the Calendar icon, found in the Main category of the Palm's Application screen.

When it appears, the Calendar starts by default in the Agenda view. This screen shows you your upcoming appointments, tasks, and the number of unread e-mail messages, as in this illustration:

The Agenda View is not just a preview of your schedule—you can tap any item to go directly to the appropriate view. Tap an appointment, for instance, to go to the Day View, or tap a task to see the Tasks application and all of the tasks that you have waiting.

TIP   *Want to change the default view? Tap Menu | Options | Display Options, and then tap the arrow next to Default View. Whatever option you select—Agenda, Day, Week, or Month—will be the first thing you see when you run the Calendar.*

The Agenda Zoom

The Agenda View is great for viewing your day's schedule, but it's also a cool way to make changes to your daily itinerary. Just tap on a calendar item to switch to the Day View so you can make schedule changes. Or tap a to-do item to go to the To Do List for editing.

NOTE   *It would be great if you could automatically start your PDA in a specific mode, such as Agenda View, all the time. Alas, you can't quite do that. But, if you set your Palm to the Agenda View and then visit another application, the Agenda View automatically appears when you return to the Date Book. If you're in a hurry, remember that you can press the Date Book button several times to cycle through the Date Book's various screens to arrive at the Agenda View.*

Navigating the Day View

The Day View is where you'll probably spend most of your time, because it lets you see all of your current appointments most easily. To get there, either tap an appointment in the Agenda View or tap the Day View icon at the bottom of the Calendar.

Once in the Day View, you can see that it shows the currently selected date in the tab at the top of the screen. Next to that are seven icons, one for each day of the week.

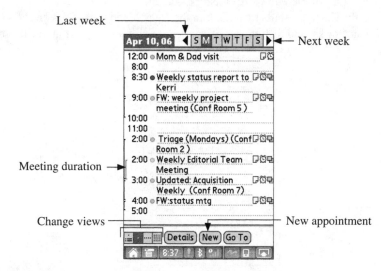

In the middle of the screen, you see the current day's calendar. You can enter new events on the blank lines. If you have any appointments already entered, note that long appointments (those that last for more than 30 minutes) have *duration brackets,* which appear to the immediate left of the appointment time and show you what time an appointment is scheduled to end.

Other icons also appear near appointments. In fact, you should get used to seeing the following three icons:

- ■ **Alarms** This icon indicates you'll get notified by the alarm sound that the appointment is due to start.

- ■ **Notes** If you attach a note to your appointment (perhaps with directions to the location or agenda details, for instance) you see this icon.

- ■ **Repeating meetings** If the meeting is configured to happen more than once, this icon appears.

If you tap any of these icons, shown in Figure 5-1, you see the Event Details dialog box, which we discuss in detail later in this chapter.

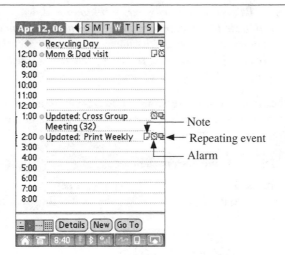

FIGURE 5-1   These icons tell you valuable information about your appointment. Tap them to edit the details.

Finally, the bottom of the screen has several important controls. You can see icons that let you change the current view, create a new appointment, view the Event Details dialog box, and go to a specific day.

Changing View Options

By default, the Day View compresses your calendar by not showing blank times of the day. This way, you can have appointments that span from 6 A.M. to 11 P.M. and have them all appear onscreen without needing to scroll at all. Whenever it can, it includes blank events between existing events for better readability.

What happens if you have such a busy day that all your appointments won't fit onscreen at once, even with your Palm's compression in place? You need to tap the scroll button at the bottom of the screen. It appears only when needed.

You can also use the scroll button or Nav Pad to move around. To change days, for instance, push the left or right direction on the Nav Pad. To see more entries in the same day, push up or down.

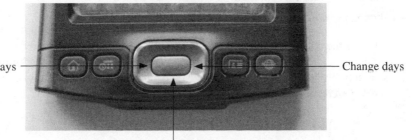

Change days

Change days

Scroll in same day

NOTE *If you have an older Palm, you can't push the scroll button down to scroll within the same day. Instead, that simply changes the view to the next day. Annoying? You bet. One solution is to do what Rick did. The 500th time he accidentally scrolled to the next day, he threw his Palm out of his car window. It didn't solve the problem, though he did have to buy a new PDA that used the new scroll method.*

Not everyone likes the Day View compression. If you frequently add events to your schedule during the day, for instance, you might want to have blank lines available for all the hours of the day. If this sounds like you, here's how to turn off compression:

1. Choose Options | Display Options from the menu.
2. Uncheck the Compress Day View option. If you have a new device like the Tungsten T5, you may have to switch to the Day tab first, such as in this illustration:

3. Tap the OK button.

Now when you use the Day View, you see all the blank lines for your day. On the other hand, using this setting virtually guarantees that you will need to use the stylus to surf around your daily schedule.

When you configure your Day View, you also have to decide what kind of person you are. Are you

■ Neat and orderly, and opt for less clutter whenever possible?

■ Impatient, and want everything at your fingertips all the time?

■ Apathetic, and don't want to bother changing the default settings?

You can change the display of the Calendar to accommodate the way you want your PDA to look. If you're the neat and orderly sort, for instance, you might want the Calendar to be a blank screen, unless it actually has appointments already scheduled for that day. If this is the case, choose Options | Preferences and set the Start Time and End Time to the same time, like 7:00 A.M.

Preferences ⓘ

Start Time: [7:00 am] ⬍
End Time: [7:00 am] ⬍
☐ **New events use time zones**
☐ **Alarm Preset:**
   Alarm Sound: ▾ Alarm
   Remind Me: [▾ 3 Times]
   Play Every: ▾ 5 minutes

(OK) (Cancel)

After configuring your Palm in this way, you should find days without appointments are essentially a blank screen with a single blank line, the time you set in Preferences.

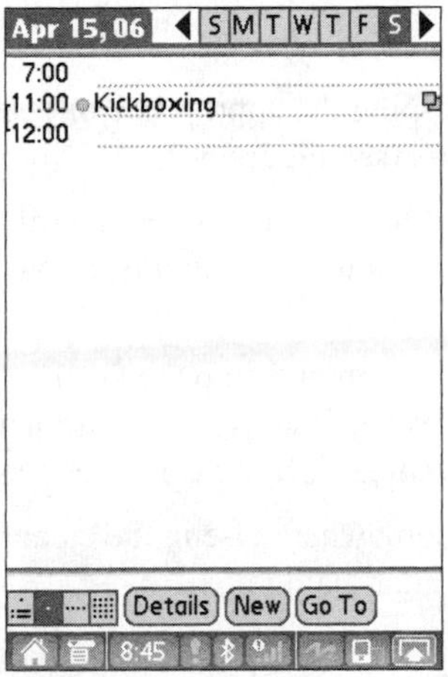

Apr 15, 06 ◀ S|M|T|W|T|F|S ▶
7:00
11:00 ⊙ Kickboxing .... 🗗
12:00 ....

(Details) (New) (Go To)

Are you more of an impatient sort? Then choose Options | Preferences and configure your Start Time and End Time to span the full range of hours you plan to use. If you ever add events to the evening, for instance, set the End Time for 10 P.M. or later. This way, you have a blank line available immediately for writing a new entry.

If all this sounds extremely pointless to you, leave the Preferences alone. The default settings cover most of the hours you routinely need.

TIP   *Don't have the greatest eyesight? You can switch to a larger font to make the calendar easier to read. Just tap Menu | Options | Font and tap the larger of the two letters, and then tap OK. This works in all the core apps, including Contacts, Memo Pad, and Tasks.*

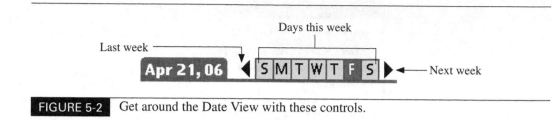

Days this week

Last week

Apr 21, 06 ◄ S M T W T F S ► ◄— Next week

FIGURE 5-2   Get around the Date View with these controls.

Getting Around the Days of the Week

As you might expect, there are several ways to switch to a different day. You can figure out most of them on your own, but we bet you can't find 'em all (if you do find them all on your own, send Dave and Rick $5 in cash as proof that you succeeded). Here's how you can do it; use the method that's easiest for you:

■ Switch to a specific day by tapping the appropriate day icon at the top of the screen, or change weeks using the arrows (see Figure 5-2).

■ To move forward or backward one day at a time, press the Scroll button or Nav Pad on your Palm. If you hold it down, you scroll quickly, like holding down a repeating key on a computer keyboard.

■ If you want to find a specific day quickly, tap the Go To button and enter the date directly in the Go to Date dialog box. When you use Go To, remember to choose the year and month first, because you go to the selected date as soon as you tap a date.

■ To get back to "today" from somewhere else in the calendar, tap Go To, and then tap Today on the Go to Date calendar dialog box.

Navigating the Week View

Now that you're used to the Day View, we'll let you in on a little secret: there's more where that came from. That's where the icons at the bottom of the screen come in. Tap the second one to change to the Week View.

TIP   *The Calendar button also serves as a view changer. Every time you press the button, the view cycles from Day View to Week View to Month View to Agenda View and back to Day View again. It's convenient to jab with your thumb as you view your various schedule screens.*

This screen uses a grid to display your appointments. The top of the grid is labeled by day and date; the left side contains time blocks throughout the day. The gray blocks represent scheduled events. Obviously, this view isn't ideal for determining your daily schedule in detail, but it's handy for getting your week's availability at a glance. Use it to pick a free day or to find a clear afternoon.

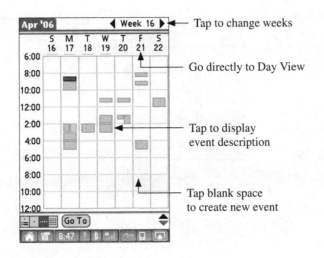

Tap to change weeks

Go directly to Day View

Tap to display
event description

Tap blank space
to create new event

TIP   *If you need to move an appointment to another time anywhere in the week, tap the event, hold the stylus down, and then drag it to another place on the schedule. As you move the block around, you can see the exact time to which the event is being moved. To abort this process without changing anything, move it back to its original location without lifting the stylus.*

Navigating the Month View

If you press the Date Book button again or tap the fourth icon at the bottom of the screen, you're transported to the Month View. This displays an entire month at a time.

Blocks of busy time are now replaced by even smaller blocks. Tapping these blocks doesn't let you see or edit specific appointment details, because these blocks don't actually represent individual events. Instead, the three possible marks represent events in the morning, afternoon, and evening, as shown in Figure 5-3. In addition, this view shows untimed events as little diamonds and multiday events as a series of dots that span several days.

NOTE   *Depending upon which Palm OS device you own, these display features may be initially disabled. If yours are turned off to begin with, turn them on by choosing Options | Display Options from the Day View screen. Then, in the Month View section of the Display Options dialog box, enable Show Untimed Events and Show Daily Repeating Events.*

Using this view takes a little finesse with the stylus. Here's what you need to know:

■ Tap and hold the stylus on a day to see a list of all the appointments at the bottom of the screen.

■ Release the stylus to automatically get taken to the Day View for that day.

■ Drag the stylus away from the day you were viewing to stay on the Month View without switching to the Day View.

Morning events — Multi-day event
Evening events — Untimed event

FIGURE 5-3   If you enable the right features in preferences, you can see untimed and multiday events in the monthly calendar.

There's one more view at your disposal: the Year View. Unlike the other views, though, this one doesn't have its own icon, nor can you get there by repeatedly pressing the Calendar button. Instead, you get there from the Year button on the Month View. Tap it and you'll see the year at a glance, like this:

To see a particular month in Month View, you guessed it. Tap it.

Using Categories in the Calendar

One of the most common complaints people traditionally had with the old Date Book was the inability to sort appointments into groups—stuff like personal and private events, or appointments for Dave and appointments for Kristen. Well, no worries. If you use a PDA with the newfangled Calendar app, categories are now yours.

Assigning Categories to Appointments

Assigning a category to an item in the calendar is a snap. If you have an existing event, do this:

1. Tap the event in the Day View that you want to assign to a category.

2. Tap Details.

3. On the Event Details screen, choose a category from the list.

4. Tap OK to change the category.

An even faster way to assign a category is to tap the bullet to the left of the appointment. These dots are color-coded so you can see what category appointments belong to at a glance.

That's all it takes. Keep in mind, though, that you can also assign categories on the desktop. Your handheld will recognize any category that you assign in either Palm Desktop or in Outlook (depending upon which program you routinely use to synchronize with your PDA).

Displaying Calendar Events According to Category

Just because you assign categories to your appointments doesn't mean you'll be able to see them that way. In fact, before you can view your appointments in color-coded category goodness, you'll need to throw a switch on your PDA. To do so, perform the following steps:

1. In the Calendar app, tap Options | Display Options from the menu.
2. Make sure that Show Category List is checked.

3. Tap OK.
4. On the Day View, look for a drop-down menu near the top of the display. It's probably set to All by default.

5. Tap it and choose the category of appointments that you want to see.

Now your calendar will show only the appointments you're most interested in seeing. Note that the categories are color-coded, so if you leave the display set to All, you can tell at a glance which events are for business, which are personal, and so on.

Switch to the other views, like the Week and Month views. Notice that your calendar items are still color-coded! Woo hoo!

> **TIP** *Want to share just your business calendar with a coworker? You can beam calendar events by category the same way you beam contacts and tasks by category, so there's no need to send your co-worker a bunch of appointments with the plumber and the veterinarian when you're getting ready for a trade show.*

Adding Some Holidays

The Date Book doesn't come with a database of holidays. When's Christmas? That one is easy. But if you want to know when we celebrate President's Day, Veteran's Day, or Arbor Day, it helps to have a calendar with holidays already nailed down for you.

Thankfully, there are several holiday databases online, many of them quite inexpensive, and all of them easy to install on your PDA. After loading the appropriate files, your Date Book will know exactly when all the major holidays are, and display them in all the various views.

Both HoliDates and Holidays at Hand cost $10, and both of these packages provide dates for every holiday through the year 2010 (by which we'll no longer need PDAs, since we'll have made first contact with alien beings that will give us some sort of technology that will make handhelds obsolete).

These holiday databases are also quite flexible. You don't have to install all the holidays, but instead get to choose just the ones that are important to you. Rick, for instance, sticks with only the holidays that include chocolate. Here is what HoliDates looks like when you choose which holidays to add to the Calendar. As you can see, you have the ability to choose exactly which holidays and important dates to show from a very large database:

Both are available on www.Palmgear.com.

The Best Sci-Fi

Dave: PDAs are like science fiction come alive, which prompts the question, which sci-fi? Rick obsesses over some of the lamest sci-fi shows ever, such as *Star Trek: Voyager* and *The West Wing*. (Martin Sheen as the president? Yeah, that's gotta be sci-fi.) I am partial to shows with plausible technology, engaging plots, and a real sense of drama. That's why *Babylon 5* and the new *Battlestar Galactica* rank up there among the best television ever. Meanwhile, Rick doesn't let the fact that *Voyager* is off the air get in his way. Stocked up on DVDs, he's watching another "very special episode" in which the ship gets attacked by the same bunch of bad guys that they fought three years ago, despite the fact that they've been flying at maximum warp back toward Earth the whole time. Hmm. Sounds like they're just running in circles.

Rick: Dave is what those of us who have lives like to call a "sci-fi snob." In his world, if it's not "plausible," it's not good. And yet he loves *Star Trek: Enterprise*, which has permanently tarnished the beloved Trek franchise by destroying the continuity between shows, solely by being implausible. (And I won't even get into the decidedly *un*-engaging plots and utter lack of drama.) Anyway, I digress. I used to rank *Star Trek: Voyager* as my all-time favorite sci-fi show, but that honor now belongs to *Battlestar Galactica*. But snob-Dave can't seem to compute that. And, obviously, anyone who doesn't like *The West Wing* must be controlled by some evil alien influence. Oh, that's right, Dave's a Republican.

Creating New Appointments

Now that you've mastered the fine art of viewing your schedule from every conceivable angle and perspective, you probably want to know how to add new events to the schedule. As you can probably guess, there are two ways to add appointments to your PDA: via the Palm Desktop or Outlook (which we discuss later in this chapter), and right from the PDA itself.

Adding Timed Events

Most of the time, your schedule will be full of meetings that take place at a specific time of day, such as

```
Meet with Susan from accounting
3-5pm in Conference Room A.
```

This is what your Palm refers to as a timed event, but most people call it an appointment. In any event, several ways exist to add an event like this to your handheld:

- **Use the New button** The only place you can actually enter data about a meeting is from the Day View. Tap the New button at the bottom of the screen. Then, within the Set Time dialog box, select a Start Time and an End Time, and then tap OK. Now, enter the meeting information on the blank line provided for you.

- **Start writing**   Tap on a blank line that corresponds to the meeting start time and write the details of the meeting on the line.

- **Pick a time from the Week View**   If you're looking for a free space to place a meeting, the Week View is a good place to search because it gives you the "big picture" of your schedule. When you find a spot you like, tap it, and the Day View should open to the desired start time. Then write the meeting info.

A Closer Look at the Set Time Dialog Box

To set a time in this dialog box, tap an hour (in the selector on the left) and a minute (on the right) for both the Start Time and End Time. You can change your mind as often as you like, but the time must be in increments no smaller than five minutes. You can't set a Start Time of 11:33, for instance.

You can also use Graffiti to set the time, a real convenience for folks who are faster at writing than tapping. 335 is interpreted as 3:35. To change between A.M. and P.M., write an *A* or a *P* in the letter side of the Graffiti area.

If you need to back up and start over, use the backspace gesture. When you want to move between the Start Time and the End Time box, use the Next Field gesture. Finally, when you've finished entering times, use the Return gesture to simulate tapping OK. Now, you're back at the Day View, ready to write in your meeting name.

SHORTCUT   *A fast way to create a new event at a specific time is to simply write the start time. A Set Time dialog box appears, and you can proceed from there. For example, writing a 4 automatically launches the Set Time dialog box for 4 P.M.*

Adding Untimed Events

If we wrote about something called a timed event, you must have assumed we'd get to something called an untimed event, right? Untimed events are pretty much what you'd expect. They're events associated with a day, but not with a specific time. You might think of untimed events as "all day events." Typical untimed events include birthdays and anniversaries, reminders to pick

How to ... Make a Date

If you're setting up an appointment with someone in particular, you can have a lot of fun with your PDA. Okay, it's not better than listening to Pink Floyd with the lights out, but it's pretty cool nonetheless. Suppose you need to meet with someone who's already in your Address Book. Switch to the Day View and tap on a blank line at the time you want to start your meeting. Then choose Options | Phone Lookup. You see the Lookup dialog box, which displays all the names in your Address Book. Find the name of the person you're meeting with and tap it. Tap Add. What do you get? The person's name and phone number positioned at the start time of the meeting.

Record Edit **Options**		Lookup	
Font...	/F	Accessories www.palmOne.com M	
Preferences...	/R	Adam's Mark Hotels 800-444-ADAM W	
Display Options...	/Y	Alamo Car Rental (800) 327-9633 W	
Phone Lookup	/L	Allstate Car Rental (800) 634-6186 W	

First screen (Day View with Options menu open):

Record Edit **Options**
Font... /F
8:00 Preferences... /R
9:00 Display Options... /Y
10:00 Phone Lookup /L
11:00 Security... /H
12:00 Year View
1:00 About Calendar
2:00
3:00
4:00
5:00
6:00

[Details] [New] [Go To]
🏠 🔍 📋 9:42 ✴ 〰 ▯ ▣

Second screen (Lookup dialog):

Lookup
Accessories   www.palmOne.com M
Adam's Mark Hotels 800-444-ADAM W
Alamo Car Rental   (800) 327-9633 W
Allstate Car Rental (800) 634-6186 W
America West Airlin (800) 235-9292 W
American Airlines   (800) 433-7300 W
Atlantic Airlines   (800) 879-0000 W
Atriedes, Evan   425 555 2398 W
Best Inns and Suites 800-BEST INN W
Best Western Intern (800) 528-1234 W
Broida, Rick   rick@broida.com E
Business Express Air (800) 345-3400 W
Comfort Inns   (800) 228-5150 W
Continental Airlines (800) 525-0280 W
Delta Air Lines   (800) 221-1212 W
Johnson, Dave   (1) 555-1212 W

Look Up: [Add] [Cancel] ⬍
🏠 🔍 📋 9:42 ✴ 〰 ▯ ▣

Third screen (Day View with event added):

Nov 4, 04 ◀ S M T W T F S ▶
▼ Unfiled
8:00
9:00
10:00
11:00
12:00
1:00
2:00 ● Adam's Mark Hotels 800-444-
        ADAM W
3:00
4:00
5:00
6:00

[Details] [New] [Go To]
🏠 🔍 📋 9:43 ✴ 〰 ▯ ▣

Now it gets even better. Does your associate have a PDA? If so, get within a few feet of it and point your PDA at theirs. Make sure the appointment is still selected and choose Record | Beam Event. You've just given your associate a copy of your meeting.

up the dry cleaning, and deadline reminders (though you might also consider putting those kinds of things in the To Do List, described in Chapter 7). To create an untimed event, perform one of these two techniques:

■ On the Day View with no time selected (in other words, the cursor isn't waiting in a blank line for you already), just start writing. The event appears at the top of the screen as an untimed event.

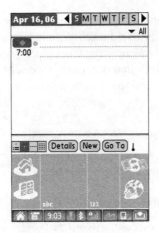

■ Tap New to display the Set Time dialog box. Instead of setting a Start Time and an End Time, though, tap the No Time button and tap OK.

Making Your Appointments Repeat

Some schedule events just don't go away. Weekly meetings, semiannual employee reviews, and the monthly dog grooming sessions are all examples of events you might want the PDA to automate. After all, you don't have the time or energy to write the same weekly event into your PDA 52 times to get it entered for a whole year. An easier way exists. To create a recurring event, do this:

1. Select the entry you want to turn into a recurring event and tap the Details button at the bottom of the Day View screen.

2. In the Event Details dialog box, the Repeat box should currently be set to None. Tap it. You can select one of the common intervals from the menu or pick Other.

3. Now you need to tap a repeat interval. Will the event repeat daily, weekly, monthly, or annually? In other words, if the event takes place only once a year, or once every five years, tap Year. If you have a meeting that takes place once a month, or every other month, tap Month. For meetings that occur every week or every five weeks, use the Week button. Finally, if you need to schedule a meeting daily, every other day, or every ten days, tap Day.

4. You now have more options, depending on which interval you choose. A common interval is Week, which would enable you to set up a weekly meeting. Tell the Change Repeat dialog box how often the meeting will occur, such as Every 1 Week or Every 3 Weeks.

5. If you chose a monthly interval, you can also choose whether the meeting will repeat by day (such as the first Monday of every month) or by date (as in the 11th of every month).

6. If the event will repeat more or less forever (or at least as long as you can imagine going to work every day), then leave the End On setting at the default, which is No End Date. If you are creating an event with a clear conclusion, tap End On to set the End Date for this repeating event.

7. Your selection is turned into a plain English description. If you agree the repeat settings are what you want, tap OK.

TIP   *If you're attending a multiday event, such as a trade show, you can display this in your handheld by creating an untimed event and setting it to repeat daily (Every 1 Day). Don't forget to set an End Date.*

Making an Appointment Private

You might not want all your appointments to be available to the public. Although we generally believe honesty is the best policy, you can flag certain appointments as private, and they'll be hidden from everyone except you. If you want to hide an appointment, do this:

1. On the Day View screen, select an appointment.

2. Tap the Details button.

3. On the Event Details dialog box, tap the Private box to add a check mark. Once you select this option, the current record is flagged for privacy.

4. Tap the OK button. A dialog box appears advising you that you've marked the record as private. Tap OK again.

You might notice the event probably isn't hidden yet. To make it go away, you need to enable the Private Records feature in the Security app. For details on how to do this, see Chapter 9. Using this feature, you can hide and show private data whenever you want.

Editing Recurring Meetings

With most appointments or events, you can make a change just by tapping and entering the needed change with a little Graffiti. Changes to repeating meetings require a little more care. In general, when you change some aspect of a meeting that repeats, the Palm asks you whether you want to change only this one meeting, future meetings, or every meeting in the series.

If you need to move a specific meeting, such as the one in November, to a different time, but all the other meetings continue to be held at the traditional time, select Current. The event is unlinked from the series, and any changes you subsequently make to the rest of the repeating event don't affect the one you changed. On the other hand, if the meeting is moving to a new day permanently, choose All:

There's an exception to this rule: if you change any of the text in the name of the appointment, then the PDA makes the change to the entire series without asking. If you want to change the text of one instance of the event without changing the rest, you need to unlink it from the series. To do that, try this:

1. Change something else about the event, such as its time.

2. You're asked if you want to change the current event or all of the events. Choose Current. The event is now unlinked from the series.

3. Change the name of the unlinked event.

4. If you need to, fix whatever you changed in step 2.

Deleting Old Appointments

As time goes on, your handheld starts to accumulate a considerable number of appointments. Often, after an event has passed, you no longer need a record of it. If that's the case, you might want to delete it to save memory. Granted, each appointment takes up a minuscule amount of memory; but eventually this can add up. Even if you don't care about memory savings, meetings do sometimes get canceled, and you need a way to delete them. A few ways exist to get these events off your Palm:

- **Erase it**   Open the Day View. Tap the stylus at the end of the line and backspace over it to delete all the characters. Or, you can highlight the text by dragging the stylus over the name of the meeting, and then use a single backspace gesture to erase it.

CAUTION   *Watch out! If you use this method to delete a repeating event, the Palm erases all the events in the series without warning.*

- **Use the Delete button**   Select the event and tap the Details button. Then tap Delete (or select the item and choose Delete from the menu).

- **Purge a bunch at once**   If you want to delete a bunch of appointments at once, a special tool was designed just for this task. On the Day View, choose Record | Purge. Then choose how much data to delete. You can choose to delete events that are more than a week old or, if you want more of a safety cushion, delete events more than a month old.

TIP   *If you purge or delete your appointments, you have the option to "save an archive copy on PC." If you do that, the PDA automatically saves your deleted data in a special archive file on your PC. You can restore those appointments on your desktop computer later by opening the archive file within Palm Desktop by choosing File | Open from the menu. In the Calendar, look for a file called Unfiled. Remember that this safety net only works if you HotSync with Palm Desktop instead of another program, such as Outlook.*

Working with Alarms

If you need a reminder about upcoming events, then you should use the built-in alarm feature. Any event you enter can be set to beep (or cause your handheld to vibrate, though not all models have this feature) shortly before the event, giving you enough time to jump in your car, pick up the phone, or start saving for the big day. You can assign an alarm setting to your events as you create the event, or at any time afterward.

Timed events play an audible sound. Untimed events don't play a sound, but simply display a screen advising you the event is pending.

5

Setting Alarms for Specific Events

To enable the alarm for a particular appointment, do this:

1. In the Day View, select an appointment.

2. Tap Details.

3. In the Event Details dialog box, tap the Alarm check box. You should see a new control appear that enables you to set the advance warning for the event.

4. Select how much advanced warning you want. You can choose no warning (enter a zero) or set a time up to 99 days ahead of time. The default is five minutes.

5. Tap OK.

Setting Alarms for Everything

By default, the PDA doesn't turn the alarm on for your appointments. Instead, you need to turn the alarm on for every event individually. If you find you like using the alarm, though, you can tell the Palm to turn the alarm on automatically for all your appointments. Then, it's up to you to turn the alarm off on a case-by-case basis when you don't want to be notified for any events.

How to ... **Pick Your Own Alarm Sound**

If, like us, you're easily bored, you might be interested in changing your default alarm sound. It's easy to do. Just visit a Palm software Web site such as PalmGear.com and search for alarm sounds. You'll find tons of downloads that give your PDA alternative sounds. Some give you special effects such as science fiction or animal sounds; others are complete songs. If you've ever wanted your Palm to sound like a Star Trek communicator, here's your chance. Of course, it's not all fun and games. A distinctive alarm sound can make your Palm easier to hear in a crowd.

To enable the default alarm setting, do this:

1. In the Day View, choose Options | Preferences.
2. Tap the check box for the Alarm Preset. Set your alarm preferences: configure the alarm time, the kind of alarm sound, and how many times the alarm will sound before giving up.

TIP *You can try out each of the alarm sounds by selecting them from the list. After you choose a sound, it plays so you can hear what it sounds like.*

3. Tap OK.

Importing Alarm Settings

Much of the time, you probably get appointments into your Palm via your PC. You HotSync them in from the Palm Desktop or Outlook. In that case, the rules are different. The PDA keeps whatever alarm settings were assigned on the PC, and doesn't use the Preference settings on the Palm. If you want a specific alarm setting, you need to change the alarm setting on the desktop application before HotSyncing or change the alarm on the PDA after you HotSync.

> *Some folks would like to have two separate sets of alarms for their appointments: one for the handheld and another for their desktop calendar program. If you have a PC and Microsoft Outlook, try Beyond Contacts. This alternative conduit enables you to configure the PDA to use a completely independent set of alarms from Outlook.*

Controlling Your Alarm

If you use an alarm clock, you surely must know that the only thing better than having an alarm is actually being able to turn it off.

Keep in mind that the PDA really isn't all that loud. If you need to hear it, don't bury it in something like a backpack, where the sound will be hopelessly muffled. But what if you're in a quiet meeting room and the last thing you need is for your PDA to start chirping in front of the CEO? That could go badly, as you can see from this hypothetical interaction:

CEO: What's that, young man?

You: Err, a Palm Z22.

CEO: What does it do?

You: It tracks my schedule and plays Space Hamsters II.

CEO: I'll expect your desk to be cleaned out by the end of the day. Wait here while I call for security.

As you can see, we need a way to temporarily silence your handheld. On most devices, open Prefs and choose the General view, where there's an option for Alarm Sound. Choose Off from the Alarm Sound list. Some Palm models even have a vibrating alarm, which is a great way to keep on top of alarms without disturbing the people around you.

On many newer models, there's a really fast way to silence your PDA: tap the clock in the toolbar at the bottom of the screen and then choose Silent from the sound settings at the bottom of the screen.

Working with Palm Desktop

If you use Palm Desktop as the calendar on your desktop PC, you benefit because it looks similar to the version on your Palm. Granted, Palm Desktop is a lot bigger than your handheld's screen, and it's in color. But aside from that, the modules share a common appearance, and the overall philosophy of the program is similar.

Using Palm Desktop's Calendar

After you start Palm Desktop, you can switch to the Date Book by clicking the Calendar (or Date, in older versions) icon on the left side of the screen. To change views, click the tabs at the bottom of the screen. You should see tabs for Day, Week, Month, and Year (Figure 5-4).

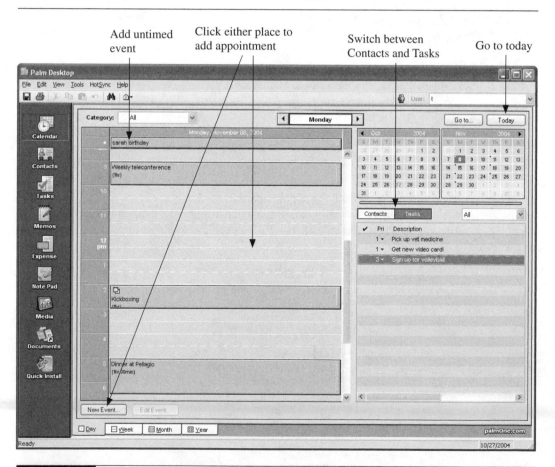

FIGURE 5-4 The Day View combines appointments with either to-dos or addresses, depending upon how you configure the screen.

Using the Day View

The Day View looks similar to the Palm display. Look at Figure 5-4 for an overview of the major elements in this display.

The easiest way to double-book a time slot is to click the Time box. A new blank appears to the right of the existing appointment.

You might recall that on the PDA, you can create an appointment by using the Phone Lookup feature. This grabs a name and phone number from the Contacts list and places it in a time slot in the Calendar. You can do the same thing in the Palm Desktop. Under the calendar, you can see the Task List and Contacts mini-lists. Choose which one you want to see by clicking Tasks or Contacts. Then drag a name (or even a task) into a time slot.

Editing Appointments

You can make lots of changes with the mouse. To change the duration of an event, drag the arrow-shaped duration handle up or down. To move the appointment, drag it by its event handle on the right edge. To see the Edit Event dialog box, which lets you edit the text and includes alarm and privacy controls, double-click anywhere in the event.

You can move an appointment to another day by dragging it via the event handle to the calendar and dropping it on the desired day.

Using the Long Range Views

The Week and Month Views are quite similar to their Palm counterparts. In the Week View (shown in Figure 5-5), though, the event blocks work a little differently than you might expect:

- To move an event to a different time, drag it by the event handle.
- To display the Edit Event dialog box and change options such as text, time, repeat settings, or the alarm, double-click the event.
- To change the duration of the event, drag its duration handle up or down.

The Month View is a bit more helpful than the one in your PDA. The Month View actually shows you what events are scheduled, not only that you have a mysterious "something" scheduled. You can't edit the events in this view, though. Instead, you can double-click the

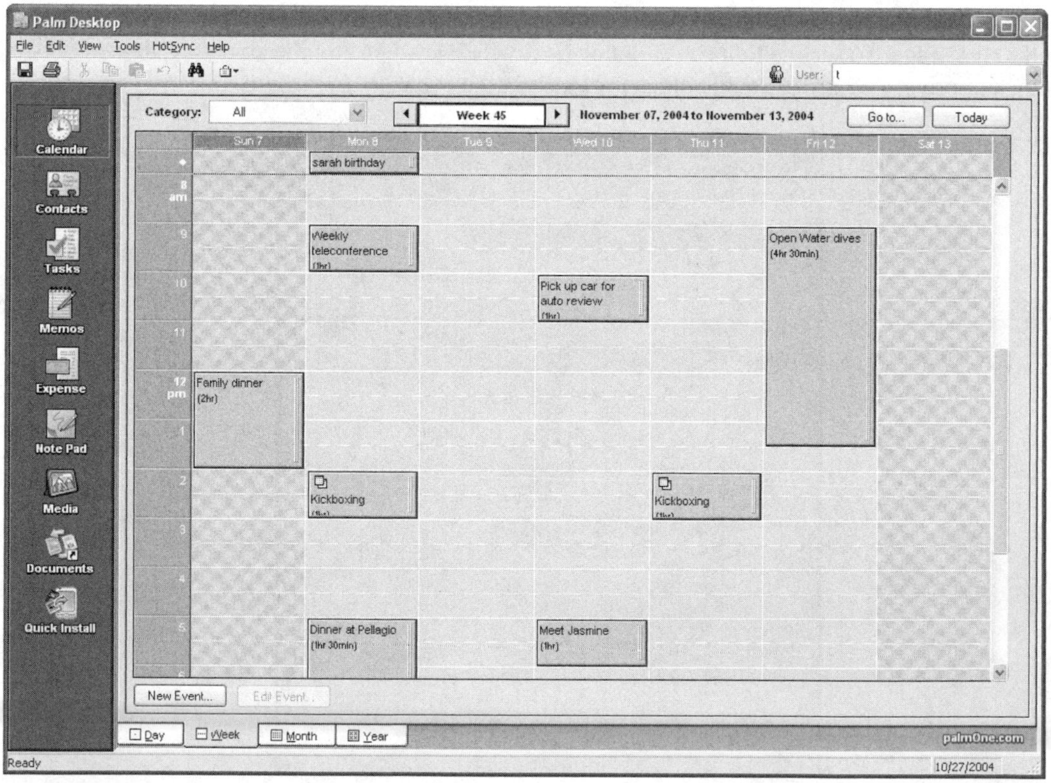

FIGURE 5-5   The Week View enables you to add and edit appointments.

appropriate day to get to the Day View, or add a new event to a specific day by right-clicking the day and choosing New Event from the menu.

Finally, the Year View lets you see 12 months at a glance. If you look closely, you'll see that the calendar marks busy days with little tick marks. To see appointments, just move the mouse so that it hovers over the appropriate day. Double-click to go directly to that Day View.

Using Alarms on the Desktop

Want to be notified about upcoming events while working at your desk? You need to use the Palm Desktop's Alarm Manager. Although Alarm Manager is linked to the Palm Desktop, it's technically not a part of it. It runs outside of the program and hangs out in the Windows System Tray, just like HotSync Manager.

To activate the Alarm Manager, choose Tools | Options and then click the Alarm tab. You'll see three choices in the Options dialog box:

- **Always Available**   When you choose this option, Alarm Manager loads when you start Windows, even if Palm Desktop itself isn't running. It ensures that you hear all of your alarms. Most folks, we think, want this option.

- **Available only when the Palm Desktop is running**   This is pretty self-explanatory, but we can't think of a lot of reasons why you'd use this option.

- **Disabled**   Alarms won't ring at all. That makes sense if you don't need to worry about event alarms or you actually use another PIM, such as Outlook.

Once you set up the Alarm Manager to your liking, you can configure alarms in the Palm Desktop when you create new events. At the bottom of the New Event or Edit Event window, you'll find the alarm options (which work just like they do on the Palm itself).

Using Outlook

Of course, Microsoft Outlook synchronizes with the Palm just fine, and many people use it instead of the Palm Desktop. We should point out, though, that some people categorize appointments in Outlook. While newer PDAs use categories in the calendar, older PDAs don't let you categorize events in the Calendar. Thankfully, if you have an older device, you can add this capability by upgrading to programs such as Chapura's PocketMirror Professional or DataViz's Beyond Contacts.

Switching from Palm Desktop to Outlook

When you first install your Palm software, you're offered the option of synchronizing with Palm Desktop or another PIM, such as Microsoft Outlook. You can change your mind later, but you'll need the original Palm Desktop installation CD-ROM.

5

To change synchronization from Palm Desktop to Outlook, or vice versa, run the Palm Desktop installation again. There's no harm in installing the software "on top of" the copy already on your hard disk. When the installer asks you which program you want your PDA to sync with, make the appropriate choice and finish the install.

Synchronizing Multiple Handhelds with Outlook

Some households or offices have more than one PDA, and each needs to sync with the same copy of Outlook. That's easy: just open Outlook and you'll see a folder called Handheld Synchronization (to get there, click the Folders icon at the bottom of the Navigation pane). You can see Outlook configured to sync with four PDAs in the following illustration, which depicts how these notes look in Outlook 2003:

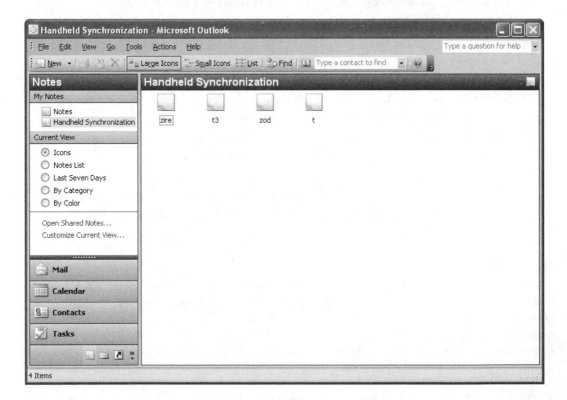

No matter which route you have to take to get here, once you arrive you'll find a note for the first Palm. It will have the same name as your Palm device. To sync Outlook with more devices, create a note for each PDA and type the device's HotSync name exactly as it appears on the top right of the HotSync screen on the Palm. The next time you sync the PDA, it will exchange data with Outlook.

> NOTE   *It's worth pointing out that if everyone logs into a single user account on your computer and you synchronize multiple PDAs with Outlook, everyone's data will be combined on the PDAs (and within Outlook) into a big, friendly broth of data. No secrets here! If you sync multiple PDAs with Palm Desktop, though, Palm Desktop keeps everyone's data separated by each device so everyone doesn't end up with everybody else's data on their handhelds. If everyone has their own separate Windows user account, all the data stays separate no matter how you sync.*

Synchronizing Your Handheld with Two PCs

Now you know how to HotSync two or more Palms to your PC. But many people have exactly the opposite problem. They want to sync a PDA to several computers, such as their home PC and office PC, all of which use Microsoft Outlook. Can it be done?

Of course it can! You simply need to throw one important little "switch" in your HotSync settings, or else you'll end up getting multiple copies of the same appointment each time you sync.

Do this:

1. Click the HotSync icon in your computer's System Tray and choose Custom.

2. Double click the entry called Calendar (Outlook).

3. Click Settings.

4. In the Outlook Calendar Settings dialog box, click Enable synchronization to multiple PCs.

Click OK.

Tweaking Alarms for the Palm

By default, every Outlook appointment comes with an alarm that sounds 15 minutes before the event. If you create most of your appointments within Outlook, you might end up with alarms you don't want on the PDA after a HotSync. To change the length of the default alarm, or to disable alarms entirely, choose Tools | Options from the Outlook menu. The Options dialog box should appear. Click the Preferences tab. In the Calendar section, edit the Default Reminder option to suit your needs. If you remove the check mark, the alarm is then disabled for new appointments.

Did you know?

There Are Better Date Books

Looking for an alternative to the Date Book that comes with your handheld? You have quite a few choices. The Palm Date Book hasn't changed much in the past decade, and it still has many of the same limitations it had back in the mid-90s. You can't categorize appointments the way you can in Microsoft Outlook, for instance, and you can't synchronize with Microsoft Exchange Public Folders. There's another annoyance. You can't "link" appointments with items elsewhere in your Palm, such as the contact information for people attending your meeting. Don't worry, though, because there are numerous alternatives available.

If you only try one, give DateBk5 a shot. DateBk5 is one of the best alternatives out there. Dave has used it for years and highly recommends it. Here are a few reasons to consider trying this alternative to the built-in Calendar:

- DateBk5 offers tons of ways to customize the display
- It lets you add alarms to tasks, which is handy if you have an older Palm that doesn't support alarmed To Dos

■ It has a new type of task optimized for telephone calls

■ You can see appointments and tasks in a split screen view

■ You can link appointments to other records, such as contacts and tasks

That said, there are several other spiffy alternatives, and they can all be installed for free, so there's no reason not to experiment and see if there's a better alternative than your Palm's Calendar or Date Book. Here are the best of the best:

■ Agendus

■ Beyond Contacts

■ KeySuite

These programs offer a wealth of features and capabilities that you won't find in the integrated Date Book. DateBk5 and Agendus, for instance, take advantage of larger screens, such as the big 320 × 480-pixel display on some Sony Cliés. They also let you attach colorful icons to appointments, making it easy to tell them apart at a glance in any calendar view. The other programs integrate with Outlook more coherently, using categories, more data fields, and other important features.

Where to Find It

Web Site	Address	What's There
Imabic	www.iambic.com	Agendus
DataViz	www.dataviz.com	Beyond Contacts
Chapura	www.chapura.com	KeySuite
Pimlico	www.pimlicosoftware.com	DateBk5
Ripple Factory	www.theripplefactory.com	HoliDates
Jampaq	www.jampaq.com	Holidays at Hand

Chapter 6

Contacts and the Address Book

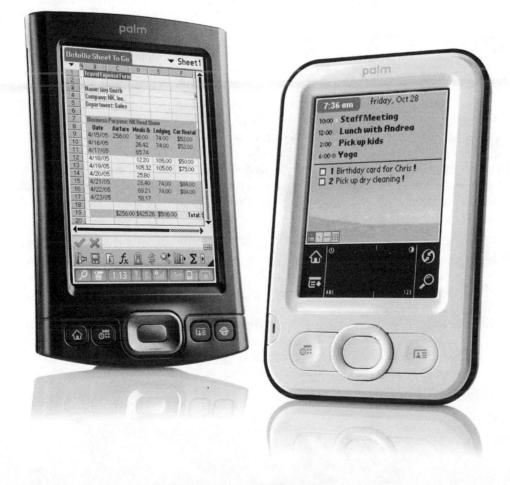

How to...

- View Address Book entries
- Customize the Address List display
- Search for an entry by name
- Search for an entry by keyword
- Create new Address Book entries
- Display a specific phone number in the Address List
- Use the custom fields
- Assign a category to an entry
- Delete Address Book entries
- Use the Windows Address Book
- Use your Palm with Outlook

What's the big deal? It's only an address book, right? Well, maybe. But as one of the four big "core" applications—the main programs that come pre-installed on your PDA—you'll use Contacts (or, in older models, the Address Book. But from here on out, we'll mostly just call it Contacts) a lot. And Contacts is an elegant program, designed to get the information you need quickly, perhaps more quickly than any other contact manager on the market.

We're sure you'll get a lot of mileage from Contacts. You can store literally thousands of entries and not run out of memory. Regardless of how many names you add to the list, your handheld never slows down to a crawl. That's a claim that many desktop applications simply can't make. In addition, Contacts isn't really a stand-alone application (though it can be if you want). It synchronizes with desktop applications such as Palm Desktop and Microsoft Outlook. This means you need to create a contact list just once, and then it's maintained on both your PC and your PDA.

NOTE   *For years, the address-book application was called Address Book (natch!). Then, Palm renamed it Contacts, just as the company changed the name of Date Book to Calendar. We'll usually call the program Contacts, but if your model has the Address Book, most of the information in this chapter still applies. What's different? Well, Contacts has a few new features not found in Address Book, but for the most part they're identical. Contacts allows you to attach a picture with each entry, for example, so you can put a name to a face, no matter how many people you need to keep track of. Contacts also has significantly better synchronization with Outlook, allowing you to include far more information about each entry than ever before.*

Viewing Your Addresses

When you switch to Contacts, the program displays all the entries in your list onscreen. As you might expect, you can start Contacts by pressing the Contacts button on your Palm, or tapping the Contacts icon in the Home screen.

NOTE *On some smartphones and PDAs with wireless capabilities, the Contacts button may actually launch the Speed Dial screen. You might have to press the button a second or third time to get your complete list of contacts.*

As you can see in Figure 6-1, the PDA lists your contacts alphabetically in a view called the Address List. Unless you have a device with a bigger screen (such as the Palm TX), there's room for 11 entries onscreen at one time; the rest appear above or below the screen, depending on where you are within the Address List. To get around in the Address List, just use the scroll buttons or the Navigator. Each time you scroll, the PDA moves the list by one complete page of entries.

You can also get around with categories. If your contacts are divided into more than one category, every time you press the Contacts button, you switch categories. You can cycle through the first page of names in each category by repeatedly pressing the Contacts button.

6

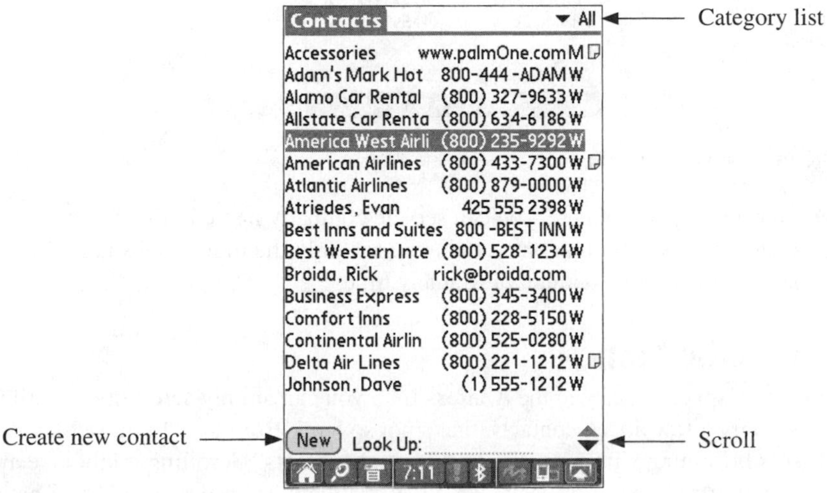

FIGURE 6-1   The Address List is a database of all your contact information.

Viewing by Company Name

For most folks, the default Address List is great. This list displays the entries by name (last, first) and a phone number. If you prefer to work with your contacts according to the company they work with, you can change the Address List.

To change the View mode of the Address List, do this:

1. Display the Address List View.

2. Choose Options | Preferences from the menu.

3. Choose Company, Last Name from the List By list.

4. Tap OK to save your changes.

Notice that after making the change, you can see the company name in the list. If no company is associated with a particular entry, then you see only the individual's name, as you did before. You can switch back to the default view at any time.

Finding a Specific Name

If you're looking for a specific entry in the Address List, you can simply scroll down until you find it. If you have only a few dozen contacts, that's not so hard. But what if you're like us and your Address List is brimming with more than a thousand contacts? Scrolling might take awhile, especially if the guy you're looking for is named Nigel Walthers or Earnest Zanthers. That's when you use the Look Up function.

To search for a specific name, start writing the person's last name in the Look Up field at the bottom of the screen. Contacts adjusts the display as you write; so if you enter the letter **J**, it displays all the names that begin with the letter *J*. If you write **JO**, it narrows the search and shows names that begin with those letters.

> **NOTE**   *If you're using the List By: Company, Last Name option in the Address List View, it's a little more complicated. If the entry has a company name, you need to search for that entry by company name. If the entry doesn't have a company name, though, you can find it by the last name.*

Once you start searching, you can keep writing letters until the PDA displays exactly the name you want, or you can write one or two letters, and then use the Scroll button to find the name you need. If you want to clear the Look Up field to write in a new name, just press one of the Scroll buttons.

> **TIP**   *If you try writing a letter, but your PDA beeps at you, this means no name in the list is spelled with the letter you're trying to add. You've probably misspelled the name.*

A Better Lookup

On some PDAs, you can locate a contact more quickly by using a fast search tool that works in conjunction with the Navigator. Tap the search icon at the bottom of the screen (which looks like the magnifying glass in the following illustration) or, if you don't have that icon (we're looking at you, Tungsten T5), press the Navigator to the right.

You'll see a new Look Up field at the bottom of the screen. Use the up and down buttons on the Navigator to find the first letter of the contact's last name, and then press the right button to move to the next letter. You can quickly filter down to exactly the name you're looking for, because the Palm only lets you select letters that spell names that are really in your Contacts. So to find Johnson, you won't have to scroll through all the letters of the alphabet to get to J. If you don't have any names in the Palm that start with C, D, E F, G H, or I, you only have to scroll down twice: from A to B, and then from B to J. It's crazy cool!

Contacts	▼ All
Allstate Car Renta	(800) 634-6186 W
America West Airli	(800) 235-9292 W
American Airlines	(800) 433-7300 W
Atlantic Airlines	(800) 879-0000 W
Atriedes, Evan	425 555 2398 W
Best Inns and Suites	800 -BEST INN W
Best Western Inte	(800) 528-1234 W
Broida, Rick	rick@broida.com
Business Express	(800) 345-3400 W
Comfort Inns	(800) 228-5150 W
Continental Airlin	(800) 525-0280 W
Delta Air Lines	(800) 221-1212 W
Johnson, Dave	(1) 555-1212 W
Johnson, Hobbes	717 555 1245 W
National Car Rent	(800) 227-7368 W
Technical Sup	www.palmOne.com... M

New   Look Up: **B E**   ◆

🏠 🔍 📋 7:12 ⚡ ☼ 📱 🖥

```
┌─────────────────────────────────┐
│             Find                │
│  Matches for "Air"              │
│ ─────────── Contacts ────────── │
│ America West Airl  (800) 235-9292 W │
│ American Airlines  (800) 433-7300 W │
│ Atlantic Airlines  (800) 879-0000 W │
│ Business Express   (800) 345-3400 W │
│ Continental Airlin (800) 525-0280 W │
│ Delta Air Lines    (800) 221-1212 W │
│ ─────────── SheetToGo ──────── │
│ ──────── Documents To Go ────── │
│ ( Cancel ) ( Find More )        │
└─────────────────────────────────┘
```

FIGURE 6-2   The Find tool is a powerful way to locate an entry even if you don't remember the person's exact name. It's also great for finding other data stored on your handheld.

Conducting a Detailed Search

You might have noticed that the Look Up field searches only by last name. What happens if you want to find someone, but you can only remember that person's first name or the company where he works? The Look Up field won't do any good.

In this case, use the Find tool. Tap the Find button, enter the word you want to search for, and then tap OK. You get a list of every entry in the handheld with that word, even items from the other applications, as shown in Figure 6-2. The current application is searched first, so make sure you're in Contacts before you start using the Find tool.

Viewing a Name

Once you locate the name you were looking for, tap on it. You see the Address View, which displays the contact's name, address, and phone numbers, as shown in Figure 6-3.

Dialing a Phone Number

If you have a wireless PDA (such as a Palm TX paired with a Bluetooth phone) or smartphone, you can dial a number in Contacts and immediately take the call. When you find the name you're looking for, tap the Quick Connect icon at the very top of the screen and then tap the phone number you want to dial. Be sure to check out Chapter 10 for details on this.

```
┌─────────────────────────────────┐
│      Quick Connect        ⓘ     │
│  Allstate Car Rental            │
│ ┌─────────────────────────────┐ │
│ │ Work: 800 634 6186          │ │
│ └─────────────────────────────┘ │
│                                 │
│                                 │
│                                 │
│                                 │
│                                 │
│  ( Done )  ( Settings... )      │
└─────────────────────────────────┘
```

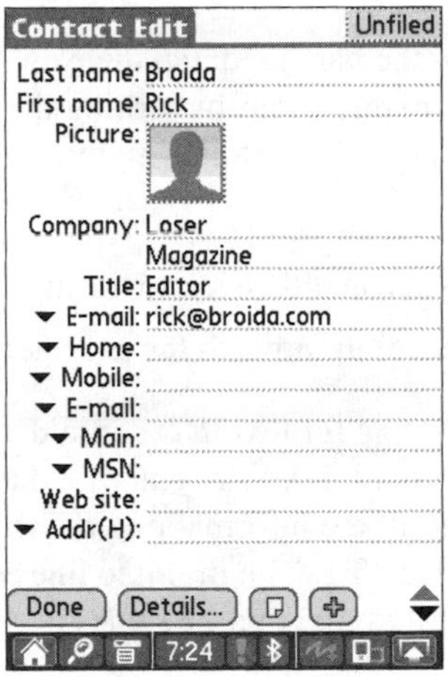

Contact Edit | Unfiled
Last name: Broida
First name: Rick
Picture:

Company: Loser
Magazine
Title: Editor
▼ E-mail: rick@broida.com
▼ Home:
▼ Mobile:
▼ E-mail:
▼ Main:
▼ MSN:
Web site:
▼ Addr(H):

(Done) (Details...) (▯) (✢)   ▲▼

FIGURE 6-3   Contacts shows you all the details about the selected individual.

The Future of Contacts

Dave: There's little doubt that thanks to Contacts, the Palm's best application, all PDAs will inevitably, someday, turn into smartphones or connected wireless devices that work with your mobile phone. After all, why carry an address book in your PDA and a totally different, incompatible phone list in your mobile phone? If your PDA were also a phone, you could tap one button and place a call using your PDA's contacts list. If you like carrying a separate phone, wireless connectivity lets your PDA communicate seamlessly with the phone. Just tap the name you want to dial on your PDA, and it automatically places the call on your phone. I do that already with my Palm TX. It uses Bluetooth to dial my Motorola Razr, and it's clearly the way of the future. In fact, I make a prediction: in the far future, only losers like Rick will carry both a Palm and some totally incompatible cell phone that you have to program separately with names and phone numbers.

Rick: Let's see … you have to carry your Tungsten, your phone, and a Bluetooth headset (the biggest "I'm a nerd" badge since the calculator watch). There's no debating the value of the Palm address book, especially when it's integrated into a smartphone. Hence, the appeal of models such as the Treo 650. Of course, you think your needs are all people's needs, so whatever you decide is right must be the future. Here in the real world (you should visit sometime!), there's no perfect smartphone (though the Treo 650 is awfully close), so there are still advantages to carrying both a non-wireless Palm and a regular phone.

Creating New Entries

To create a new Address List entry on the handheld, tap the New button at the bottom of the screen. From there, start filling in the blanks. Start by writing the last name of the person you're adding. When you're ready to move on to the first name, you need to change fields. You can do this in two ways:

- Tap the next field with the stylus, and then start writing.
- Use the Tab gesture (shown here) to move to the next field.

Even though you see only a single line for text in each field, the Address List secretly supports multiple lines of text in each field. If you're entering the company name, for instance, you can use two or more lines to enter all the information you need about the company, department, and so on, for the individual. To write multiple lines of text in a field, use the Return gesture to create a new line. You won't see the multiple lines in the Address List, but you can see them when you select the entry and view the Address View.

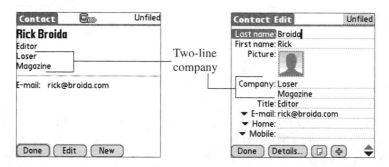

When you've finished adding information about this new person, tap the Done button.

On most new Palms, you can add pictures to your contacts. To see if your PDA supports pictures in its address book, tap an entry and see if you have a picture frame, like the one in the illustration above.

To set the picture for an entry, tap the frame and choose Photos from the menu. You'll be able to choose a picture from your handheld's internal memory, or from the expansion card, if you have one installed.

> TIP
>
> *To get pictures onto your PDA, use the Palm Desktop to transfer images using the Media button. Or you can drag and drop pictures directly to the memory card (place them in a folder marked DCIM). The advantage of using Palm Desktop is that it can automatically resize your images, which makes them take up less room and display faster.*

If you are using the newest version of Outlook, which also supports pictures in contacts, you can easily add a picture to entries from the desktop. Your PDA automatically recognizes pictures in Outlook contact entries and associates them with your contacts on the handheld.

> TIP
>
> *What if you're Canadian, French, or living in some other non-American location? The Palm defaults to address details such as city, state, and ZIP code, which might not be appropriate for your locale. The solution is to tap on the Prefs icon in the System category of the Home screen and select Formats from the menu. Then, set the Preset To: menu to whatever country you desire.*

Using Multiple Phone Numbers

The Address List gives you a few options when you enter contact information. Specifically, you can set what kinds of phone numbers your PDA has for each contact. Conveniently, this needn't be the same for everyone. For one person, you might list a home phone and a pager, for instance, and another entry might have a work number and an e-mail address. The PDA keeps track of everything for you.

To control these numbers, tap on the phone number list and choose the desired label. Then, write the number or e-mail address in the field next to the label. You can specify up to five entries for each person in your Address List.

Contact Edit | Unfiled
Last name: Johnson
First name: Dave
Picture:

Company: PC World's Digital Focus
Title: Editor
▼ Work: (1) 555-1212
Work | ne (1) 555-1213
Home | ail: dave@bydavejohnson.co
Fax | m
Other | ail:
E-mail | in:
Main | iN:
Pager | te:
Mobile | V): 123 Elm Street

(Done) (Details...) (▯) (✛)   ▲▼

If you're on the ball, you might wonder which of those numbers shows up in the Address List View. Remember, the list shows the name and a phone number for each contact. This means you might not have to open an entry simply to dial a phone number, because it's right there in the List View. The answer, though, is that the first phone number you enter into the Edit View is the one that appears in the List View, no matter where it appears in the list of phone numbers.

If you later decide you want a different number to appear in the List View, tap the Details button and select the number label you want from the Show in List menu.

TIP *Don't like the font? You can choose from four font sizes by selecting Options | Font in the Contacts menu. You can even set the display and edit screens differently.*

Using Extra Fields

The Address List has plenty of preconfigured fields (such as name, company, and phone numbers) for most users, but it's also flexible enough to accommodate the special needs of everyone else. You might want to track birthdays, Web pages, spouse names, or other personal information. If so, you're in luck—nine custom fields are available at the bottom of the Address Edit View, which you can rename as you like. If you have an older Palm, you'll have four custom fields to work with, not nine.

To label these bonus fields as something more useful, do this:

1. Open Contacts. Any view will do.

2. Choose Options | Rename Custom Fields from the menu.

3. Select the text on the first line (which should say Custom 1) and write a name for the field. Name the other fields, or as many as you need, in the same way.

Rename Custom Fields ⓘ
To rename any custom field below, enter a new name:

Shoe Size	Custom 5
Spouse	Custom 6
PADI	Custom 7
Custom 4	Custom 8
	Custom 9

(OK) (Cancel)

4. Tap OK when you finish.

Once you create labels for these fields, you can find them at the bottom of the list of contact info in the Address Edit View.

> **NOTE** *The custom fields are global. This means you can't have different custom fields for each entry or even for each category. Once named, the custom fields apply to all entries in the Address List. You needn't fill them out for every entry, though.*

Duplicating an Entry

If you have multiple entries that are quite similar, such as different people in the same company or in the same household, you might want to use the Duplicate command to streamline data entry. Suppose you just meticulously entered the data for Susan Jackson, and then you wanted to create an entry for her husband, Bob Jackson. Do this:

1. Select the entry you want to duplicate.

2. Choose Record | Duplicate Contact from the menu.

3. Open the new duplicate entry and make the changes you need to customize it.

Assigning Categories

Your new contact can easily get lost within a sea of names and addresses if you aren't careful. With only a few names to manage, this isn't a big deal. But what if you have 500 or 1,000 contacts in your address list? This is where categories come in handy.

6

Choosing a Category

As you might remember from Chapter 2, categories are simply a way of organizing your data more logically into groups that you use frequently. To assign a contact to a specific category, do this:

1. From the Contact Edit screen, tap Details. The Contact Details dialog box should appear.

```
┌────────────────────────────────────────┐
│ Contact Edit              ┊ Unfiled │
│ ▼ Addr(W): 123 Elm Street              │
│        City: Wordan                    │
│       State: UT                        │
│    Zip Code: 98562                     │
│     Country: United States of America  │
│ ┌──────────────────────────────────┐   │
│ │ Contact Details              ⓘ  │   │
│ │ Show in List: ▼ Work             │   │
│ │    Category: ▼ Personal          │   │
│ │     Private: ☐                   │   │
│ │ ( OK ) ( Cancel ) ( Delete... ) (▯)│  │
│ └──────────────────────────────────┘   │
└────────────────────────────────────────┘
```

2. Tap the Category list and choose the category name you want to assign to this contact.

3. Tap OK to close the dialog box.

Of course, you needn't assign a category if you don't want to do so. By default, new contacts are placed in the Unfiled category.

Editing and Deleting Addresses

In this fast-paced world, a contact once entered in an address book isn't likely to stay that way for long. After all, think of how briefly J-Lo's name stayed in Ben Affleck's Treo. (Note to Halle Berry: Dave promises never to erase your name from his Palm.) Anyway, you might commonly find yourself needing to update an address, phone number, or e-mail address, or delete an entry entirely.

To edit an entry, all you must do is find the entry in the Address List and tap it. You're taken to the Address View where you can see the existing information. Then, tap on the screen and the display changes to the Address Edit screen, which you can change to suit your needs.

If you have a contact you simply don't need anymore, you can delete it from the PDA to save memory and reduce data clutter. To delete a contact, do this:

1. Choose the entry from the Address List. You see the Address View.

2. Choose Record | Delete Contact from the menu.

NOTE   *If you check the box marked Save Archive Copy on PC, then a copy of this entry is preserved in a file called "archive" on your PC, which you can load into Palm Desktop using the File | Open menu. In general, you probably needn't archive your data, but this option lets you restore deleted data in a crisis.*

Creating and Beaming Your Business Card

As we mentioned in Chapter 4, one of the coolest things about taking your handheld to meetings and trade shows is the capability to beam your personal information into other peoples' PDAs. This is a lot easier and more convenient than exchanging a business card. Heck, a paper business card? That's so . . . 80s! Use your Palm instead.

Before you can beam your personal information around, though, you need to create a business card. That's not hard to do. Find your own personal information in the Address List (or, if you haven't done this yet, create an entry for yourself). After you select your card and you can see your personal information on the Address View screen, choose Record | Select Business Card from the menu.

From here on, you can beam your card to others either by choosing Record | Beam Business Card from the Address List menu or, more simply, by holding the Contacts button down for two seconds.

By the way: You can do more than just beam entries, too. On some models, you can choose Send Contact or Send Category from the Record menu and you'll see this screen:

You can use e-mail, text messaging, or Bluetooth to send contacts wirelessly.

Is your personal entry selected as your business card? It's easy to tell. In the Address View, you can see an icon representing a business card at the top of the screen, to the right of the title.

How to ... Create a Contacts Entry

In summary, here's how you can create entries in the Address Book:

1. Press the Contacts button or tap the Contacts icon on your PDA to switch to that app.
2. Tap the New button on the bottom of the Address List View.
3. Enter all the information to create an entry for the person in question.
4. Tap the Details button and assign the entry to a category, and then tap OK.

Working with the Palm Desktop

The Palm Desktop obviously has its own counterpart to the Contacts program found on your PDA. Using the Palm Desktop, you can not only create, edit, and refer to entries on your PC, but you can also put them to use in ways unavailable on the Palm itself. Next, we look at the Palm Desktop.

The Palm Desktop Contacts

Using the Contacts module in Palm Desktop is a radically different experience than using it on your handheld (see Figure 6-4). In most respects, it's better because the larger desktop screen, keyboard, and mouse enable you to enter and use the data in a more flexible way. After you start Palm Desktop, you can switch to Contacts by clicking the Contacts icon on the left side of the screen.

The Contacts interface enables you to see both the Address List and Address View simultaneously. To see a specific record's contents, click it in the list, and the information then appears in the column on the right.

We highly recommend printing a hard copy of your Contacts for those just-in-case situations, like if you lose your handheld or its memory gets wiped and you're away from your PC. You can print a detailed address book by choosing File | Print.

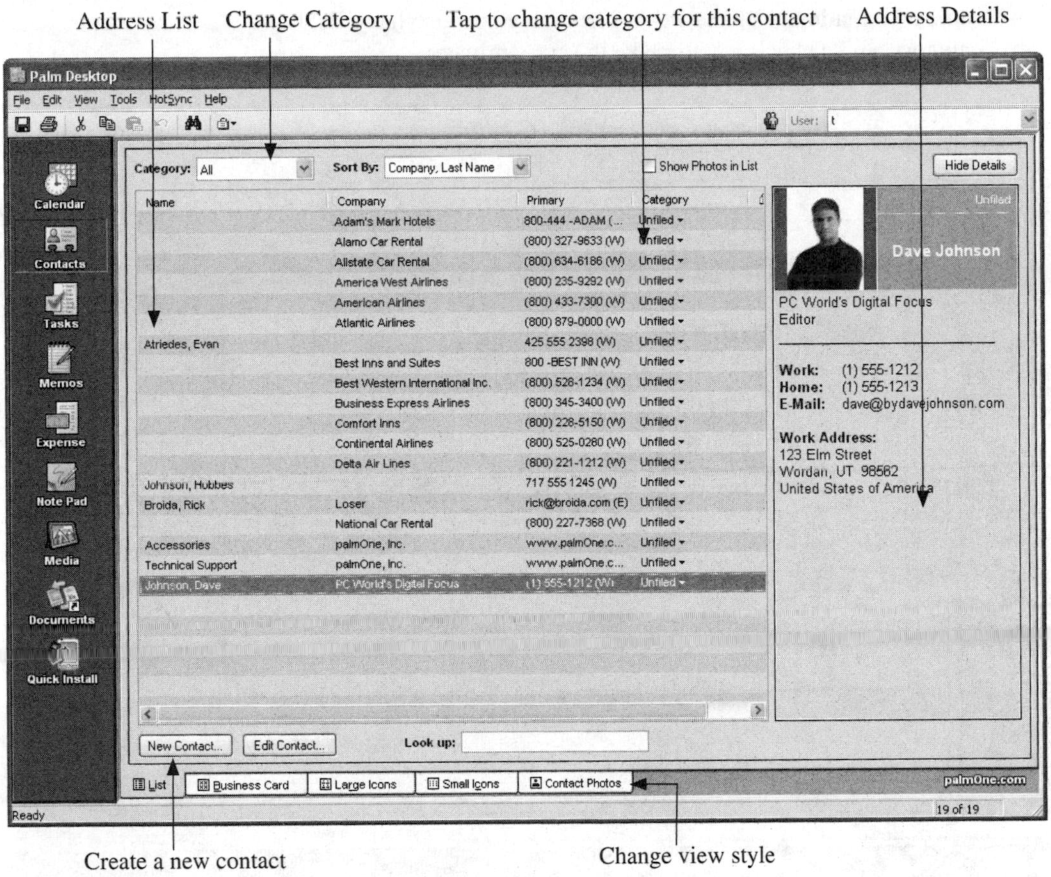
Address List
Change Category
Tap to change category for this contact
Address Details
Create a new contact
Change view style

FIGURE 6-4 Contacts looks sparse, but has more features than the Palm itself.

Creating and Editing Entries

There are a few dramatic differences in the desktop version of Contacts. Here are a few things to look out for:

- To create a new entry, click the New button at the bottom of the screen or double-click a blank spot in the Address List.

■ The Edit and New dialog boxes (the former is shown next) allow you to enter the same information as on the PDA. The dialog box also has a list box for specifying the category, and a check box to make the entry private.

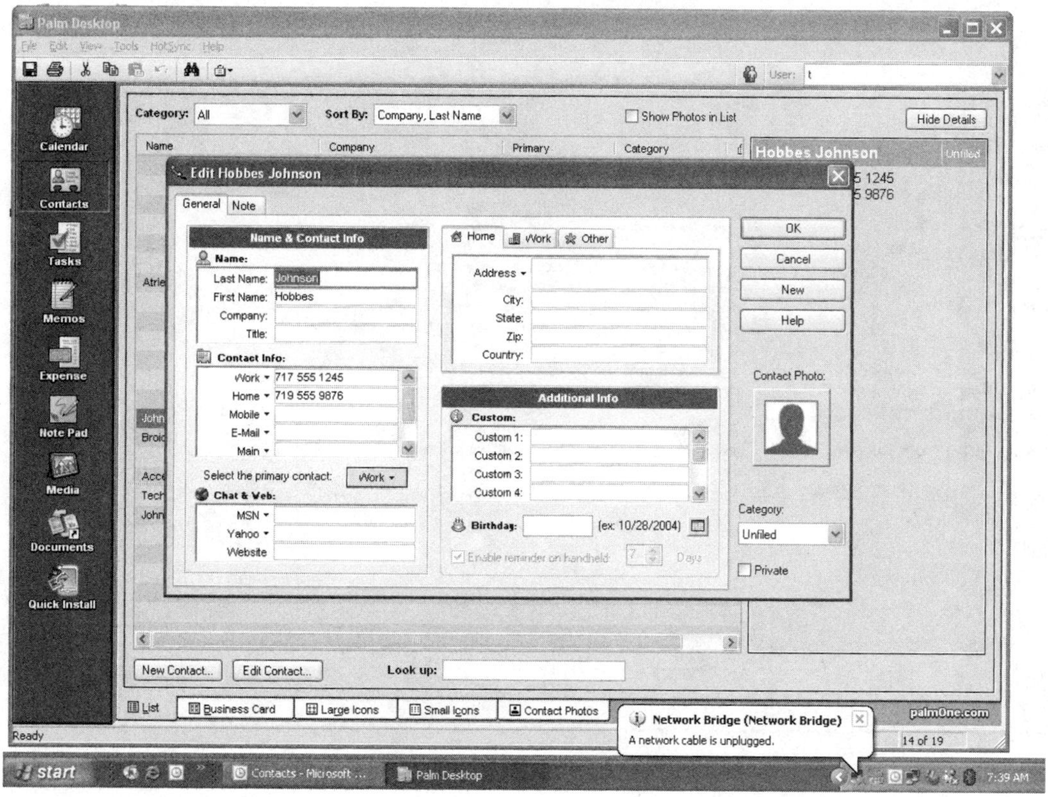

■ To specify which phone number will appear in the Address List, click the radio button to the left of the appropriate phone number.

■ To edit an existing entry, either double-click the entry in the Address List or its equivalent in the Address View on the right.

■ You can also change the custom fields on the Palm Desktop. To do that, choose Tools | Preferences.

Importing Contacts into the Palm Desktop

If you have a history with another contact manager, you could have dozens or even hundreds of names and addresses that should be copied over to the Palm Desktop to be synchronized with the Palm. Thankfully, the Palm Desktop makes importing all those contacts possible with a minimum of fuss. All you need is a contact manager capable of saving its data in either a comma-separated values (CSV) or a tab-separated values (TSV) format. (Palm Desktop can also import Address Book Archive (ABA) files, which are created when you export contacts from Palm Desktop.) To import your data from another program, do this:

1. In your old contact manager, find the menu option to export your data in either CSV or TSV format. If the program gives you an option to remap your data as it's saved, don't worry. We'll map it properly as it's imported into the Palm Desktop. Save the exported data to a file on your hard disk. Make a note of where you save this file, because you will need to find it again in about two steps.

2. In the Palm Desktop, choose File | Import. The Import dialog box should appear.

3. Select the file you just created with the old contact manager. You might have to choose the proper file extension (such as CSV or TSV) from the Type of File list box to see the file you created. Choose Open.

4. Now you see a Specify Import Fields dialog box, as shown in Figure 6-5. This is the hardest part of the process and the one part that isn't terribly automated.

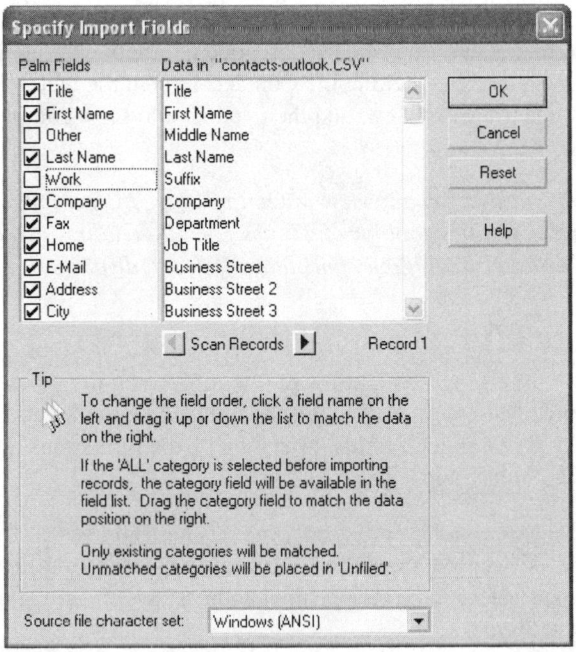

FIGURE 6-5 Carefully rearrange the fields in the Specify Import Fields dialog box so your old data is imported properly into the Palm Desktop.

Here's the deal: The data in a typical contact entry includes items such as name, phone numbers, and address. But those fields won't be in the same order in any two contact management programs, so you need to help the Palm Desktop put the old data in the right fields as it imports. To map the fields properly, drag each field on the left (which is the Palm Desktop) until it's lined up with the proper field on the right (which represents the old program). Line up last name with last name, for instance, and match phone numbers, e-mail addresses, and any other important fields. If you don't want to import a certain field, deselect its check box.

TIP   *You can use the arrows to cycle forward through the database and make sure you assigned the fields properly.*

5. When you finish lining up the fields, click the OK button.

If you did everything right, you should see your contacts in the Palm Desktop. Any newly imported entries are highlighted. If you messed something up, all isn't lost. Simply delete all your records, and then try to import your contacts file again.

Using Outlook

As we mentioned in Chapter 5, Outlook is a perfectly good alternative to the Palm Desktop. To see your contacts in Outlook, start by clicking the Contacts icon in the Outlook Shortcut bar. Outlook should switch to the Contacts View, and then you should see a complete list of your names and addresses.

SHORTCUT   *To find a contact quickly from any view in Outlook, type the person's name in the Find a Contact field on the Outlook toolbar and press ENTER. Outlook displays a list of names that matches your criteria or, if only one name appears, displays its entry.*

Outlook and Your PDA

Outlook can hold a wealth of information, but it's important for you to understand the Palm's limitations when synchronizing to Outlook. Not all the fields in Outlook get transferred to the PDA because there simply aren't enough fields. Specifically, the limitations in the HotSync from Outlook to the PDA are the following:

- On many Palms, especially older ones, only the business address is stored on the Palm. You can get a new device, like the Palm TX, or just upgrade to a different HotSync conduit that lets you synchronize the personal address. Specifically, try PocketMirror Professional or Intellisync.

■ Work, Home, Fax, Mobile, and E-mail are typically the only contact fields transferred to the Palm. If you create a contact with alternative fields, such as Business 2 or alternative e-mail addresses, Palm tries to include these entries, space permitting.

■ None of the data from the Details tab is stored on the handheld.

This illustration should help you see how Contacts entries correlate to Outlook:

Did you know?

Contacts Alternatives and Enhancements to Look For

Don't think you have to stick with Contacts just because it came with your trusty old PDA. Personally, we prefer the Palm Contacts to most of the alternatives, but here are a few you might want to look into if you feel like expanding your contact management horizons:

- **KeySuite** This program from Chapura could well be the answer to every power user's dreams. The ordinary Contacts doesn't synchronize many of Outlook's fields, but KeySuite is a replacement that transfers absolutely everything, including all those extra fields in the other Outlook Contact tabs and all the categories as well. Visit www.chapura.com.

- **Agendus** This replacement combines the Tasks, Contacts, and Calendar to deliver a single integrated interface for tracking, alarming, and viewing your daily itinerary. This program has lots of diehard fans because of its many powerful features for managing contacts. You can try it out at www.iambic.com.

- **Beyond Contacts** Yet another aggressive alternative, Beyond Contacts, comes with a slew of cool features, the most important of which is a comprehensive, integrated interface that does the work of all four Palm apps, making it work more like Microsoft Outlook. It even has an Outlook-like Today screen that summarizes your appointments. Visit www.dataviz.com for more information.

Where to Find It

Web Site	Address	What's There
Chapura	www.chapura.com	PocketMirror Professional and KeySuite
DataViz	www.dataviz.com	Beyond Contacts
Iambic	www.iambic.com	Agendus
Intellisync	www.intellisync.com	Intellisync

Chapter 7

Tasks, the To Do List, and Memo Pad

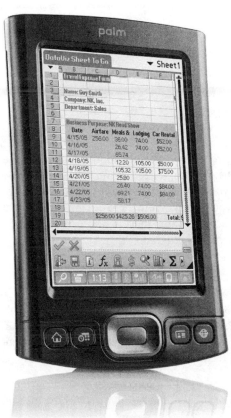

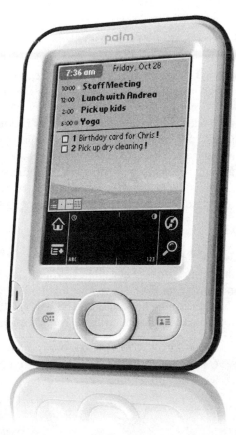

How to...

- View Task entries
- Create new Tasks
- Prioritize your Tasks
- Add notes to Tasks
- Customize the Tasks View
- Beam Tasks to others
- Use the Palm Desktop for Windows
- Use Outlook with the Palm
- Create new memos
- Cut, copy, and paste text in a memo
- Assign categories to memos
- Customize the Memo List
- Make memos private
- Import text files into Windows

Two other programs constitute the core features of your PDA's personal information management, Tasks (also called the To Do List in older PDAs) and the Memo Pad. For a lot of folks, these programs don't get the same constant workout as the Contacts and Calendar, and that's too bad. These programs are great for making your day smoother, more efficient, and less troublesome. Well, think of it this way. Would you be more organized if you actually carried a list of things you needed to do, big and small, with you all the time? Would you stay on top of your tasks and remember important brainstorms if you simply wrote them down as they occurred to you? That's the magic of these little guys. In our never-ending quest to improve your life, we've dedicated this next chapter to illuminating these two programs.

Viewing Tasks (a.k.a. the To Do List)

As with the other core applications in your Palm, you can start Tasks by tapping its icon on the Application screen. If you have an older model with a Tasks button, you can press that—it's usually the one to the right of the scroll buttons. If your Palm doesn't have a Tasks button, but you use Tasks a lot, you can even reprogram one of the buttons to start Tasks automatically (see Chapter 2 for details).

TIP   *On some newer PDAs, the To Do List is called Tasks, and has a few extra features that we'll talk about later in the chapter.*

FIGURE 7-1   The Tasks list displays all of your pending to dos.

On many newer models, the Tasks button has been eliminated in favor of other apps. The Tungsten W, for instance, makes the third button an e-mail launcher, whereas the TX reallocates buttons to a Home screen and a Web browser, so there's no room for poor old Tasks. If you have such a device, you have two choices:

1. Always start Tasks from the Main category of the Apps screen.

2. Reassign one of the buttons to launch Tasks. For details on that, see Chapter 2.

As you can see in Figure 7-1, the handheld lists your Tasks in a fairly straightforward list that you can use to see what tasks you have coming up or, in some cases, past due (you might want to take care of those pretty soon).

Each time you scroll, the PDA moves the list by one complete page. This means that if you scroll down, the bottom entry on the page becomes the top entry after scrolling.

Another way to get around is by using the categories. If your tasks are divided into more than one category, every time you press the Tasks button, you switch categories. You can cycle through the first page of tasks in each category by repeatedly pressing this button.

Did you know?

The Agenda View Is Handy!

You don't have to start Tasks to see the list of things you need to do. You can also view your Tasks in the Calendar. The Calendar's Agenda View lets you see all of today's appointments and upcoming tasks at a glance, all on the same screen. See Chapter 5 for the whole scoop.

Choose Your View

Tasks makes it easy to filter your list of tasks. This can be really handy if you create a lot of them, using the three tabs at the top of the screen:

When you select the Date tab, use the drop-down menu to see only those items that have due dates in a particular time period, such as due today, due in the last week, due in the next week, or past due.

When you select the Category tab, you can display just those tasks that are assigned to a specific category, again by making a selection from the drop-down menu.

Finally, don't forget about the Note button at the bottom of the screen. It lets you quickly attach a note to any task. To use it, tap on an item in the list and then tap the Memo button. The Memo Pad opens automatically. Enter the note and tap Done. You've just attached a note to your selected task!

Creating a Task

To add a task, just start writing. The text appears automatically in a brand new entry.

 *If you want to create a task with a specific priority, tap on an entry that has the priority you want, and then tap New. The new To Do takes the priority of the previously selected task, saving you the trouble of choosing a priority later.*

Although most tasks can be summarized in only one line of text, there's no reasonable limit to how long you can make one. If you need more than one line of text to describe your task, you can use the Enter gesture to get the PDA to display a new blank line in the same task. Remember, though, creating multiline tasks might make it hard for you to read them later, as you can see next:

Instead of making long, multiline tasks, we recommend you add a note to your task instead (explained in the next Tip).

Friends Are a Chore

It's true! Having friends and coworkers can be actual work. Suppose you need to meet with Ed Grimpley from accounting sometime this week to talk about why you've gone through 18 mouse pads in the space of one week. You don't have an appointment in your calendar. You'd rather pop in sometime when it's convenient. The Tasks List is your answer. Create a new task and choose Options | Phone Lookup from the menu. Find Ed in the Phone Number Lookup dialog box and tap Add. You get Ed's name and phone number in the Tasks entry. It's a handy way to remind yourself to call someone without setting up a rigid appointment in the Calendar.

Adding Some Details

Once you finish entering the name of the task, tap elsewhere on the screen to save the entry. If you prefer, you can add extra information, such as a priority, category, and due date. You don't have to enter any of these special settings, but using them enables you to track your tasks with greater accuracy. The following explains what you need to do.

1. Select the task you want to edit by tapping the name of the task.

2. Tap the Details button.

3. Tap a number to represent the priority of your task. You can select any number from 1 to 5 (the lower the number, the higher the priority).

4. Choose a category from the Category list.

5. Choose a due date from the Due Date list. You can choose to make a task due today, tomorrow, or in a week, or you can choose a date directly from the Calendar dialog box.

6. Tap OK to save your changes to the task.

To Do or Appointment?

We know what you're thinking—if you can assign due dates to items in the To Do List, why bother with appointments? Or, from the other perspective, why use To Dos if you have the Date Book? That's a good question. We use the To Do List whenever we have tasks that need doing by a certain date, but not at a certain time of day. If it requires a time slot, we put it in the Date Book. So, stuff like "buy the new *Raconteurs* album" and "finish Chapter 12" (hint, hint, Rick . . .) are To Dos. "Meet with Laura for lunch at 11:30" is a Date Book entry. There's also the matter of alarms. Your handheld can attach alarms to appointments, but not to To Dos.

> **TIP**
>
> *Although you can make a task almost any length, most people find it's better to keep them short, and add a note for all the gory details. To add a note to a task, select it, tap the Details button, and then tap Note. Or just tap the handy new Note icon, if your handheld has the newer Tasks app in place of the Tasks List.*

Working with the List View

When you switch to Tasks, all of your existing tasks are arranged onscreen, usually in order of importance (as determined by the priority number assigned to each one). As you can see in Figure 7-2, several elements are associated with each task:

- **Check box**   If you complete a task, you can indicate it's done by tapping the check box. That places a check mark in the task. Depending on how you configured the To Do Preferences, the entry either disappears or remains onscreen, but is marked as done.

- **Priority**   Not everything is the most important thing on your task list. If you want to arrange your tasks by importance or urgency, use the priority numbers, from 1 through 5. Tap the number to get a list of all the priority choices.

> **TIP**
>
> *We recommend that you use priority numbers for your tasks—they help you sort through the clutter of your various to dos and determine what's really important from one day to the next.*

- **Description**   You can edit the description of the task by tapping in this field and editing the existing text.

 FIGURE 7-2   The Tasks list lets you modify your tasks without tapping the Details button.

■ **Note icon**   If you already created a note for the task, you can read the note or edit it by tapping the icon to the right of the name field. If no note already exists, you can add one by selecting the task and choosing Record | Attach Note from the menu.

■ **Due date**   You might have tasks that need to be accomplished by a specific date. If this is the case, you can track them easily using the Date tab.

■ **Category**   If you assign categories to your tasks, you can track them via the Category tab at the top of the screen.

NOTE   *Some of these columns aren't displayed by default. To enable them, tap the Show button and choose the columns you want to appear in the Preferences dialog box.*

Changing the View Options

If you're anything like us (and that could be a very, very bad thing, if you know what we mean), you might be perfectly happy with the default look of the Tasks list. It's easy to modify, though. Tap Options | Preferences and you will see the Preferences dialog box. Here are your options:

Sorting Options

The first item you encounter in the Preferences dialog box is a Sort By list. This determines the way the Tasks list shows the tasks onscreen.

■ **Priority, Due Date**   This groups all the priority 1 tasks first, then priority 2, and so on. Within each priority group, the earliest deadlines are listed first, and no-deadline tasks are listed last. This option works best if you need to work on tasks with the highest priority, and if due dates aren't particularly important to you.

■ **Due Date, Priority**   This selection arranges all the tasks by due date, with the soonest due dates listed first and no due dates listed last. If several tasks have the same due date, they're listed by priority order. This is probably the best display option for most people. It lists your tasks with the ones due soonest at the top of the page and, within each due date, you can see the top priorities arranged first.

- **Category, Priority** Arranges your tasks by category. The categories are arranged in alphabetical order. If you have more than one task in a given category, they're arranged in priority order within the category. Use this category if seeing tasks visually arranged into different categories, such as work and personal, is more important for you than arranging them by due date or priority.

- **Category, Due Date** This selection also arranges your tasks by category, and the categories are arranged in alphabetical order. If you have more than one task in a given category, they're arranged by due date within the category. Soonest deadlines appear first, and no-due-date tasks are placed last within each category.

Using Filters to Customize the Display

The next section in the Preferences dialog box controls what kinds of tasks are displayed onscreen. Actually, that's not true, but we're trying to apply some logic to the way PDA chooses to group the items on this screen. The following explains what each of these three items does.

- **Show Completed Items** As you check off tasks you complete, slowly but surely they clutter up your screen unless you do something about them. If you uncheck this option, completed items are hidden. If you need to see items you have completed, simply check Show Completed Items and they reappear.

NOTE *If you hide completed tasks in this way, they're not deleted. They still take up memory on the handheld. See later in this chapter to find out how to delete old tasks.*

- **Show Only Due Items** If you're concerned only about tasks due today, check this item. Any tasks with a due date after today disappear from the screen and reappear only on the day they're due. (If you don't see this option, you're not going nuts. It just means you have a new Palm, which unfortunately doesn't have this option.)

CAUTION *Be careful with this option because it hides tasks from the screen that aren't due today, regardless of priority. It's easy to get caught off guard by a major deadline this way.*

- **Record Completion Date** This interesting little feature changes the due date of a completed item to the date it was completed. If you didn't assign a due date to a task, the completion date becomes the due date. In this way, you can track what day you completed each of your tasks.

CAUTION *This option overwrites the due date with the completion date. You can't get the original due date back, even if you uncheck the task or turn off the Record Completion Date option.*

Modifying the Task Columns

As you probably already saw, you can tweak the data the Task list shows you for each task in the list. That tweaking occurs here, in the last three options of the To Do Preferences dialog box. Your Tasks list can look sparse, highly decorated, or anything in between by changing the Show options, as explained next.

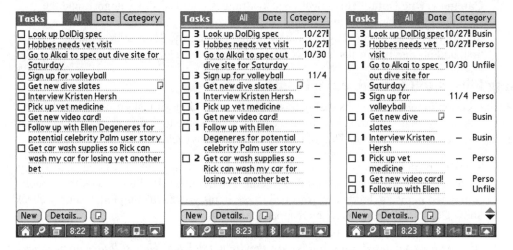

- ■ **Show Due Dates**   The due date format is day/month, which takes some getting used to. If you don't assign a due date to a task, you see a dash instead. On the Task List, if you tap a due date you see a list for changing the date.

- ■ **Show Priorities**   This displays the priority to the left of the task name. The priority can be adjusted by tapping the number on the Task List.

- ■ **Show Categories**   The category of the task appears on the right edge of the Task List if you use this option. You can assign a category to an unfiled task (or change the category of a previously filed entry) by tapping the category name on the Task List view.

> **TIP**   *As you can see, these views can get very cluttered. In our opinion, it's easier to turn off most of those columns and use the All, Date, and Category tabs at the top of the screen to see just the tasks you're interested in.*

Deleting Old Tasks

For most people, tasks are not like diamonds—they don't last forever. After you check off a task that says "pick up a loaf of bread," how long do you need a record of having accomplished that grand feat? That's why your PDA provides a method of removing tasks you no longer want. The Palm offers you two ways to eliminate tasks:

- **Delete them one at a time** If you need to delete only one task, select it. Then choose Record | Delete Task from the menu and it's gone forever.

- **Delete a whole bunch at once** If you use Tasks a lot, and occasionally develop a back list of dozens or hundreds of completed tasks, axing them one at a time could become a full-time job. Instead, purge them. A *purge* deletes all completed tasks. To purge, choose Record | Purge from the menu. The Purge dialog box appears, asking if you really want to delete your completed to dos. Tap OK.

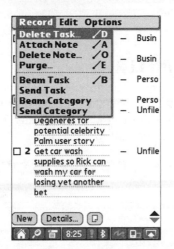

How to ... **Create Tasks on Your Handheld**

We've talked a lot about Tasks, so here's a summary of how to create tasks:

1. Press the Tasks button on the Palm (or tap the Tasks or To Do icon).
2. Start writing—this creates a new entry.
3. If you want to further customize the task, tap the Details button.

If you want to, assign a priority, category, and due date on the Details dialog box. Tap OK to close this dialog box.

TIP   *If you want to preserve a copy of your completed tasks, check Save Archive Copy on PC when given the option. If you later want to refer to deleted tasks, load the archive file (which is automatically created using the name of the category the item belonged to on the PC when you HotSync) into Palm Desktop when you need to refer to the entries. This works only if you do, in fact, synchronize with Palm Desktop instead of Outlook or another program.*

Using Tasks in Palm Desktop

Who says the only place you can enter to dos is on your PDA? Not us! The Palm Desktop has a module dedicated to tracking your tasks. Using the Palm Desktop, you can enter tasks and have them appear on your handheld when you're away from your desk.

The Palm Desktop To Do List

The Tasks interface is a bit more spacious than the one in your PDA. As a result, the Palm Desktop pulls off a cool trick—it displays both the list itself and the contents of the Details dialog box onscreen simultaneously. Click a task and the details automatically update to show you more information about the particular task you selected.

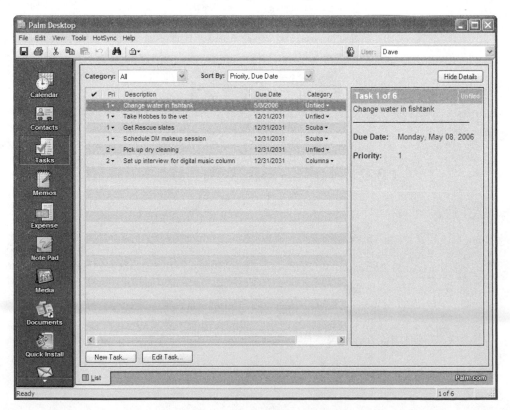

How to ...   Turn Tasks into Appointments

Your PDA understands that there's a tight relationship between your calendar and your tasks. Switch to the Calendar in the Palm Desktop and you'll find that the right side of the screen has a window for displaying either contacts or tasks. Click the Tasks box to show your upcoming to dos; click Contacts to return to the Phone Number Lookup mode. What good is that? Well, you can actually grab a task and drop it into a calendar appointment. That lets you turn a task into a bona fide appointment. You can't go the other way, though, and turn an appointment into a task.

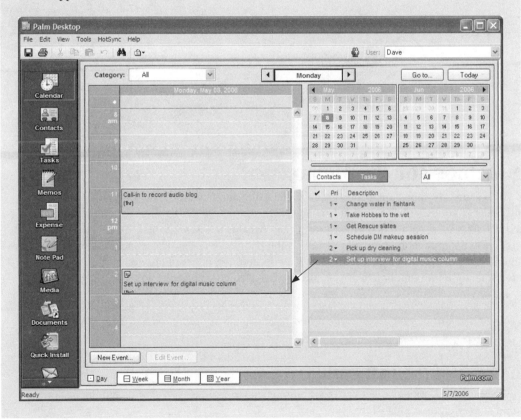

Creating and Editing Tasks

To create a new to do, just click the New Task button at the bottom of the screen. You'll see the New Task dialog box, where you can enter text, assign priorities, and even set a due date for your task.

Using To Dos in Outlook

If you're an Outlook user, you probably already know that your Palm tasks items become Outlook Tasks when you HotSync. In fact, that's pretty much all you need to know to use Outlook with your PDA. To see your tasks in Outlook, click the Tasks icon in the Outlook Shortcuts bar. The tasks are also displayed in the Taskbar section of the Calendar.

Understanding Task Priorities

Your PDA and Outlook use two slightly different ways of assigning priority to tasks. Thankfully, the two systems work together and are easy to figure out. You can use the following guide to correlate the Palm and Outlook systems:

PDA	Outlook
1	High
2	Normal
3	Normal
4	Normal
5	Low

Using Memos (or the Memo Pad)

As you've already seen, applications such as the Calendar, Contacts, and Tasks let you attach long notes to your entries. A note in Contacts, for instance, enables you to list directions to the person's house, the names of all their kids, or ten reasons not to visit them for Thanksgiving. But there's also an application designed to do nothing but create notes. These memos can be memory joggers, information you need to take on a trip, or anything not explicitly connected to an address, an appointment, or a to do. Memos is your chance, in a sense, to color outside the lines and leave yourself any kind of message you want.

NOTE *Depending upon which model Palm you have, this application will either be called Memos or the Memo Pad.*

The Saga of the Last Button

You know the drill by now; there are four buttons on the front of your Palm, and the last one should start Memos, right? Right.

Unless it doesn't. Depending upon which model you own, it might be that your Palm is preprogrammed to launch the Note Pad, which we cover in Chapter 8. And some other models assign that button to something else entirely, like a Web browser. See Chapter 2 if you need a button refresher.

The solution, especially if you've already read about Tasks, is obvious. After you get comfortable with your PDA and decide which apps you use most often, you can leave your handheld the way it is, or, if you prefer, you can reassign a button to launch the Memos instead.

Viewing Memos

Memos has two views—the Memo List (which is, not surprisingly, a list of all the memos you created) and the Memo View, which shows you the contents of whatever memo you select from the Memo List. When you start Memos, it always starts in the Memo List view. As you can see in Figure 7-3, the PDA displays each of your memos in a list, with the first line of the memo visible as a kind of title that lets you know what's inside. Getting around is easy—just scroll up or down to see more memos.

SHORTCUT *If your memos are divided into more than one category, and if you have Memos assigned to one of the four buttons, every time you press the Memos button, you'll switch categories. You can cycle through the first page of tasks in each category by repeatedly pressing the button.*

FIGURE 7-3 The Memo List displays all of your memos.

Cool Things to Do with Memos

Do you know what surprises us? Lots of things, actually. Dave is surprised Rick has no appreciation for the fine arts—specifically, bands such as *Pink Floyd,* the *Velvet Underground,* Kristin Hersh, and the *Throwing Muses.* Recently, Dave has had to add *The White Stripes* to the list of bands that Rick doesn't get. (Inexplicably, Rick has an entirely different definition of "fine arts.")

More to the point, we're surprised at how many people can't seem to come up with good uses for Memos. They let it languish while they use Contacts and Calendar all the time. To help you fully realize the potential of this cool little application, here are some helpful suggestions for how to use Memos:

- **A "Million Dollar Idea" memo**   Create a memo with a header that says **Million Dollar Ideas**. No matter when or where you come up with one of those incredibly amazing ideas to help you retire before you turn 50, pull out your PDA and jot it down.

- **Trade show category**   Got a lot of booths to visit at next month's lawn care trade show? Create a category and put all the memos for that event in the category. As you walk the show floor, you can reference your notes about the show in one easy-to-find set of memos.

- **Store passwords**   This one is dangerous, so be sure you make it private. But, if you have a lot of passwords you routinely need—for your ISP, Web sites, computer logons, and that kind of thing—you can store them all in one place in a memo for passwords. Note, we have to reiterate this is kind of dangerous. If your Palm is stolen, you can give all your passwords away if they're not protected properly. No IT department on Earth would sanction this particular tip, and we won't even admit to writing it down if questioned in court. A better alternative is a password keeper program (see Chapter 8), but this is a fast and free alternative.

- **Meeting notes**   Take notes during a meeting and beam the memo to others when the meeting is over.

- **A "Phone Messages" memo**   Name a memo "Phone Messages" and when you check voice mail, jot down the notes in your handheld in this memo. If you're diligent about this, you won't end up with a million yellow stickies all over your desk after each VM-checking session. And names and phone numbers will be in your Palm where you need them, not splayed out all over your desk.

- **Store your new words**   Dave makes up new words in an effort to evolve the English language at a grassroots level. If you, too, make up new words frequently (and that's a *beautiquious* thing to do), store them in a "New Words" memo so you don't accidentally forget them. *Chizzy!* (Rick is working on a way to delete that particular memo from Dave's Palm, perhaps by using a large hammer.)

Creating New Memos

Sure, there's a New button at the bottom of the Memo List, but you don't need to use it. Start writing in the Graffiti area, and the PDA automatically switches from the Memo List View to the Memo View.

The memo can be as long as you want—sort of. On older devices, you have a limit of 4,096 characters, or about 700 words. On PDAs running OS5 or later, the limit is dramatically higher—32KB. That's pretty long, and it should suit your needs most of the time. You can include blank lines and divide your memo into paragraphs, anything you need to make it logical and readable. If you require longer documents, consider getting an office suite, which we cover in Chapter 11.

TIP *You can't name your memos in the sense that you can save files on the PC with a specific filename, but the first line of the memo is what appears in the Memo List. To keep things neat and organized, you can write a brief description of the memo on the top line, and then start the memo itself on the next line.*

7

Using Editing Tools

The familiar cut, copy, and paste tools are available in every handheld app, but nowhere are they more important than in Memos, where you're likely to be writing more than a sentence or two. Remember, you don't have to create text from scratch all the time. Using these edit tools, you can move text from other applications and rearrange it to suit your needs.

Suppose, for example, you previously had a Calendar appointment that read

```
Meeting with Ted
```

Within that appointment, you might have created a note that looked like the following:

```
Discuss performance review
Get feedback on budget for 2Q
Agree on approach for marketing plan
```

If you want to have a record of your meeting with Ted, take notes in a memo. Open the appointment note and select the three lines of text from the note. With the text selected, choose Edit | Copy from the menu (or you can use the Command gesture and write **C**). Then switch to Memos, create a new memo, and paste the text into the memo using Edit | Paste (or COMMAND-P using the Graffiti shortcut).

After pasting the text into the memo, you can use it as your agenda items, and insert notes as needed, giving you a complete record of the meeting. After you HotSync, you can paste that data into Word or some other application and generate a formal report.

Assigning Categories

After you accumulate a few memos, you might find the Memo List View getting a bit crowded. Clean it up with the Palm's ever-helpful category filing system. Assign a category by doing the following:

1. Create a new memo.

2. Tap the Details button. The Memo Details dialog box appears.

3. Choose a category from the Category list.

4. Tap OK to close the Memo Details dialog box.

After your memos are arranged into categories, you can cycle through them easily by pressing the Memos button on the Palm case.

Making a Memo Private

If you have private information stored in a memo, you can easily hide specific memos from prying eyes. The procedure is essentially the same as with other applications. Do the following:

1. In the Memo List, select a memo by tapping it.

2. Tap the Details button. You see the Memo Details dialog box.

3. Tap the Private box to add a check mark. Now the entry is marked as private. Tap OK and you see the following dialog box:

4. Tap OK to close the dialog box.

The memo probably isn't hidden yet, meaning you still have one more step to go. To make your memo disappear, you need to enable the Private Records feature in the Security app. For details on how to do this, see Chapter 10.

Deleting Memos

No matter how much you like your memos, eventually you might need to delete some. To delete a memo, tap the memo you want to delete. Then choose Record | Delete Memo from the menu. The memo is then deleted from your handheld.

Arranging Memos in the Memo List

Some computer users can be fanatical organizers. People like Rick tend to spend hours straightening up the Desktop so icons appear in exactly the right place when the computer starts each morning. If you're one of those folks, you probably want to organize your memos as well. This isn't pointless busy work: if you need to open the same memo over and over, having the memo appear at the top of the list whenever you open the Memo List can help. At the very least, we're sure you'll want to understand how to take control of the way memos appear onscreen.

When you add memos to the Memo List, by default, the newest ones always appear at the end of the list. The default order of Memo List entries is essentially chronological, with the oldest entries at the top and the newest ones at the bottom.

It's a little more complicated than that, though. You can specify the sort order of memos by choosing Options | Preferences. You get two choices:

- ■ **Manual**   This is the default mode your PDA uses out of the box. New memos are added to the bottom of the list, but you can actually drag and drop memos to different positions in the list. Suppose you have a frequently used memo that you want to appear at the top of the screen. Tap and hold the stylus on the entry, and then drag the stylus up to the position where you want it to appear. You should see a line move with the stylus, indicating where the memo will land if you release the stylus.

- ■ **Alphabetic**   This option sorts all entries into alphabetical order. If you select this option, the drag-and-drop method of moving memos won't work unless you revert to the manual method.

How to ... Add Blank Lines for Emphasis

Here's a trick you can try if you think the Memo List is too cluttered. If you use the manual ordering method and arrange your memos in a specific order in a near-fanatical way, you might be bothered by the fact that memo number 4 is "touching" memo number 5. Rick, for instance, is adamant about not eating his mashed potatoes if they come into contact with his peas. Maybe you suffer from the same kind of problem with your PDA. If so, perform the following steps:

1. Create a new memo with a blank first line.

2. Enter at least one character on the second line, because the Palm doesn't let you create a completely blank memo.

3. Close the memo and you see you've made a new memo with a blank header.

4. Drag this memo between two memos you want separated, and voilà—you've found a way to separate memos.

```
Memos              ▼ Personal
1. Favorite novels
2.
3. Meals
4. New Words
5.
6. 30 Top Movies
7.
8. The top 10 restaurants you wo...
9. Top 5 reasons to get a PDA
10. Top 5 Reasons to Get A Comput...
11. Top 5 Best Things About Weara...
12. Top 5 reasons Laura asked me ...
13. Top 5 Reasons to get a PDA
14. Top 5 Reasons for taking the Di...
15. Top 5 Best things About Bluetoo...


 New 
🏠 🔍 📋 8:37 ⚡ 🔵 〰 📇 🔲
```

Using Memos in Palm Desktop

You can create and review your memos on the Palm Desktop. That's good, because many kinds of memos might come in handy on the desktop. If you took our advice from earlier in the chapter to create a Phone Messages memo, for instance, you'd appreciate the capability to type directly into the PC when the phone rings.

Using Memos in Palm Desktop

Because the handheld has pretty limited real estate on the small screen, you have to switch between the Memo List and Memo View. But, on the Palm Desktop, you can see both at once. To see a memo, click the header on the left. The memo's contents then appear in the window on the right, as you can see in Figure 7-4. Double-clicking a memo opens the memo in its own window if you prefer to see it that way.

Most of the Memos operation is obvious. The controls aren't identical, though. Here are some things to remember:

- You can't rearrange memos; you can sort them alphabetically or by the way they appear on the PDA. Use the Sort By drop-down menu at the top of the screen.

- You can display memos in a list or by icons (like Outlook's Notes) using the tabs at the bottom of the screen.

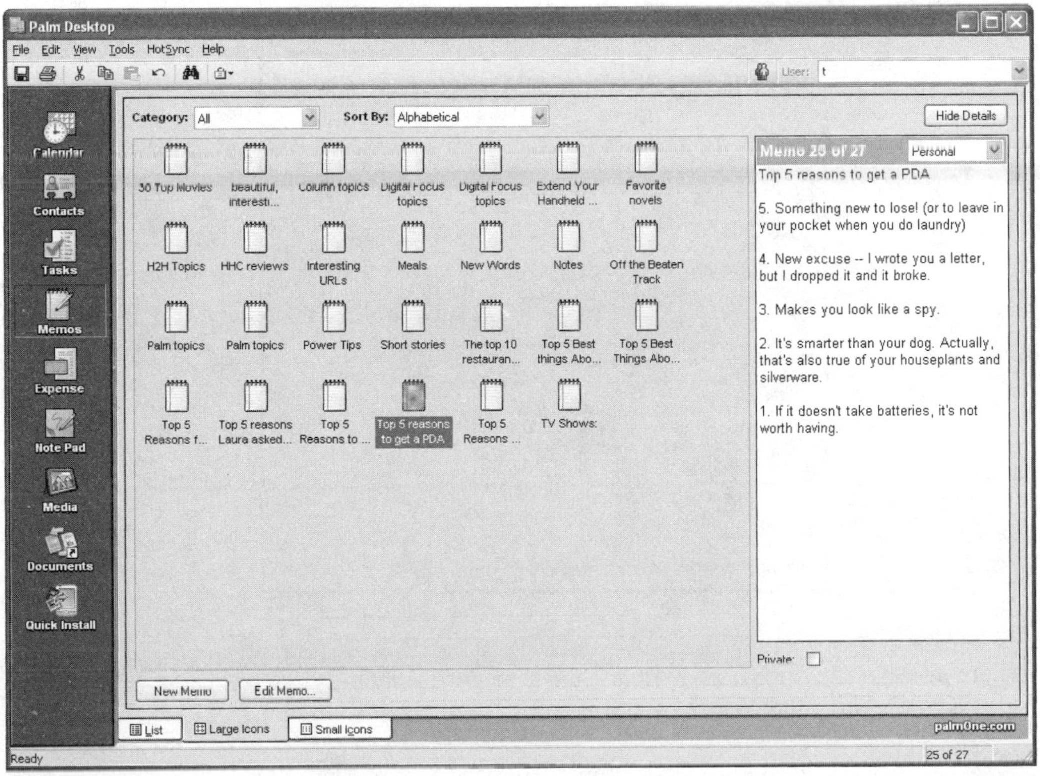

FIGURE 7-4   Memos lets you view your memos on the desktop, where you can edit them with your full-sized keyboard.

Importing and Exporting Memos

You don't need to create memos from scratch. Heck, you don't even have to cut and paste to create a memo. The Palm Desktop lets you import text files from elsewhere on the computer. To import a text file, perform the following steps:

1. Choose File | Import. The Import dialog box appears.

2. Choose Text (*.txt) from the File of Type list box.

3. Find the file you want to import. It has to be a plain text file in ASCII format—no Word or other specially formatted file types are allowed. Select the file and click the Open button. You then see the Specify Import Fields dialog box.

4. The text file should be ready to import, with the text lined up with the Memo field. If it isn't, drag the Memo field on the left until it lines up like the one shown here:

5. Click OK.

6. If your text file is too large to fit in a single memo, the Palm Desktop automatically divides it into multiple memos.

7. Click OK.

What about the other case where you have a memo and you'd like to get it into Microsoft Word? Piece of cake! Just right-click a memo and choose Send To | MS Word from the menu. The text will automatically appear in a new blank document in Word.

Using Memos in Outlook

Outlook's Notes View is, like Memos, a place to store free-form notes of any kind. You can use it to record phone messages, jot down reminders, leave long-term documents (such as things to bring on a trip), or to remind yourself about Web sites you want to visit. It doesn't matter what you put in these notes. By default, Outlook's notes look like little sticky notes.

Quirks between Outlook and Palm

Although the Outlook Notes View and Palm Memos are perhaps the simplest of all the features in these two programs, there are a few things you should know to ensure that everything works smoothly when you HotSync:

1. Memos has a size limit, but Notes in Outlook doesn't. This means you can create a very long note in Outlook that doesn't transfer properly to the PDA. If you create a huge note in Outlook, only part of it may appear in the Memo Pad, depending upon how old your PDA is. You also see a warning saying this occurred in the HotSync log.

2. The Palm's categories aren't used by Outlook. This means your Palm memos, when they appear in Outlook as notes, are unfiled. The same is true in the other direction.

3. Outlook memos can contain special elements that aren't transferred to the Palm. What kind of stuff are we talking about? Things like "digital ink" created on Tablet PCs or Pocket PC PDAs, or audio clips recorded using a microphone on your computer or Pocket PC.

Look Ma, No Scroll Bar!

Outlook's notes have an annoying glitch. Lacking scroll bars, it's hard to read a long note that trails off the bottom of the sticky note window. Don't know what we're talking about? Copy a long Word document into a new note. Or create a really long Palm memo and HotSync. You'll find that the text extends beyond the bottom of the note window in Outlook and there's no scroll bar to scroll down to read it all.

The solution is deceptively simple: click in the note window to place the cursor in the note, and then use the down arrow key on the keyboard to scroll through the document. Or make the note's window larger, so it can show more text.

Why do we mention this? Rick didn't realize that there was any way to scroll through the document at all. He thought anything that didn't fit in the sticky note window was totally inaccessible—until Dave showed him the keyboard arrow trick. So, if you were ever perplexed by the missing memo text, now you are at least as smart as Rick (fill in your own jokes here).

Chapter 8

Note Pad, Expense, and the Rest of the Palm OS Team

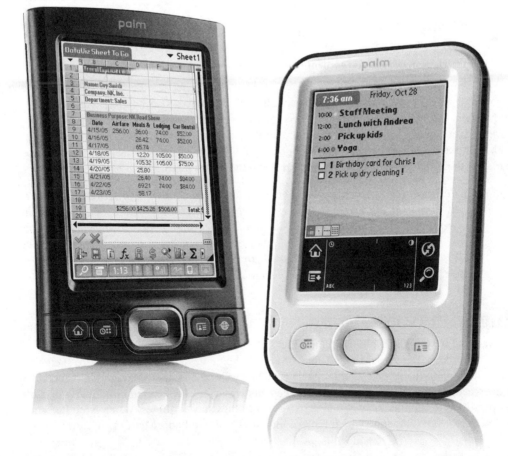

How to...

- Scribble handwritten notes
- Access notes on your PC
- Access security features
- Set records as private
- Hide or show private records
- Password-protect your PDA
- Find third-party security measures for your PDA and data
- Use the Find feature
- Use the calculator
- Find third-party calculators
- Use your PDA to track expenses
- Use Expense to track mileage
- Export your expenses to Excel
- Find other expense-management software and solutions

Now that we've looked at the stars of the Palm OS—Contacts, Calendar, Tasks, and Memos—let's turn our attention to the supporting cast. We're talking about the Security program, which enables you to hide private records and "lock" your PDA; the Find feature, a search tool that helps you quickly sift through all your data; the calculator, which, big surprise, calculates; the often-ignored Expense program; and the beloved Note Pad.

NOTE *We designed this chapter as a kind of catch-all, a place to cover programs that don't really fit into specific categories or require their own chapters. That said, there might be programs bundled with your handheld that aren't covered here—or anywhere else in the book. That's because different manufacturers (and even Palm) bundle different software with different models, and it's impossible to cover everything. We do, however, cover the really important extras that are common to all models.*

Working with Notes

The Note Pad is very similar to the Memo Pad, at least in that they both have "Pad" in their name. The major difference is this: instead of writing text notes with Graffiti, you're sketching or writing directly on the screen, as if the stylus is a pen writing on paper. Though Note Pad gives you the freedom to write anything on the screen any way you like, keep in mind that you can't transform this "digital ink" into actual text. Your scribbles stay scribbles. When Note Pad starts, you'll see the Note List view (which looks a lot like the Memo Pad's Memo List view).

Don't confuse Note Pad notes with Outlook's notes. The latter are paired up with Memo Pad, synchronization-wise. As we discuss in the next section, Note Pad notes sync only with Palm Desktop.

Creating a Note

To create a note, tap the New button at the bottom of the screen (you can also just start writing in the Graffiti area). Start your note by giving it a name. Unlike memos, all notes get their own unique subject line. By default, this subject begins with a "time stamp," though you can erase that if you want to.

When you're ready to draw, just write or sketch in the main part of the screen. The following shows the controls at your disposal:

Tap this box to access the three different pen sizes and the eraser

When you tap the box in the lower-right corner, a pop-up toolbar gives you a choice between three different pens, each offering a different line thickness, and an eraser. These tools are pretty self-explanatory; the best way to learn them is via experimentation. As for the notes themselves, you can categorize, beam, and delete them pretty much the same way you do with memos.

Adding Alarms to Notes

Unlike those yellow sticky notes you leave all over your office walls (hey, clean up already—it looks like a pigsty!), the notes you leave in your PDA can actually buzz you at a certain time and date. Why on earth would you want that to happen, you ask? Well, here's a good example.

You're stopped at a red light when you hear on the car radio that Diana Darby is playing a show in town in a few weeks. You'd love to go to the concert, so you whip out your PDA. The light will turn green in a moment, though, so you don't have a lot of time to write. Instead of trying your luck with Graffiti, you simply press the Note Pad button and scrawl "Diana Darby" on the screen. Then you quickly tap Menu | Options | Alarm, and choose Saturday, 4 P.M., which is when the tickets go on sale. Tap OK, and when Saturday morning rolls around, your PDA will turn on, bring your note to the front, and play the alarm. As you'd probably expect, you can accept the alarm or tap the snooze button.

8

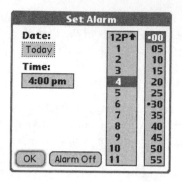

Notes in Palm Desktop

As with the other core apps, Note Pad items are copied to your PC when you HotSync. However, that's where the similarities end. Note Pad necessarily requires the use of Palm Desktop, meaning you can't access your scribbles in Outlook (even if you use that program for addresses, appointments, and the like). What's more, you can't create new notes in Palm Desktop; you can only view them and edit their settings (such as category, alarm, and so on).

You can also export notes to a graphics program. Don't expect to stick one of these sketches into a PowerPoint presentation, though; a Note Pad image measures just 152×352 pixels, which is not nearly enough to fill a computer screen. But getting your handiwork into a graphics program is easy. Just do the following:

1. Press the Note Pad button on the left side of the Palm Desktop display. You should see the Note Pad window appear.

2. Find the note in the list that you want to export.

3. Right-click the note, whether in the list view or on the image itself and choose Copy from the menu.

4. Open your favorite image editing program and choose Edit | Paste from the menu.

TIP   *Looking for a good image editor for your PC? One of our favorites is IrfanView (www. irfanview.com), which lets you make basic changes to your images (resize, rotate, and so on). Best of all, it's freeware!*

PDA Security

At the risk of sounding like a spy novel, listen up, 007. If your data falls into the wrong hands, it could spell disaster for *M, Q,* and lots of other letters of the alphabet. Fortunately, we've outfitted your PDA with foolproof security measures. Only you will have the access codes. Only you can view Naomi Watts' phone number. (Can we have it? Please? Please?)

In all seriousness, it's not unlikely that you'll be storing some sensitive information in your PDA, information that should be kept private. Important passwords, account numbers, meeting locations, and contact data, are among the items you'd be loath to let a stranger see. Fortunately, the Palm OS offers two effective ways to protect your data: marking individual records as private, and "locking" your handheld every time you turn it off.

In both scenarios, you, or anyone who's trying to access your device, must supply a password. It's a bit of a hassle to have to enter it over and over again, but at least you have the comfort of knowing that your PDA and data are totally secure.

> TIP   *Although you might want to familiarize yourself with the Palm OS's built-in security capabilities, we prefer some of the third-party solutions you can download and install. See "Other Security Software" later in this chapter for the scoop on those appealing alternatives.*

Security 101

To get started with security, head to the main Applications screen, tap the Prefs icon, and then the Security option.

> NOTE   *In older Palm models, Security had its own icon and was accessible from the Applications screen, not Prefs.*

You'll see the screen shown in Figure 8-1 (or something like it—it might look a bit different depending on which version of the Palm OS you have). The first step is to choose a password. Notice that the Password box currently says "Unassigned," meaning simply that you haven't entered your password yet. Before you do, read a little further.

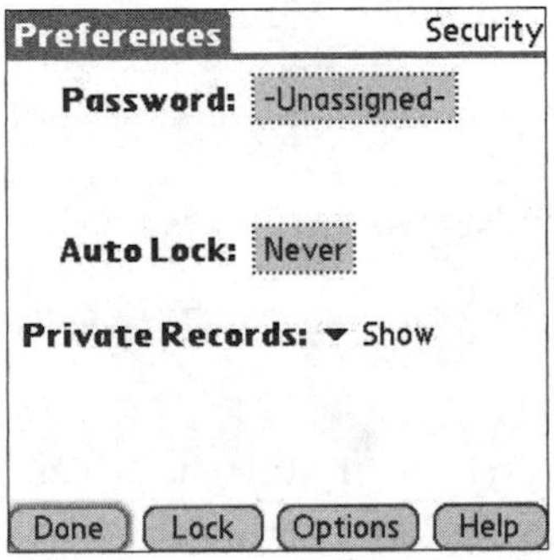

8

Preferences	Security
Password:	-Unassigned-
Auto Lock:	Never
Private Records:	▼ Show

(Done) (Lock) (Options) (Help)

FIGURE 8-1   In Security, you select a password for use in hiding private records and locking your PDA.

What You Should Know about Passwords

The password you choose can be any combination of letters, numbers, symbols, and spaces. You can make it "Spock" or "H4T*Q" or "The quick brown fox." Ideally, it should be something reasonably short, as you'll probably wind up writing it frequently. Don't make it too obvious, like "123," but you could use something as simple as the last four digits of your Social Security number or your favorite *Battlestar Galactica* character.

NOTE *Capitalization doesn't matter. Even if you make a point to capitalize "Spock" when you enter it as your new password, you can write "spock" to unlock your PDA and it'll work just fine.*

CAUTION *Whatever password you decide on, it's vital that it be something you can easily remember. If you forget it, you could wind up unable to access certain records, or even your entire PDA! Thus, if you have even the slightest concern that you might forget your password, write it down on a piece of paper and store it in a safe place. Better safe than sorry.*

Working with Passwords

Okay, let's enter a new password on your PDA. Just tap the Unassigned box, and then use Graffiti or the onscreen keyboard to enter your desired password.

NOTE *At this time, you're also asked to supply a hint. If you use, say, your mother's maiden name as your password, you should put "mother's maiden name" in the hint field. This hint appears when an incorrect password is entered.*

Note the warning that's included here: "If you assign a password, you must enter it to show private records." This sounds a little scary, but don't worry—none of your existing records will immediately be affected by your selection of a password. Only when you mark one as private, as we explain later, does your password enter into play.

After you tap OK, you'll be asked to verify the new password by entering it again. And you'll see another warning about what'll happen if your password is forgotten. The moral of the story is, *don't forget your password!*

Tap OK again, and notice that the Password box now reads Assigned.

TIP *You can tap this box again at any time to change or delete your password, but you have to supply the original one first.*

Now, when you mark records as private, they become hidden from view, requiring your password to reveal them. Additionally, if you use the Lock & Turn Off option (as detailed in the following section), you'll need to supply your password the next time you turn on your PDA.

SHORTCUT *If you tap the abc button in the corner of the Graffiti area, the onscreen keyboard will appear. You can use this to enter your password!*

The "Lost Password" Button

Oh, the perils of the forgotten password. For the last time, just don't forget yours, okay? If you do, there's a scary but effective way to reestablish access to those records you've marked as private. In Security, when you tap the Assigned button under Password, you're prompted to enter your password. You also see a Lost Password button. Tap it, and your password will be deleted—and all your marked-as-private records along with it. Zoiks! However, those deleted records will be restored on your PDA the next time you HotSync.

Password-Protecting Your Entire Handheld

If you really want to secure what's stored in your PDA, you need to password-protect the entire thing, not just certain records. That's where "locking" comes into play. When activated, your device becomes locked the next time it's turned off. Translation: When the PDA is turned on again, a screen pops up requiring the password (see Figure 8-2). Without it, there's no getting past that screen.

8

NOTE   *You can modify the information that appears on this "locked" startup screen by going to Prefs | Owner (see Chapter 2 for a refresher). We recommend including your name and phone number, and maybe even a reward offer—all so that anyone who might find your lost PDA would have an easier time returning it (and an incentive to do so). What's a good reward? Considering how much a new PDA would cost you, we think no less than $20.*

FIGURE 8-2   When you "lock" your PDA, only the correct password will unlock it. (This shows the latest version of Palm OS Security. Your password screen might look a bit different.)

Auto Lock Handheld

Palm OS 4.0 and later includes several automated locking options, all of them accessible by tapping the Auto Lock Handheld button in the main Security screen. The following's a quick rundown:

- **Never**   No automatic locking.
- **On power off**   The moment you turn your handheld off (or it shuts off after a few minutes of inactivity), it locks.
- **At a preset time**   Set the handheld to lock at an exact time. For example, if you use it a lot during the day, but rarely at night, you might set it to lock at, say, 6 P.M. That way, you won't have to keep entering your password all day.
- **After a preset delay**   This is our favorite option. It locks the handheld after a period of inactivity—ten minutes, three hours, whatever you choose.

The "Current Privacy" Menu

We've saved the Current Privacy option till last because it relates to the upcoming section on hiding and masking individual records. Simply put, when the *Hide* option is selected, all records you've marked as private will disappear from view. When you select *Mask,* private records are hidden but still listed. When you select *Show,* which you need your password to do, private records are made visible.

> **NOTE**   *The Mask option was added to Security in Palm OS 3.5. If you have an earlier version, you might want to consider upgrading, as masking is a far better solution than hiding.*

Advanced Security Options

The latest Palm handhelds (like the Tungsten T5) sport some new and improved security features, not the least of which is 128-bit data encryption, your choice of AES or RC4 algorithms, the same kind used by corporations to protect valuable desktop and server data. You have the option of encrypting all the data. There's also optional intrusion prevention, meaning that if someone enters the wrong password a certain number of times, your data or private records will be deleted. To access these features, tap the Options button or Menu | Security Options.

> **NOTE**   *Not all Palm models have the level of security that would require Marshal from* Alias *to crack. Lower-end models like the Z22, for instance, have lower-end security features. They're probably sufficient for most users, but if you need to meet stringent corporate standards, you might have to upgrade to a more secure model.*

> **TIP**   *The Tungsten T3 didn't come with these advanced security features, but they're available for download. Head to the Support section of the Palm Web site and look for Palm Security 5.0p.*

Unless you're carrying lots of sensitive corporate data on your PDA, you probably don't need such drastic security measures as these. If you do, however, check with your company's IT manager for advice on when and how to make use of them.

Hiding and Masking Your Records

In the main applications—Contacts, Calendar, Note Pad, Memos, and Tasks—any record can be marked private, meaning it suddenly becomes masked or invisible and, therefore, inaccessible. The following shows you how:

1. Select a record (just by tapping it) in any of the aforementioned programs.

2. Tap the Details button. (In Contacts, you have to tap Edit to get to the screen with the Details button.) You'll see a window containing some options for that record, and a box labeled Private.

3. Tap that box, noticing the check mark that appears. This indicates that the record will become private after you tap OK.

4. Tap OK.

Remember, marking a record as private has no effect unless you've chosen one of the two privacy options in the Security program. If it's set to Mask Records, records you've marked as private will turn into solid gray bars. If you choose Hide Records, records will just plain disappear. (Don't freak out. They're still in memory, just not visible.)

The Difference Between Masking and Hiding

The *Mask Records* option provides a middle ground between the visibility of "shown" records and the total invisibility of "hidden" records (which appear to have been wiped from existence— great security, but awfully inconvenient). Masked records still appear in your phone list, memo pad, and so forth but appear as solid gray bars (see Figure 8-3). This remains a less-than-stellar solution, as there's still no way to know what lies beneath until you tap the record and enter your password.

FIGURE 8-3 When you choose Mask Records, all records marked as private are hidden by gray bars.

The *Hide Records* option goes a major step further, removing marked-as-private records from view altogether. To make them visible again, you must return to Security and select Show Records. Naturally, you'll need to supply your password at this time.

Passwords on the Desktop

Security isn't limited to the PDA itself. It also extends to Palm Desktop, working in much the same ways. Thus, you can hide certain records or password-protect the entire program. The same password you've selected for your PDA will automatically be used in Desktop.

> **CAUTION** *Only Palm Desktop is affected by masked and hidden records. If you synchronize with Microsoft Outlook or another third-party contact manager, records marked as private on your PDA will still be visible on your PC.*

Hidden Records

Whenever you HotSync, any records marked as private on your PDA will become hidden in Palm Desktop, and vice versa. To change whether private records are visible or not, click the View menu, and then select the desired option: Hide, Mask, or Show.

Password-Protecting Palm Desktop

Just as you can lock your handheld, so can you lock Palm Desktop. When you do, and then exit the program, your password will be required the next time it's started by you or anyone else. The following explains how to activate this setting:

How to ... Keep Others from Accessing your Palm Desktop

Suppose you step away from your desk for lunch or a meeting. You don't want coworkers or corporate spies poking around through your records. Fortunately, there's an easy way to password-protect Palm Desktop for Windows (alas, the Macintosh version has no security features). Choose Tools | Options, click the Security tab, and check the box marked Require Password To Access The Palm Desktop Data. Now, whenever someone starts Palm Desktop, they must input the correct password (which is the one you created on your handheld) to access their data.

1. Make sure Palm Desktop is running, and then click Tools | Options.
2. In the tabbed dialog box that appears, click the Security tab.
3. Click the box that says "Require password to access the Palm Desktop data."
4. Click OK, and then exit Palm Desktop.

> **NOTE** *This security setting applies only to your data. If multiple users are sharing Palm Desktop on a single PC, they'll need to implement password protection for their own user profiles.*

Other Security Software

While the Palm Operating System's built-in security features are fairly comprehensive, there's always room for improvement. Hence the availability of numerous third-party security programs, which generally offer greater versatility and/or convenience. Here we spotlight some of the more intriguing solutions.

eWallet

Your PDA can be a handy place to store account numbers, PIN numbers, passwords, and other secret codes, but stuffing them all into a memo isn't the most practical solution. Ilium Software's eWallet, one of Rick's personal favorites, is designed expressly to organize and protect your important numbers and passwords. You need to remember only one password (different from the one used by Palm OS Security) to access all this neatly categorized information. eWallet also has a Windows-based counterpart, so you can manage and access the information on your PC.

8

While Rick is a fan of eWallet, Dave likes Chapura's TurboPasswords (formerly known as Cloak)—a similar product. It's worth checking out if you're interested in this kind of security. And these two are by no means the only choices. Visit Handango.com or PalmGear.com and search for security software to see some others.

TealLock

Like Security on steroids, TealLock locks your PDA automatically whenever it's turned off. There are lots of security programs like it, but none quite as comprehensive. For instance, TealLock supports 128-bit encryption, meaning no one without James Bond-level government clearance will be hacking their way into your Palm (and we think even 007 might have trouble). It can even encrypt and password-protect your SD memory cards, a huge plus for anyone who stores sensitive data there.

If you're at all concerned about what would happen if you lost your Palm, a program like TealLock is absolutely indispensable.

The Find Feature

The more you use your PDA, the more data you're likely to wind up storing. And the more data you have, the harder it can be to find what you're looking for expediently. Some examples:

■ You know you have a dentist appointment coming up, but can't remember if it's this month or next. Must you page through your calendar a day at a time to find the entry?

■ You've got dozens of memos and need to find the ones containing the word "sponge." Must you open each memo individually?

■ You have 1,500 names in your address list and want to quickly find the record for that guy named Apu whose last name and company you can't remember. How will you locate him?

Using the Palm Operating System's built-in Find feature, you can unearth all this information in a snap. True to its name, *Find* sifts through your databases to ferret out exactly what you're looking for, be it a name, a number, a word, a phrase, or even just a few letters.

As we showed you in Chapter 2, Find can usually be found in the lower-right corner of the Graffiti area, represented by a little magnifying-glass icon. (On some models it's located in the toolbar.) Using it couldn't be simpler: Tap it (at any time, no matter what program you're running), and then write in what you want to search for (see Figure 8-4).

NOTE   *Capitalization doesn't matter. Even if you're looking for a proper name like "Caroline," you needn't capitalize the first letter.*

8

TIP   *If you use your stylus to highlight a word or chunk of text (done in much the same way you select text using a mouse), that text will automatically appear in the Find field when you tap the Find icon.*

The search process should take no more than a few seconds, depending on how many records you've got on your Palm and the complexity of your search criteria.

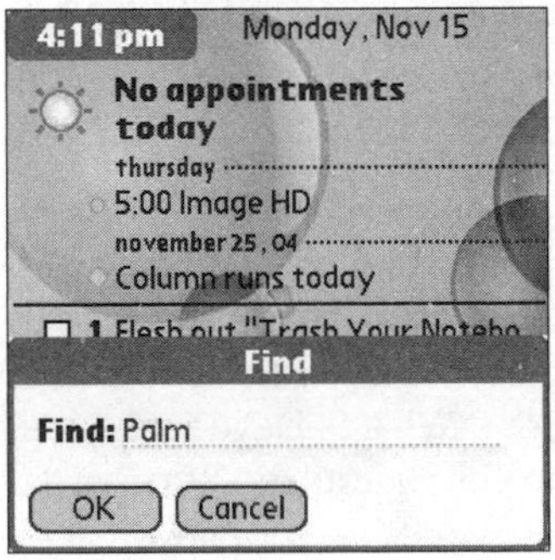

FIGURE 8-4   Looking for a specific word? Just write it in the Find box and your PDA will find it for you.

How Find Works

When you execute a search, the Palm OS looks through all stored records (except those marked as private) for whatever text you've specified, starting with whatever program you were in when you tapped the Find icon. It looks not only in the main databases—those used by Contacts, Memo Pad, and so forth—but also in the databases associated with any third-party software you might have installed.

> TIP   *If you're looking for, say, a phone number, you can save a lot of time by loading Contacts before tapping Find. That's because Find starts its search in whatever program is currently open.*

Keep in mind that Find searches only the beginnings of words. Thus, if you look up "book," it will find "bookcase" but not "handbook." Third-party programs can perform much more thorough searches. We talk about some of them in the next section.

> TIP   *You can make your data a bit more "Find friendly" by using special modifiers. For instance, you might use the letters AP to preface any memo that has to do with Accounts Payable. Then, when you do a search for "AP," you'll quickly unearth all the relevant records.*

Running a Search

After you've written the desired search text in the Find box and tapped OK, your PDA will get to work. You'll see items appear in a categorized list as they're found. If you see what you're looking for, you can halt the search immediately by tapping the Stop button. Then, simply tap the item to bring up the corresponding record in the corresponding program.

If your PDA finds more instances of the desired item than can fit on the screen at once, it will stop the search until you tap the Find More button. This essentially tells it to look up another screen's worth of records. There's no way to backtrack (return to the previous screen) so make sure you need to keep searching before tapping Find More. (You can always run the search again if need be, but that's a hassle.)

A Better Way to Search

Many users feel that Find isn't nearly as robust as it could be. If you want to maximize the search potential of your PDA, a third-party alternative might be in order. It's called IntelligentFind, and, true to its name, it's quite possibly the most sophisticated Find replacement ever. IntelligentFind allows you to ask questions in English ("What is Dave Johnson's phone number?") and displays the results ranked by the relevance to your questions. When in "simple" mode, IntelligentFind will search your handheld for multiple words and/or phrases at the same time, just like a Web search engine. We'd have to call this the power-user's find tool.

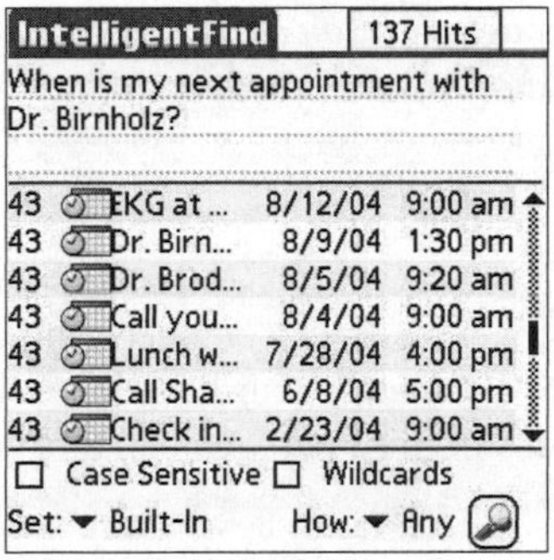

IntelligentFind	137 Hits	

When is my next appointment with
Dr. Birnholz?

43	EKG at ...	8/12/04	9:00 am
43	Dr. Birn...	8/9/04	1:30 pm
43	Dr. Brod...	8/5/04	9:20 am
43	Call you...	8/4/04	9:00 am
43	Lunch w...	7/28/04	4:00 pm
43	Call Sha...	6/8/04	5:00 pm
43	Check in...	2/23/04	9:00 am

☐ Case Sensitive ☐ Wildcards
Set: ▼ Built-In   How: ▼ Any

The Calculator

What's an electronic organizer without a calculator? Not much, so let's take a quick peek at the one included with the Palm OS. Activated by tapping the Calc icon, Calculator operates like any other (see Figure 8-5). In fact, it's so self-explanatory that we're not going to insult your intelligence by explaining how to use it.

There are, of course, one or two features we feel obligated to point out. First, you can use the standard Palm OS copy option to paste the result of any calculation into another program. Second, you can review your last few calculations by tapping Menu | Options | Recent Calculations. (On some models, tap Menu | Edit | Show History.)

If the calculator's basic functions aren't enough for you, try Advanced Mode, which is accessible by tapping Menu | Options | Advanced Mode. Presto—a calculator that's capable of math, trigonometry, finance, logic, statistics, and many other fancy functions. (Tap Menu | Options again to access these features, or to return to Basic Mode.)

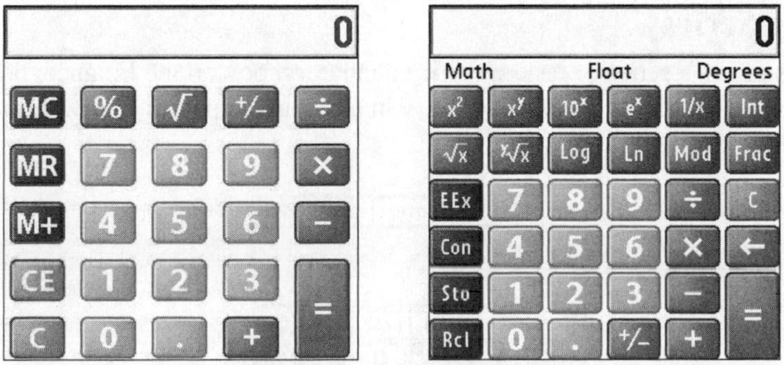

FIGURE 8-5   The Palm OS calculator functions like every other calculator you've ever used. Switch to Advanced Mode and gain and wealth of advanced functions, like trigonometry, logic, and finance.

8

Calc's buttons are large enough that you can tap them with a fingernail, so save time by leaving the stylus in its silo. Just keep in mind that oil and dirt from your fingers will grubby-up the screen.

Third-Party Calculators

Whether you're a student, realtor, banker, or NASA engineer, there's no debating the value of a good scientific and/or programmable calculator. Your PDA has ample processing power to fill this role, and the proof is in the dozens of third-party calculators currently available. Let's take a look at some of the best and brightest.

LoanMax

Think the car salesman is sharking you? Need an amortization schedule to maximize your house payments? At times like these, a good loan calculator is worth its weight in gold. LoanMax makes it simple to calculate payments based on interest rate, loan term, down-payment amount, and so on. It can also generate on-the-spot amortization schedules (though, unfortunately, you can't save or print them). Not bad for a $10 piece of software.

The powerOne Series

Infinity Softworks offers a series of task-specific calculators: powerOne Finance, powerOne Graph, powerOne Scientific, and so on. They vary in price and capability, so visit the company's Web site to see which one meets your needs.

Just Don't Take Away My...

Most people come to have a single favorite program for their handhelds, be it the address book, the expense program, or, in Dave's case, his beloved Hello Kitty game. In case you're wondering what else we'd be loath to live without:

Rick: I'm a huge fan of e-books, and the combination of eReader (see Chapter 15) and the eReader.com e-bookstore allows me to read just about any mainstream book on my Palm. In fact, if there's a new book out that sounds appealing, instead of heading to Amazon, I'll visit eReader.com and see if it's available. I can read an excerpt online or even download it to my handheld. You can take away my calendar, note pad, and expense program—just don't take away my e-book reader.

Dave: As much as I can't do without Hello Kitty—oh, wait, that's Rick making things up again—I am truly lost without AvantGo. Each and every day I fire it up at lunch to read the Joke of the Day, The Onion, *The New York Times* tech articles, and other bits of news that help me wile away my lonely existence as I eat lunch. Eventually, though, I know that Halle Berry will answer my letters, and then we can read AvantGo together at lunch.

And Many More

There are more third-party calculators available for the Palm OS than you can shake a stick at—and than we can fit in this book. To see what else is out there, visit Handango.com or PalmGear .com and do a search. If there's number-crunching you need done, chances are there's a program that'll do it on your Palm.

Expense Management

Expense is an often overlooked but decidedly valuable addition to the Palm software arsenal. With it, you can track and manage all your expenses and mileage, whether for personal reconciliation or reimbursement from your company or clients. While a bit on the rudimentary side, Expense does afford quick and easy item entry and direct synchronization with Palm Desktop. It can also export items to Microsoft Excel.

NOTE *Not all models come with Expense. If yours doesn't, see "Alternatives to Expense" later in the chapter.*

Getting Started with Expense

Put simply, Expense is like an electronic folder for your receipts and a logbook for your mileage. Whenever you buy something, you simply add it to your expense list. Whenever you take a business-related road trip, you do the same. On the PDA side, using Expense is a piece of cake. Using it with Palm Desktop is just as easy, but we'll talk about that a little later.

Creating New Expense Items

Adding new expense records is a snap. Here's the basic process:

1. Tap New to create a blank expense item. You see a line appear with the date, the words "-Expense type-", and a blank field next to a dollar sign. Note that your cursor appears in that field.

Expense		▼ All
11/5 Breakfast	$	78.93
11/15 Lunch	$	12.00
11/15 Mileage	mi	325.00

(New) (Details...) (Show...)

2. Write in the amount of the purchase or, if you're recording mileage, the number of miles driven.

3. Now, tap the words "-Expense type-" to see a predefined list of expense categories, and choose the one that most closely matches your purchase. If you're recording mileage, select that option, noticing that the dollar sign changes to the abbreviation "mi."

Expense		▼ All
11/5 Breakfast	$	78.93
11/15 Airfare		
Breakfast		
Bus		
Business Meals		
Car Rental		
Dinner		
Entertainment		
Fax		
Gas		
Gifts		
Hotel		
New Incidentals	↓	

NOTE *Unlike most lists that appear in Palm OS applications, the Expense list cannot be modified or expanded. In short, you're stuck with the categories provided. If you can't find one that fits the situation, there's always the "other" category.*

4. By default, any new expense is created with the current date. If, however, you're catching up on previous purchases, you can tap right on the date that's shown to bring up the calendar and select whatever date is appropriate.

There, wasn't that easy? You've just recorded a new expense. Now let's talk about recording the more specific details of that expense.

You can save yourself a step when you create a new expense by not tapping the New button first. Instead, just start writing the dollar amount in the numeric portion of the Graffiti area. A new expense item is created instantly. This same practice also works in Date Book, Memo Pad, and To Do List.

Modifying Expense Details

Obviously, any expense report worth its salt needs to have more than just the date, expense type, and amount. As you probably guessed, your next stop after entering these tidbits is the Details button.

Before tapping it, make sure you select the expense item you want to modify. You know when an item is selected because the date is highlighted and a cursor appears in the Amount field.

The Receipt Details screen (see Figure 8-6) lets you specify the minutiae of your purchase, from the category to which it belongs, to the type of currency used, to the city in which it took place.

Expense in Palm Desktop

As with the other core applications (Contacts, Memo Pad, and so on), Expense synchronizes its data with Palm Desktop every time you HotSync. Likewise, any additions or changes that you make in Palm Desktop are reflected on your handheld.

Older versions of Palm Desktop don't include direct synchronization with Expense—one more reason to upgrade. Visit Palm's Web site (www.palm.com/us/software) to download the latest version of Palm Desktop.

Receipt Details

Category: ▼ Unfiled
Type: ▼ Lunch
Payment: ▼ Credit Card
Currency: ▼ $
Vendor: Quizno's
City:
Attendees: Who...

(OK) (Cancel) (Delete) (Note)

FIGURE 8-6 You can record any or all of the crucial details of your expense in the Receipt Details screen.

8

As you can see in Figure 8-7, Palm Desktop keeps your Expense entries in a neat list. If you click the tabs at the bottom of the screen, you can view the items as icons (large or small), which can help you get an at-a-glance overview of the kinds of expenses you've incurred. If you need a hard copy, just choose Print from the File menu. You can choose to print an expense summary, a list of expense details, or both.

Copy Data from Expense to Excel

You can also export your Expense data to Microsoft Word or Excel, provided you have those programs installed on your PC. This can be helpful if you need to include your Expense data in

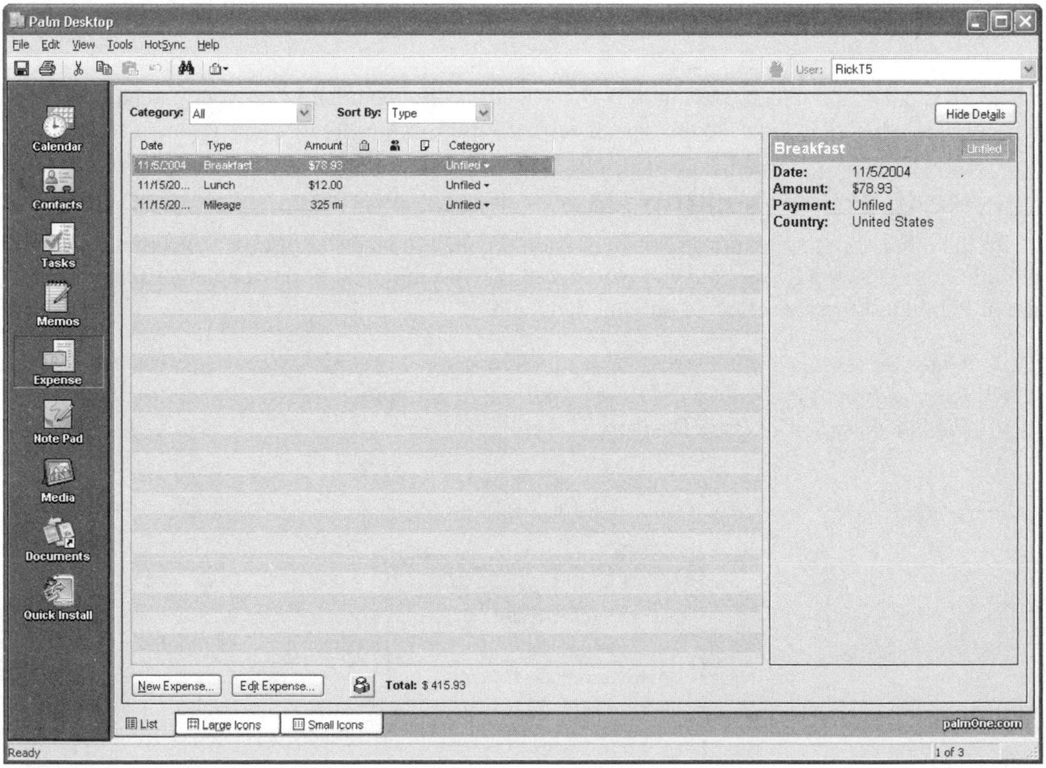

FIGURE 8-7   Palm Desktop displays and organizes your Expense data, just as it does with your addresses, appointments, and so on.

a pre-formatted invoice or spreadsheet. To start the process, select one or more of the expense items you to want to copy (or press CTRL-A to select them all), click Edit | Send To, and then choose MS Word or MS Excel from the list that appears. That's all there is to it!

Alternatives to Expense

Truth be told, Expense isn't the most robust expense-management program, especially relative to some of the software created by third-party developers. If your needs extend beyond what Expense has to offer—and for businesspeople who rely heavily on reimbursement reports, they probably do—you should definitely check out one of the many available alternatives.

We've spotlighted some of the major programs, but keep in mind that these are designed for expense tracking only. Other programs manage billing as well as expenses, and allow you to track your bank accounts and stock portfolios. So don't be discouraged if none of these packages fit your particular bill. Chances are good there's a program out there that will.

- **ExpensAble** ExpensAble began as a PC application and eventually migrated to the Palm OS. LandWare's software makes it a snap to record rcimbursable, non-reimbursable, and personal expenses, and it supports split transactions. Also present is the ever-popular AutoFill feature, a Quicken staple that simplifies repetitive data entry. Naturally, the Palm version of ExpensAble integrates seamlessly with the computer version. The latter offers report submission via e-mail or the ExpensAble Web site.

8

- **ExpensePlus** One of the most robust and versatile expense managers available, WalletWare's ExpensePlus uses an icon-based interface to simplify the selection of expense types, and automation to fill in dates and amounts for things such as hotel stays and car rentals. More important, it can link directly to any existing company expense forms created in Excel or FileMaker (including the Mac versions), so you needn't contend with nonstandard forms. And, if your company's forms aren't based in Excel, WalletWare can design a custom link (for a fee) to other software programs.

■ **TimeReporter**   Iambic Software's TimeReporter is more than just a business-expense manager, though it offers plenty of power in that area. The program also tracks time, which is helpful if your business requires you to bill clients that way.

Other Software on Your Palm

In addition to Calc, Expense, and Find, you've no doubt discovered other icons on your Palm's Applications screen. Let's take a look at some of the other programs that might have come preloaded on your device.

We said "might" because different models come with different programs. Your device might not have everything listed here, or it might have some programs not listed here.

■ **Addit**   Addit is a nifty little utility that lets you try out new software without having to go to all the trouble of downloading, expanding a Zip file, installing, etc. It works a bit like a Web browser: Just tap the Shopping tab, browse the available options (like "Browse Software Catalog"), and tap a program you might like to try. The next time you HotSync, Addit will fetch and install the program (a trial version) for you, easy as that.

As you explore Addit, you'll also discover that you can buy programs outright (helpful when the trial version has expired), read news stories (which are as timely as your last HotSync), and get help and tips on using your PDA. Cooler still, if you have a wireless model like the TX, you don't even have to HotSync; you can download and install new apps wirelessly, no PC required.

8

■ **Card Info**   Want to know how much storage space is left on the memory card you added to your Palm? Tap the Card Info icon and you'll find out. This little utility tells you the overall storage capacity of the card, the amount of used and free space, and other handy bits of info. You can also use Card Info to rename or format a memory card (tap Menu to access these options).

■ **Dialer** As you'll discover in Chapter 10, Bluetooth-equipped Palms can wirelessly communicate with Bluetooth-equipped cell phones and headsets. Dialer lets you leverage this arrangement by dialing a phone number even while your phone is nestled in your pocket. It's designed primarily for dialing numbers not already in your address book, as those numbers can be dialed directly from the Contacts app. We suspect few users will make much use of Dialer.

■ **Drive Mode** Found only on the LifeDrive and Tungsten T5, Drive Mode turns your device into the equivalent of a portable hard drive. Just tap the icon, enable Drive Mode, and plug your Palm into one of your computer's USB ports (you'll need your USB cable, of course). The device will show up as a new drive; just drag and drop whatever files you want to copy. This is a handy way to transport files between computers or even make a backup of some important data. However, keep in mind that this is not the way to install new programs on your Palm. For that, you have to follow the method outlined in Chapter 2. Meanwhile, you can find out more about Drive Mode in Chapter 11.

■ **Favorites** Tapping this icon takes you to the application launcher of the same name. However, you needn't go to all the trouble of finding the Favorites icon and tapping. You can simply press your handheld's Home button to go right to it. (A second press might be required, depending on how you've configured the Home button in Prefs—see Chapter 2.) You can find out more about Favorites in Chapter 2.

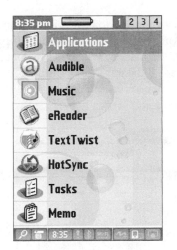

■ **Media** Palm's Media applet is the place to view photos stored on your handheld or a memory card, and watch certain kinds of videos. Find out more in Chapters 15 and 14, respectively.

■ **SMS** SMS stands for Short Messaging System, also known as text messaging. If your Palm is connected to your cell phone via Bluetooth (see Chapter 10), you can use the SMS applet to compose, send, receive, and view messages. Why would you want to do this on your Palm instead of your phone? Simple: Your Palm has a much bigger screen, and it's much easier to enter text on a Palm than it is on most phones. Just establish a connection to your phone (see Chapter 10), run the SMS applet, and then tap New to create an outgoing text message or Send & Check to retrieve messages and send any that might be in your outbox.

■ **VersaMail** VersaMail is Palm's e-mail program. You can use it to send and receive e-mail wirelessly or via your computer. See Chapter 10 for more details.

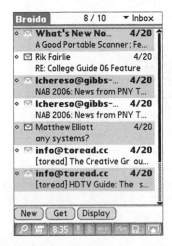

■ **Voice Memo**   If you're lucky enough to have a Palm with a built-in microphone, you can record voice memos. After running the Voice Memo applet, tap New, and then tap the big red Record button. Start talking. When you're done, press the stop button (which is represented by a square box—the universal consumer-electronics symbol for "stop"). In the highlighted field that appears, enter a name for the recording (if desired—you can also leave the timestamp that's automatically provided), and then press Done.

■ **Web**   All this and the Web, too? Sure enough, many Palms come with a Web browser. All you need to do is supply a wireless connection: cell-phone-via-Bluetooth or Wi-Fi will do. Find out more in Chapter 10.

■ **World Clock**   You probably already know what time it is in your part of the world. But what about Tokyo? Beijing? Paris? The way-cool World Clock applet shows you the time in three different cities—anyplace from Amsterdam to Washington, DC. Just tap any of the three pop-up city lists to choose one; select Edit List if there's a city you want to add. You can also use World Clock as an alarm clock by tapping the corresponding icon in the top-right corner of the screen and setting the time you want your Palm to "go off." Tap Menu | Options | Alarm Preferences to choose a sound and volume for the alarm.

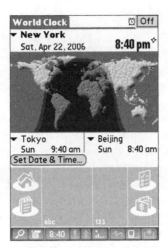

Voices from the Community

Expense Management in the Real World

Rick met Steve Gray a few years back in a kickboxing class, where he graciously provided his head as a target (we'll leave it up to you to decide whose head). Alas, the class is no more, but Rick and Steve remain buddies (which just goes to show that nothing breeds friendship like weekly throw-downs). In addition to being a fierce boxer, Steve travels frequently and uses his Palm OS–based smartphone to manage expenses. Here the man reveals his methods.

My occupation as a regional manager for an industrial chemical company requires me to be on the road working with clients, prospects, and sales representatives. Travel requirements vary from week to week, but I am usually out of my home office more than 70 percent of the time.

For those of you in similar circumstances, you know how challenging it is to keep an accurate tally of the various business-related expenses incurred while on the road. With both companies and the government incorporating and enforcing stricter rules with regards to the class and amount of business-related expenses, I wanted a reliable way to record, track, and recall what I was spending.

In the past, I would keep copious records in a Franklin Planner. However, the planner was too cumbersome to take on plane trips, so I had to resort to scraps of paper to record various expenditures (sound familiar?).

(continued)

Having purchased a Kyocera 7135 Phone/PDA, I found the ideal way to effectively track and manage my expenses. Conducting a search of the Handango Web site for "Expense" programs returned a plethora of choices. While each program touts its various features and benefits as being the greatest thing since sliced bread, you cannot really determine if the program is right for you until you try the demo.

I selected two programs to evaluate: Expense-N-Go from Solid Rock Software and ExpensePlus from WalletWare, Inc. Expense Plus is available for both Mac and Windows users, while Expense-N-Go is primarily for Windows, because if you want to produce reports on your PC, this program requires an additional application called Expense-N-Go Reporter, which works only on Windows systems.

Expense-N-Go is the application I have used most extensively. It offers a simple, clean interface with numerous pull-down menus regarding expense types, sources, and notes. All of the pull-down menus can be modified to suit your tastes and needs. There is even a built-in calculator for quick calculations without having to leave the program.

You can create and manage as many expense reports as required. However, I found there is quite a bit of lag as you switch from one report to the other. This issue is the only downside I've found with this program.

Upon completing an expense report, you can generate a report directly to the handheld's built-in memo application. I preferred using their Reporter program on my mobile PC. This program converts the data to an Excel spreadsheet format and is quite easy to work with.

ExpensePlus is a much more graphically rich program. It uses icons to represent expense categories and its numerous pull-down menus make entering data very quick and simple.

Both programs offer mileage calculators and will compute reimbursements based on company-paid mileage programs, but ExpensePlus has a more comprehensive mileage feature that tracks your start mileage from the previous entry. It also has the ability to separate your non-reimbursable expenses from those that are reimbursable from your employer.

These two programs will print to predesigned Excel spreadsheets. ExpensePlus has the ability to transfer data directly into your company's form (or your own). But, you have to submit the form in question to WalletWare so they can build a template for you.

Both programs will save you time in tracking vital personal and business expenses. You might also save some money by being able to keep a more accurate accounting of your expenditures. The programs are helpful at tax time and for getting your reimbursable expenses back from an employer on a timely basis.

Expense-N-Go sells for $19.95; Expense-N-Go Reporter costs $9.95. The mileage feature is okay, but I needed a more comprehensive program and purchased QuickMile for this purpose.

ExpensePlus is the full-featured program in this category, offering comprehensive reporting and mileage tracking in one program. However, the cost for all this wonderfulness is $49.95.

Where to Find It

Web Site	Address	What's There
Chapura	www.chapura.com	Cloak
Iambic Software	www.iambic.com	TimeReporter
Ilium Software	www.iliumsoft.com	eWallet
Infinity Softworks	www.infinitysw.com	powerOne calculators
IntelligentFind	www.intelligentfind.com	IntelligentFind
LandWare	www.landware.com	ExpensAble
PalmGear	www.palmgear.com	Tons of Palm OS software
WalletWare	www.walletware.com	ExpensePlus
XiY Technologies	www.xiy.net	LoanMax

8

Chapter 9

Go on a Trip

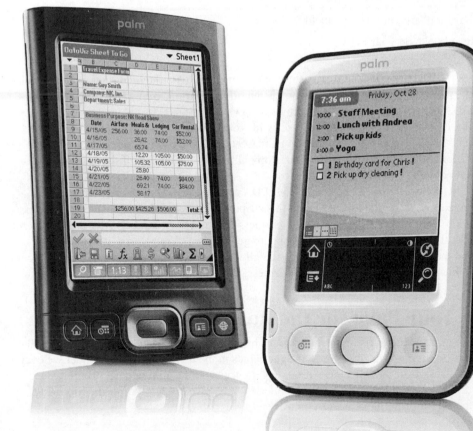

How to...

- Organize your PDA's categories and data for travel
- Pack smartly so you're prepared for trouble
- Make sure your handheld doesn't run out of power during the trip
- Prepare for HotSync opportunities away from home
- Enhance the core apps for life on the road
- Load your PDA with essential travel phone numbers
- Use the Palm as an alarm clock
- Use your PDA as a subway map
- Communicate in a foreign language with your handheld
- Turn your PDA into a USB flash drive
- Use your PDA as a compass
- Get star charts on your handheld
- Read books on your PDA

Some people find their handhelds so useful that—imagine this—they put them in their pocket and take them on trips away from the home and office! Daring, we know. And, as it turns out, your PDA is even designed for these kinds of "away missions." Its batteries mean you needn't plug it in, and because it synchronizes with your desktop PC, you can bring important information with you wherever you go. The Palm OS even has a built-in clock in case you forget your watch, and a scheduling app so you can stop pulling your calendar off the wall when you travel. What could be better?

Seriously, we know you already carry your PDA around town. But, if you plan to take it on an extended trip, you might want to read this chapter. We have all kinds of suggestions for how to prepare your handheld for a grueling business trip, and what kind of software you might need to make the trip a little smoother. Planning to go camping? Your trusty little handheld might not be the first accessory that springs to mind when you consider roughing it in the Rocky Mountains, but it has a lot to offer in the wilderness, too.

Preparing Your Palm for the Road

When we go on a business trip, it's usually such absolute pandemonium, running around at the last minute, throwing power cords and HotSync cables in the travel bag, it's a wonder we ever make it to the airport in time. Because of our experiences with forgetting data, bringing dead batteries, and being unable to connect to the Internet in strange cites, we offer the following checklist to you for bringing your PDA on trips.

Setting Up Your Data

Make sure your PDA is ready for the details of your upcoming trip. Specifically, consider the kinds of data you need to create while you're on the road and prepare your handheld ahead of time. The following shows you how to make sure you're ready:

1. In Tasks or Memos, consider creating a "trip checklist" and use it to enter everything you need to do before you leave, and what you need to bring with you. If you have a comprehensive checklist that is always right on your Palm, you'll finally stop forgetting important things when you travel.

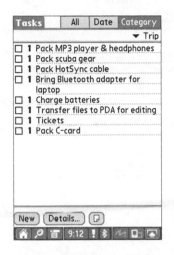

9

TIP

You probably don't want to build your travel list from scratch each time. Instead, create a comprehensive list of travel tasks and leave it in Memos. You can copy the entire travel checklist memo and paste it into a new, blank memo before a trip, and then erase individual lines as you complete them. The master list is still safely stored in a different memo entry.

2. Create a category just to store information related to your trip. If you're going to Chicago for a convention, for instance, create a category called Chicago. (Of course, if you want to call it something else, that's okay, too.) By using a special category on the road, you can find stuff related to your trip more quickly; both during the trip and after you return home. When you get back, you can recategorize the data any way you like.

3. Enter your itinerary in the Calendar. If you're flying, enter each flight's number, departure, and arrival time in your handheld so it's available when you need it. An easy way to do this is to enter the flight number in the Calendar at the scheduled departure time, and note the arrival time there also. That way, you can check your PDA in-flight to see how much longer you have to grit your teeth, eat peanuts, and make sure Kiefer Sutherland isn't planning to take over your plane.

```
Oct 27, 04  ◀ S M T W T F S ▶
                        ▼ Unfiled
 8:00
 9:00 ................................
-10:00 ● Leave for airport ........
-11:00 ................................
 12:00 ................................
 1:00 ................................
 1:30 ● United 6875 dep 125 arr LAX
        242
 2:00 ................................
 3:30 ● United 1416 dep 345 arr 459
 4:00 ................................
 5:00 ● Weston Hotel ............... ▯
 5:30 ................................
 7:00 ● Throwing Muses play at Slims
 9:00 ................................

 ⬚ · ─ ▤  (Details) (New) (Go To)
 ⌂ ♂ 🗑  9:27  ! ✴  🗠 🖳 📭
```

TIP

Planning a trip? You can block out the dates of your upcoming travel using a multi-day untimed event. The trip appears at the top of the Calendar's Day View and still lets you schedule actual appointments during those days.

Having a Backup Plan

Call us Luddites, but we don't like to rely 100 percent on a fragile piece of electronic gizmotry. (And yes, that's a word. Don't look it up, just trust us.) What if you drop your PDA in the airport and it shatters on the pretty marble floor? You'd better have a Plan B.

Dave: For me, the most important document to have access to on a trip is my flight itinerary. I always buy e-tickets, so I have no written record of my flight, and then I enter the flight information in my PDA. But, to be on the safe side, I also print a copy of my flight info and stick it in the back of my bag somewhere. That way, if my Palm batteries die before I finish my trip, or if my handheld falls out of a five-story window, I can always refer to the piece of paper and get myself home. This is less of a problem with my Palm TX, because if the batteries die during the trip, a little recharge brings it all back to life without the need for a HotSync. If you have a PDA with more traditional memory, though, all bets are off.

Rick: Your handheld probably has an expansion slot—use it. Do yourself a favor and purchase a memory card and one of the many backup utilities available from sites like Handango and PalmGear. With just a few stylus taps, you can back up the complete contents of your handheld's memory. Then, in the event that some catastrophe left you with a wiped handheld (it's been known to happen), you could pop the card in and restore everything in a matter of minutes. It's well worth the $30 to $40 you'll spend for the card and software. Better still, print and carry a hard copy of your contact list and appointment calendar, which can really save the day if your PDA up and dies—something else that's been known to happen (just ask Dave).

Getting the Hardware Ready

When you leave on a trip, you should make sure your Palm is fully prepared to go the distance. There's nothing like being a thousand miles from home and remembering you forgot to bring some data from your desktop PC, discovering you forgot an important cable, or finding that the Palm is only half-charged.

To save yourself from calamity, remember these tips:

- *Always bring a stylus with a reset pin.* Most PDAs include some kind of reset pin. Some incorporate a reset pin in the metal stylus—just unscrew the end to get to it. Others let you reset the device with the pointy end of the stylus, as with some Tungsten models. If neither of those options works for you, bring a paperclip or a thin pin in your travel bag (see Figure 9-1), and test the pin before you go! Rick once traveled with a toothpick that proved in a moment of crisis to be too thick to fit in the hole. D'oh! Bottom line: There's nothing worse than having your handheld crash when you're away from home and discovering you have no way to reset it. Find out more about resetting your PDA in Chapter 17.

- *Perform a HotSync right before you leave.* This way, you're sure to have the latest info on your PDA, and you also have a current backup in case something unfortunate happens to your trusty handheld while you're away.

9

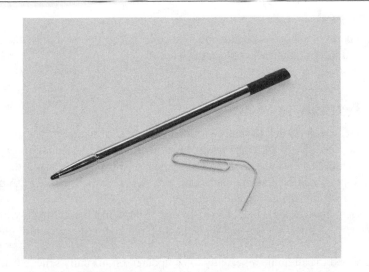

FIGURE 9-1 Your stylus is probably designed to reset your Palm, but a thin paperclip will work in a pinch

■ *Do you plan to do a lot of typing?* If so, pack a keyboard. You have many options to choose from, such as Palm's Universal Wireless Keyboard or Think Outside's Stowaway Universal Bluetooth Keyboard, both of which fold up to about the size of a deck of cards (read about the best choices in Chapter 16).

■ *Be prepared to restore.* Call us paranoid, but ... hey, wait a minute, did you just call us paranoid? Sheesh, the nerve. ... Anyway, if your PDA should lose all its data for some reason, you might want to have the capability to restore it while you're on the go. If you have a new model like a Palm TX or a recent-model Treo, all the memory is *non-volatile,* meaning it can't be wiped out by a power loss, so the chances of a catastrophic problem on the road are significantly less. But for everyone else, depending on what model you have, you can do that in a few ways. A HotSync cable can let you restore data from a laptop, for instance, but a better bet might be a backup on a memory card. Some PDAs come with a backup program that lets you create a perfect copy of the PDA's contents on a memory card and recover your data at any time, even when you're far away from your PC. Any handheld with an SD card slot can take advantage of Palm's Mobile Backup Card, which lets you recover your device's data without the need for a HotSync.

NOTE   *Even a Palm with non-volatile memory can still be rendered unusable by a corrupt program file or a virus that causes the device to continuously reset or fail to start properly. If something like that happens, your only recourse might be to perform a hard reset, wiping out your data. Thankfully, such a catastrophe is extremely unlikely.*

Staying Powered

A dead Palm is no good to anyone except people that collect dead Palms and use them in modern sculptures. And we don't think those people actually exist.

Real-Life Tragedy

A while back, Dave spent a week in sunny Florida in the dead of winter to see a photography trade show and do a bit of scuba diving. While there, his trusty PDA held all his data—contact info, schedules, even flight information for the return trip. Well, thanks to a bitterly frustrating glitch in a wireless modem attachment, two days into the trip, the PDA performed a hard reset, erasing all the data on the device.

"I had thrown caution to the wind," Dave reports. "I thought I could trust my Palm, and I had no backup of any kind—no laptop, no backup module, not even a printout of my schedule."

In fact, Dave had to call home repeatedly to be updated on his daily schedule and to know what time to show up to the airport at the end of the trip. Frustrating? You bet. He has since learned to better heed his own advice and always travels with some sort of data backup for his PDA.

Anyway, a dead Palm is of no use to anyone. And it surprises many users to learn that most PDAs use battery power even when turned off, meaning you can come back to an unused handheld after a week or so and find it totally dead, even if it was fully charged when you left it. Therefore, take these steps to keep working when you're away:

- *Recharge your PDA right before you leave.* Leave the PDA connected to its cable or cradle overnight, and pop it into your travel bag right before you head out to the airport.

- *Bring backup power.* If you plan to be away for more than two days, bring some sort of charging solution with you. For example, we like the ones available at SF Planet, which work with a wide variety of Palm models, including the Treo, LifeDrive, and Tungstens. Check out the Battery Travel Charger Extender at http://sfplanet.com/product/C-PT5-BX .Another one of our favorites is Tech Center Labs. These guys offer a variety of charging solutions that covers just about every Palm model around. Still have an old Palm V? Then get the Palm V Emergency Charger, which relies on a pair of AA batteries. Or the USB Emergency Charger, which works with models like the LifeDrive, T5, and Treo 650. Also be sure to check out Palm's online store, which sells a variety of charging solutions, including USB chargers (which plug into laptops or desktop PCs for charging power), car chargers, and more.

- *If your handheld uses replaceable batteries, check them before you go.* There aren't many of these kinds of PDAs left in the world, but if you have one, heed this advice. If you're going to be away for a week or more, bring a spare set of batteries with you— better safe than sorry. If you generally leave a spare set of batteries in your travel case, score ten points for preparedness. But use a battery tester before each trip to make sure your backup batteries are still in good shape.

- *Bring batteries for any accessories you use.* This includes your keyboard, cell phone, GPS receiver, and any other gadgets.

Road Tips

We've done our share of traveling, and we've amassed a few handy tips for making the best use of your PDA on the road. Not all of these suggestions will appeal to you, but you're sure to find a few things to make your next trip a little more enjoyable.

- **Make time**   If you're planning to stay at your destination for more than a few hours, fix the time on your PDA. Otherwise, all your appointments will have their alarms set to the wrong time and you'll show up late everywhere you need to be. The exact method varies depending upon which model you own, but most new devices work like this: tap the Prefs icon in the Home screen and choose the Date & Time page, as in the following illustration. Tap the Location menu and select your new city. Other models may require you to tap a Set Time Zone box, or—for really old models—you may have to simply change the time via the Prefs app.

CAUTION *Remember, if you travel to a different time zone and don't change your handheld's clock, your appointment calendar and alarms won't do you much good—they'll still be running on your old time zone. Likewise, when you get back home, don't forget to change the clock back again.*

■ **Avoid battery disasters** Some PDAs can accidentally run their battery down very easily if you're not careful. Why? Packing the PDA in your pocket or a crowded travel bag can result in things getting pressed against the power button or application buttons, causing a constant power drain. There are several solutions, depending upon which model you own. For instance, you can get a hard-shelled case to enclose your PDA, which keeps the power button from getting triggered accidentally. But the best solution: many newer models have a page in the Prefs app called Keylock. Tap Keylock and choose to disable all the buttons on your device either manually or automatically. When Keylock is activated, the quick-launch app buttons won't turn on the device (though they'll function normally once the device is on), and the power button turns on the device only after you also tap a button onscreen. It's a great way to avoid killing your battery before you even reach your destination.

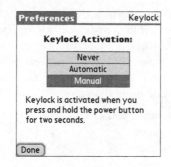

■ **Flight rules** Obviously, your handheld is considered a "portable electronic device," so you shouldn't use it at the beginning or the end of a flight. You probably already knew that, but your handheld can get you in trouble anyway if you're not careful. Specifically, don't enable any alarms—especially for the flight—or your PDA will come to life and start beeping during the Forbidden Times. If you want to be a real stickler for FAA rules, you should be sure to turn off any wireless features, such as Bluetooth and Wi-Fi. You can find the master toggle for these functions in the Prefs application. Look under the Communication category. On some models, wireless can be turned on and off directly from the status bar at the bottom of the screen.

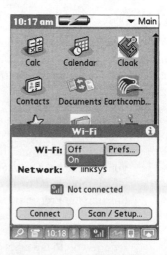

Turn Your Palm into an iPod

We can see it in your eyes—that iPod envy. No matter how much you love your PDA, there's something alluring about a little metal box the size of a deck of cards capable of playing your entire music collection anytime, anywhere.

Well, lust no longer, because you don't need a stinkin' iPod. Your Palm is every bit as capable a portable music machine as Apple's ubiquitous music player. So over the next few pages, let's see exactly what you need to do in order to get music onto your Palm and then into your ears.

THE ROAD FROM PALM TO iPOD

1. Rip your music collection onto your computer.

2. Create some playlists to make it easier to select music on the Palm.

3. Transfer music from your computer to your Palm.

4. Sit back and enjoy—we recommend using Pocket Tunes Deluxe, the enhanced version of the music player that comes with many Palm models. In fact, we'll assume you're using Pocket Tunes.

Get Your Palm Ready

What's it take to turn your Palm into an iPod? Well, clearly, you're going to need a lot of storage. Music takes up a lot of space, even when compressed into MP3 or WMA files. We recommend buying the biggest card you can afford. And believe it or not, you can probably afford quite a bit. Memory cards have plummeted in price in the last year or two. Check out pricegrabber.com for good prices on SD cards: as this book was going to print, we found deals like 4GB cards for well under $100—in fact, for as little as $80. By the time you read this, prices will no doubt be even better. What does 4GB get you? Apple likes to claim that their 4GB model fits about 1000 songs, and that's not a bad estimate. Equip your Palm with one of these cards, and you've got days worth of music in your pocket.

Pick Some Music Software

There are several digital music players available for the Palm (for details, see Chapter 14) but our favorite is Pocket Tunes. The Deluxe version lets you play MP3s, WMA, Ogg Vorbis (which is great if you're the one guy on the planet that uses that format), and even protected music that you've bought online via download services like Napster, Rhapsody, and Yahoo. You can download Pocket Tunes at www.normsoft.com.

Go Bluetooth

You should also invest in good headphones. Dave is very fond of the freedom of movement that Bluetooth affords him, so if your Palm is Bluetooth-ready, then try headphones like the Motorola HT820 Bluetooth headphones and the AudioGate Bluetooth software, available from www.softick.com.

AudioGate is actually a snap to get up and running. After you install it, do this:

1. Tap Configure and set it to the highest quality level (304 kbps). After all, this is music we're trying to listen to, not talk radio.

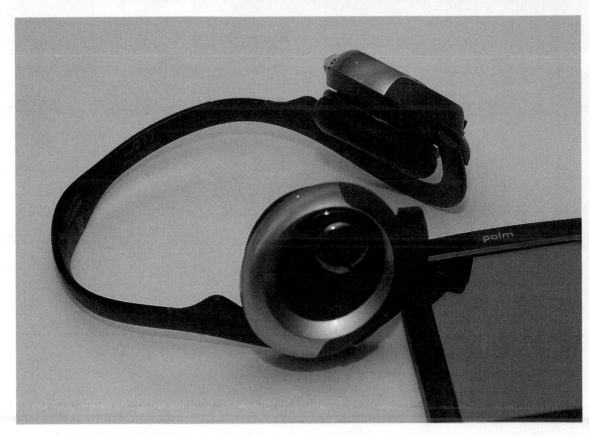

Figure 1. The Motorola HT820 headphones let you listen to music up to 30 feet from your Palm.

2. Tap Done.

3. Tap Remote. This connects the Palm to the headphones.

4. You're done. Now just start listening to music.

Well, kind of. First we should get some music on that Palm of yours. That's the first step.

Rip Your Music Collection

The term "ripping" confuses people who are new to digital music. It sounds complicated

and perhaps even a little violent. In reality, it's just a slang term that refers to the process of transferring a copy of a song from CD to your computer. When you "rip" music, you're making a perfect copy, identical to the original in every way (and that explains why the record companies are somewhat nervous).

Pick a File Format

Ripping music is pretty simple, really, but you need to make a few decisions before you start your music collection. First of all, digital music is a generic term that includes a lot of different kinds of file formats. Just like the term "digital photo" could mean TIFF, JPG, RAW, or any of another dozen computer file formats, digital music could be WAV, WMA, MP3, and more. Which do you choose? Well, in our opinion, there are really only three important files: WAV, WMA, and MP3.

If you're a long-time PC user, you probably have already heard of WAV files. They are important because the format is *lossless*. A lossless file format does not sacrifice any information in the file to compress data or save space, so a WAV file will sound exactly like the original CD.

On the other side of the proverbial coin, there's MP3 and WMA audio. These formats are called lossy because they discard some information when you rip your music. That sounds bad, but it isn't; the compression algorithm strips away information humans can't hear—or can't hear well—as long as you compress your music at a typical bitrate. The advantage of an MP3 or WMA file is that it takes a small fraction of the space required by a WAV file.

How big is the file size difference between WAV and MP3 files? This chart can help illustrate:

File Format	File Size for 10 minutes of audio
WAV	100MB
256 kbps MP3 or WMA	20MB
64 kbps MP3 or WMA	5MB

Some folks will tell you that WMA files sound better than MP3, and they're probably right. The differences are small enough, though, that we don't worry so much about that. Instead, pick your music format based on where and how you plan to play your music. If, for example, you own Pocket Tunes Deluxe, consider WMA. But the basic version of Pocket Tunes doesn't support WMA files, so you'll have to stick with MP3.

Ripping Music

The process of ripping tracks from a CD is pretty straight-forward. Essentially, here's the rundown:

1. Insert a CD in your computer's CD or DVD drive.

2. Start your software (more on that in a moment).

3. If necessary, specify the file format and bitrate that you want to capture.

4. Press the Record button and watch the magic as your computer reads the music from the CD and stores it on your PC in digital form.

Ripping with Windows Media Player

We'll be honest: We love Windows Media Player. If you're new to ripping your music, look no further than this little gem, which, conveniently enough, comes with your Windows XP or Vista computer.

> **NOTE**
>
> When you actually rip music from CD, you might initially be surprised at the speed. Most software can read many, many times faster than the ordinary playback speed of the CD, so you can rip an entire CD in just a couple of minutes.

If you have had your computer for a while, it's a really good idea to visit Microsoft.com and download the latest version of Media Player (which was version 11 as we wrote this book).

To rip a CD, do this:

1. Start Windows Media Player.

2. Verify your burn settings. To do that, click any menu and then choose More Options. Click the Rip Music tab and choose your preferred settings—MP3 or Windows Media Audio (WMA), and choose a bitrate from the Audio quality slider. We recommend either 192 or 256 kbps, which will give you sound quality

that's essentially indistinguishable from CD. Make sure the Copy protect music checkbox is not selected, and then click OK to make these settings your default.

3. Insert a CD in your CD or DVD drive, and then click the Rip button at the top of Windows Media Player.

4. After the disc information appears on the screen, click the Start Rip button at the bottom of the screen.

5. When it's done, click the Library button to see your songs displayed in the Windows Media Player music library.

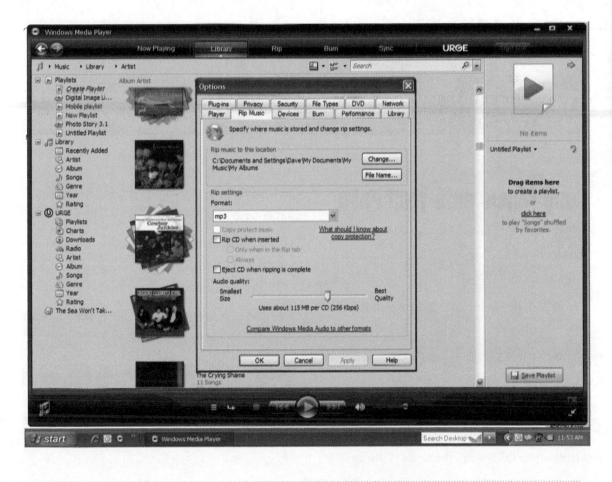

Copy Music onto Your Palm

So now you're ready to take your music collection and put it on your Palm. There are two ways to do this:

- Copy music manually onto your Palm's SD card

- Use Windows Media Player to synch your music library with your Palm

Copying Music Manually

If you don't use Windows Media Player, or if you simply prefer to do things the hard way, then moving music to the Palm is no different than copying any sort of file onto a floppy disk, CD, or another hard drive. Do this:

1. Insert the Palm's SD card into your computer's desktop media card reader.

2. When AutoPlay appears, choose Open files to view folders and click OK.

TIP

If neither of these solutions excites you, you can also drag music files to the Palm's Quick Install window. For details on that, see Chapter 4.

3. Drag the music files and playlists from the My Music folder on your computer to the SD Card folder.

That's it; insert the SD Card in your Palm and you're ready to roll.

Sync with Windows Media Player

If you're using Windows Media Player, it's easier to sync with your Palm because you can see all your music in the Media Player library. Do this:

1. Start Windows Media Player and insert your Palm in its docking cradle or connect the docking cable.

2. In Windows Media Player, click Sync at the top of the screen.

3. Drag all the songs and playlists that you want to copy to the Palm into the Sync list pane on the right side of the screen.

4. When you're ready, click Start Sync. All the selected music will be copied.

Play Music on the Palm

F inally! We've got music on your Palm, and we want to hear it. Start Pocket Tunes and choose Action | Open. You'll see a list of all the music on your Palm's memory card. You can select as many songs as you like (each time you tap a song, it gets selected) and then click OK, or you can simply click Select All and bring all of your song into Pocket Tunes at once. From here, just operate the player controls and enjoy listening to music on your new Palm music player!

Make Some Playlists

Finally, don't forget that a few playlists can dramatically enhance your music listening experience. Playlists are lists of songs that you can use to quickly choose music on the Palm--think of them like radio setlists that you have total control over. Here's what to do:

1. In Pocket Tunes, click Action | Manage Playlists.

2. Click New and then, in the Name field, enter a name for this playlist (like "Workout music" or "Showtunes").

3. Tap Add Song.

4. Tap songs in the list. You can add as many songs as you like to the playtlist. When you're done, tap OK.

5. When your playlist is complete, tap Save List.

That's all there is to it. To actually play one of your new playlists, select the playlist and tap Select. All the songs in that playlist will appear automatically in Pocket Tunes and start playing.

■ **PDA printing**   You might need to print something stored on your PDA while you're on your trip. There are several ways to print. The easiest solution is to get a print driver for your Palm such as PalmPrint, PrintBoy, or one of the print solutions from IS/Print, especially if you have access to a portable printer. If that's the case, just aim your PDA and print. If you do a lot of printing, it is a good idea to buy a portable printer and carry it with you (see Chapter 11 for details). If you can get to a printer, but it isn't IR-capable, you still have options. First, if you have a few extra bucks, you might want to carry the PrintBoy InfraReady Adapter or the Belkin Bluetooth Wireless USB Printer Adapter, both available from Bachmann Software. These little devices fit easily into a travel bag and plug into your printer. The InfraRed Adapter has an infrared port that lets you instantly convert almost any printer into an IR-ready printer. Likewise, the Bluetooth adapter lets you turn any USB printer into a Bluetooth device, ideal if you have a Bluetooth enabled Palm. When you're finished printing, remove the adapter and put it back into your travel bag. Either one is a very cool solution for printing anything anywhere you can find a printer when you travel.

Software to Bring Along

Don't rely on the software that comes with your PDA to get you through your extended trips away from home. Most of the software we discuss in this next section is available from PalmGear.com. Experiment and see what applications are useful.

9

CAUTION   *Don't install a new application as you're walking out the door to go to the airport. Some applications might cause your handheld to misbehave. Others can change the way your PDA operates or make it hard to access data you've already created unless you know some new tricks. You don't need to discover those kinds of things after you're already on an airplane bound for Topeka. Bottom line: install and experiment with new software well in advance of a trip.*

Calendar and Contacts Enhancements

Sure, you love the Palm's Contacts and Calendar, but by enhancing these core applications, you might find you can significantly improve the way you work when you're away from home.

Synchronizing with the Web

Believe it or not, you can synchronize your Contacts and Calendar with Yahoo's Web-based information managers. Why would you want to do that? Well, when you're on the road, you might want to access your schedule and contacts from a PC that isn't yours. And, if you can get to a Web-enabled PC, you can log on to your Yahoo-based calendar and address book. Here are some cool reasons to try this:

- Send e-mail from a Web-based e-mail system using contact information culled from your PDA.
- Add calendar appointments on the PC and synchronize it to your handheld later.
- If something happens to your PDA on a trip, access all your data from a PC that's connected to the Internet.

Yahoo.com currently offers the only PDA synchronization support on the Internet. By installing a small utility—Intellisync for Yahoo—on your home or office-based PC, you can sync Calendar, Contacts, and Memos with equivalent applications on the Yahoo site. Because Yahoo also offers free e-mail, you can use your Contacts to send messages without reentering any data.

To get started with Web synchronization, visit www.yahoo.com. If you don't already have an account there, create one—it's free. You'll then need to find the site's synchronization tools, which are actually buried a few layers deep. Navigate to Yahoo's Address Book or Calendar, and then click the Sync link, which you can see at the top right of the Web page (see Figure 9-2).

Getting Common Phone Numbers

Your handheld can hold lots of phone numbers, so why not take advantage of this? Several databases of phone numbers exist to services like rental car companies, airlines, and hotels. Here are some examples of what you can find at PalmGear.com:

Topic	What You'll Find
Rental cars	You can find a handful of downloads at PalmGear that include all the major rental car companies. In particular, check out two programs called Travel Telephone Numbers and Car Rental 800 Numbers.
Hotels	If your travel plans often put you in strange cities unexpectedly, it's handy to have a list of phone numbers for popular hotel chains on your Palm. You'll find a few such collections on PalmGear. Check out Hotel 800 Numbers, for example.
Golf courses	Believe it or not, we found a slew of downloads at PalmGear.com that pour phone numbers for golf courses in major cities into your handheld, so you can easily find the numbers you need when you travel. Be sure to download US Golf Courses Pocket Directory Database, which has information on 15,000 courses.
Restaurants	Want a guide to restaurants in major cities? You'll find that online as well. The Finer Life Restaurant Guide is available at PalmGear for cities such as San Francisco and L.A. Of course, if you want a really good guide to local restaurants when you travel, you'll want a city guide, which we cover later in this chapter.
Emergency Credit Card Contacts	You're in Berlin and you lose your Visa card. What do you do? If you have an app called VISA/MasterCard Emergency Numbers installed on your Palm, you just look up the correct phone number for your location and call.

FIGURE 9-2 Yahoo lets you synchronize your Palm with an online calendar

Itinerary Tracking

Although you can certainly store your itinerary information in the Calendar, using a specialized program is more efficient for many people. There are many applications at sites such as PalmGear that fit the bill. Our hands-down favorite is a program called Trip Boss, which you can see below. Trip Boss is an all-in-one travel manager that lets you track your travel expenses, log mileage, plan your trip, keep a running travel journal, convert currency, and more. There's a tremendous wealth of things you can do with Trip Boss, but it's pretty easy to use. If there's simply more here than you need, you might also want to look at some of our other favorites, like TravelTracker and TravelPal.

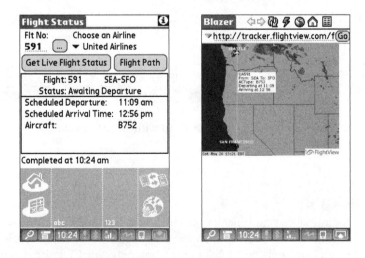

Another cool program that has quickly become an essential tool for us is called Flight Status. If your Palm has Internet access, either via Wi-Fi or Bluetooth (see Chapter 10), you can use Flight Status to retrieve live, up-to-date status on your upcoming flight in seconds. All you need to enter is the flight number and the name of the airline. Flight Status does the rest. It will tell you arrival and departure times and current flight status. You can even see the plane's position on a flight path map. Best of all, it's a lot faster than retrieving the same information via a Web browser on your computer.

In Search of the Ultimate Alarm Clock

You can set alarms with your PDA, but the somewhat anemic alarm system built into the Calendar isn't terribly useful in a lot of situations (the clock that comes with the now sadly discontinued Tapwave Zodiac is a notable exception). Instead, you might want to download a copy of a specialized clock program. A program just to tell the time? When your PDA already comes with a clock? Surely we jest.

We don't, and stop calling us Shirley.

Note to selves: That joke simply doesn't work in print.

The Palm software universe is filled with some excellent clocks and alarm clock applications. These programs tend to offer more advanced features than those that come with the PDA itself, such as multiple alarms that aren't tied to specific Calendar events, snooze buttons, countdown and stopwatch modes, and world time displays. Here are some programs worth investigating:

■ **BigClock**   BigClock is the granddaddy of alarm clock apps for the Palm. It's free, yet has a wealth of useful features. Not only does it display the time, but it has a timer and four independent alarms. It also lets you easily change time zones—a boon if you're still using an older device without OS 5's easy time zone adjustment. It also allows you to change the look of the program and display your own favorite background images behind the clock using the program's themes feature.

■ **WorldMate Professional**   This gorgeous program isn't just great for travelers—it's eye candy for your PDA as well. At its core, WorldMate lets you compare four world clocks to your local time and features a beautiful map display that animates the day/night terminator. It also synchronizes your PDA with an online atomic clock at each HotSync, retrieves weather forecasts, and includes a currency converter.

■ **MegaClock**   This is a must-try. MegaClock is a multifunction clock app that has a huge collection of alternative views; you can see the time in a variety of analog and digital clock faces, display a world globe with day/night terminator, and more. It has no fewer than 20 alarms and four programmable daily timers.

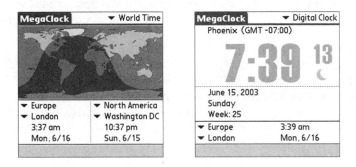

■ **CityTime**   Like WorldMate, CityTime has a gorgeous color display that shows the day/night terminator graphically as it moves across the globe. CityTime displays four world clocks and lets you change your location and time easily without entering the Prefs app. It offers sunrise and sunset times and moon phase information, and performs time and distance calculations between locations.

■ **Time 2.0**   For those who want a simpler, calendar-based view, Time 2.0 shows the time and a calendar along with a second time zone and upcoming appointments.

Finding Your Way Around

Many Palm tools can help you find your way around in a strange place. In fact, you can actually connect your PDA to a GPS navigation system! (See "PDA Survival Tools" later in this chapter.) Most people need more mundane assistance, though, so we've collected a few interesting applications for you here.

Having a Better Time with City Guides

City Guides have become virtually indispensable for frequent travelers. These programs deliver up-to-date, trustworthy information about things to do in cities you travel to. Such info includes restaurant, nightclub, shopping, and sightseeing advice. The following describes a few to check out:

■ **Vindigo**   We list Vindigo first for a reason: it has become the single most popular city guide in the world. It supports more than 50 cities and has categories for food, shops, services, museums, movies, essential services such as banks and ATMs, and more. The program has maps and provides directions to wherever you're trying to go; it also features reviews to help you make good choices about where to go. Alas, it's not a one-time fee; Vindigo costs $25 per year.

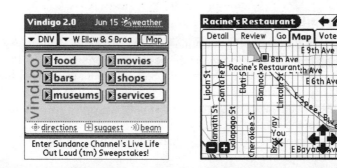

■ **Earthcomber**   If you are a fan of both city guides and things that are free, then you'll like Earthcomber. Here you'll find navigation, mobile mapping, and community networking. If your Palm has GPS navigation, it can guide you to specific locations and make recommendations about nearby points of interest. But even without GPS, it's a powerful guide. The program has street maps of the entire US, 1.5 million points of interest, and the ability to load detailed city guide-style information on specific cities (though these add-ons are not free). When this book went to print, there were guides available for Boston, Vegas, Chicago, LA, Miami, New York, and several other cities.

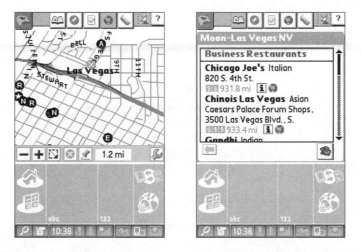

■ **Zagat To Go**   The popular Zagat restaurant guide is available for the Palm. Its database includes about 65 cities and has reviews of dining and nightlife in the same familiar form as the paper version.

■ **Qvadis Envoyage**   Looking for a free city guide? Live or travel in Canada? Try Envoyage, which has some of the same features as Vindigo and Zagat for a handful of cities, such as Toronto, Vancouver, Montreal, and Ottawa.

Getting Metro and Subway Routes

Do train, bus, and subway routes leave you scratching your head? Those maps they put in the train stops aren't exactly intuitive, and finding the best route from one end of Paris to the other can be a nerve-wracking experience. That's why you might want to search a site such as PalmGear for metro aids. These programs help you find your way around strange towns when you travel. The best ones let you enter two stations and simply tell you what train to get on. Others include digital maps and displays to help you navigate. To get started, search PalmGear for terms like "metro" and "subway" to locate apps that interest you. The following includes some of the better ones we dug up:

Region	Service	Program Name
200 cities worldwide	Displays best routing information for finding your way by subway or bus.	MetrO
Paris 3.1P	Shows Metro paths between monuments, museums, and stations.	Paris
Versions available for New York, Boston, London, Paris, Chicago, and others	Map that plans the best route between metro stops; combined with a street map for easier route planning.	TUBE
Databases available for select cities in California, Washington, New York, and others	Comprehensive bus and train schedules.	Transit
19 cities, including New York, Paris, and London	Computes the best route between any two stations.	Route Expert
New York	Enter a Manhattan address and the program provides the nearest cross street.	X-Man
Southern California	Offers the MetroLink schedule.	MetroLink

Language Translators

In the past, traveling abroad often resulted in serious communication difficulties. Do you know how to ask for the bathroom in French? If not, try one of these applications.

■ **Small Talk** This program is a real-time, two-way translator. Hold your handheld up to the person you want to communicate with. Small Talk presents you with complete sentences organized into situation-based categories such as Basics, Lodging, Emergency, Food, and Entertainment. Select a phrase in English and it's translated into the target language, as you can see in Figure 9-3. The person you are communicating with can then select a response from a menu, which is translated back into English. Small Talk supports French, Italian, Spanish, German, and Japanese.

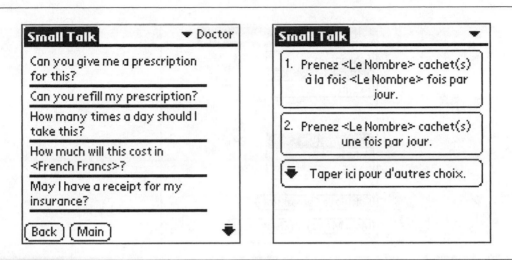

FIGURE 9-3   Choose a phrase from a list, divided by topic (left), and your associate can choose a response (right) that is translated back into English for you.

- **TourMate**   Available in several versions (including English-Spanish, English-Italian, English-French, and English-German), TourMate is easy to use. Choose a common greeting, expression, or question in English, and read the phonetically spelled foreign-language equivalent expression to the person with whom you're trying to communicate.

- **MyTourPal**   This program offers a list of common phrases and their accompanying phonetic equivalents so you can read foreign phrases off the Palm's screen. A single program includes seven languages: German, Japanese, Hindi, French, Italian, Spanish, and Urdu.

- **Translate**   This application enables you to enter a word and instantly translate it among 18 languages. The translator works in both directions, so you can go from English to Italian or Italian to English, for instance.

Unit Conversions

If you're an American in Europe, you need to contend with an alien set of measurements: not only is the currency different, but even the length, weight, and volume of common items are unusual. Heck, unless you're a scientist or an engineer, you may not know if 40 degrees Celsius is hot or cold. Try Conversions (see Figure 9-4) or Conversion Master. Both are calculators that let you instantly make conversions among units and measurements such as currency, temperature, length, area, and volume.

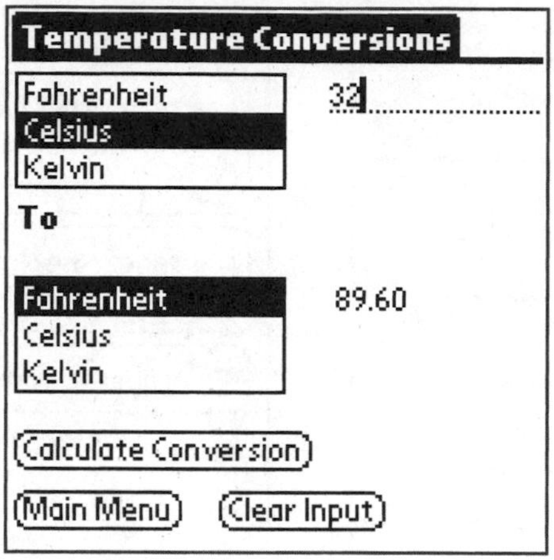

Temperature Conversions

Fahrenheit   32
Celsius
Kelvin

To

Fahrenheit   89.60
Celsius
Kelvin

(Calculate Conversion)

(Main Menu)   (Clear Input)

FIGURE 9-4   Conversions makes it easy for an American to get by in a metric world.

Using Your PDA as a USB Flash Drive

Some new Palm models (as of when we went to print: the Tungsten T5 and the LifeDrive) can actually do double duty, both as a PDA and one of those cool USB flash drives that lets you transfer data between two PCs. That's cool, since you don't have to remember to carry your USB flash drive wherever you go. As long as you have your PDA and a USB HotSync cable, you can transfer files between computers.

To turn your PDA into a flash drive, tap the program called Drive Mode, and you'll see a screen like the following:

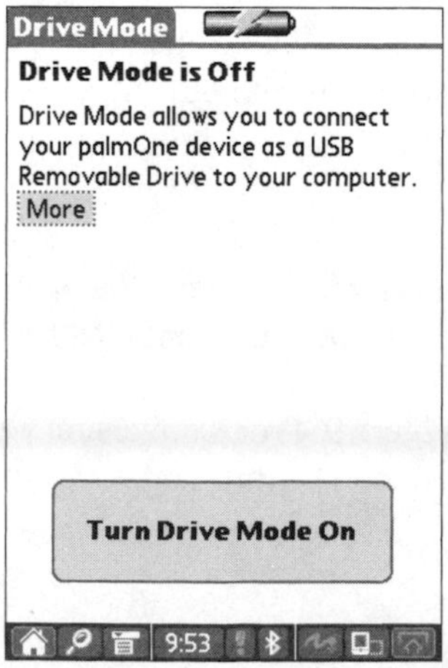

Drive Mode

Drive Mode is Off

Drive Mode allows you to connect your palmOne device as a USB Removable Drive to your computer.
More

Turn Drive Mode On

9:53

Obviously, the next step is to tap Turn Drive Mode On. If you haven't already, plug in the USB cable to your PDA and computer now. After the cable is connected, you'll see this screen:

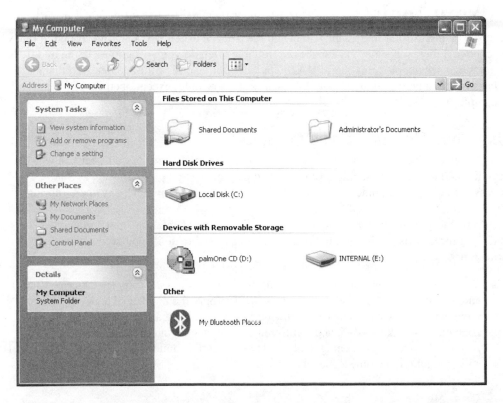

Finally, open the My Computer folder on your PC and look for your new removable storage, which will be labeled INTERNAL.

9

Double-click this icon and you'll see a number of folders on your PDA—Applications, Music, Documents, and so on. You can drag and drop any files from your computer into these folders (or even add new folders). When you're done, tap Turn Drive Mode Off on your PDA and you can ferry these files to another computer and repeat the connection process to copy them.

Also, remember that you can see any files you copied to your PDA by tapping the Files app. This program shows you all the files stored on your PDA, and you can use the File menu to copy, move, delete, and rename any files you find here.

PDA Survival Tools

It's not surprising to walk into a fancy hotel and see a dozen executives standing around in fancy suits, checking their schedules via handhelds. But how often do you go camping in the middle of the woods and see people bring their PDAs? Not that often, we're willing to bet. And that's too bad, because it's a handy survival tool. It does almost everything, except open cans of beans or start campfires.

Using Your Handheld as a Compass

Although we're quite sure you know a PDA won't open a can of beans, we suspect you wouldn't believe it could be a compass, either. But you'd be wrong. Using a program such as Sun Compass, you can get an immediate onscreen indication of north any time, anywhere (during daylight hours).

Unfortunately, Sun Compass comes with virtually no documentation, which may make it confusing for new users. To use Sun Compass, all you need to do is input a few pieces of information:

- ■ **Tz**   This is the time zone you are in currently. Time zones are calculated from −12 to 0, and then on up to +12. Your time zone value is simply the number of hours away from Greenwich, England (home of Greenwich Mean Time) you are located. GMT is a time zone of 0. New York is −5, and California is −8. You can find a complete list of time zones in Windows by opening the Date/Time Properties dialog box (in the Control Panel) and looking on the Time Zone tab.

- **La** Enter your latitude. Latitude is measured from 0 degrees (the equator) to 90N and 90S.

- **Lo** Enter your longitude. Longitude is commonly measured from 0 (at the longitude line that cuts through Greenwich, England) to 180E and 180W.

Looking for your latitude and longitude? Visit www.census.gov/cgi-bin/gazetteer. Enter your city or ZIP code to find out your latitude and longitude.

- **DSI** DSI stands for Daylight Saving Time, and it needs to be set to either on or off, depending on the time of year. Daylight Saving Time is on between the first Sunday in April and the last Sunday in October.

A few locations in the United States don't observe Daylight Saving Time at all. These include Arizona, Hawaii, and parts of Indiana.

Once you enter these values, point the front of your PDA at the sun (but be sure to keep it level with the ground), and the compass indicates which way is north. That's all there is to it!

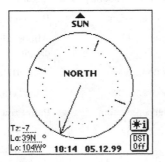

Finding Stars

You can also use Sun Compass to find the North Star. Choose Misc | Polarstar from the menu and you'll see a dark screen with the Big and Little Dipper constellations. By aligning them with what you see in the sky, you can find the North Star, and thus get a northerly orientation even at night.

That's great, but you can also use your PDA for some real star gazing. Here are a few programs you can try the next time you're far away from city lights with your Palm (there are many more at PalmGear):

- ■ **Planetarium**   This program calculates the position of the sun, the moon, the planets, and more than 1,500 of the brightest stars and deep sky objects in the sky. You can enter any location and any time period—you needn't use the present system clock. In addition to using this program for stargazing, it can also be used as a compass when the sun or moon is visible (much like Sun Compass).

- ■ **Star Pilot**   This program lets you specify your location, and then see the planets, the moon, and 500 stars in a compact star map. You can identify objects by clicking them, and you can search for celestial objects by name.

Reading Late at Night

When all of your tent buddies are trying to sleep while wondering if that odd sound is an approaching bear, you can relax in your sleeping bag and read a good book—with your PDA. Its backlight makes it easy to read in total darkness. You need a document reader. See Chapter 15 for details on electronic books and document readers, but we think it's worth pointing out right now that there's nothing like curling up with a good e-book on a camping trip. You can store lots of reading on one device, so you can travel right and still have a lot of things to read on those quiet, lonely nights.

Where to Find It

Web Site	Address	What's There
Bachmann Software	www.bachmannsoftware.com	PrintBoy
BigClock	www.gacel.de/palmpilot.htm	BigClock
Instant Power	www.instant-power.com	Instant Power Charger
IS/Complete	www.iscomplete.com	BtPrint and IrPrint
PalmGear	www.palmgear.com	Almost all the software mentioned in this chapter
RGPS	www.rgps.com	StayOffHack
SilverWare	www.silverware.com	TravelTracker
Stevens Creek Software	www.stevenscreek.com	PalmPrint
Tech Center Labs	www.talestuff.com	Battery chargers
Vindigo	www.vindigo.com	City guide software
Yahoo!	www.yahoo.com	Web-based information management that HotSyncs to the Palm

Chapter 10

E-Mail, the Internet, and More

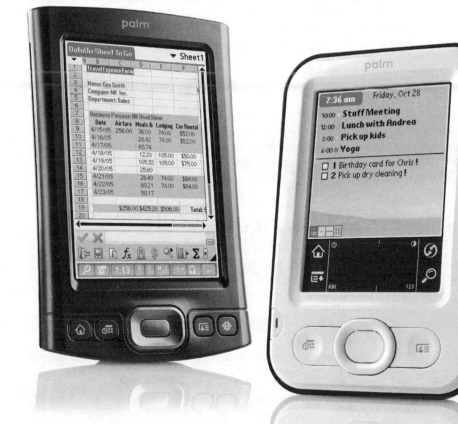

How to...

- Understand different wireless options
- Connect your cell phone to your handheld
- Configure your handheld for Web and e-mail access
- Find Wi-Fi hotspots
- Work with e-mail programs
- Access America Online
- Use AvantGo to take the Web with you
- Choose and work with handheld Web browsers
- Make the most of your Treo 650/700p

It's a little-known fact that when Jeff Hawkins (remember him from Chapter 1?) first conceived of the PalmPilot, he envisioned it as a device for sending and receiving e-mail. Unfortunately, the technological limitations of the time prevented that idea from getting much traction, but nowadays, e-mail and PDAs go together like peanut butter and jelly.

> **NOTE** *Do not, under any circumstances, apply peanut butter or jelly to your PDA. Learn from Dave's mistake.*

In fact, most modern Palm handhelds are downright savvy when it comes to e-mail, the Web, and the Internet in general. They're even good at communicating with cell phones, GPS receivers, and other wireless devices. In this chapter, we're going to teach you the ways of the wireless PDA. We'll also delve into smartphones like the Treo 650 and Treo 700p, which are, of course, inherently wireless. Get ready to get online ... pocket-style!

What Constitutes a Wireless PDA?

Believe it or not, some crazy people still buy PDAs just for organizing their contacts and calendars. They're actually surprised to learn that the little gizmos have wireless capabilities. Well, maybe that's not too surprising, as it's not always immediately obvious just what those capabilities are. Let's start by defining the three basic kinds of wireless technology and what they're used for.

> **NOTE** *You may notice that we don't include infrared, or IR, in this discussion. Although technically this is a kind of wireless technology, one possessed by all Palm handhelds, it's not really used for Internet connectivity. Instead, it's used primarily for beaming contacts, memos, and other bits of data from one handheld to another, as discussed in various chapters prior to this one.*

■ **Bluetooth**   Yeah, we think it's a dumb name, too. What some ancient Danish king has to do with short-range wireless technology is beyond us. Anyway, Bluetooth has become something of a staple in cell phones, headsets, GPS receivers, and PDAs. That's because it enables wireless communication between those devices, and consumes relatively little power in the process. Can you use a Bluetooth-enabled Palm (like the Tungsten E2 or TX) to access the Internet? Yes, but only if your cell phone is configured for data services (like e-mail and Web access) and has built-in Bluetooth so it can function like a wireless modem for your PDA. We'll tell you just how to make that happen later in the chapter.

■ **Wi-Fi**   Short for "wireless fidelity" and also known by its technical name, 802.11x (where the x can stand for a, b, g, or n, all just varieties of the technology), Wi-Fi is the greatest thing to happen to PDAs since the stylus. With a Wi-Fi-equipped Palm, you can access the Internet anywhere there's a "hotspot"—a publicly accessible wireless network. This could be in your home, at your office, or in a hotel, airport, or coffee shop. You can also use Wi-Fi to wirelessly HotSync your PDA (cradles? We don't need no steenkin' cradles). We're sad that Palm has chosen to integrate this technology in so few models (at press time, only the LifeDrive and TX had it), but once you have it, you'll never want to be without it again. Read on to learn more about Wi-Fi, hotspots, and cool tricks you can perform with both.

■ **Cellular**   Although the word "cellular" is something of a misnomer nowadays (most mobile-phone networks rely on different technology), it's still the best way to describe the third flavor of PDA wireless. Basically, if you have a smartphone like the Treo 650 or 700p, you can take advantage of its voice-oriented wireless capabilities to access the Internet. Keep in mind that this isn't the same thing as Bluetooth, which simply serves to link your PDA to your phone. Cellular connections tend to be slower than Wi-Fi, but they have the advantage of being accessible from just about anywhere.

10

NOTE   *Why do we knock the Treo smartphones for not including Wi-Fi? Simple: Even though they offer wireless Internet access anywhere there's a signal (which is just about everywhere these days), there are other advantages to Wi-Fi. For starters, it's usually much faster than traditional cellular Internet connections. Also, when you're connected to a hotspot, you're not paying by-the-minute data charges. And finally, Wi-Fi can be used for wireless HotSyncs; cellular wireless can't. When Palm announced the Treo 700p just before press time, we were sure it would have Wi-Fi—the one feature Treo 650 fans had been clamoring for. Alas, it wasn't to be. Why do you forsake Wi-Fi, Palm? Why?!*

Now that you know the three major wireless technologies, let's take a look at which one(s) are found in current Palm models (as shown in Table 10-1).

Model	Bluetooth	Wi-Fi	Cellular	Notes
Z22	No	No	No	The only model in Palm's lineup without wireless capabilities.
Tungsten E2	Yes	Optional	No	Built-in Bluetooth adds versatility to this model, and you can even add Wi-Fi via an expansion card.
TX	Yes	Yes	No	Our favorite Palm, the TX offers Bluetooth and Wi-Fi in a super-slim design.
LifeDrive	Yes	Yes	No	Bluetooth and Wi-Fi, plus a whopping 4 gigabytes (GB) of storage.
Treo 650	Yes	No	CDMA or GSM/ GPRS	Palm's super-popular smartphone is awesome, but it lacks Wi-Fi.
Treo 700p	Yes	No	EV-DO	The latest Treo offers high-speed "cellular" connectivity, but no Wi-Fi.

TABLE 10-1   Palm Wireless Capabilities by Model

All About Bluetooth

Years ago, Rick and Dave would argue endlessly (and, many would say, pointlessly) about the future of Bluetooth. Dave was convinced it would change the world, finding its way into everything from toasters to toothbrushes. Rick, who's always been much better at predicting the future, pooh-poohed Bluetooth, saying it would never amount to anything more than a niche technology. In the end, they were both wrong. Except for Dave's toothbrush, which actually does have Bluetooth.

Still, Rick will admit, Bluetooth has evolved into a pretty useful niche technology. Let's take a look at some of the cool things you can do with a Bluetooth-equipped Palm:

■ **Link to a cell phone for e-mail, messaging, and Web browsing**   As discussed previously, one of the main advantages to Bluetooth is leveraging your cell phone's wireless data capabilities. Your phone (see Figure 10-1) acts as a modem; Bluetooth links your Palm to your phone. You can then check e-mail, load Web pages, and so on. The key ingredient in this equation is a Bluetooth-equipped phone. More on that later.

FIGURE 10-1   If your cell phone has a Bluetooth radio, you might be able to use it as a wireless modem for your Palm.

■ **Link to a cell phone and headset**   You know those people who look like they're talking to themselves? Some of them actually are, sure, but an increasing number are carrying on phone conversations. They reason they look crazy is that you can't see the Bluetooth headset clipped to their ears. These nifty gizmos let you keep your phone in your pocket while making and taking calls, as the two devices are connected wirelessly. Where do Palms fit in? Instead of relying on your phone's clumsy, hard-to-read contact list for making calls, you can tap your way into your Palm's address book and dial just by tapping a contact's name. Of course, you still have to contend with looking like a geek, a crazy person, or both (Dave feels your pain), but once you get accustomed to this kind of convenience, it's hard to go back to the old way of doing things.

■ **Link to a hands-free car kit**   You can also use your PDA as the intermediary between your phone and a hands-free car kit like the Parrot EasyDrive (www.parrot.biz).

■ **Link to a GPS receiver**   Before you spend big bucks on an aftermarket GPS navigation system for your car, consider turning your Palm into one. Software like TomTom Navigator 5, when used with an inexpensive Bluetooth GPS receiver, can navigate you door-to-door, complete with voice prompts ("Turn left in 200 yards," etc.), points of interest, and so on. Rick has been using his Palm TX for this and it works splendidly. See Chapter 16 for more information on GPS solutions for your PDA.

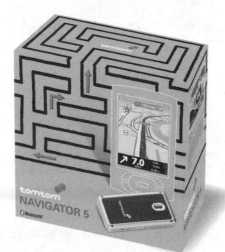

■ **Link to Bluetooth headphones**   As you'll learn in Chapter 14, your Palm can serve as a mighty fine jukebox. But you don't want to be tethered to your Palm with *wires*, do you? You can roam free (well, a few feet, anyway) with a set of Bluetooth headphones, the kind that are becoming popular with iPod users. All you need is a program called Softick Audio Gateway (www.softick.com), which enables your Palm to "stream" audio to Bluetooth headphones. See Chapter 16 for more information on accessories like these.

■ **Play games with other Palm users**   In the "old" days, two Palm users wanting head-to-head gaming action had to rely on their devices' infrared ports—and hope that the ambient light wasn't so bright as to interfere with the connection. With Bluetooth, a pair of players can sit comfortably, several feet apart, and compete in games like Monopoly and Scrabble.

10

■ **Swap data with other Palm users**   Speaking of infrared, in other chapters we've talked about beaming data from one handheld to another via their IR ports. You can accomplish the same thing via a Bluetooth connection between handhelds. However, you have to go through the extra steps of pairing the devices first, which makes this a less practical option than regular old beaming.

■ **Print wirelessly**   There aren't many Bluetooth-equipped printers out there, but if you can find one, you can print memos, calendar entries, Documents To Go documents, and more—no wires required.

TIP   *Want to make your printer wireless? Products like the Belkin Bluetooth Wireless USB Printer Adapter and D-Link Bluetooth USB Printer Adapter plug into your printer's USB port (in the case the name didn't clue you in to that fact) and turn it into a Bluetooth device. Now you can print from your Palm!*

Cool stuff, huh? Now let's talk about a few things you *can't* do with Bluetooth:

■ **Connect directly to the Internet**   There's no such thing as a "Bluetooth hotspot." Well, okay, that's not entirely true. You can actually buy a Bluetooth Access Point, like Belkin's F8T030 Bluetooth Access Point, which, if you connect it to your home computer network, lets Bluetooth PDAs connect to the Internet kinda like Wi-Fi. But honestly, there are more *Joey* fan clubs than Bluetooth Access Points. As you'll discover, Wi-Fi is much better for that. Read on to find out more.

■ **HotSync wirelessly**   Actually, this *is* possible, but it's neither easy nor convenient. For starters, few computers have Bluetooth radios, so you'd probably have to install third-party hardware if you wanted to enable Bluetooth HotSyncs. Even then, Bluetooth's limited range (about 30 feet) would force you stay close to your PC. But the bigger issue is configuration. We've never been able to successfully HotSync via Bluetooth, despite our incredibly high IQs and immeasurable modesty. In our minds, it's a hassle, and it just ain't worth it.

> TIP
>
> *You can learn more about your Palm's Bluetooth capabilities (and get instructions on setting up Bluetooth HotSyncs—but, trust us, it won't work) at Palm's support site: www.palm.com/us/support/bluetooth.*

Connect Your PDA to Your Cell Phone

Ready to use your cell phone as a wireless modem for your PDA? Here's what you need to get started:

- A Bluetooth-equipped Palm like the TX, Tungsten E2, or LifeDrive.

- A compatible Bluetooth-equipped GSM or GPRS cell phone (check the instruction manual if you're not sure your phone has this capability). Which phones are compatible? Check Palm's Web site (www.palm.com/us/support/bluetooth) for a list. Even if your model isn't on the list, it's pretty likely to work.

- A phone subscription plan that includes data services. Check with your carrier (Cingular, T-Mobile, etc.); you might have to pay a few dollars extra per month if data services aren't part of your current plan.

- VersaMail, the e-mail program that's included with most Palm handhelds.

- A Web browser. Most Palm handhelds come with one called Blazer.

> NOTE
>
> *To take advantage of your phone as a wireless modem, you might need to download and install a software update for your Palm. Head to this Web site to see if there's an update required for your model: http://tinyurl.com/gzj6.*

10

Pairing Your Palm and Phone

With those items in place, your first step is to *pair* your PDA with your cell phone. Pairing is the act of establishing a link between two Bluetooth devices. Specifically, you're going to designate your PDA and phone as a *trusted pair*, meaning whenever one tries to communicate with the other, they'll automatically get the go-ahead.

The latest Palm models (such as the Tungsten E2, TX, and LifeDrive) make it very easy to pair devices. Here's how to do it on a Palm TX; your model may have slightly different screens, but the overall process should be nearly identical.

1. On your phone, turn on Bluetooth and make the phone discoverable. You might have to consult the phone's manual for instructions on how to do this, because the people that make phone interfaces used to design the nuclear reactor control panels in Soviet submarines.

2. On your Palm, tap the Bluetooth icon in the status bar at the bottom of the screen (it looks like a really jangly, angular B) and then tap Prefs.

3. Tap Setup Devices.

4. On the Setup Devices screen, tap Phone Setup.

5. Select Phone Connection and follow the wizard to establish a connection between your Palm and your phone. Along the way your Palm will ask you to create a 4-digit passkey. Create it, then enter it on your phone when prompted.

6. Continue to follow the prompts in selecting your network service (such as Motorola or Cingular).

That's all there is to it!

Making the Bluetooth Connection

Now that your phone and PDA are paired, you need to finish the job by configuring the handheld to actually connect to the Internet so you can surf the Web or check e-mail. Depending upon

Understanding Passkeys

Upon connecting your Palm to any Bluetooth device, you're very likely to be asked for a passkey—an alphanumeric code that's essentially a password designed to keep unauthorized users from connecting to your devices. Sometimes you get to make up the key, such as when you connect your Palm to a phone. Sometimes, such as when you're connecting to a gadget like headphones that doesn't have any sort of keypad for entering numbers, the key already exists. Not sure what the passkey is for a particular device? Look in the device's user manual. If it's not handy, try '0000' or '1234' (without the apostrophes), the most common passkeys.

which model you have, this can sometimes be a major pain in the beehive. The Palm devices that include Phone Link do this step for you automatically. Just go to the Bluetooth icon in the status bar, tap Setup Devices, and follow the wizard. If you have a less cooperative PDA, however, you might need to call your mobile phone service provider (like Cingular, Verizon, or Sprint) and get some important bits of information before you can proceed.

Do this: Call them up and explain to the tech support operator that you are setting up a Palm OS PDA and need to be told how to configure it for Internet access. The tech folks will give you some essential bits of information, including:

- Username
- Password
- Phone number or access string

Use the info they give you to finish your setup. When you're done, you'll have a working Bluetooth connection to your mobile phone, and you're just an e-mail program away from checking messages on the go.

10

Where to Find Help with Your PDA/Phone Connection

We'll be the first to admit it: Creating a successful PDA-to-phone link isn't always easy. There are lots of variables that can gum up the works: Bluetooth's persnickety nature, Palm's cryptic network settings, the huge number of different phone models out there, and on and on. If you can't get connected using the steps outlined here, you have three options. First, you can call Palm for help. Second, you can call your carrier for help. Third, you can turn to other users who have been down a similar road and come up with a solution. We highly recommend the latter option, as we usually get much better results from fellow Palm owners than we do from know-nothing tech support reps. Visit the Wireless forum at 1src.com, create a new message (you might have to register first), and describe in detail the equipment you own and the problems you're having. Chances are good the whip-smart users there will help you resolve the issue. At the same time, try posting messages at Brighthand.com and PalmInfocenter.com. There are lots of smart users at those locations, too.

What to Do After You've Established the Link

Now that your phone and PDA are making sweet, sweet wireless music together, you can use your PDA for e-mail, Web browsing, instant messaging, and more. To learn about these and other applications, skip ahead to the sections titled E-Mail on Your PDA, Web Browsing on Your PDA, and ... well, you get the idea.

All About Wi-Fi

If you're lucky enough to own a Palm Tungsten C, LifeDrive, or TX, you can experience firsthand the joys of Wi-Fi on a PDA. Rick, for instance, will often use his TX for a quick e-mail check when he's roving around the house (or, more likely, sitting on the couch). And that's the beauty of Wi-Fi: As long as there's a network in range, you can enjoy fast and easy Internet access. You can also wirelessly HotSync your Palm, though only when you're connected to the same network as your PC.

> **TIP** *If you own a Tungsten E2, T3, or T5 or Zire 72, you can take advantage of Palm's $99 Wi-Fi Card. Just pop it into your handheld's SD slot to add instant Wi-Fi. Just one catch: You have to remove your memory card, meaning you can't have both Wi-Fi and extra storage. Sigh ... If only Palm had been smart enough to equip those models with Wi-Fi in the first place.*

Enable Wi-Fi on Your Device

The Wi-Fi radio in your Palm is either on or off. To turn it on, do the following:

1. Tap the Wi-Fi icon in the toolbar.

2. In the window that appears, tap next to where it says Wi-Fi and choose On.

3. Tap the Connect button—but only if you're already set to connect to a known network. If not, read on to learn about finding Wi-Fi hotspots.

Now check your e-mail, hit the Web, send an instant message, and all that good stuff.

Finding Hotspots

The only thing more important than having a Wi-Fi radio in your Palm is being near a Wi-Fi *hotspot.* Otherwise there's nothing for your Palm to connect to. Most Wi-Fi networks have a range of about 300 feet, which is why they tend to be localized in places like homes and coffee shops. Of course, now that entire cities are adding Wi-Fi networks, you may be able to find connectivity just about anywhere you go.

To see if there's an open network in the vicinity, do this:

1. Tap the Wi-Fi icon in the toolbar, then turn Wi-Fi on as described in the previous section.

2. Tap the Scan button. With any luck, you'll see one or more networks listed. Find one that doesn't have a padlock next to it (indicating that it's a closed, password-protected hotspot), tap it, and then click Connect.

3. If your Palm cannot connect to that network, pick another one and try again. Maybe the signal was too weak, or the network had some other kind of protections.

You might need to perform one additional step. Some public Wi-Fi hotspots, like those found in libraries and Panera Bread bakeries, require you to agree to their terms of use before you can start surfing or checking e-mail. To do this, fire up the Blazer Web browser. The first page that loads will likely be the network's welcome page. Read the instructions and tap whatever "I Agree" button is presented. From there you should be able to surf and e-mail normally.

NOTE   *Finding an open hotspot is no guarantee that you'll be able to get online. Hotels, for instance, have notoriously flaky networks, and we've had trouble connecting to them on several occasions. The harsh reality is that PDAs are not PCs, and sometimes you just might not be able to connect to a hotspot, even if it's free and public. As the French have been known to say,* sacre bleu!

10

> TIP
>
> *After you disconnect from a Wi-Fi network, your Palm's Wi-Fi radio remains on. This just drains the battery, so remember to manually turn Wi-Fi off when you're done with your online activities.*

Plan Ahead: Find Hotspots on the Road

You can't always count on finding a hotspot, so it pays to plan ahead, especially if you're traveling. Say you're headed to lovely Colorado Springs for the weekend (you couldn't have chosen a better vacation spot). Wouldn't it be great if you had a list of hotspots so you could quickly find Internet access when you need it?

Head to JiWire (www.jiwire.com) and you can find just such a list. As shown in Figure 10-2, this Web site lets you input a city or ZIP code, then gives you a list of free and fee-based hotspots, complete with addresses, maps, and driving directions. Print the results page and you're good to go!

> TIP
>
> *JiWire is also available as an AvantGo channel (see "Channel Surfing with AvantGo" later in this chapter), meaning you can find hotspots right on your Palm. Of course, you have to be connected to a network for the search to work, so you still need to plan ahead a bit.*

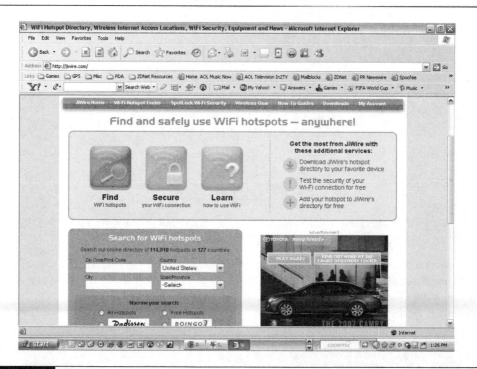

 FIGURE 10-2 At JiWire, you can find a list of hotspots, free and otherwise, for any city or ZIP code.

Create Your Own Hotspot

If you have broadband Internet access your home (via a cable or DSL modem), you can easily turn your entire house into a hotspot, one accessible not just from your Palm, but also from desktop and notebook PCs that have Wi-Fi capabilities. All you need is an inexpensive wireless router, which plugs into your modem and PC. We recommend a router based on 802.11g technology, which you can pick up for as little as $25. We've had good luck with the Netgear WGR614, though just about any model will do.

After you get your router up and running, use your Palm's scan feature to detect and connect to the new network. Presto! You should have speedy Internet access in the Palm of your hand. (Can you believe this is the first time we've made that awful pun? Just goes to show how much restraint we have, pun-wise.)

TIP   *To discourage neighbors and passers-by from "stealing" wireless Internet access from you (and possibly even hacking into your PC), you should password-protect your router. Read the manual to learn how to enable its security features. From there you'll need to enter that password on your Palm, but only the first time it tries to connect.*

Wi-Fi HotSyncs   If you have a Wi-Fi network set up in your home or office, you can use it to HotSync your Palm wirelessly. And trust us: Once you've done it, you'll never go back to syncing with a cradle or cable.

Before you learn how, there are a few considerations:

- Your desktop or notebook PC must be on and connected to the network (it doesn't matter if it's a wired or wireless connection).

- Your Palm must be connected to the same network as your PC. In other words, you can't get online at, say, Panera Bread and HotSync to your home PC.

- If you've enabled WEP or WPA security on your router, you'll need to enter the password on your Palm (that's if you haven't already entered it as discussed in the previous section).

So, how do you configure your PDA and PC for Wi-Fi HotSyncs? Palm has published very good instructions, so rather than reinvent the wheel, we invite you to access the online directions at http://tinyurl.com/7uptz.

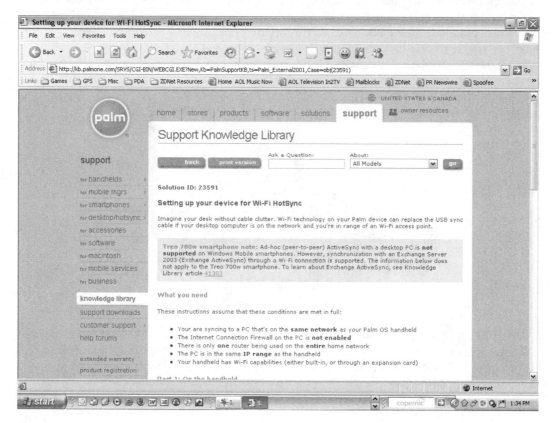

NOTE

Depending on how your home network is configured, your PC occasionally might inherit a different IP address than the one you entered into your Palm. That means subsequent Wi-Fi HotSyncs won't be successful, because the Palm will continue to look for your PC at the old address. You can remedy this by starting the HotSync applet on your Palm, making sure Network is selected, and then tapping the little arrow beneath the large HotSync icon. Tap Select PC and follow the instructions to reconnect with your PC.

Hotspots: Free or Fee?

Not all hotspots are free. Walk into any Starbucks, for instance, and you'll see signs touting T-Mobile HotSpot access—for a price. (That's why we get our coffee at Panera Bread, where Wi-Fi is free.) We think you should pay for Wi-Fi only when it's an emergency, like you desperately need to receive an e-mail or check NCAA basketball scores. Usually it's much more economical

Did you know?

You Can Beam Data to Your Phone

Here's a little-known secret about many cell phones—well, those that have infrared ports, anyway. Many IR-equipped phones can receive contact info beamed from your handheld, and can also beam their own address book entries to your handheld. Although you're limited to sending one contact at a time, this can be a timesaving way to transfer important phone numbers into your phone (much quicker than entering them manually). Consult your phone's instruction manual for information on beaming (it's a little different on each phone). We've tested this on Nokia and Sony Ericsson phones, and it works like a charm. On the Sony Ericsson T68i, for instance, just turn on the phone's IR port in the Connections prefs, and then beam. The phone receives the address info automatically and files it in its own phone list.

to pay for data services on your phone (which usually costs only $4-5 per month) and use the Internet connection method described earlier in this chapter. T-Mobile HotSpot access costs $9.95 for a one day password or $29.95 for unlimited use. That's pretty steep for something you can get free up the street!

Wi-Fi Security

When you connect to a public hotspot, all the data that's sent and received from your PDA—e-mails, instant messages, files, and the like—floats around the ether for anyone to intercept. If you use your PDA for business purposes, you might want to protect sensitive information. In that case, consider using a Virtual Private Network, or VPN.

Basically, a VPN routes your Internet connection through a private, protected "tunnel." There are several VPN programs available for Palm handhelds. Visit www.palm.com/us/wireless/vpn for details, and see if you can get your company to foot the bill for the software. After all, it's their precious data you're protecting.

E-Mail on Your PDA

It's hard to remember life before e-mail, isn't it? Imagine, having to actually pick up the *phone* every time you wanted to communicate with someone. Now we just fire off e-mail messages.

Most Palm handhelds come with an e-mail program called VersaMail. Once you've configured it to access your mail account(s), all you have to do is establish an Internet connection (via Bluetooth, Wi-Fi, or whatever) and you can send and receive messages right on your handheld.

10

Why not just use your data-enabled cell phone for e-mail? For starters, we're willing to bet it has a much smaller screen than your Palm. What's more, using a telephone keypad to compose text is like trying to pull a sock onto a wet foot. In comparison, writing on a Palm is a breeze, and much faster to boot.

What if your Palm has no wireless capabilities to speak of, meaning it can't connect directly to the Internet? VersaMail still has you covered—in a way. The program can send and receive e-mail when you HotSync, leveraging your PC's Internet connection for the actual receipt and transmission of messages. For instance, suppose you want to write Dave a love letter, but you're nowhere near your PC. Just compose the e-mail on your Palm, then HotSync when you get back to your desk. The letter will get sent via your computer's mail program. On the flip side, VersaMail can copy all newly received mail to your Palm so you can read and reply on the go. Cool, huh? In fact, while we're on the subject, let's take a look at some of the programs VersaMail can sync with:

- Microsoft Exchange ActiveSync (used for many corporate e-mail systems)
- Microsoft Outlook
- Microsoft Outlook Express
- Eudora
- Lotus Notes (local databases only)
- Domino server mail

Other noteworthy VersaMail features include:

- Support for multiple POP and IMAP e-mail accounts.
- Support for AOL and Yahoo e-mail.
- Support for attachments: you can send and receive them.
- Support for HTML e-mail (meaning messages that have fonts, photos, graphics, and other visual elements).
- Automated message retrieval—the software can check for and download new messages at scheduled times.

Needless to say, VersaMail does just about everything a PDA user could want. It's very easy to configure and use, especially if you have version 3.0 or later, which comes with the LifeDrive, TX, and Treo. Once again, we don't want to reinvent the wheel; you can find excellent VersaMail setup instructions in the Getting Started guide that's included with your Palm.

Of course, we're here to turn you into a power user. Once you've got VersaMail set up for your e-mail account(s), you should familiarize yourself with the program's options, which are accessible by tapping Menu | Options | Preferences. You'll see the following screen:

Let's take a look inside Preferences and how these options can affect your VersaMail experience.

- **Display** Also accessible by tapping the Display button when viewing your list of mail, this setting lets you modify various aspects of the VersaMail display. Choosing "1 line view," for instance, fits more messages on the screen at once, but shows you only the subject. "2 line view" shows both the subject and sender, but you see fewer messages at a time. This is also the place to choose a font and font size. We recommend Gill Sans MT 6, which is the smallest available size—it lets us cram the most amount of info onscreen.

■ **Auto Sync** Check the "Sync automatically" box and you'll see settings you can adjust for automatic e-mail retrieval. Set the days, times, and frequency you want, and then tap Alerts if you want your Palm to beep (or vibrate, if it has that option) when new mail arrives.

■ **Reply Options** Want your replies to include the text of the original message? Want the recipient to see a different reply-to address? This is the screen to set these options. You can also check "Always BCC a copy to:" if you want to have "blind" (i.e., secret) copies of your replies sent to another e-mail address.

■ **Server** By default, VersaMail will retrieve only copies of your messages, leaving the original messages on the server so you can still retrieve them normally via your PC. You can uncheck this option if you don't want your Palm to leave mail on the server. Likewise, if you want e-mail to be deleted from the server after you delete it from VersaMail, check the corresponding box.

VersaMail Folders

By default, VersaMail offers the usual selection of e-mail folders: Inbox, Outbox, Drafts, Sent, and Trash. You can see the contents of these folders by tapping the arrow in the top-right corner of the screen and selecting the desired folder:

Notice the option at the bottom of the list: Edit Folders. Tap it and you'll see this screen:

This works exactly like the Edit Categories option (used to organize applications) discussed in Chapter 3. Tap New to create a new folder, Rename to rename one, and Delete—oh, come on, you don't need us to explain *that* one, do you? Ah, but why aren't Inbox, Outbox, and all the other existing categories listed here? Simple: They can't be modified.

So let's create a new folder called Business. Tap New, input the folder name, and then tap OK. Tap OK again and you're back at the main VersaMail screen. How do you move one or more e-mails to the new folder? Like this:

1. While viewing your Inbox, tap the little circle next to a message. You'll see a checkmark appear.

2. Repeat this if you want to move more than one message at a time.

3. Tap Menu | Message | Move To...

4. Choose the Business folder, and then tap OK.

E-Mail Client	Where to Find It	Features
Aileron Mail— Personal Access	www.corsoft.com	This outstanding e-mail client provides access to just about any kind of e-mail: corporate, AOL, Hotmail—you name it. Plus, it has robust support for attachments. Good stuff if you need something a bit more powerful than VersaMail.
GlimmerMail	www.sunroomsoft.com	A Palm e-mail program designed specifically for accessing Hotmail and MSN accounts.
SnapperMail	www.snappermail.com	Our favorite third-party e-mail client, SnapperMail has a great interface and can easily handle a wide variety of attachments thanks to "plug-in" applications. It can display JPEG images and comes with SplashPhoto 4, a popular photo viewer.

TABLE 10-2   E-mail Clients for Your PDA

What happens if you're actually reading an e-mail and want to move it to a specific folder without returning to the Inbox? Just tap Menu | Options | Move To... and follow the same procedure. Of course, this works for only one message at a time.

> **TIP** *The aforementioned method of putting checkmarks next to multiple messages can also be used for other functions. For instance, you can tap Menu | Message and then choose Mark Read or Delete. The selected messages will be marked or deleted accordingly.*

E-Mail Alternatives

You don't have to stick with the e-mail client that comes with your PDA. There are several alternatives available, Most of which are commercial applications that cost a small amount of money. Table 10-2 lists some of the best options currently available.

Accessing America Online

At last count, America Online (AOL) had something like 70 billion subscribers. Okay, we might be off by a few billion, but there's no debating the popularity of the service. With AOL for Palm, you can access your e-mail account(s) and some of the service's more popular areas: file cabinet, instant messaging, buddy lists, and so on. Get it from within AOL at keyword Anywhere, or on the Web at mobile1.aol.com (click the AOL for PDAs link to find the appropriate software for your handheld).

There are several different versions of the AOL software, all priced at $19.95. Keep in mind that you must already have an AOL account to use the Palm OS version of the software:

- ■ **AOL 3.1 for Palm** This version is for models with any version of Palm OS 3.52 through 4.x (the *x* being any number).
- ■ **AOL 3.2 for Palm OS 5.x** This version is for models with Palm OS 5.0 and later.
- ■ **AOL 3.3 for Treo 650** At press time we weren't able to determine if this version would also work with the Treo 700p, but rest assured Palm will have a compatible version before long.

Web Browsing on Your PDA

Web browsing? On a PDA?! Bwa ha ha ha ha ha ha ha ha ha ha, don't be ridiculous. Viewing Web pages squished into a tiny screen is no one's idea of a good time. Except Dave's. He's happy as long as he has access to his many Britney Spears fan sites. Actually, there are times when Web access comes in mighty handy, regardless of screen size. News, stock reports, movie times, sports scores, blog access. You don't want to walk around without all this stuff, do you?

The latest Palm models come with a Web browser called Blazer. It's fairly powerful, with desirable features like bookmarks, cookies, VPN support (so you can access your company's Virtual Private Network, if it has one), file downloading, multiple views, and so on. Don't expect to watch streaming video in Blazer, but it's more than qualified for most everyday Web tasks.

Let's take a look at Blazer's toolbar so you can get familiar with the program's operation:

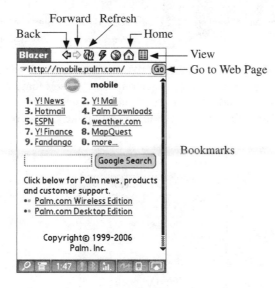

- ■ **Back**   Just like your regular browser's Back button, tapping this takes you back to the previous page.

- ■ **Forward**   Just like your regular browser's Forward button, tapping this takes you forward one page.

- ■ **Refresh**   Tap here to reload the current page

■ **View**   Tap here to switch between Blazer's two views: Optimized (which fits everything to the width of the screen) and Wide Page (which retains the Web site's original proportions—and forces you to scroll horizontally in addition to vertically). In some versions of Blazer, this option has been replaced with Fast mode/Normal mode. Fast mode strips all images, thus enabling pages to load faster.

■ **Go to Web page**   Although you can type Web addresses into Blazer's address bar, it's faster to enter them here. Tap "www." to automatically insert that important prefix. Then enter the main part of the address (such as "yahoo") and tap ".com" to insert the suffix. That's a lot less writing than you'd need to do writing the full address manually.

■ **Home**   Tap here to immediately return to the Home page specified in Preferences (Menu | Options | Preferences).

■ **Bookmarks** Blazer's bookmarks let you quickly surf to your favorite sites. As you'll see, Blazer comes with a handful of bookmarks already set up. To add a new one, tap an empty square, then input the name, description (this part's optional), and address of the site. Tap Use Current if you want the site you're currently viewing to become this bookmark.

TIP   *If your Palm didn't come with Blazer, there's a third-party browser that's almost as good: Xiino (www.mobirus.com). It's not quite as pretty as Blazer and it'll set you back $25, but it definitely gets the job done.*

Palm-Friendly Web Sites

Remember how we were griping about how Web pages don't generally fit well on a PDA's smallish screen? Well, some sites are designed specifically for phones, PDAs, and other diminutive devices. Here's a list of sites you might want to bookmark:

- **Amazon (www.amazon.com/mcommerce)** So you're listening to NPR and hear about this really cool book. By the time you get home, you'll have forgotten the name—maybe even the book itself. Don't wait! Just head to Amazon's PDA-friendly site and order right from your Palm.

- **Google (www.google.com/pda)** All the glories of the Google search engine shrunk down to PDA size.

■ **MapQuest (www.mapquest.com/pda)**   Need maps or driving directions? This stripped-down version of the mega-popular MapQuest gives you just the essentials.

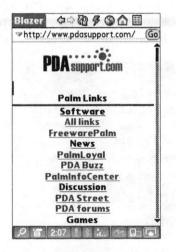

■ **PDASupport.com (www.pdasupport.com)**   Links to several dozen PDA-friendly Web sites.

10

Other Ways to Web

Web access isn't limited to Web browsers. Let's take a look at some cool Web-enabled apps that are a bit more specialized:

■ **AvantGo**   We love AvantGo's ability to download content from the Internet and store it for "offline" reading anytime we like (see "Channel Surfing with AvantGo" later in this chapter). But AvantGo is a rudimentary Web browser in its own right, so once you install it, you can surf with it as well. It's definitely one of our all-time favorites, and it's free.

■ **Mobileplay** Designed to bring Web content to your PDA, Mobileplay is kind of like AvantGo, but prettier. The browser-like applet provides up-to-date information from channels like BusinessWeek, Gizmodo (one of our favorite tech blogs), PC World, The Weather Channel, and the infamous Wonkette blog. Like AvantGo, Mobileplay can fetch updates wirelessly or when you HotSync with your PC. At press time, Mobileplay was undergoing beta testing and was free for users to try out.

■ **MobiTV** TV on your Palm? Yep, it's possible, though with a few limitations. The MobiTV service works with the LifeDrive, TX, and Treo 600/650/700p. It comes with about a dozen channels, including Comedy Time, ESPN, Toon World Classics, and Fox News (which some of us would pay extra *not* to have). MobiTV costs $9.99 per month.

■ **Pocket Express** Designed with Treos in mind (but compatible with any Palm that can connect to the Internet), Pocket Express provides free access to customized news, sports, and weather. By upgrading to the subscription version of the service (which costs $6.99

per month or $69.90 per year), you get lots more data: street maps, driving directions, movie times, portfolio tracking, expanded news, and business/residential phone and address lookups. But before you pay for this admittedly polished service, we recommend trying AvantGo and/or Mobileplay, which offer a lot of the same info for free.

Channel Surfing with AvantGo

Let's face it: The Web wasn't designed to fit on a three-inch screen. That's why we love AvantGo (www.avantgo.com), a free service that not only delivers Web-based content to your Palm, but also formats it to look pretty (and readable). With every HotSync, the software downloads your preselected channels—everything from news and stock reports to driving directions and movie showtimes—using your computer's modem to ferry the data. Pretty slick, and did we mention it's free? You get 3MB of content. That can be up to a dozen channels, depending upon how much data is included in each. Want more? You can upgrade to 8MB of AvantGo service for $20/year.

Setting Up AvantGo

To install the AvantGo software, visit the AvantGo Web site at www.avantgo.com and download the software. Install it using the directions that come with AvantGo and configure your AvantGo account, which you'll need to set up complete with username and password.

FIGURE 10-3   AvantGo lets you transfer Web "channels" to your Palm for offline reading.

NOTE   *AvantGo is included on the installation CD-ROM with some devices, but you're better off visiting the AvantGo site and installing the newest software, because it is occasionally updated with new features.*

To set up the channels you want to transfer to your PDA, go to the AvantGo Web site and log in. The AvantGo site should look something like the one shown in Figure 10-3, in which your currently selected channels appear on the left in a column called My Channels. You can browse the AvantGo Web site and click any channel you'd like to add to your personal AvantGo hotlist.

Editing Your Channel Content

Most AvantGo channels are configured to work well on a handheld device with limited memory. Sometimes you might want to customize the way channel content is delivered to your PDA, though. Take *The Onion,* for instance. Dave loves to read this news parody Web site each week while eating lunch, but the site is so large that many of the stories often aren't downloaded to the PDA in their entirety. The solution? Dave increased the Maximum Channel Size from the default of 100 KB to 500 KB so it all fits on his Palm. To edit your channels as cleverly as Dave, open the AvantGo Web page, log in, and click a channel in the My Device tab. You should see the Edit Personal Channel page, as shown in Figure 10-4. Make your changes and click the Save Channel button.

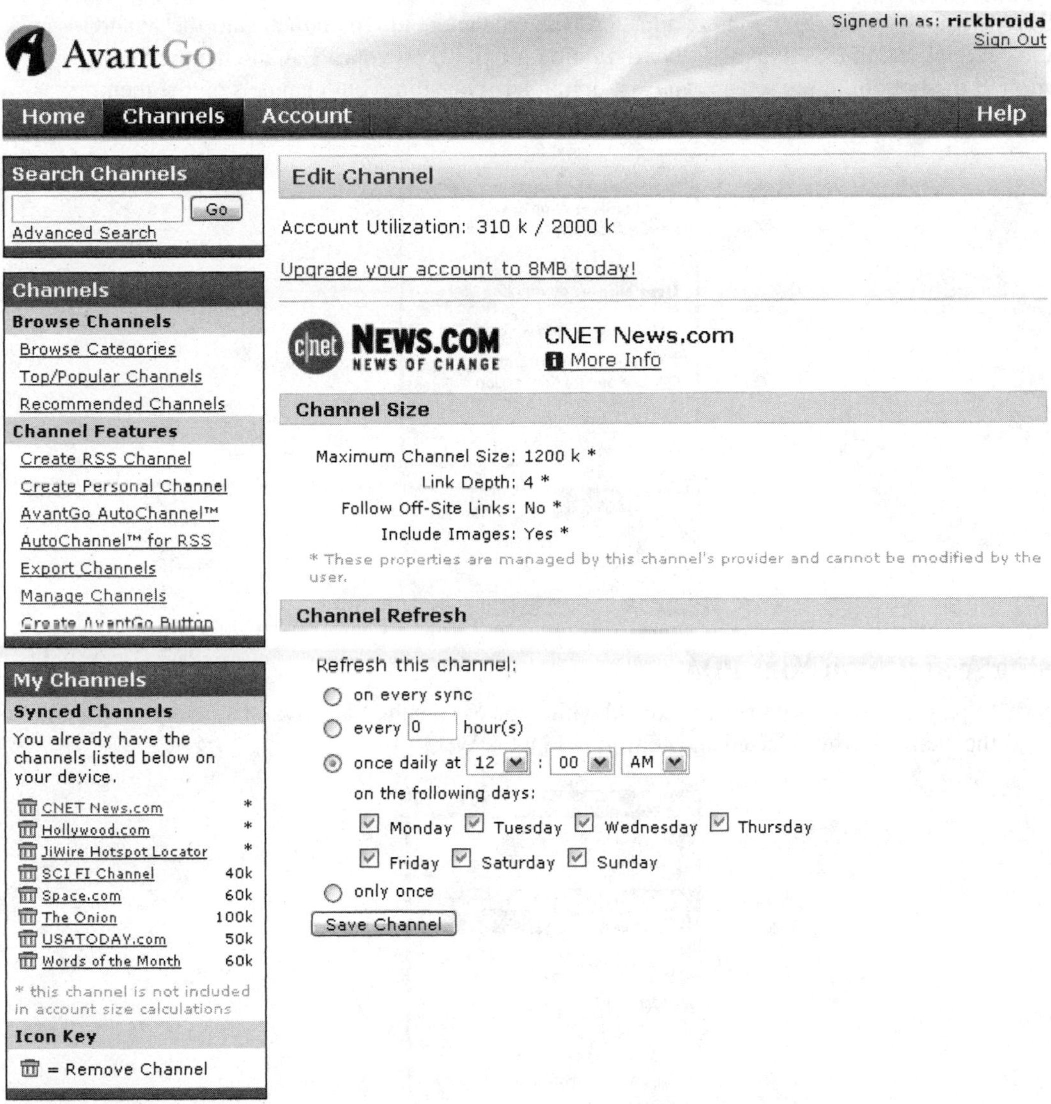

Signed in as: **rickbroida**
Sign Out

AvantGo

| Home | Channels | Account | | Help |

Search Channels

[_____] [Go]
Advanced Search

Channels

Browse Channels
Browse Categories
Top/Popular Channels
Recommended Channels

Channel Features
Create RSS Channel
Create Personal Channel
AvantGo AutoChannel™
AutoChannel™ for RSS
Export Channels
Manage Channels
Create AvantGo Button

My Channels

Synced Channels

You already have the channels listed below on your device.

🗑 CNET News.com	*
🗑 Hollywood.com	*
🗑 JiWire Hotspot Locator	*
🗑 SCI FI Channel	40k
🗑 Space.com	60k
🗑 The Onion	100k
🗑 USATODAY.com	50k
🗑 Words of the Month	60k

* this channel is not included in account size calculations

Icon Key

🗑 = Remove Channel

Edit Channel

Account Utilization: 310 k / 2000 k

Upgrade your account to 8MB today!

CNET News.com
NEWS.COM CNET News.com
NEWS OF CHANGE ℹ More Info

Channel Size

Maximum Channel Size: 1200 k *
Link Depth: 4 *
Follow Off-Site Links: No *
Include Images: Yes *

* These properties are managed by this channel's provider and cannot be modified by the user.

Channel Refresh

Refresh this channel:

○ on every sync
○ every [0___] hour(s)
◉ once daily at [12 ▾] : [00 ▾] [AM ▾]
   on the following days:
   ☑ Monday ☑ Tuesday ☑ Wednesday ☑ Thursday
   ☑ Friday ☑ Saturday ☑ Sunday
○ only once

[Save Channel]

10

FIGURE 10-4 You can modify the amount of data contained in each channel from this page.

Low on internal memory? You can store your 2 MB or so of AvantGo channels on your PDA's memory card, preserving precious RAM in the handheld. To do that, start the AvantGo Connect application (it's AvantGo's configuration program) on your PDA and tap the Settings button at the bottom of the screen. The last option lets you store your channels on the memory card.

Using AvantGo on Your PDA

Ready to read some news on your handheld while you eat lunch? Start AvantGo and you should see all the channels you selected and configured on the Web.

NOTE *If you don't see any channels in AvantGo, it's probably because you haven't HotSynced yet.*

To use AvantGo, just tap on one of the channels in the My Channels list. You can read text, view pictures, and drill deeper into the channel by tapping on links. There are several navigational tools built into AvantGo, as described here:

- ■ Tap the navigational arrows to move forward and backward through the current channel.

- ■ Tap the Home icon to return to the My Channels list.

- ■ AvantGo also let you navigate using whatever special navigation controls are on your PDA, such as the Navigator on Tungsten models.

In addition to reading cached channels on your Palm, AvantGo can also be used to open live Web pages if you have a modem attached. To do that, perform the following steps:

1. Start AvantGo.

2. Choose Channels | Work Online from the menu. This tells AvantGo to activate your modem.

3. Choose Channels | Open Page from the menu. Enter the URL you would like to visit and tap OK.

NOTE *AvantGo isn't your only option. Some users prefer HandStory or Plucker (available at PalmGear.com, of course).*

10

Instant Messaging

For those times when a phone call or e-mail just won't satisfy your communication needs, you can always fall back on instant messaging. Admittedly, it's not our idea of a good time, as writing out your messages is slow going, even if you have a keyboard-equipped smartphone like the Treo. But if you're online and want the capability, it's there for the asking.

There are several instant-messaging programs available for Palm handhelds, but there's one we think is head and shoulders above the rest: Causerie Unified Messenger for AIM/Yahoo/MSN/Jabber/Google Talk (see Figure 10-5). Yes, it's a mouthful, but at least the name tells you which instant-messaging services the program supports. It also provides "bots," which leverage your IM accounts to fetch news, weather reports, stock prices, and so on.

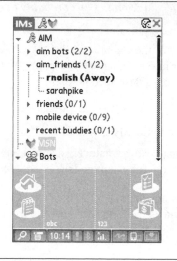

FIGURE 10-5 Causerie Unified Messenger supports just about every popular instant-messaging service.

Making the Most of Your Treo

If you own a Treo 650 or 700p, count yourself lucky. These smartphones rank among the top products in their class, and with good reason. They're not only great phones, they're also equipped with the venerable Palm Operating System, meaning they can run the vast majority of programs we've discussed in this book, and a host of programs we haven't discussed. Indeed, let's take a look at some Treo-specific software. Don't leave home without these killer apps, all of which can be found on Handango and/or PalmGear:

> **TIP** *Looking for a good online hangout where you can read reviews of Treo-related gear and interact with other Treo users? Start with TreoCentral (www.treocentral.com), which also has a store where you can buy a wide variety of Treo accessories.*

■ **Butler**   A collection of several handy utilities, Butler includes an alarm clock, an "attention grabber" (which lets you know about received calls, voicemail messages, SMS messages, and so on), an application launcher (you can start any program just by holding down a button), and improved control over the volume buttons (using them to scroll pages of text or switch back and forth between previously used applications). All in all, some darn good stuff, especially considering the $7.95 price tag.

■ **CallFilter**   Like a spam filter for your phone, CallFilter lets you allow or disallow calls based on phone number, name, company, and other criteria. Disallowed calls will go straight to your voicemail. This is great when you're in a meeting and don't want to be disturbed unless it's something critical. CallFilter also allows you to use MP3 files as ringtones, a way-cool feature. It costs $29.95.

■ **funSMS 4**   Your Treo comes with a fairly basic SMS (Short Message Service) applet, thus allowing you to send short text messages to other devices. funSMS 4 provides a much more attractive interface and a host of handy features. It's a must have for anyone who lives and dies by SMS. funSMS 4 costs $24.95.

■ **Pocket Tunes Deluxe**   You'll learn more about Pocket Tunes Deluxe in Chapter 14, but suffice it to say, this is the killer music app for Treo users. That's because it not only lets you play and manage MP3 and WMA files stored on your device, it also lets you wirelessly stream music from ShoutCast Internet radio stations. The program costs $27.95, and it's worth every penny, in our humble opinions.

10

■ **TapDial**   Wouldn't it be great if you could call someone just by tapping an icon? That's the idea behind TapDial, a $9.95 utility that effectively creates speed-dial buttons right in your Applications screen. (And here's a somewhat obvious tip: create a "Speed Dial" category so your phone icons stay separate from your apps, thus cutting down on icon clutter. See Chapter 2 if you need a refresher course in using categories.)

■ **VeriChat**   Like instant messaging? You'll love VeriChat, which makes it possible for you to hold real-time chat sessions with users on AOL, ICQ, MSN, and Yahoo networks. It supports multiple chat sessions, user alerts (meaning it can notify you when a particular user comes online), and even file exchanges. It also comes with a boatload of nifty emoticons—essential for any serious IM-er. VeriChat costs $24.95.

■ **Voice Dialer**   If there's one key feature the Treo sorely lacks, it's voice dialing. Wouldn't it be great if you could just say the name of the person you want to call? With Voice Dialer, a $19.95 program, you can. (Treo 600 users must install a firmware update in order to use this program. See Palm's Web site for details.)

■ **VolumeCare**   Many people (Rick included) find the Treo's volume to be seriously lacking. VolumeCare lets you increase the volume beyond what the hardware normally allows. Dozens of demerits to Palm for requiring a third-party utility to fix this annoying problem.

■ **WiFile**   Though it sounds like it has something to do with Wi-Fi, WiFile is actually designed for wireless access to files and folders stored on your desktop PC or company server. (For what it's worth, it supports any kind of wireless connection, Wi-Fi included. But where Treos are concerned, access comes via the cell network.) This proves mighty handy when you need to retrieve an essential file and you're nowhere near your PC. Cooler still, if you use WiFile in conjunction with Pocket Tunes, you can stream your entire MP3 library right to your Treo. We also recommend Avvenu, a similar program— and a freebie!—discussed in Chapter 12.

TIP   *At PalmGear.com, you can find a special section devoted to Treo software. Just look for the Treo Smartphones tab near the top of the home page, click it, and browse the items. This is by no means the only Treo-specific software available on the site. It's merely a collection of some of the more popular programs.*

Where to Find It

Web Site	Address	What's There
Aileron	www.corsoft.com	E-mail software
AOL	www.mobile1.aol.com	AOL software
AvantGo	www.avantgo.com	AvantGo
Brighthand	www.brighthand.com	News and information
Handango	www.handango.com	Huge selection of Palm OS software
PalmGear	www.palmgear.com	Huge selection of Palm OS software
PalmInfocenter	www.palminfocenter.com	News and information
SnapperMail	www.snappermail.com	E-mail software

Chapter 11

The Palm Office

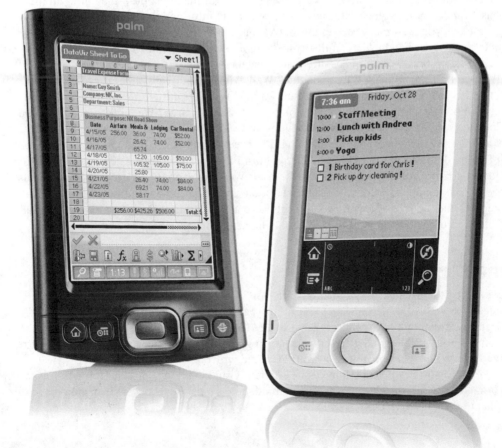

How to...

- ■ Use your Palm as a complete business application computer
- ■ Read and edit Word and Excel documents on your PDA
- ■ Distinguish between Palm Doc and Word .doc files
- ■ Import Palm documents into Microsoft Word
- ■ Generate graphs and charts on your PDA
- ■ View Adobe Acrobat files
- ■ Project PowerPoint slides via your handheld
- ■ Print to wireless printers
- ■ Print to serial and parallel printers

The core programs that come with your PDA are fine for many people—they offer all the basic functionality you need to stay on top of contact information and schedules while on the go. But, as you've already seen in this book, your PDA can do so much more. In fact, it's possible to use your handheld as a full-fledged alternative PC, capable of running applications as varied as a word processor, a spreadsheet, and a database program.

Why on Earth would you want to do that? Well, which would you rather carry around, a PDA that fits in your pocket or a seven-pound laptop? Which is easier to store in a hotel room? Which is more easily stolen? Which lasts longer on a single charge? We think you get the idea. Obviously, using a suite of "office" applications on your PDA isn't for everyone and won't work all the time. After all, your handheld has a lot less storage space than most laptops, so you can't fit a hard drive's worth of files on it. And most PDA-sized document editors don't support as wide an array of formatting options as Microsoft Word, so even if you exchange documents with your desktop apps, your text and format options might be somewhat limited. But, if you're intrigued by the thought of leaving your PC at home and traveling only with a PDA, then read on. This chapter is all about creating the perfect handheld office.

Building the Perfect Beast

No, we weren't really big fans of that '80s-era Don Henley solo album either. But that does describe your PDA if you want to outfit it to be a mobile office, complete with office applications. The name of the game when it comes to creating a handheld office is convenience and compatibility. What good is it, for instance, to generate documents on your Palm if they're not readable by the word processor on your PC? And why bother trying to do office-style work on your Palm if you can't do it easily, efficiently, and in all the apps and formats you're accustomed to on your desktop? With this in mind, here's a list of products you should have if you plan to do serious work on your PDA:

■ **Your PDA** Stock up on memory—lots of memory. Working with Word documents, databases, and spreadsheets soaks up memory, so you should invest in a PDA with plenty of memory or the capability to upgrade to more, or you might get stopped short. If you still have an old device that lacks an SD card slot, definitely consider upgrading to a modern device. Equipped with a large expansion card, you can store lots of files on your PDA without ever running out of memory. How much memory does your PDA have? Find out by tapping Menu | App | Info from the Home screen. You can then check how much free space is available on the Palm's main memory (called Device) and on the SD Card, if you have one inserted.

```
┌─────────────────────────────┐
│            Info             │
│ Device: ▼ Device            │
│ Free Space: 50.2M of 63.8M  │
│ ┌─────────────────────────┐ │
│ │ ▓▓▓▓▓                   │ │
│ ├─────────────────────────┤ │
│ │ Addit              26K ▲│ │
│ │ Addit Vault       910K  │ │
│ │ Address            27K  │ │
│ │ Adobe Reader      605K  │ │
│ │ BFViewer          104K  │ │
│ │ Bgnd Service       48K  │ │
│ │ Blazer Cookies      3K  │ │
│ │ Bluetooth Device…   4K  │ │
│ │ Bluetooth Library   4K  │ │
│ │ Bluetooth Prefs B…  4K  │ │
│ │ Calc                5K  │ │
│ │ Calendar           23K ▼│ │
│ └─────────────────────────┘ │
│ (Done) (Version Size Records)│
└─────────────────────────────┘
  🏠 🔍 📋  8:46  ⚙  🔲 🖥
```

■ **A keyboard** As much as we love Graffiti, the fact remains you'll hate writing long documents or entering more than few bits of data into a spreadsheet with the stylus alone. The solution? Invest in a portable keyboard. There are a lot of compact, yet comfortable keyboards available for Palm-powered PDAs; the Palm Universal Wireless Keyboard is one of our favorites. It works superbly with almost any Palm model in both portrait and landscape orientations. See Chapter 16 for a rundown of the best ones.

■ **Document reader** If you mainly need to read documents on your PDA and don't care about creating or editing them, then you can get by with a document reader such as Palm Reader (which lets you read electronic books), Picsel Proviewer, or RepliGo (both of which enable you to view everything from Word and Excel files to Adobe PDF documents). But what you probably want is a full-featured office application, or, in other words, a document editor. Which brings us to ...

■ **Office suite** If you want to create new documents or edit files you've already made in Microsoft Word, then a simple document reader won't be enough. You should try an office suite instead. Though these PDA applications are not quite full-featured suites—at least not in the sense that Microsoft Office on the desktop is—some programs deliver sophisticated tools such as spell checkers, rich text formatting, charting tools for your spreadsheet, and more. Most important, these programs break through the file-size limit imposed by the Memo Pad and let you edit documents of almost unlimited length that can be shared with Word and Excel.

11

- ■ **Adobe Acrobat** If your office makes extensive use of PDF files, you should have a program like Adobe Reader on your PDA so you can view those documents on the go.

- ■ **Database** Yes, database applications are available even for the Palm. There are a slew of popular programs available for your PDA that let you create new databases from scratch, and most even let you import existing databases from programs such as Access, FileMaker, and other ODBC-compliant applications. Some of the most popular database engines for the Palm include HanDBase, JFile, MobileDB, ThinkDB, and dbNow. FileMaker also has its own PDA "companion" to FileMaker, called (not too surprisingly) FileMaker Mobile. If you're a FileMaker user, FileMaker Mobile might be all you need.

Top Ten Reasons to Use a PDA

Dave: With all the really neat office-like applications available for handhelds, it got us thinking. What are the top ten reasons to use a handheld computer? So, here goes (and if you imagine us reading this off blue cards at your local book store, you've pretty much experienced a *How to Do Everything with Your Palm Handheld* book signing):

10. New excuse at work: I was writing the weekly status report, but I dropped it and it broke.

9. Something new to lose!

8. Makes you look like a spy.

7. It's smarter than your dog. Wait—that's also true of houseplants and silverware.

6a. As a "Star Trek: The Next Generation" fan, you like to pretend you're an Enterprise crewmember on an away mission.

6b. As a "Star Trek: The Original Series" fan, you like to pretend you're an Enterprise crewmember in a landing party.

You know, for me, the funny thing is you have to be a "Star Trek" fan to even appreciate the difference between those last two items.

Rick: For me, it's funny to hear Dave describe any of his half of the list as "funny."

5. Gives you a great pickup line: "Hey, let's HotSync!"

4. When tipping the pizza guy, now you can calculate 15 percent of $36.87 to the exact penny.

3. No one can tell you're reading trashy romance novels (Dave has a thing for those).

2. You can look busy in a board meeting when you're actually playing a game of SimCity.

1. They don't put a single penny into Bill Gates' pocket! (Rick has a thing for pennies.)

Dealing with Documents

If you're like most business travelers, you're used to carting a laptop around with you to edit Word documents. If you have a 14-inch or 15-inch display, then you know what it's like trying to get the laptop screen open in the cramped space on an airplane seat. Heck, sometimes we can't get it open far enough to read what we're typing.

Thankfully, there's an easier solution. Your handheld, combined with a keyboard, can take the place of your laptop for text entry. You can even synchronize specific Word documents with your PDA, edit them on the road, and update your desktop PC with the latest versions of your work when you get home.

Look but Don't Touch

Sometimes you don't need or want to edit a document on the Palm, you just want to read it. And though it might be nice to know that you can tweak the fonts, add a paragraph, or recalculate a figure, those sorts of frills are unimportant. For times like that, you might want to have a document viewer.

Document viewers are especially handy if you need to see the document exactly the way God—or your boss—intended it, with no minor variances caused by the conversion tool or rendering system.

In particular, document viewers excel at showing you one of the most common kinds of business documents, Adobe PDF files. PDF files are incredibly popular because they're self-contained text-and-graphic documents that display exactly the same no matter what kind of computer you view them on. They also aren't easily edited, so you can distribute a PDF secure in the knowledge that some clown in a different office won't make changes to your handiwork.

Here are the most common document viewers that we recommend:

- **Documents To Go Professional**   Yes, Documents To Go is a full-fledged document editor, with word processing, spreadsheet, and presentation document programs. But it also has its own PDF viewer. The latest version shows PDFs complete with images, so if you have an older version of Documents To Go, this might be a good time to upgrade.

- **Adobe Reader for Palm**   This is a free program from Adobe that lets you download PDF files to your PDA. As the name suggests, Adobe Reader does one thing and one thing only—it shows PDF files. So good news: it's free. Bad news: if you want to read other documents as well, you will need Documents To Go or another app. Adobe Reader is handy because it lets you choose to include or strip out graphics, so you can save memory on your PDA by leaving out non-essential graphics, or leave them in if they're needed to understand the document. Unfortunately, that's where the good news ends. Adobe Reader must convert PDFs on the Windows desktop and then transfer them to the Palm, so you can't use Adobe Reader to open files you get in e-mail or just copy via an SD Card. Worse, it uses a crazy bad interface and doesn't support full-screen mode on 320x480-pixel models. Ugh.

11

■ **Picsel Proviewer**   Make no mistake: this is the program we recommend. Simply put, Proviewer blows away Adobe Reader and any other document viewer, for that matter. It is a great way to view PDF files. The program accurately reproduces the PDF in exacting detail, including all text and graphics. You can zoom in, zoom out, and pan around with great ease. Moreover, Picsel Proviewer can display a variety of other kinds of files, including all the Microsoft Office document formats. And there's no conversion needed. Just copy a Word file to your SD Card or get it via e-mail, and you can immediately view the document.

■ **RepliGo**   Much like Picsel Proviewer, RepliGo re-creates your graphics-filled PDFs and other common documents on the small screen with the ability to pan around, zoom in and out, and view the documents any way you like. Unfortunately, RepliGo is not nearly as convenient as Picsel. You pretty much have to plan ahead with RepliGo. There isn't even a handy desktop converter tool that you can drag files into. Instead, you need to open a file in its original program—such as Word, for example—and then click a conversion button in the toolbar. For Adobe PDF files, you must choose to print the file and then select RepliGo from the list of printers. The result is a great experience on the Palm (you can even perform searches inside the document), but the only way to make the program less useful (especially compared to Picsel Proviewer) would be to have someone hit you repeatedly with a stick whenever you tried using it.

    In our humble opinion, these are the best, but you can find other programs that do this
as well. If you want to experiment, check out programs such as Ansyr Primer PDF Viewer,
RichReader, and PDF2Doc.

Using an Office Suite

Pocket PC users have one tiny advantage over Palm users—a Microsoft-branded office suite
that includes Pocket Word and Pocket Excel. People can trust those apps to be very compatible
with Microsoft Office on the desktop. But in reality, Pocket PCs are no more (and often less)
compatible with Office documents than the Palm.

    A lot of people don't realize, though, that there also are several excellent Office-compatible
suites for the PDA. Most models come with one right in the box, in fact. That's Documents
To Go, from DataViz. If your Palm-powered PDA didn't come with an office suite, or yours is
getting long in the tooth and you want to try another, you'll be happy to know that there are a
couple of popular suites to choose from:

- **Documents To Go** (www.dataviz.com)   Documents to Go is quite popular by virtue of
  the fact that Palm has chosen to put it in the box of every new model it sells. In addition
  to a word processor (Word To Go) and spreadsheet (Sheets To Go), the Professional
  edition of Documents To Go includes the capability to view PowerPoint slides and
  Adobe Acrobat (PDF) files.

11

■ **Quickoffice** (www.quickoffice.com)   This suite includes Quickword and Quicksheet for reading and editing Word and Excel documents. Quickword has its own thesaurus and spell checker, and you can install custom fonts, too. Quickoffice also allows you to collaborate wirelessly on documents via cell phones and modems, so you can invite other people to view and make changes to a document even if you're in different cities.

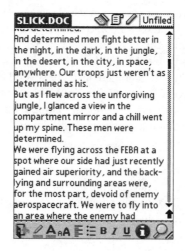

■ **Wordsmith** (www.bluenomad.com)   Wordsmith is not a suite; it's a stand-alone word processor for the Palm. But we decided to mention it here anyway, because it's so good at what it does. If you don't need spreadsheets or presentations on your Palm, but just need a good word processor that can read Microsoft Word documents and render them accurately on screen with support for multiple fonts and advanced formatting, give this one a try.

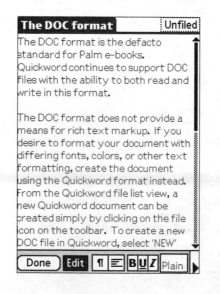

If you don't want an entire suite but aren't passionate about Wordsmith, you can buy Quickoffice's word processor and spreadsheet separately. Or you can just install one specific app in the suite of your choice and disregard the others.

Transferring Documents between the Palm and Desktop

PDA office suites of old weren't quite so flexible. But these days you can choose several ways to transfer documents from your computer to the handheld:

- **Use the desktop converter** This is generally the least convenient method, but it's the traditional way, dating back to the age when office suites on the Palm didn't understand Microsoft Office file formats and had to be converted first. Just drag the documents you want to move into the suite manager on the desktop (you can see several of them in the following illustration), and they will be copied to the PDA at the next HotSync.

- **Put your PDA in Drive Mode** If you have a PDA like the Tungsten T5 or the LifeDrive, you can start drive mode and copy files to the device as if it were a memory card reader or USB Flash Drive. The advantage? You can copy documents from strange PCs without drivers, Palm Desktop, or even e-mail. All you need is an open USB port and your Palm's HotSync cable.

■ **Put the documents on an SD Card**   This is handy, especially if you have an SD Card reader on your desktop PC. Drag the documents to a folder on the SD Card, put the card in your PDA, and voilà, instant office documents.

■ **Use Quick Install**   Drag your documents from the desktop to the Expansion card section of the palmOne Quick Install application. After you HotSync, you'll have access to the files.

■ **Get it in E-mail**   This method is handy because it works anywhere, anytime. Just send Word, Excel, and PowerPoint files to yourself and check the mail on the PDA. You can access those attachments with Documents To Go or Quickoffice.

TIP

Bachmann Software's FilePoint is a file management program for the Palm that lets you install documents from the desktop. So if you have several different Office-style applications, you can transfer files on the PDA to all of them by using just one program—FilePoint—instead of loading each office suite's desktop component separately.

What if you create a new document from scratch on the Palm? No problem. On the next HotSync after you create the document, you'll find that it has been synchronized with the desktop. To find it, just open your suite manager software and double-click the new file; it'll automatically open in Word.

Working with Documents and Spreadsheets

If you want to leave your laptop at home and just carry a PDA, it's absolutely essential to be able to read and edit Word and Excel files on the go. Although most PDA word processors try very hard to preserve all of the formatting in your document, keep in mind that these programs do it with varying levels of success. You may sometimes find, for instance, that group annotations or graphics such as "boxes" around text may be stripped out when the files are synchronized back to the PC. As a consequence, word processing on the PDA is often best reserved for documents that have fairly conservative levels of formatting. In addition, some word processors have more formatting features than others.

Because all office suites have a free trial period, we recommend installing all of them and seeing which one you like best.

CAUTION   *Many handheld word processors don't support some advanced formatting features, and they're stripped away when you synchronize documents. When we tested these programs, Documents To Go did best with wacky stuff like text with Track Changes; Quickoffice sometimes made a real mess out of the text. Documents To Go keeps the desktop version of the document intact even when it has truly unusual formatting elements (such as images) that don't display on the PDA.*

11

How to ...   Work with Palm Documents

In a nutshell, here's what you need to know to work with text documents on the PDA:

- To create or edit long documents on your PDA, you need a program such as Documents to Go, Quickoffice, or WordSmith.
- On the desktop, open your office suite's manager application.
- Click the button to add a file, or just drag and drop a document into the suite's manager window.
- Close the program and then HotSync to transfer the files to the Palm.
- Edit the files on your PDA.
- HotSync to carry the changes you made to the Palm back to the desktop versions of the affected files.

Better Software for Bigger Screens

If you feel constrained by the anemic width of your handheld's screen, you're not alone. That's why virtually all new Palm devices offer better resolutions than earlier devices, either 320×320 or 320×480. And because all of the office suites support these higher resolutions, along with a variety of fonts and font sizes, you can pack a lot more data on the screen, provided you have strong enough eyesight to see all those little letters. Check out the difference between editing a Word document on a Zire 71 (on the left) and a Palm TX:

PowerPoint on Your Palm

The last piece of the puzzle is PowerPoint. If you lug your laptop around so you can deliver slideshows on the road, well, we have some good news for you. Your PDA is capable of pumping slides directly to a projector in their entire 1024×768, full-color glory.

Actually, depending upon your needs and which PDA model you own, you have a few choices:

- ■ **Documents To Go Professional**   This program just won't go away! It seems like we've mentioned it a dozen times in this chapter alone. The professional version includes a PowerPoint viewer. You can't broadcast these slides on a projector or even edit them once they're on your device, but you can use this viewer to view the slides in both a text-only and graphic mode.

- ■ **iGo Pitch Duo**   If you want to plug your Palm into a projector to display presentations on a big screen without lugging around a laptop, try the Pitch Duo. This gadget lets you display PowerPoint presentations stored on your PDA directly on a VGA screen. Pitch is a small, PDA-sized gadget that connects to your Palm wirelessly via Bluetooth, so your Palm must have Bluetooth for this to work.

- **Margi Presenter-to-Go**   Now discontinued, you can still find Presenter-to-Go online, and it's worth looking for if your Palm doesn't have Bluetooth. This device plugged into your Palm's SD Card slot (other versions also fit in Compact Flash and even Memory Stick slots, depending upon your Palm model) and then, in turn, jacked into your projector.

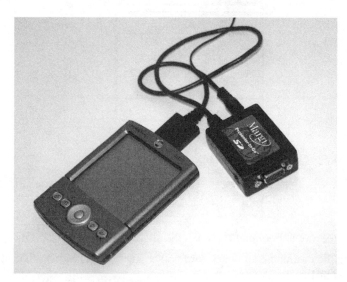

11

Get Your Files from the Road

Up until now we've been kind of assuming that as long as you have some sort of program on your Palm to read or edit your documents, you're all set. In other words, the files you need are already on your Palm, either because you copied them to an SD Card before you left town, or someone e-mailed them to your PDA.

But what if that's not the case? What if the files you need are still tucked away on your PC at home? Does your Palm has some kind of Internet access, such as via Wi-Fi or a Bluetooth phone? Sounds like it's time for Avvenu.

Avvenu is a free file access solution that you download and install on your desktop PC. When it runs, you can see the Avvenu icon in the System Tray:

Avvenu

And whenever Avvenu runs, you can fire up your Palm's Web browser, log in to share.avvenu.com, and access any files on your computer. Here's what the process looks like:

1. Start your Palm's browser, such as Blazer or AvantGo. We'll assume you're using Blazer in this procedure, but any browser will do.

2. Tap the Bookmarks icon in the upper right corner of the screen and then tap an empty bookmark. Enter "Avvenu" in the Name field and enter "share.avvenu.com" in the URL. Tap OK to save it.

3. Tap your new Avvenu bookmark to open the site.

4. Log in using the user name and password you created when you established the Avvenu account on your PC.

5. In the Web browser, tap the links to navigate around your PC. You'll see the same folder structure as you have on your home computer, so you'll probably want to tap My Documents and then tap additional folders until you reach the file you need.

6. Tap the file you want to copy to your Palm.

7. Tap Download.

8. Choose whether to install the file on your Palm or the card slot, and then tap Yes to download.

9. Finally, tap Save to save the file to your PDA, after which you can open it in any document viewer or suite that you have installed on your Palm.

Printing from Your Palm

The ultimate handheld PC would probably look a lot like the Palm, but with one important difference: it would have a paper-thin printer embedded inside, enabling you to print anything you see on the screen. Although that's mere science fiction for the time being, this doesn't mean you can't print stuff from a PDA. Quite the contrary: armed with a print driver, you can send a wide variety of documents from your Palm to a desktop printer or to a portable, pocket-sized printer.

To print anything from your handheld, you need to add a print driver. There are several available, and selecting one isn't as easy as it sounds. You need to consider two ingredients:

- ■ **What you want to print** Some print drivers only print data from the Palm's four core apps, whereas others can print documents from certain office suites.

- ■ **What kind of printer you want to print to** If you have your eye on a compact, battery-operated portable printer, you'll need to find a print driver that works with that printer.

This chart outlines some key data for the most common Palm print drivers:

Print Driver	Printers	Software
InStep Print	Prints to almost all portable and desktop printers	Supports the broadest range of document types, including Documents To Go, Quickoffice, WordSmith, and the Palm's own built-in applications.
IrPrint	Prints to almost all portable and desktop printers	Supports Documents To Go, WordSmith, and other apps. Has some problems printing from Handspring Visors, though.
PalmPrint	Supports most portable and desktop printers	Prints from the Palm's core apps, and from a few third-party programs, including Quickword.
PrintBoy	Prints only 8.5 × 11-inch pages, which means it doesn't work with very compact printers such as the Sipix Pocket Printer	Largely prints only from the Palm's core applications.

As you can see, getting a good match with your device, the software you want to print, and the printer you want to use can be tricky. Be sure to visit the Web site of each of these print-driver vendors to check their latest list of compatible programs and printers.

Infrared Printers for Your Palm

The easiest way to print from your PDA to a nearby printer is via infrared. Your Palm's IR port (the same one that you can use to beam apps and data to other PDAs) can communicate directly with compatible printers. There are a small handful of lightweight portable and IR-enabled printers, and even some full-sized desktop printers that have infrared ports built in. If you like the idea of printing wirelessly from your Palm, or if you travel frequently and want to print from wherever you happen to be, you might want to look for one of these. To be perfectly honest, not a lot of printers have infrared ports built in, so you'll have to look carefully to find a model. Here's a list of printers we've found, but be advised that not all of these are still being sold. Even so, we had no trouble finding these models for sale on the Internet—sometimes new in the original packaging, sometimes refurbished.

Manufacturer	Printer	Comments
Desktop printers with Infrared		
Canon	PIXMA iP90	Desktop photo printer
Hewlett-Packard	LaserJet 5P, 6P, 2100	Out-of-production desktop laser printers. You can still find these for sale online.
Portable, laptop-oriented printers		
Canon	BJC-55, 85	Out-of-production lightweight mobile printers
Handheld-sized portable printers		
Brother	Mprint	Handheld thermal printer
Pentax	PocketJet 3	Handheld thermal printer, compatible with IrDA adapter
Sipix	Pocket Printer A6	Out-of-production handheld thermal printer

11

Did you know?

About IrDA?

Technically, IrDA stands for the Infrared Data Association, which is just a bunch of companies that make IR-enabled products. More important, though, IrDA represents the industry-standard infrared port you can find on most laptops, handheld PCs, and printers with IR ports. If you find a printer with an IrDA port, chances are excellent that it'll work with one of the Palm's print drivers. Bottom line: IR, or infrared, is a wireless technology built into most mobile gadgets. As long as they are fairly close and pointed at each other, IR lets you share data easily.

Bluetooth Printing

If you have a Bluetooth adapter for your Palm (or you have a model with Bluetooth built in), you can print wirelessly to a Bluetooth-enabled printer. As we wrote this chapter, our Bluetooth options in the printing world were still rather limited, but we hope that will start to change.

Right now, there are rather a limited number of printers that have Bluetooth built in. If you don't want to shop for a printer based entirely on whether it has Bluetooth or not, you can try adding a Bluetooth adapter to your existing printer. There are quite a number of such adapters around. Just plug them into the back of your printer, and any Bluetooth-enabled Palm device can print to it. Here are a few to check out:

Adapter	Web site	Connects to
Belkin Printer Adapter	www.belkin.com	USB port
Bluetake BT200	www.bluetake.com	Parallel port
Bluetooth Printer Adapter	www.mpitech.com	USB port

Printers for Your Pocket

If you expect to do a lot of printing and want to have easy access to a portable printer, you have a few excellent choices. Forget about having to track down a desktop printer when you're on the road. Just carry your printer in your pocket. Here are two models we highly recommend:

■ **Brother MPrint** This thermal printer measures $4 \times 6.4 \times .7$ and weighs just 10 ounces, yet it holds 50 sheets of 3×4-inch paper in an internal tray and prints about 100 sheets on a single charge of its Lithium-Ion battery. It comes with IS/Complete's IrPrint software.

■ **Pentax PocketJet** A bit longer than the others at $10 \times 2 \times 1$ inches, the PocketJet uses thermal imaging to print 300 dpi on either sheets or rolls of paper. Though the Pentax may be bigger, it lets you print real letter-sized documents. It, too, employs serial and IrDA, and uses AC power or internal rechargeable batteries for power.

Of course, if you get a Bluetooth printer, you'll also need a Bluetooth-aware print driver for your PDA. There are two, and both worked great in our testing:

- ■ PrintBoy Anywhere (bachmannsoftware.com)
- ■ BtPrint (iscomplete.org)

Printing to a Parallel or Serial Printer

What if you don't have access to an infrared printer? That's when things can get dicey. If you own a serial port printer (such as any Apple ImageWriter), plug the Palm's HotSync cradle into the printer and, with the handheld docked, send jobs to the printer.

Most Windows users don't have serial printers, though. They use parallel printers. In that case, you need a special serial-to-parallel converter (available from Stevens Creek, the manufacturer of PalmPrint).

You have another option. The PrintBoy InfraReady Adapter from Bachmann Software is a small plug that fits into the parallel port of any printer. A small IR port turns the printer into an IR-ready device that you can use with your Palm. It's small and light, so you can carry it with you when you travel.

> NOTE *It doesn't make any difference if you print via the PC or via your PDA. The print quality is identical, and everything prints out fine on standard 8.5 × 11-inch paper. If it's more convenient to print via your PDA, go for it!*

Where to Find It

11

Web Site	Address	What's There
Avvenu	www.avvenu.com	Avvenu file sharing
Bachmann Software	www.bachmannsoftware.com	PrintBoy and the InfraReady Adapter
Blue Nomad	www.bluenomad.com	WordSmith
Brother	www.brother.com	MPrint
Cerience	www.cerience.com	Repligo
Cutting Edge Software	www.cesinc.com	Quickoffice
DataViz	www.dataviz.com	Documents To Go
InStep Print	www.instepgroup.com	InStep Print
IS/Complete	www.iscomplete.com	IRPrint and other print drivers
Picsel	www.picselpowered.com	Picsel Proviewer
SnapperMail	www.snappermail.com	SnapperMail
Stevens Creek	www.stevenscreek.com	PalmPrint

Part III

Beyond the Box

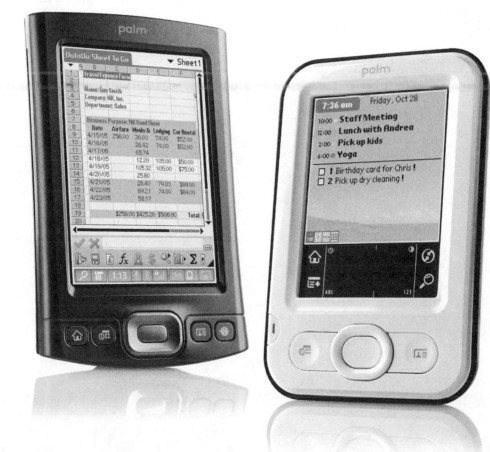

Chapter 12 Utilities

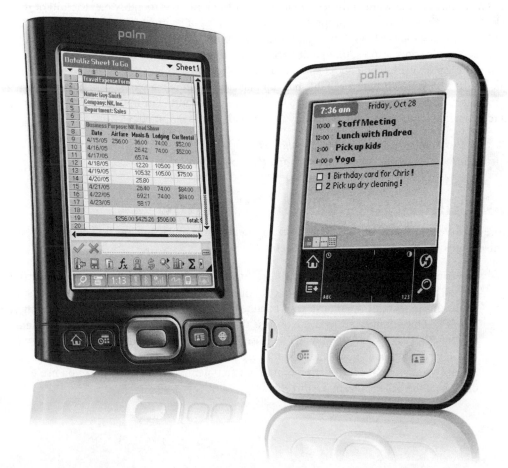

How to...

- Access your PC from your PDA
- Back up your PDA
- Add a screensaver
- Keep your device from accidentally turning on
- Manage and uninstall files and programs
- Choose a launcher
- Write your own Palm OS software
- Improve handwriting recognition
- Find Graffiti alternatives

When you hear the word "utilities," you probably think of your monthly electric bill or those four worthless Monopoly properties (hey, $150 isn't gonna break anybody's bank). In the world of computers and PDAs, however, utilities are programs that add capabilities and fix problems. They're power tools, though not necessarily limited to power users.

In this chapter, we tell you about some cool and worthwhile Palm OS utilities. When we're done, you'll find yourself with a reliable backup that can overcome any data-loss disaster, a great file manager, some excellent alternatives to Graffiti, and lots more. Utilities might sound boring and technical, but they're actually fun, easy to use, and extremely practical.

> **NOTE** *Most of the utilities listed in this chapter can be purchased and downloaded from software sites like Handango.com and PalmGear.com.*

10 Cool Utilities to Check Out Right Now

Before we dive into specific utilities like backups and Graffiti replacements, let's take a look at 10 miscellaneous programs you may find useful.

- **Avvenu** As discussed in Chapter 10, Avvenu enables you to access your home or office PC via your Treo, Palm TX, or any model that has a live Web connection. The utility itself runs in Windows; you use your handheld's Web browser to establish a link with your PC. Once connected, you can browse the files on your hard drive, download them to your PDA, and share them with other users. Avvenu could come in mighty handy if you're on the road and realize you forgot an important document. Or it could just simplify sending a PowerPoint presentation to a potential client. However you use it, you can't beat the price: Avvenu is a freebie.

TIP *You're not limited to using Avvenu on your handheld. You can also use it to remotely access your PC from another PC.*

■ **Fonts4OS5** OS 5 doesn't offer much in the fonts department. If you'd like to change the way text looks on your PDA, check out this nifty font collection. The program comes with 26 different sets and lets you choose a different font for each application.

■ **PocketCopy** So you've decided to abandon the Palm camp in favor of Windows Mobile (a.k.a. Pocket PC). Or maybe you've just decided to stop using Palm Desktop in favor of Outlook. Whatever the case, a utility like Chapura PocketCopy makes the migration quick and painless. PocketCopy moves your Palm Desktop appointment calendar, address book, memo pad, and task list to Outlook's Contacts, Calendar, Notes, and Tasks sections, respectively. It's compatible with Palm Desktop 3.0 and higher and Outlook 98 and higher.

12

■ **Pocket DVD Studio** Calling all movie buffs! This invaluable utility copies your DVD movies so they can be viewed on your handheld. Yep, you guessed it, this is actually a utility for your PC, one that produces a video file you copy to your PDA's memory card. We talk more about Pocket DVD Studio and similar programs in Chapter 14.

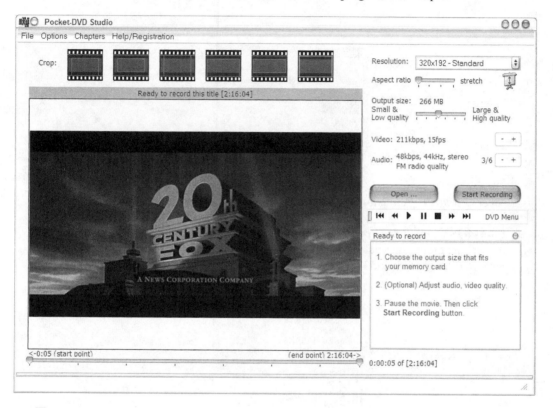

■ **Resco Explorer** The ultimate utility for power users, Resco Explorer provides a file manager, program launcher, document launcher (meaning you can create icons that launch documents directly instead of having to run the corresponding program first), image viewer, backup utility, text editor, and more. Not bad for a program that costs just $15.

■ **PowerOn for OS 5** It's a common scenario: you slip your PDA into a pocket or purse, only to find it dead a few hours later when you pull it out. The cause? Something was pressing against one of the buttons, causing the unit to power on and the battery to drain. PowerOn reduces the chance of that happening by disabling the hard buttons. Or, more accurately, by requiring two quick presses of one of them to turn the unit on. Before you plunk down your $12 for this handy utility, however, check to see if there's a Keylock option in your Palm's Prefs screen—it accomplishes a similar goal (see Chapter 2).

■ **QLaunch** Your handheld has just four hard buttons, but you probably use a lot more than four programs regularly. QLaunch lets you launch up to three applications from each button. You can also use it to access special functions, like the built-in keyboard or the Bluetooth radio (if your model has one).

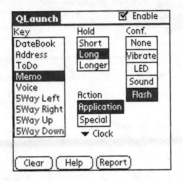

■ **VolumeCare 5 Pro** This one's only for Treo owners, but it's quite possibly the single most important utility you can get. VolumeCare magically overcomes the Treo's volume problem, enabling you to make the speaker much louder than normal. It works not only with the handset itself, but also with the speakerphone and wired headsets. If you've ever found yourself wishing that you could crank the volume on your Treo (and we don't know a Treo user who hasn't), VolumeCare is the best $20 you can spend.

■ **XTNDConnect** If your synchronization needs to extend beyond Microsoft Outlook, check out XTNDConnect. Designed for business users (particularly those who work in medium-to-large offices), the software lets you synchronize your handheld with ACT!, Lotus Notes, Lotus Organizer, Novell GroupWise, and other applications.

■ **ZLink** Ever wished you could create an icon—or "link"—for a particular document, image, movie, e-book, or even phone number? ZLink is designed to do exactly that. It integrates with the Palm launcher, effectively creating a new category ("Links") containing your newly created icons. ZLink is a bit on the pricey side at $17.95, especially considering that Resco Explorer offers a similar capability (and much more) for a couple bucks less. But as with most Palm software, you can try before you buy, so if you like the idea behind ZLink, give it a try!

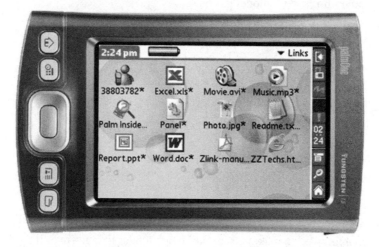

Two Great Utilities for Tungsten T Users

Much as we like the cool sliding design of the Tungsten T, T2, and T3, it's kind of a hassle to open the unit every time we want to access the Graffiti area. Fortunately, we found a pair of utilities that virtually eliminate the need.

■ **Graffiti Anywhere** This handy utility frees you from the Graffiti area, enabling you to write anywhere on the screen. It's a freebie, too!

■ **SlideFree** When you draw a special stroke on the screen, SlideFree pops up a command bar containing all the icons found in the Graffiti area—Favorite, Find, Brightness, and so on.

Backup Utilities

One of the really cool things about the Palm OS is the way it keeps a complete copy of your data on your PC. Every time you HotSync, it's like you're making a backup of your important info. If something terrible befalls your handheld—the batteries die, or it gets lost, stolen, run over, sat on, or inexplicably wiped clean—at least you know your data lives on on your PC.

Of course, what happens if you're a thousand miles from home and your PDA piffles? To reduce the chance of a major crisis, consider using a backup utility and a memory card. There are numerous utilities that can make backups of absolutely everything. If your handheld gets wiped, you simply insert the card, run the backup utility, and hit "restore."

NOTE *The Palm TX, Tungsten E2, Tungsten T5, and Treo 650 aren't affected by dead batteries in the same way that other Palm OS devices are. That's because they rely on non-volatile RAM, which doesn't require continuous power to retain its contents. To put it another way, if your handheld or smartphone dies, all you have to do is charge it up again, and all your data will still be there. Nevertheless, a backup utility may still be worthwhile for these models, as you never know when you'll accidentally delete a vital file or experience a memory-wiping crash.*

Memory Cards

First things first: you need a memory card. If you're not familiar with them, skip ahead to Chapter 16 for some basic info. The key thing is to make sure you have a card with at least as much storage space as your Palm OS has RAM. If you have a Palm TX, for instance, you need at least a 128 MB card. (Of course, you'll probably wind up with a 256MB or 512MB card anyway, as they're the best deals, so you should be more than adequately covered.) It's worth noting, however, that some backup programs compress your files, so you won't necessarily need to devote, say, every inch of space to your backup.

Indeed, the card you use for your backup needn't be used for that exclusively. You can still use it to store extra applications, MP3 files, photos, and other stuff. You just need to be sure there's enough space available to store a copy of the contents of your device's internal memory.

Backup Software

Once you're outfitted with a memory card, you need a backup utility to go with it. There are several programs that get the job done with a minimum of fuss. Usually it's just a matter of tapping Backup, then waiting a few minutes for the process to complete. If you need to restore your data, tap Restore and wait again.

That said, you might want to look for certain features when choosing a backup utility:

■ **Scheduled backups** Some programs can make backups for you automatically at predetermined times. This can be quite helpful if you're the forgetful sort, as it ensures that you'll always have an up-to-date backup ready.

- ■ **Partial backups**   Although it's nice to have a backup of every single bit of data in your PDA, you might want to save time (or storage space) by backing up a select few files. Some programs let you pick and choose which files to copy; others make it an all-or-nothing proposition.

- ■ **Incremental backups**   Making a complete backup of everything in RAM takes time. If your software supports incremental backups, only those files that have changed since the last backup will be copied during subsequent backup sessions. That can save you a ton of time and storage space.

- ■ **Password protection**   Suppose you were to lose the memory card containing your backup files. Whoever finds it might have easy access to all your data. But if your backup program offers password protection, you can keep the data secure.

A search of PalmGear reveals a multitude of backup utilities. Most have free trial versions that you can download; we recommend checking out BackupBuddyVFS (pictured next), BackupMan, and FlyBackup, but feel free to try some others.

Wireless Backups with BackupBuddy.Net

Just before we completed work on this book, Blue Nomad unveiled a new backup service that's the first of its kind. BackupBuddy.Net, an online version of the BackupBuddyVFS software we mentioned previously, is designed to give Treo users a way to back up their data wirelessly. Instead of copying the data to a memory card or your PC, everything is transmitted to a BackupBuddy server. One of the chief advantages to this is that if you lose or break your Treo, you'll still have a current backup to restore to the replacement Treo. And because BackupBuddy.Net automatically updates your backup every time you add or change information, even your most recent data gets restored. A 12-month subscription to BackupBuddy.Net costs $34.95.

The Problem with Prequels

Palm, schmalm . . . let's talk about the really important stuff—namely, treasured sci-fi franchises that have been ruined by prequels.

Rick: First there was the colossal disappointment of *Star Trek: Enterprise*, the blandest, most uninteresting *Trek* series ever. Now, George Lucas continues to make a mockery of the *Star Wars* trilogy by serving up pabulum like *Attack of the Clones*. Maybe I'm too old, maybe I'm jaded, maybe I just expect fresh writing and decent acting, but these prequels have left me colder than a polar bear in January. They're just not *fun.* The magic is gone. And I think this is a problem inherent to the prequel formula—when you know the outcome, there's no suspense. I *knew* Anakin would turn into Darth Vader in *Episode III*. For me there's no excitement in watching it happen. And don't get me started on all the ways *Enterprise* has destroyed the *Star Trek* canon . . .

Dave: You, my friend, have been abducted by mind-controlling body snatchers. First, *Enterprise* when it started, was fresh, fun, and engaging, though it soon went as flat as day-old soda ... but that's a different problem. As for *Star Wars,* are you too cool to like stuff anymore? All the million-dollar book royalties gone to your head? What do you expect? To be knocked off your feet like you were watching *Star Wars* when you were 12? Not going to happen. That film is a classic, and you were lucky enough to see it for the first time at the perfect age. *Episode III* was a decent enough film—aside from the FrankenVader monster tearing loose from the table towards the end—but the bottom line, dude, isn't with the concept of prequels. Prequels can be done really well, and it's often fascinating to see what happened before the story we already know. *Star Wars* and *Enterprise* deserve to be criticized. But as usual, you're criticizing them for all the wrong reasons, claiming that the very fact they're prequels is what doomed them to mediocrity.

12

Screensavers

A screensaver for your PDA? Why not? Although its screen certainly doesn't need "saving"—the traditional definition of a screensaver is a program that prevents burn-in on a computer monitor, but your PDA's screen can't get "burned in"—there's nothing wrong with looking at some pretty images while the unit is resting in its cradle. (You did buy a cradle, right? If not, see Chapter 16 to learn all about them.)

There are two pretty cool screensavers that take advantage of your PDA's color screen:

■ **The Matrix Screensaver**   Say what you will about the second and third *Matrix* movies (we agree, they were terrible), the first one was among the coolest sci-fi films ever made. You can bring a little of the magic to your PDA by installing The Matrix Screensaver, which turns your screen into that cool green drizzle of Matrix code, and even includes a Matrix-y clock. Best of all, it's a freebie!

■ **Riverland**   From the same company that brought you The Matrix Screensaver, Riverland is a lavishly animated, Disney-caliber screensaver. The scene is fully animated and changes from day to night. Pretty nifty, and an impulse buy at just $6.95.

How to ...   Beam Software to Another Palm OS User

Suppose you're enjoying a game of Text Twist (one of our favorites), and a fellow Palm OS PDA user says, "Hey, I'd like to try that!" Generous sort that you are, you agree to beam a copy of the game to him (which is perfectly legal because Text Twist is shareware). To do so, tap the Home button to return to the Applications screen, and then tap Menu | Beam. Find Text Twist in the software list, tap to highlight it, and then tap the Beam button. Point your PDA at the other person's handheld, and then wait a few seconds for the transfer to complete. Presto! You've just shared some great software—wirelessly!

Keep in mind, however, that not all software can be beamed. In many cases you'll see a little padlock next to programs listed in the Beam menu—that indicates a copy-protected program that ain't going anywhere.

Putting an End to File Clutter

The more programs you install on your PDA, the more files you end up with. A new game, for instance, might include the game itself, a high-score database, and various other files the game requires (or produces). If you decide to delete the game, however, it's possible that some of those files will get left behind. (A shining example of this is AvantGo, which, while not a game, litters your PDA with countless files.) This leads to a messy PDA, and Rick, for one, doesn't like messy.

Uninstall Manager keeps things neat and orderly by monitoring programs as they're installed on your device, then enabling you to uninstall those programs, and all associated files along with them. This is one of those necessary-evil utilities, one that you hate to have to spend money on (it's $17.95), hate even needing, but should really consider using. If you do, make sure to read the accompanying manual in detail because Uninstall Manager has some rather complex features, and it's important that you learn how to use them correctly.

Removing Duplicate Entries

If you routinely work with ACT!, Outlook, or some other third-party contact manager on your computer, it's not uncommon to wind up with duplicate entries on your PDA. This can also happen if you import additional databases into Palm Desktop. Whatever the cause, the last thing you want to have to do is manually delete these duplicates from your records. UnDupe does it automatically, ferreting out duplicate entries in Address Book, Date Book, Memo Pad, and To Do List, and then eliminating them in one fell swoop.

Ah, but before you spend $9.95 on this decidedly handy utility, why not let Palm Desktop (which is free) do the work instead? The program's Delete Duplicates function works much like UnDupe, enabling you to find and remove duplicates in the four core apps.

12

To access this function, run Palm Desktop, and then click Tools | Addins | Delete Duplicates. Check the boxes for the applications you want it to search, and then click the Search button. In no time you'll see a list of matches, all marked by default for deletion. Remove the checkmarks from any entries you don't want deleted, and then click the Delete button.

TIP *Need more information about any given entry in the search results? Click it once to highlight it, and then click the Details button. You'll be able to look at each individual entry and make sure it's something you want to delete.*

When you're done, HotSync. This will remove all the duplicate entries from your handheld that were just removed from Palm Desktop.

Managing (and Beaming!) Your Files with FileZ

The more you work with software, the more you need a good file manager. FileZ lets you view, edit, copy, move, delete, and beam virtually any file on your handheld. It's not the most user-friendly program of its kind, but it does have one feature that makes up for it: it's free.

Beaming is one of FileZ's most admirable capabilities. As you might recall from Chapter 4, beaming programs and data to other PDA users isn't only practical, it's just plain fun. But the Palm OS is a bit limited in terms of what it can beam. Specifically, it can't beam e-books or certain kinds of programs and databases. That's where FileZ comes in—it can beam just about anything.

> **TIP** *If you're an advanced user, you can also use a program like FileZ to find and delete the extraneous files that are sometimes left behind when you delete an application. The standard Palm OS Delete tool usually doesn't show these "behind-the-scenes" files. Of course, you should take caution when deleting files, as you could accidentally remove something important. Make a complete backup first so you can restore files if necessary.*

The Wonderful World of Launchers

As you know from poring over Chapter 2 (you did pore, didn't you?), the Palm OS enables you to assign applications to different categories; the idea being to help keep your icons organized and more easily accessible. However, a variety of third-party programs take this idea to a much higher level and with much better results. In this section, we introduce you to a few of our favorite launchers—programs that organize your apps, simplify certain features, and, in some cases, slap on a much prettier interface.

What should you look for when choosing a launcher? A couple key features to consider are described in the list that follows.

- **Support for memory cards** If your handheld has an expansion slot (as most do nowadays), your launcher should have direct support for memory cards. That means you can install applications on a card, but still organize them as you see fit from within the launcher.

- **Support for big screens** A good launcher should take full advantage of your screen's capabilities, meaning it should extend the full length of your screen (if you have a model with a virtual Graffiti area, like the Palm TX). You'll be able to fit more icons on the screen at a time (if you desire to) and enjoy a nicer-looking interface.

- **Support for themes** Part of the fun of using a launcher is customizing your handheld's interface. Some launchers let you install themes (also known as "skins") that dramatically alter their appearance while maintaining the same basic layout and functionality. The standard Palm OS interface looks downright stark in comparison to these nifty themes, which are usually free to download (though the launchers themselves cost a few bucks).

- **Support for jog dials and navigators** If you have a handheld with a jog dial or navigator, make sure to choose a launcher that supports it. That way, you can still enjoy the benefits of one-handed operation.

A Few of Our Favorite Launchers

We've tried most of the launchers out there, including the one that attempts to re-create the—horrors—Windows desktop on your handheld's screen. Rest assured, that one isn't among our favorites (but if the idea intrigues you, by all means check it out—it's called WinLauncher). These include the following:

- **Launcher X** Though it's looking a bit long in the tooth these days, Launcher X remains one of our favorites. It quickly and easily organizes your icons into tabbed windows, thus enabling you to switch categories with a single tap of the stylus. Plus, you can drag and drop your icons between tabs—no irksome category menus to deal with. Launcher X is packed with other helpful features, ranging from onscreen memory and battery gauges to a built-in file manager. It costs $19.95.

■ **MegaLauncher**   In addition to its crackerjack support for memory cards and high-resolution color screens, MegaLauncher offers a wealth of advanced features (including one-tap beaming, deleting, and copying) and comes with a handful of attractive themes. It costs $19.95.

■ **SilverScreen**   Dave's launcher of choice, SilverScreen offers the most glamorous interface of any launcher and a growing library of way-cool themes. It's also the only launcher to replace the core-app icons with icons of its own, thus creating an even more customized look. In short, if you're big on bells and whistles, this is the launcher for you. However, we should point out that SilverScreen is a bit on the slow side—the unfortunate by-product of its graphics-laden interface.

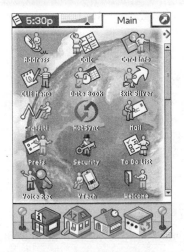

■ **ZLauncher**   Neither Rick nor Dave care much for ZLauncher (see Figure 12-1), but that hasn't stopped it from becoming one of the bestselling Palm apps of all time. Admittedly, it does have more features than just about any other launcher, and you can choose from dozens of cool themes to seriously spruce up the interface. We find it over-cluttered and complicated, but that doesn't mean you shouldn't try it out for yourself.

12

FIGURE 12-1   ZLauncher gives you countless tools for organizing your icons, beautifying your interface, and, of course, launching your programs.

As with most Palm OS software, you can try demo versions of these launchers before plunking down your hard-earned cash. We recommend you use each one for at least a week so you can really get to know it.

Palm Antivirus Utilities

Unless you've been living under a rock, you know that computer viruses can wreak havoc on a PC and even propagate from one system to another without users' knowledge. Viruses are an unfortunate fact of computer life. They aren't, however, a part of PDA life, at least not at press time. While a few companies have introduced virus-protection software, do yourself a favor and don't bother wasting any money or energy on them.

Creating Your Own Palm OS Programs

Ever wonder why there's so much third-party software available for Palm OS devices? Maybe because it's so easy to write programs for the platform. While the more sophisticated applications do require programming experience and professional development tools, utilities are available that enable you to design basic software with ease. Indeed, if you're willing to tackle a short learning curve, you can create customized applications for your personal or business use.

If you're looking for software to create databases, see Chapter 11.

The following offers a quick rundown of some of the tools available to budding Palm software developers:

- **AppForge Crossfire**   A powerful development tool (available in Standard and Professional editions), AppForge Crossfire lets you write for the Palm OS, using Microsoft Visual Basic 6.0.

- **NS Basic**   Remember that BASIC programming class you were forced to take in high school or college? Now you can put the knowledge to practical use. NS Basic (see Figure 12-2) lets you create Palm OS apps with everyone's favorite programming language. Okay, show of hands: who remembers what BASIC stands for?

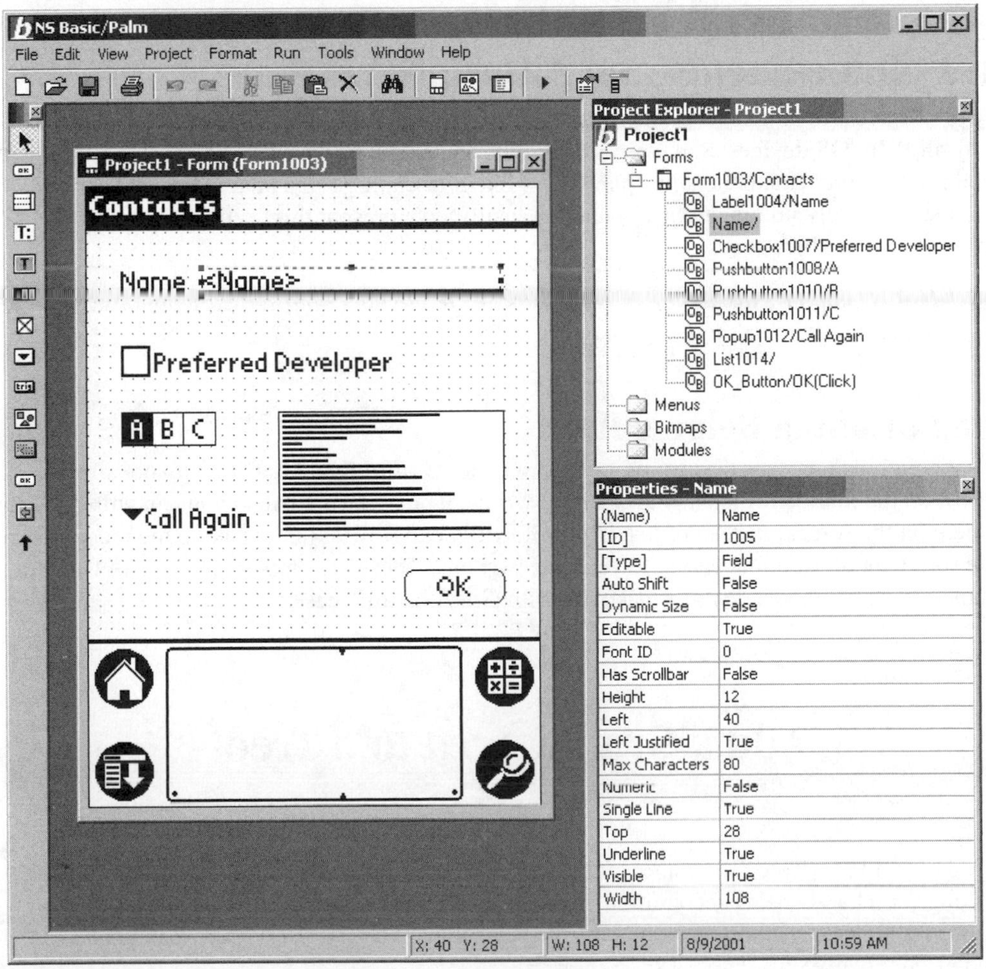

FIGURE 12-2   If you can remember your BASIC training, you can program for the Palm OS with NSBasic/Palm.

- **PDA Toolbox**   Formerly known as PalmFactory, PDA Toolbox doesn't require much in the way of programming knowledge. Rather, the software employs a graphical interface and makes software design as easy as dragging-and-dropping elements on to a simulated Palm screen. You can even create your own icons for your programs.

- **Palm OS Development Suite**   This free, open-source C/C++ Integrated Development Environment (if you're a software developer, you'll know what all that means) is probably the first place any serious Palm OS developer should start. Find it here: www.palmos.com/dev/tools/dev_suite.html.

- **SuperWaba**   Okay, we don't pretend to understand Java, but if you do, SuperWaba is a "Java Virtual Machine" that runs on the Palm OS (among other platforms). It's free, it supports OS 5, and it gives you the opportunity to say "waba" a lot.

Graffiti Enhancements and Alternatives

Many of us have a love/hate relationship with Graffiti, the handwriting-recognition software used by all Palm OS devices. Some users take to it right away, finding it a speedy and convenient method for entering data. Others just plain don't like it or can't get the knack. For those folks (who have absolutely nothing to be ashamed of, really), we present this section on Graffiti enhancements and alternatives.

> NOTE   *In this chapter's discussion of keyboards, we're talking about software options. We look at actual keyboards in Chapter 16.*

Giving Graffiti a Helping Hand

Here's a novel idea: Rather than trying to build a better Graffiti than Graffiti, why not simply cut down on the number of letters necessary to write a word? Or make it so you can write anywhere on the screen, instead of just in the Graffiti area? How about tweaking the recognition engine so it's more accommodating to your handwriting? These are among the goals of Graffiti assistants—software tools that just make life with Graffiti a little easier.

How to ...   Add a Graffiti Area to a Treo

If you own a Palm Treo (or another model with a built-in keyboard), you might find yourself wishing for a handwriting-recognition option. Consider installing a utility like Graffiti Anywhere: It lets you write anywhere on the screen, just like some keyboard-equipped models do already.

How to ... Improve Graffiti Recognition

For all its quirks, Graffiti is actually an excellent handwriting-recognition tool. If you plan to stick with it, you can use these tips to improve accuracy. By the way, if your handheld has Graffiti 2, the first three tips still apply.

- Write big. If your characters fill up the bulk of the Graffiti area, they're more likely to be accurately recognized.

- Don't write on an angle. Many of us do just that when writing with pen and paper, but that's poison to Graffiti. Keep your strokes straight.

- Take advantage of the built-in Graffiti Help application, which provides a graphical cheat sheet for all Graffiti strokes. Go to Prefs | Buttons | Pen, and then choose Graffiti Help from the list of available options. Now, whenever you draw a line from the Graffiti area to the top of the PDA's screen, the Help applet appears.

- Having trouble with the letter *T?* That's because most people draw the downstroke first, then the crossbar. By default, Graffiti likes it the other way around. If you'd rather make your *T*s the normal way, head to Prefs, then tap Graffiti 2. Tap the letter *t* to "tune it," and then uncheck the box labeled "Use this form of 't.'"

- Having trouble with the letter *G?* Forget trying to draw it Graffiti's way, write the number 6 instead (on the left side of the Graffiti area, of course, otherwise you'll get a 6!).

12

Was *This* the Word You Were Looking For?

Remember the old game show "Name That Tune"? The host would describe a song, and the contestant would say, "I can name that tune in three notes." Imagine if Graffiti could adopt that precept, guessing the word or phrase you're writing as you write it. By the time you entered, say, the *e* in "competition," the software would have figured out the rest of the word, thereby saving you six additional pen-strokes.

That's the appeal of *TextComplete,* a utility that helps you write faster by helping you write less. As you enter characters, a box containing possible word matches appears. If you spy the word you're after, just tap it. The more letters you enter, the closer you get to the correct word (if it's in the software's database).

Obviously, for little words like "the" and "to," the program won't help much. But for longer words, it can indeed save you some scribbling. And TextComplete lets you add your own words and/or short phrases to its database, which can definitely save you time in the long run.

Goodbye, Graffiti Area!

Ever notice that the Graffiti area is kind of, well, small? Most of us aren't used to writing in such a confined space, and that alone can be a source of Graffiti contention. Fortunately, there's a utility that can liberate your stylus from that tiny box, effectively turning the entire Palm screen into one big Graffiti area. It's called Graffiti Anywhere, and, true to its name, it enables you to write, using Graffiti characters, anywhere on the screen. What's more, it leaves a trail of "digital ink" beneath your stylus tip, which goes a long way toward helping you produce more accurate characters. You see what you write as you write it, just as you would with a pen on paper. It's a freebie (www.escande.org/palm/GrfAnywhere/), so grab it today!

Graffiti, Your Way

Finally, we come to the one product that really manhandles Graffiti, that says, "Look, can't you just learn to understand *my* writing?" It is TealPoint Software's TealScript, a utility that lets you tweak Graffiti so it's more responsive to your hand, or replace it altogether with a customized character set.

　　If you're willing to battle one of the steepest learning curves we've encountered in a piece of Palm software, the benefits are truly worthwhile. TealScript works its wizardry through the use of custom profiles, which contain the Graffiti character set as you define it. In other words, you teach TealScript how you like to write, and it teaches Graffiti to accommodate your penmanship.

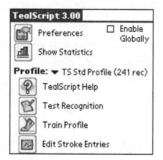

　　As confusing as TealScript can be to work with, it's not totally out of the question for novice users. That's because it comes with an already-built profile that helps you overcome the most commonly miswritten Graffiti characters. So, right out of the box it's useful. And while TealScript might not be the friendliest program around, it's by far the best way to make Graffiti an ally instead of an obstacle.

TIP   *If you've upgraded to a Palm OS handheld that has Graffiti 2 but miss good old Graffiti 1, TealScript lets you switch back, after a fashion.*

Ditching Graffiti Altogether

Ready to show Graffiti the door? Hey, it's okay; you gave it your best, tried counseling, and all that. The good news is, if you still like the idea of handwriting recognition, there are plenty of Graffiti alternatives to try:

- ■ **Decuma V4**   For many users, the problem with Graffiti lies in having to draw one character on top of the other, which is totally contrary to the way we all learned to write. Decuma V4 not only gives you an entire blank line on which to write, but also recognizes ordinary handwriting. We think it's by far the most sophisticated and capable Graffiti alternative, though you might find that paper-like writing (that is, left to right) on a small PDA screen isn't all that great. Fortunately, there's a trial version available, so you can see for yourself!

12

- ■ **MobileWrite**   MobileWrite is somewhat unique in that, like Decuma V4, it interprets both uppercase and lowercase letters, and most common punctuation marks. However, it's more like Graffiti in that it uses the standard Graffiti area, but also allows you to write anywhere on the screen. Another nice perk: you can write letters one on top of the other or across the screen, as on paper.

■ **QuickWrite**   QuickWrite is not unlike TextComplete, except that it relies on an onscreen keyboard for data entry and uses a cool dynamic-recognition system that predicts words as you tap-type. It's even smart enough to keep track of words you use frequently, giving those words future priority in the "guess list." Definitely worth checking out.

Where to Find It

Web Site	Address	What's There
AppForge	www.appforge.com	AppForge Crossfire
Decuma V4	www.zicorp.com	Decuma V4
Handy Entertainment	www.handyent.com	Riverland, The Matrix Screensaver
Inkmark Software	www.inkmarksoftware.com	MobileWrite
Little Mobile Creations	www.launcherx.com	LauncherX
MegaSoft 2000	www.megasoft2000.com	MegaLauncher
MobileSystems	www.mobi-systems.com	QuickWrite, TextComplete
NorthGlide	www.northglide.com	Uninstall Manager
Nosleep Software	www.nosleep.net	FileZ
NS BASIC	www.nsbasic.com	NS Basic
PDA Toolbox	www.pdatoolbox.com	PDA Toolbox
PocketSensei	www.pocketsensei.com	SilverScreen
SuperWaba	www.superwaba.com.br	SuperWaba
TealPoint Software	www.tealpoint.com	TealScript

Chapter 13 Playing Games

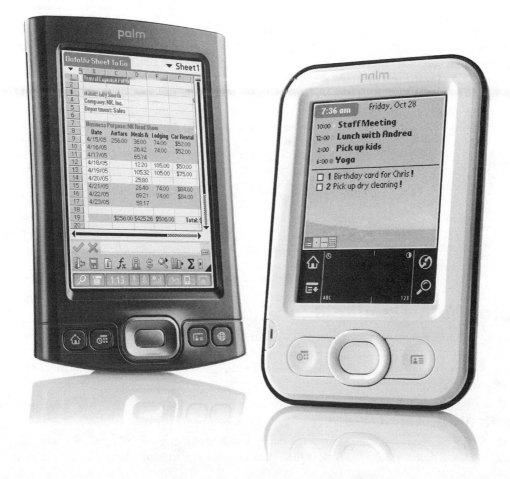

How to…

- Adjust your handheld's volume for games
- Install new games
- Control games on your handheld
- Play action, board, and card games
- Play sports, strategy, and word games
- Play two-player games on two handhelds
- Play interactive fiction games
- Use your PDA as a substitute for dice

Spreadsheets, databases, document readers, and memos are all well and good. If that's all you ever plan to do with your PDA, that's fine—you're just unlikely to ever get invited to one of our parties.

Your PDA is a miniature general-purpose computer, and, as a result, it can do almost anything your desktop PC can do, including play games. Sure, there are limitations. The display is pretty small and the processor isn't nearly as fast, but the fact remains your Palm is a great game machine for passing the time in an airport, on a train, in a meeting (where it looks like you're taking notes), or any other place you're bored with doing productive activities. In this chapter, we discuss what you should know to get the most out of your handheld as a gaming machine, and we recommend some of the best games for you to try.

NOTE   *As PDAs have evolved, so have their capabilities. Various models have different resolutions. Some have limited audio hardware; some have special audio hardware optimized for gaming. Some have Palm OS 4, some have Palm OS 5, and so on. As you look around for games (and even check out those that we recommend), you might find some that are not completely compatible with your particular model. Of course, most games are universally compatible, but you should always check the system requirements before installing anything on your PDA. (The most notorious games are those written specifically for the now discontinued Tapwave Zodiac, which run only on that particular gadget.)*

Prepping Your Handheld for Gaming

No, playing games isn't exactly rocket science, but before you get started with them, you should learn a few things that'll come in handy. You should know, for instance, how to control your PDA's volume, install applications, and enable beaming (some games let you play against other handheld users via the IR port).

Controlling Game Volume

At the top of the list is the Palm OS sound system, which includes a control for how loud to play game sounds. Logic dictates you'll want to set this loud enough to hear what's going on in your game, but this might not always be the case. As much as we like to play games, we don't always want others to know that's what we're doing. Fortunately, it's possible to set the game sound level low or to even shut it off completely. This means you'll play your games without sound (which, if you're at work, is probably a wise decision).

To tweak game sounds, do the following:

1. Tap the Prefs icon to open your Preferences application.

2. In the general section, tap the Sounds & Alerts category. If you have an older device that doesn't have Sounds & Alerts, switch to the General category instead.

3. Find the Game Sound entry and choose the volume level you're interested in.

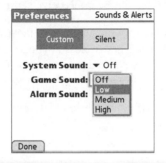

Silencing Your Palm Quickly

If you have a newer model, there's a fast way to change the sounds settings. Let's say that you want to silence your Palm so you can play games in public without making noise. Simply tap the time in the status bar at the bottom of the screen and tap Silent from the sound options at the bottom of the screen. You can return to your previous sound level when the game is over by tapping the time again and choosing Custom.

13

If you find that a game still squeaks and squawks even if the Palm OS volume setting is set to off, the game must have its own sound preferences, and it ignores the sound settings of your Palm's prefs. Check its options menu for a control to set the sound volume. Indeed, many games have built-in volume controls that eliminate the need to futz around with the settings in Prefs.

Enabling Beaming

If you know other Palm OS handheld users, you might want to try your hand at some head-to-head games, which are made possible thanks to the devices' infrared ports. It's fun and addictive, and very nearly qualifies as being sociable. For two games on different handhelds to "find" each other, though, you need to make sure that the Beam Receive setting in Prefs is enabled.

1. If you have a wireless keyboard for your Palm, start the keyboard app (usually called Keyboard) and disable the driver. The wireless keyboard driver often interferes with other programs, like games, that want to use the Palm's IR port.

2. Tap the Prefs icon to open your Preferences application.

3. Switch to the Power category. (If you have an older device, choose the General option instead.)

4. Look for the entry called Beam Receive and make sure it's set to On. (By default, it is.)

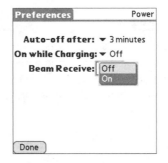

If you have a PDA with Bluetooth, you might be able to multiplay some games via Bluetooth. Quite a few games for the Tapwave Zodiac, for instance, are designed to allow several people in the same room to take part wirelessly with Bluetooth.

Installing Games

Installing games is a snap. We discussed how to install applications onto your handheld in Chapter 4, and working with games is no different. After all, a game is just another kind of application. Need a refresher? We won't make you go all the way back to Chapter 4. Turning pages can be such a drag, so we'll offer it here.

Game Packs

Occasionally, you might find game compilation discs in stores or online that promise to deliver hundreds of unbeatable Palm OS games for just 10 or 20 bucks. Should you invest in one of these packages?

Our opinion: probably not. The collection might sound promising, but anyone with a halfway decent Internet connection can get all of the games they like from a site like PalmGear.com or Palmgamingworld.com just as easily, and without spending a dime. Remember: PDA games are tiny compared to games for the PC, and they download in seconds, even if your Internet connection is powered by hamsters.

Also, keep in mind that you won't get the full, registered version of shareware games even though the disc itself cost you cash. Instead, these discs are sort of like samplers for folks who want a guided tour of someone else's idea of the "best" games for your PDA. If you like a game you find on the disc, you'll still have to pay to play it beyond the first few levels, just as if you downloaded it from the Internet.

Let's assume you're dealing with games you want to download from the Web. (Some computer and office-supply stores sell game bundles, most of which have their own installation programs. You don't need us for those.) If you're new to downloading, you need to know that most apps come compressed in one of two popular formats:

- **Zip**   This is the standard way of managing files in Windows. To install a Zipped file, you need a program capable of unzipping it first. Windows XP and Vista can automatically extract the contents of Zip files, but if you're using an older version of Windows, you might want to try a utility such as WinZip.

- **SIT**   Macintosh files are compressed in the SIT format, which can be uncompressed with a program such as Aladdin Stuffit Expander.

Once you expand the compressed file, you'll probably end up with a folder containing several files. Installation instructions typically come in one or more file formats:

- **Plain text files**   These are usually called something clever like readme.txt or install.txt, and will tell you which file(s) to install.

- **HTML pages**   These will probably have an Internet Explorer icon (or whatever Web browser you use), and usually contain the game's instructions. Double-click them to see the instructions in your Web browser.

- **PDF files**   You need Adobe Reader to read these files, though it's probably already installed on your computer. If not, visit adobe.com to get this popular document reader.

- **Files with a PRC extension, and possibly PDB also**   These are the actual game files that you need to install on your handheld. Open the Install tool and use the Add button to mark these files for installation during the next HotSync.

13

How to ...   Control Your Jet / Race Car / Submarine / Spaceship

Now you're all set to start playing some games, but where's the joystick or game pad? There isn't one, silly (unless you have a very special model that caters to games, like the old Tapwave Zodiac). Many games use the handheld's buttons to control the action. While the game is running, the Calendar, Contacts, Memos, and Tasks buttons typically are diverted to game controls and won't switch you to the usual apps. To find out which buttons do what in a given game, you can experiment (that's our favorite way) or check the game documentation. In most games, you can find basic instructions by checking the game's built-in Help screens (tap Menu to find them). A handful of newer games take advantage of the Navigator control found in the most recent handhelds. And some PDAs (like Zire models) have only have two buttons, which might be a problem for games that expect your PDA to have the four standard buttons. If you have such a model, many games (especially action games) might not work for you.

SHORTCUT *A fast way to install game files is simply to double-click the PRC and/or PDB files from within the zipped folder. That will save you the extra step of having to unzip the files first. Alternatively, you can just drag Zipped files directly into the Install Tool window if you have any but the oldest of PDAs.*

CAUTION *If you reset your PDA while a game is paused, the game session you were playing will be lost and you'll need to start over.*

Gone But Not Forgotten

Rick: Frogger, Galaxian, Pac Man—these were household names back in my youth, and they're just a few of the arcade classics that have been resurrected for Palm OS handhelds. Of course, your PDA's buttons don't compare too favorably with traditional coin-op controls, so longtime favorites like Spy Hunter, Joust, and Sinistar are a bit tricky to control. Still, it's a blast to revisit my youth with these favorites of yesteryear. And I don't even need to pump quarters into my PDA.

Dave: I love the old arcade classics as much as the next geek, but it's time to move on, dude! It's the 21st Century! I've put childish games like those well behind me and today, I play mainly just the mature, modern classics. Like Bejeweled. And Astro.

Rick: Don't call me "dude."

A Few (Dozen) of Our Favorite Games

Games account for a pretty healthy chunk of all software sold for Palm OS handhelds, so it should come as no surprise that you can find hundreds upon hundreds of titles spanning every genre. Card games, action games, puzzle games—you name it, it's out there. Of course, we can't list all of them without doubling the size of this book. It's big enough already, don't you think?

As with other kinds of Palm software, games are easy to try before you buy. Most have a trial period, usually from two weeks to a month, after which the game becomes disabled unless you register it (that is, pay for a code to unlock it permanently). Games usually cost $10–20, though a few will set you back $30. There's also a treasure trove of great freebies like these (most of them available at www.freewarepalm.com):

- **Cribbage**   Sure, you could pay 12 bucks or so for one of the commercial Cribbage games, but why? (Okay, okay. The PDA *does* tend to cheat a bit with this freeware, but otherwise it's a gem.)

- **IBE Chess for Palm**   Play chess against your Palm or another person.

- **IMR-Bombers**   Fans of the arcade classic Bomberman will enjoy this faithful Palm recreation.

- **Mulg vIIq**   Use your stylus to guide a marble through a maze within a fixed amount of time. Devilishly addictive.

- **Patience Revisited**   An amazing collection of Solitaire games—21 in all, all in color, and all free, free, free!

13

- **PilOth**   A clone of the classic game of Othello.
- **Pocket Video Poker**   Why take a trip to Vegas when you can gamble all you want for free? There's also Pocket Video Blackjack, if that's more your speed.

- **Sea War**   A nice implementation of the beloved game Battleship. There's even a high-resolution version.
- **Solitaire Poker**   One of many variations on Solitaire, this one involving poker hands.
- **Vexed**   One of the most addictive puzzle games ever, and a Palm OS freeware classic. The latest version includes multiple puzzle packs with over 600 levels.

NOTE   *Many of these freebies are pretty old, meaning they might not even offer color graphics. And a few might not work on newer Palms. But even the oldies are worth checking out.*

These freebies are a great place to start for anyone interested in a little fun on the run. In fact, there are enough freeware games to keep you entertained almost indefinitely. On the other hand, if you're willing to shell out a few bucks, you'll find some of the best mobile entertainment money can buy. In the following sections, we've listed some of our favorites, all divided into a few major categories.

Action and Arcade Games

Did you pump an untold number of quarters into arcade machines in the 80s? We sure did. These action games will make you long for the classics of yesteryear—and, in some cases, revisit them.

- **Galax**   An excellent retread of the inimitable (but often imitated) Galaxian.
- **Midway Arcade Classics**   Five flawless re-creations of arcade greats: Defender II, Joust, Root Beer Tapper, Sinistar, and Spy Hunter.

■ **Astro Defence** Unbelievably addictive, we've been playing this game on our PDAs for years and still can't put it down. Modeled after the old classic Missile Command, Astro puts you in charge of the moon's defenses. Save it from falling asteroids and passing UFOs.

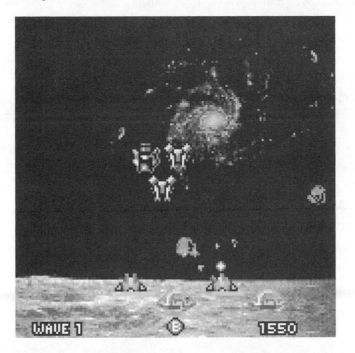

■ **Sonic the Hedgehog** Sega's console classic is now available for Palm OS 5 handhelds. Your kids will be in hog heaven.

■ **Zap!2016** A scrolling space-shooter with gorgeous graphics and terrific sound effects.

13

An Ode to Astraware

Any Palm user with even the slightest interest in games should head straight to Astraware.com. This site is home to Palm versions of the some of the most popular puzzle and action games ever to hit the Web, including Bejeweled, Bookworm, and Zuma. Many of our other all-time favorites also can be found there: Text Twist, Sudoku, Warfare Incorporated, and Zap!2016. The company generously offers trial versions of all its titles, and several quality freebies (some of which, like Bang! Bang!, can be lots of fun for younger kids).

We can't say enough good things about Astraware. The company has kept us entertained for years with its outstanding games. Keep up the good work, guys!

Card Games

Card games adapt well to handheld PCs because they don't require fancy graphics or complicated controls. They're games you can relax with, and maybe play in the bathtub. (On second thought, the bathtub is probably not the best place for your PDA. Try the shower.) Poker, Hearts, Blackjack—there are versions of just about every classic card game you can think of.

- **AcidFreecell** Freecell is one of our favorite Solitaire games, and this version includes sound effects, photographic backgrounds, and other nifty perks.

- **KidzTalk GoFish** A memory game not unlike Concentration, the goal is to match pairs of cards from a spread-out deck of 20. As you make matches, a picture is revealed underneath. This OS 5-only game also talks to you in a real human voice. Great for little kids.

- **Texas Holdem Poker** Rick isn't much of a card player, but he is a big fan of the movie *Rounders,* hence his interest in this great little poker game.

- **Vegas Blackjack** Without a doubt the best-looking Blackjack game for the Palm OS, Vegas Blackjack plunks you down at a casino-style table for some serious hands of 21. Double down!

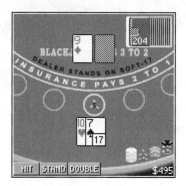

Board Games

There's a reason games such as chess, Risk, and Monopoly have been around forever: they're fun, no matter where, or even how, you play them. Lots of big-name board games are available for the Palm OS. These are the ones we like best:

- **Aggression** Remember Risk? Aggression is a visually striking re-creation of the beloved board game. It looks best on high-resolution color screens, but you can play it even on older grayscale Palm devices.

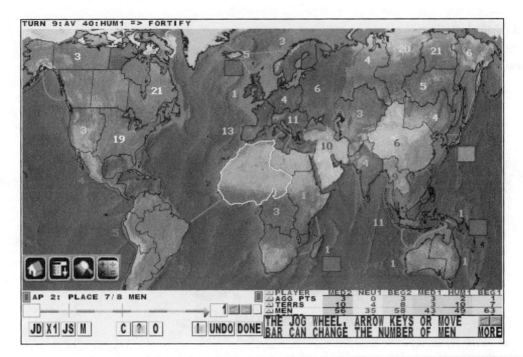

- **Monopoly**   This needs no explanation, other than to say that one to four players can partake, human or computer, on the same handheld or several of them (the game supports play via infrared).

- **Rook's Revenge**   Almost too fast-paced to qualify as a board game, Rook's Revenge is like chess with a jolt of caffeine. Move your pieces as fast as you can (they still have to be legal moves), without waiting for your opponent to make his moves. A great change of pace from boring old chess.

- **Chess Genius**   If you prefer boring old chess, here's the real deal. And Chess Genius is one of the best. It runs full screen on 320x480-pixel Palms (like the TX) and has features you'd usually expect to find only on a big PC version, like a tutorial mode that warns you if you're about to do something dumb. Infrared and Bluetooth even let you play with another human.

- **Scrabble**   Like Monopoly, no explanation needed here. But how cool to play this old favorite anytime, anywhere, without having to worry about tiles spilling all over the place.

13

Puzzle Games

Some of the very best Palm OS games, bar none, are puzzle games. They're generally easy to learn, seriously addictive, and endlessly entertaining.

■ **Bejeweled**   Like TNT's "New Movie Classics," this game has been around for just a few years, but it's already achieved Tetris-like classic status. It requires zero time to learn to play, and all your free time once you do. If by chance you've never heard of it, trust us and give it a try. It might just be the perfect game for PDAs.

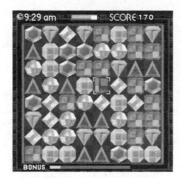

■ **Sudoku Master**   The biggest craze to sweep the nation since line dancing, Sudoku is an addictive puzzle game in which you must fill in a grid of numbers by deducing which numbers are missing. This version has a billion unique puzzles, and it includes some modes that use pictures instead of numbers, plus great features that make it easy to mark up the screen as you figure out what goes where.

■ **Bounce Out**   If you get tired of Bejeweled, try Bounce Out. It's the same game, only with balls instead of jewels, and the chance to work diagonally.

■ **NetWalk II**   An oldie but goodie, NetWalk challenges you to make successful connections between your servers and your computers. Sounds like a tech-support nightmare, but it's actually a ton of fun.

■ **Triclops**   How best to describe this game? There's a big triangle, see, and lots of little triangles fall into it, and you have to try to remove three or more like-colored triangles with each tap of the stylus. Okay, it sounds a little kooky, but it's a blast.

Word Games

Dave's not much for word games—too much stress on the brain—but Rick loves 'em. Nothing like keeping the old noodle active while you're passing the time.

■ **Bookworm**   Make as many words as you can from Bookworm's wall of letters. The trick is, the letters must be adjoining. We're not sure it'll actually increase your word power, as the developer claims, but it's definitely an enjoyable challenge.

■ **Crossword Puzzles for Palm OS**   Whether you're a crossword-puzzle fanatic or you haven't looked at one in years, this excellent collection, derived from *Washington Post* puzzles, is an ideal way to pass the time. Sure beats carrying a big book of puzzles or getting newspaper ink on your fingers!

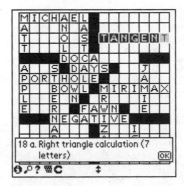

■ **Word Monaco Solitaire**   Here's a clever mash-up of card game and word game. You play it like solitaire. You move cards from column to column. But instead of creating a sequential stack of playing cards, you make words. Surprisingly addictive, and it looks very pretty on your color Palm screen.

13

■ **Text Twist** The first game Rick reaches for when he has five minutes to spare, Text Twist is a bit like Boggle. You're given six scrambled letters and a time limit; try to make as many words as you can from the letters *and* unscramble the six-letter word.

Strategy and Role-Playing Games

You might think a PDA isn't the best place to play a strategy or role-playing game, but you'd be wrong. Although some strategy and RPGs do benefit from the big screens afforded by desktop computers, those clever Palm OS developers have created some mighty compelling stuff for handhelds. Witness the following:

■ **Warfare Incorporated** If you're a fan of the real-time strategy genre, like Command and Conquer or Age of Mythology, you'll be tickled to learn that you can finally command an army on your PDA. Warfare, Inc is the first RTS for the tiny screen, and it actually plays quite nicely.

■ **Tradewinds** Want to become a pirate? Tradewinds is part strategy, part action, part simulation—think of it as a sort of "pirate tycoon" game for your PDA. Your goal is to build up a fleet, make money, and dominate the seas. Our take: we still can't believe a game this cool fits on a PDA!

■ **Lemmings**   Show of hands: who remembers the Amiga? Lemmings was one of the all-time great games to emerge from that system. In this perfect re-creation, you must guide the dumb little guys to safety. It supports high-resolution screens, sound, memory cards, and so on—and it's a freebie! (The level packs will cost you a few bucks, though.)

Sports Games

Anyone for tennis? How about racing? Maybe even a little Quidditch? Sports games (even fictional ones based on an amazing book) aren't always ideal for a screen as small as the one on your PDA, but that hasn't stopped developers from making some admirable efforts. Golf, basketball, football, and even bowling are among the other sports represented as PDA games. Whatever your athletic passion, even if it's darts, you're sure to find a game to match.

■ **TableTennis3D**   This is one of the most impressive titles we've seen—it's simply a way-cool Ping Pong simulator. You can play against your PDA or another player via infrared.

13

■ **Darts Deluxe II**   This dart-tossing simulation has great-looking graphics and an excellent throwing simulation that's not entirely unlike the way you swing a golf club in PC golf games.

■ **Bike or Die!**   Sure, the title is a little goofy, but this is the only game you can install on your PDA that lets you become a stick figure and ride a bike.

Games for Which We Haven't Figured Out a Category

Okay, how would *you* classify a game that involves a fish tank? Some games just don't fit the standard mold. Nevertheless, don't miss these amazing titles:

- **Billiards**   If you like pool, you'll love this dazzling interpretation. It's particularly great on big 320 × 480-pixel screens.

- **Insaniquarium**   Running a fish tank is hard work. You have to keep all the fish fed, gather up the coins they drop, fend off alien attackers—the usual stuff. Insaniquarium is like no other game we've seen, but it's definitely lots of fun. Your "tweens" and teens will love it, too.

Two-Player Wireless Games

As we already mentioned, two-player games are a cool way to pass the time when you're traveling with another handheld-equipped person. IS/Complete offers perhaps the largest collection of infrared- and Bluetooth-enabled games, including Palm OS versions of Battleship, checkers, chess, and even Hangman. They all work more or less the same way. You make a move, and then tap a button. Your move is then beamed to your opponent's handheld, where the board is updated to reflect the new data. Then you perform the same process in the other direction.

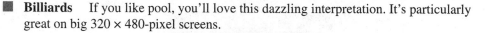

The games and graphics are nothing spectacular, but they're still kind of cool. And you don't need to pre-arrange a gaming session with another player. That is, if you've got one of the IR games and your buddy doesn't, no problem—just beam it to him. Of course, there might be a few limitations, depending on whether the game in question is commercial or freeware. If it's commercial, the beamed copy will often work only with the one from which it was beamed. Or, it might stop working after a short period of time, like two weeks (this is to encourage "player 2" to buy his own copy).

If you're interested in more sophisticated IR games, check out Handmark's excellent versions of Monopoly and Scrabble. Both can be played either on a single device (with multiple players) or via IR.

Using Your Palm to Play Classic Arcade Games

The great thing about computers is that, with the right *emulator* software, any computer can be made to pretend to be any other computer. That means that if you have the right software installed, your Palm can actually become an arcade machine and play all of the old classic arcade games you grew up with. The following illustration, for example, shows the old arcade classic Donkey Kong running on a Palm.

Although it's possible—and really not all that hard to do—keep in mind that this whole area of Palm gaming lies in tricky legal territory. To play Pong, Dig Dug, or Time Pilot on your Palm, you need two things, the arcade emulator software and a copy of the original game. It's the second part that's problematic. The arcade game files, called ROMs, are available on several Web sites. But to download and use them, you generally need to acknowledge that you already own the original arcade game. So if you try this out, you're pretty much saying that you have a garage full of old arcade games.

If you want to try your hand at emulating arcade games on your Palm, you have a few good options to choose from:

- **Palm MAME** The Multiple Arcade Machine Emulator is considered one of the best game emulators. It's available at www.pocketdimension.com/PalmMAME.html.

- **XCade** A company called CodeJedi offers XCade, which works much like MAME and is available from www.codejedi.com.

So where do you get the arcade game ROMs? Several Web sites offer these, and one of the best legal resources we know of is www.pdroms.de.

Playing Text Adventures

Remember Zork? How about Douglas Adams' Hitchhiker's Guide to the Galaxy text adventure? What about Trinity? These games were popular decades ago, at the dawn of the modern computer age. Text adventures put you in a text-based world, with flowing narratives and extensive descriptions of your surroundings. When it was time to make your hero do something, you typed instructions into your PC, and the computer then moved you along through the story based on your decisions. These games were often fiendishly clever, being composed largely of logic puzzles and intellectual challenges.

So, why are we telling you all this? Text adventures are long-lost icons for the museum, right?

Not quite. Text adventures have made something of a comeback in the last few years, largely because handheld PCs are an ideal platform for playing them. And although their identity has changed with the times—they're now usually called *interactive fiction* instead of text adventures—they're still a lot of fun to play. No serious gamer would consider his Palm complete without one or two interactive-fiction games installed for a rainy day at the airport (see Figure 13-1).

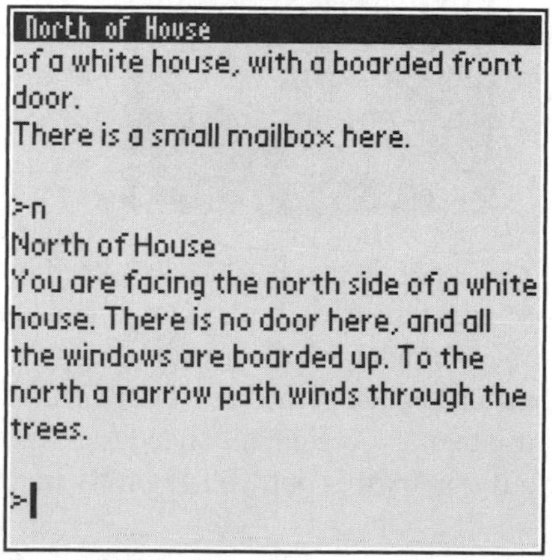

FIGURE 13-1   Interactive fiction combines good old-fashioned storytelling with a bit of brain-teasing puzzle solving.

Unlocking Interactive Fiction Files

You can find hundreds of interactive fiction titles on the Internet. But these files aren't playable all by themselves. They usually come encoded in a format called *Z-Code*. Like a spreadsheet or document file, a Z-Code file is useless without the appropriate reader app. In this case, you need a program like Kronos (from www.CodeJedi.com), CliFrotz (from http://zodiacstuff.sourceforge .net/clifrotz.html), or Pilot-Frotz (or Frotz, for short, from palmgear.com.). Install one of these apps, and you can play any interactive fiction games you find and transfer to your PDA.

Any of these programs will give you the same experience you got when you played those text adventures years ago. They display the game's text on the screen and provide you with a text prompt in which to enter your next move. If you use Frotz, for instance, you see the Frotz list view when you start, along with any games you have currently installed. To play a game, tap its name, and then tap the Play button.

From there, you're taken to the game view, where you actually play the game. Unlike those early text adventures, though, Frotz gives you a few graphical tools that make these games easier to play. The following offers a few pointers on how to use Frotz:

- If the game displays a long text description, you might see the word "MORE" to indicate that more text occurs after this pause. Tap the screen to continue.

- To enter your text command, write it in the Graffiti area.

- You can display a list of common verbs and nouns (shown on the right in Figure 13-2) by tapping the right half of the screen in any spot where no text exists. Instead of writing **Look**, for instance, tap for the menu and tap the word "Look."

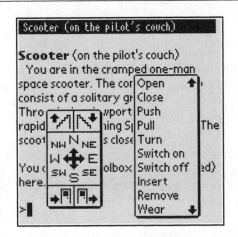

FIGURE 13-2   Frotz helps you play interactive fiction titles by displaying common commands and mapping tools.

13

■ You can tap any word in the story to make that word appear on the text prompt line. Thus, you can assemble your command from the menu and words already onscreen, instead of writing it all from scratch with Graffiti.

■ If you want your character to move, tap any blank space on the left half of the screen. You'll see a map window, like the one on the left side of Figure 13-2. Tap the desired compass direction. Other icons help you Enter, Exit, and go up or down stairs.

Getting Started with Text Adventures

So, you want to try your hand at interactive fiction, but that text prompt is a little too intimidating? Fear not, because entering commands in a text adventure isn't too hard. You can enter just a verb—such as **Look**—or a complete sentence, such as **Pick up the compass**. Each game has something called a *parser* that's designed to decrypt your input. Here's a primer to get you started:

Directions

Compass points are frequently used: north, south, east, west, or any combination thereof, such as northeast or southwest. You can also use one- and two-letter abbreviations, such as *n* and *se*. Also good are up, down, in, out, enter, and exit.

Looking Around

To look around, use the old reliable command Look. Thus, you can combine Look with anything that makes sense: "look up," "look down," or "look inside."

Action Verbs

Action verbs include just about anything: push, pull, open, close, take, pick up, pump, give, swim, turn, screw, burn. When you deal with more than one object, you can use the word All, as in "Take All the coins."

Making Sentences

You have to combine nouns and verbs to form complete sentences to accomplish much in interactive fiction software. Manipulating objects is the name of the game and the way to solve the puzzles, as in "Take the money," "Pick up the compass," "Read the book," or "Close the gate with the red key."

TIP *You can add custom words and phrases to the word list. Enter the desired word or phrase at the text prompt and select it with your stylus. Then choose List | Add from the menu. To see custom words, open the list menu and then tap on the first entry, USER LIST.*

Your position is automatically saved when you leave the game to do something else with your handheld. If you want to switch to another title, choose File | Force Quit to go back to the List view to select another game. If you do that, though, your position in the current game is lost.

Finding Interactive Fiction Titles

Interactive fiction is scattered around the Web. The following offers a few sites to try:

- www.refalo.com/palm/interactive.htm
- www.csd.uwo.ca/~pete/Infocom/

If you're really diligent, you may be able to find some of the classic Infocom adventures (such as Zork and Planetfall). Check eBay to see if anyone is selling them used, or do a Google search for Infocom. There might even be a site or two where you can pay for the adventures and download them directly without having to purchase an actual CD. Look for bundles such as Lost Treasures of Infocom and Masterpieces of Infocom, which include multiple games.

Using Your PDA as a Pair of Dice

If you like to play board games in the real world, you might be interested in using your handheld as a virtual pair of dice. After all, the PDA is harder to lose (we always misplace the dice that go with our board games). Several apps are available, but many of them have the disadvantage of requiring run-time modules of programming languages such as Forth or C. We don't care for that approach, because it's just extra stuff you have to install.

Some dice simulators you might want to try include Gamers Die Roller, DicePro, and Roll Em.

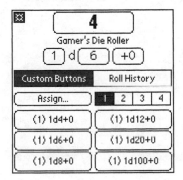

Where to Find It

Web Site	Address	What's There
Aladdin Systems	www.aladdinsys.com	The Stuffit Expander file compression tool for the Mac
Astraware	www.astraware.com	Bejeweled, Bookworm, Bounce Out, Text Twist, Zap!2016, and many of our other favorites
FreewarePalm	www.freewarepalm.com	Freeware games (and other software)
CodeJedi	www.codejedi.com	XCade
Handmark	www.handmark.com	Midway Arcade Classics, Monopoly, Scrabble
IS/Complete	www.iscomplete.com	Several two-player-via-IR games
PalmGamingWorld	www.palmgamingworld.com	One-stop surfing for all sorts of Palm OS games
PalmGear	www.palmgear.com	Most of the games mentioned in this chapter
PD ROMs	www.pdroms.de	Arcade game ROMs for emulators
Pocket Dimension	www.pocketdimension.com	Palm MAME
WinZip	www.winzip.com	A WinZip file compression tool for Windows

Chapter 14

Music, Movies, Podcasts, and More

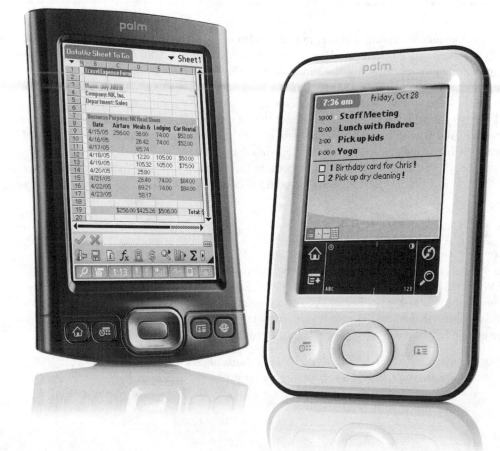

How to...

- Listen to music on your PDA
- Choose good headphones
- Work with memory cards
- Work with music download services
- Listen to audiobooks
- Make your own music
- Listen to podcasts on your PDA
- Watch movies on your PDA
- Decide what movie viewer to use
- Deal with file formats
- Find movies to watch

Hey, is that an entertainment center in your pocket or are you just glad to see us? Oh, it's your PDA—well, same difference. Many of the latest and greatest Palm OS-powered PDAs can play music and movies, meaning you can always have a little entertainment at your disposal. (If you're more of a bookworm, see Chapter 15.)

It might surprise you to learn just how multimedia-savvy your handheld is. When we say it can play music, we're not talking about the happy little jingles you hear when playing Bejeweled. And when we say it can play movies, we're talking actual DVD movies, not 15-second silent clips that look like glorified slideshows. Heck, the little buggers can even play audiobooks purchased from Audible.com. In this chapter you'll learn all about these and other miraculous multimedia feats (including podcasts!).

Where to Store Everything

Before we get started with the particulars of music and movies on your PDA, you'll need to equip yourself with at least one high-capacity memory card—unless, of course, you have a LifeDrive, which has oodles of space (4GB, to be exact) for storing your tunes and flicks. Obviously, the exact capacity is up to you and your checkbook, but we recommend a 1GB card as a bare minimum, and a 4GB card if you can swing it. Music, and especially movies, will eat up the available space in a hurry. See Chapter 16 for more information about memory cards.

We usually find the best deals on memory cards at eCost.com. At press time, a 1GB Secure Digital (SD) card was selling for only $9 (after a $30 mail-in rebate). And a 4GB card was on sale for $78 (after a $50 rebate). That would give you as much storage space as an iPod Nano!

Just how much space do music and movie files consume? It varies quite a bit, but here's a table that illustrates the storage needs for MP3 files recorded at various *bit rates* (more on those later):

Common MP3 Storage Scenarios	Average Number of Songs on a 512MB SD Card	Average Number of Songs on a 1GB SD Card
64-Kbps MP3s	256	512
128-Kbps MP3s	128	256
160-Kbps MP3s	90	180

As you can see, a 512MB card holds "only" about 128 songs encoded at the popular 128-Kbps bit rate. That's the equivalent of roughly ten albums, or ten hours of music. That sounds like a lot, and it is, but if you're traveling for a week or two, those ten albums could get old pretty quick. That's one reason to consider a larger card, or at least a second one filled with more tunes. Spring for one of those 4GB cards and you'll be able to store a whopping 1,000 songs.

As for movies, it's impossible to say exactly how much space they consume because of all the variables involved. We talk more about this in the upcoming "Movies" section, but suffice it to say, you'll want the largest SD card you can get.

NOTE *Users often wonder if it's possible to mix and match items on a memory card. In other words, can you load applications, e-books, music, movies, and other stuff onto the same card? The answer: yes! As long as everything's organized correctly (meaning the items are stored in the right folders so their corresponding applications know where to look for them), you can mix and match to your heart's content. Space permitting, of course.*

Music

Not all Palm OS handhelds can play music, but many can. If you're not sure if your model has this capability, look for a headphone jack (a little one, like the kind you'd see on a Walkman). If it has one, you're golden. If not, well, time to start shopping for a new model.

NOTE *By "music" we mean songs and albums in a digital format, usually MP3—currently the most popular format for digital audio. A select few handhelds, like the Z22, can play alarms and game sounds that sound musical, but that's not the same thing as playing your personal music library. Look for models that expressly mention MP3 support.*

Another option is to look for one of two preinstalled programs: Pocket Tunes or RealPlayer. If your handheld has either of these programs, you'll be able to play MP3 tunes stored on memory cards. Regardless of which program your Palm has, however, you'll want to upgrade to Pocket Tunes Deluxe. To find out why, see the sidebar, "Online Music Services."

14

Online Music Services

You've heard of iTunes, right? Apple's 99-cents-per-song download service proved beyond a doubt that music fans were willing to pony up for digital music instead of stealing it off the Internet. Great, thanks for the history lesson, you say, but what does that have to do with Palm handhelds?

Until recently, not much. Although Palms have long had the ability to play MP3 tunes, they didn't support Digital Rights Management (DRM) protection, meaning they couldn't play songs purchased from online music stores. But that changed with the introduction of NormSoft's Pocket Tunes Deluxe, which supports not only DRM-protected tracks purchased from any number of stores, but also DRM-protected downloads from a growing number of music-subscription services. Oh, and it still plays MP3s, too.

Translation: Your Palm can now do a pretty good iPod imitation.

All you need is Pocket Tunes Deluxe ($24.95 if your Palm came with Pocket Tunes Basic, $34.95 if it didn't), a memory card (unless you have a LifeDrive), and, of course, a compatible Palm model (see the NormSoft Web site for a list). Armed with those items, you can stock up on 99-cent and/or subscription downloads from AOL Music Now, MTV Urge, Napster, Rhapsody, Virgin Digital Red Pass, Yahoo Music Unlimited, and other stores/ services (see Figure 14-1). Why isn't iTunes on the list? Because the only portable players compatible with iTunes tunes are iPods.

Rick is a huge, huge fan of subscription services like Napster To Go and Yahoo Music Unlimited To Go, which cost $14.95 per month and $9.99 per month, respectively, and allow you to download an unlimited number of songs from their multi-million-track libraries. You can then copy any of these songs to your Pocket Tunes Deluxe-equipped Palm; the only limitation is storage space. That's a pretty unbeatable deal considering it costs little more than the price of a single CD per month. The only downside is that if you terminate your subscription, your downloaded tunes (those you didn't buy outright) will stop playing, usually after 30 days.

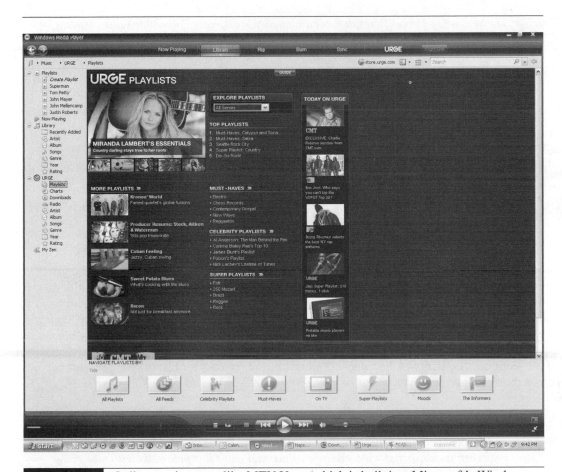

FIGURE 14-1   Online music stores like MTV Urge (which is built into Microsoft's Windows
Media Player 11) are compatible with many Palm handhelds, but you need
Pocket Tunes Deluxe to get the most from them.

14

If you already have a library of MP3 tunes on your computer, skip ahead to the "Getting
Songs onto Your PDA" section later in this chapter. If you're new to the concept of MP3s,
however, and need to know where they come from and how to get them on your PC, read on.

Where Do Digital Music Files Come From?

Okay, so just where do MP3s come from? Well, when a mommy and daddy love each other very
much, they—oh, sorry, we thought you said *babies*. Most commonly, MP3 files originate on
ordinary audio CDs. We've both completed the rather daunting task of converting our hundreds
of CDs into MP3s; meaning our music collections now reside on our computers' hard drives,
where we can copy them to memory cards for on-the-go listening on our PDAs.

NOTE
The version of Pocket Tunes that comes bundled with many Palm handhelds supports WMA files in addition to MP3s. For the uninitiated, WMA stands for Windows Media Audio. Basically, it's Microsoft's file format for digital music, one that promises (and mostly delivers) equivalent sound at half the bit rate. In other words, a 128Kbps WMA should sound just as good as a 256Kbps MP3—and it requires half the storage space, too.

This process of converting audio CDs is usually called ripping, and you can perform it on any PC that has a CD-ROM drive (or, for that matter, CD burner, DVD drive, and so on) and the right software.

TIP
Got a bunch of old LP records and/or cassettes lying around? You can "rip" those too. A little Googling will help you find all the information you need to make it happen.

Digital music can also come from the Internet. Perhaps you've heard of Napster, the infamous "service" that once enabled Internet users to download MP3s from other users' hard drives. The original Napster was litigated out of existence, but has since been reborn as a legal music-download service. But other so-called file-sharing services still exist, and people still download copyrighted music illegally. In case you're wondering, we think artists deserve to be paid for their work (and, yes, that even applies to Britney Spears, regardless of how much money she already has).

Okay, but what of legal Web-based services like Apple iTunes, Rhapsody, Yahoo, and the aforementioned Napster? See the sidebar "Online Music Services" for details. For now, just be aware that for most music you want to copy to your PDA, you should be looking to your CD collection.

TIP
A few services do sell their songs in MP3 format, including Bleep.com, eMusic.com, and LiveDownloads.com. Only eMusic has artists you're likely to have heard of, and even then its library isn't too extensive. Plus, you can't just pick and choose the songs you want to buy. You have to subscribe to the service and pay a monthly rate. Still, these services are worth checking out if you want to buy MP3s online.

Ripping Your Own Music Collection

If you're new to the digital music scene, getting started with ripping is pretty simple. Admittedly, the term "ripping" tends to confuse people, as it sounds complicated and perhaps even a little violent. In reality, it's just the term everyone uses to refer to the process of making a copy of a song, CD, or some other musical source. The technical term is Digital Audio Extraction, but, of course, that's not cool enough for everyday use.

Ripping is a digital process, meaning it creates a perfect copy that's identical to the original in every way. (This explains why record companies are so hoppin' mad.) So when we refer to ripping music from a CD to your computer's hard drive, what are we really talking about? A few key steps, really:

■ **Rip**   Your software reads the audio data from the CD and transfers it to your PC in digital format, without losing one iota of quality.

■ **Encode**   Next, the program needs to encode it into your desired file format (in this case, MP3). MP3 is a compressed format, meaning there's a loss of quality in the process. (How much depends on the bit rate used for encoding. The lower the bit rate, the poorer the sound quality.) Another popular format is WMA, which offers roughly the same sound quality as MP3 at half the bit rate (and, therefore, half the file size). A 2MB, 64-Kbps WMA file sounds about the same as a 4MB, 128-Kbps MP3. So, why not use WMA? You can, but you'll need Pocket Tunes, which is currently the only Palm OS player that supports the WMA format. (Pocket Tunes Deluxe adds support for DRM-protected WMAs, like the kind you buy or download from online services.)

■ **Tag**   As the music data is read from the CD, your software checks the Internet for information about each song—album title, artist name, and so on. All of this handy info is stored in a database within the MP3 file, where it can be read by any music player that happens upon it. This data is called the ID3 tag.

■ **Catalog**   The tracks are finally entered into your software's library. You can use the library to select music for playback on your PC.

Ripping Software

Ripping music is easy, all you need is the right software. We recommend one of the popular jukebox programs, such as Napster, RealPlayer, or Windows Media Player (just be sure to upgrade to at least version 10, which includes support for ripping to MP3, unlike version 9). You can rip a fairly large CD collection in just a day or two if you don't mind standing near your PC with a stack of CDs and turning yourself into a robot, removing one CD, inserting another, closing the CD drive, and clicking the copy button over and over.

> **TIP**   *This is a great job for kids. Pay your kid, neighbor, cousin, or grandson a quarter per CD (or something) to transfer your music collection to your PC.*

Before you begin, though, you should make sure that the encoder is set up the way you like. Specifically, set the file format (MP3 or WMA) and sound quality (that is, bit rate—we recommend at least 128 Kbps) as well as the destination folder for where the music will be stored.

14

Converting Music Files to MP3

What happens if you already have a large music collection in a non-MP3 format like WMA? Can you salvage those tracks for your PDA, or do you have to rip them all over again from scratch? Thankfully, you can indeed convert them—if you have the right software.

NOTE *If your music library consists of DRM-protected WMA files (see "Convert Protected Songs to MP3 Format" later in this chapter), you cannot convert them using this method. It works only with unprotected WMAs.*

We like using RealPlayer for this job (though you must upgrade to the premium version to do it). To convert a slew of WMA tracks to MP3s, just open RealPlayer and follow these steps:

1. Click My Library so you can see your songs.

2. Select the tracks you want to convert to MP3. To do that, click a track, hold the SHIFT key, and again click the last track that you want to convert.

3. Right-click the list of files and choose Convert Media Format from the context menu.

4. Ignore the left side of the dialog box—it simply indicates that you have multiple files selected. On the right, choose MP3 from the format menu and pick a quality, such as 160 Kbps Stereo.

5. If you want to replace the old file with this new one, click the check box for "Erase the current clip from my hard drive when done with Convert Media Format." If you want to keep both the old and new music files, leave this checkbox unchecked.

6. When you're ready, click OK and wait for the files to be converted.

When it's done, you can load these new MP3 files onto your PDA.

TIP   *If you'd rather not install RealPlayer (a large and rather intrusive program) just to convert your audio files, there are plenty of utilities that can accomplish the same task. We're partial to Media Monkey (www.mediamonkey.com), an excellent freeware music manager that includes a converter.*

Choosing a Music Player for Your PDA

As we've discussed, many Palm PDAs come with Pocket Tunes (though not the Deluxe version—that costs extra), a perfectly capable MP3/WMA player. It includes shuffle and repeat modes, and it can play in the background (meaning you can continue listening to music while performing other tasks on your PDA). It also enables you to create *playlists* right on your device. (A playlist is exactly that: a list of songs grouped together and given a name, such as "Rock Classics," "Workout," or "Mellow.") You can even gussy it up by downloading fancy skins that overhaul that interface.

How to ...   Convert Protected Songs to MP3 Format

So let's say you've purchased a bunch of songs from iTunes, Napster, or some other online store. Most of the files will be in an encrypted WMA format (or AAC, in the case of iTunes), meaning they're "locked" with digital rights management (DRM) protection. Translation: you can't convert them to MP3 format using conventional means.

You can, however, take a slightly unconventional approach. Almost all the online music stores allow you to burn purchased songs to CDs. And you now know how easy it is to rip songs from a CD to MP3 format. That's all you have to do—burn your songs to CD, then rip them back to your PC again. This two-step process effectively kills the DRM protection that keeps you from playing your music on your PDA.

The downside? You may notice a slight reduction in sound quality in your newly ripped MP3s. That's because the songs are being "processed" twice—once in the move to CD, and again in the ripping to your PC. However, unless you have a truly keen ear, you probably won't notice much difference.

14

However, as with virtually all Palm OS programs, there are alternatives. Let's take a look at a few Pocket Tunes replacements and why you might want to consider them:

■ **AeroPlayer**   A gorgeous-looking MP3 player with extensive skin support, so you can change the way the program looks in very dramatic ways. Seriously, if you're into skins, this is the player for you. AeroPlayer also includes a graphic equalizer, support for the Ogg Vorbis format (do a Google search if you're not familiar with it), and many other nifty features. It costs $14.95.

■ **goMP3 Player (Busker)**   goMP3 Player (formerly known as Busker) doesn't have lots of flashy skins or high-profile features. It's just a solid MP3 player that happens to include some nice perks. For instance, you can tap QuickMix to instantly start playing a random mix of 15 tunes. You can view album art (copied from your PC or downloaded wirelessly from your handheld!) while listening to songs. And you can easily build a list of favorites for one-tap playback. Busker costs $19.95.

■ **MMPlayer**   Not the prettiest or easiest audio player around, but MMPlayer is unique because it also plays video files. As you'll learn later in this chapter, it's a crucial piece of software if you want to watch movies on your handheld. But there's no reason you can't use MMPlayer for movies and another player for music. That's what we do.

■ **Pocket Tunes Deluxe**   As we've noted previously, Pocket Tunes Deluxe adds the enviable capability to play DRM-protected WMA files—a pretty huge deal. It plays all the major formats, including MP3, WAV, WMA, and Ogg Vorbis. It's packed with cool features, like integration with Windows Media Player for synchronizing songs with your PDA; a built-in equalizer; and cross fading between songs. Our favorite feature is bookmarks, which is ideal for anyone who likes to listen to MP3 audiobooks. And as with AeroPlayer, you can choose from an extensive library of skins.

Getting Songs onto Your PDA

Okay, let's review. Memory card? Check. Music player? Check. Updated last-will-and-testament listing us as beneficiaries? Check. (Aw, c'mon, throw us a bone.) Looks like you're ready to play that funky music (or, if you're Dave, that harsh, depressing music). All that's left is to actually move the songs from your PC to your PDA, or, more accurately, to your memory card, which you'll then pop into your PDA.

14

Actually, there might be slight variations in that process, depending on what music format you're loading on your handheld and what audio player is installed on it. For example, if you're using Pocket Tunes Deluxe to load songs downloaded from a subscription service, you can't just drag and drop files to your memory card. Let's take a look at the different methods of mobilizing your music.

Copying MP3s

Because MP3s are unprotected, you can play them using any Palm OS player, and copy them using whatever means is most expedient. We highly recommend a memory-card reader, which many PCs have built-in. If yours doesn't, it's easy and inexpensive to add one. We've seen USB memory-card readers selling for around $10—well worth the investment if you have a PDA, a digital camera, or any other device that uses memory cards.

Using Windows Explorer or your favorite method of copying files, just drag and drop the MP3s from your hard drive to the memory card. (Check your music player's instructions to see if it requires music files to reside in a specific folder.) When the process is complete, pull the card out of the reader, pop it into your PDA, and fire up Pocket Tunes or whatever music program you're going to use.

 While it is possible to HotSync songs to your PDA (just use the Palm Install Tool as you would for programs and data), we don't recommend this option—mostly because it takes significantly longer than the drag-and-drop method.

Copying Purchased and Protected Tracks

As noted earlier, the only way to listen to DRM-protected songs downloaded from online stores and services is with Pocket Tunes Deluxe. However, you can't just drag and drop these songs to your memory card as you can with MP3s. That's because the pesky Digital Rights Management system used to protect (i.e., restrict) the files requires you to use either Windows Media Player or the store's desktop music manager (like Napster or Yahoo Music Engine). Within those programs, however, you can usually drag and drop to the PDA, set up automatic synchronization, create playlists, and so on. So it's actually kind of a good thing.

Hey, My Tunes Won't Play Anymore. What Gives? The DRM-protected songs you download from subscription services have built-in licenses designed to keep you from making unauthorized copies, burning them to CDs (which you can do only if you've purchased them outright), and so on. They're also time-protected, meaning if you don't "update" the license on a regular basis (which usually requires nothing more than starting your desktop music manager and syncing with your Palm), the tunes will stop playing. What's a regular basis? It varies depending on the subscription service, but most of them give you 30 days.

How to ...   **Listen to Audiobooks and Internet Radio on Your PDA**

Rick is a nut for books on tape, or, more accurately, audiobooks (as "tape" is rapidly becoming an outdated medium for the material). But you won't catch him carrying around a bulky tape or CD player. Instead, he now listens to audiobooks on his PDA. You can too, with a little know-how.

First stop: Audible.com. This site is like the Amazon of audiobooks, where you browse and purchase titles online. Audible stocks thousands of fiction, non-fiction, radio, and even newspaper titles, most of them much less expensive than their tape or CD counterparts (and many of them not even available on tape or CD). But instead of waiting for your books to arrive in the mail, Audible downloads them directly to your PC, where you can then copy them to your PDA for anytime, anywhere listening.

Audible content is delivered in a proprietary format, meaning you need a special player to listen to it. Fortunately, the company offers just such a program: AudiblePlayer for Palm OS, which is compatible with most of the latest Palm handhelds and smartphones. In fact, your model may have come with the software already loaded, or at least contained on the accompanying software CD. (Even so, check the Audible Web site at www.audible.com to see if a newer version is available.)

Much as we love Audible, we're suckers for free (or at least really cheap) stuff. That's why we visit sites like AudioBooksForFree.com, which, true to its name, offers a vast library of free audiobooks in MP3 format (meaning they're ready to roll in RealPlayer or

(continued)

14

whatever software you care to use). Most of the titles are old, public-domain works (like Jules Verne and Mark Twain), but you can't beat the price. There's also Audiobooksonline. com, which offers some relatively high-profile titles on MP3 CDs (meaning the CDs are shipped to you in the mail, then you copy the MP3 files from them to your memory card). Finally, don't forget your local library. Many libraries now allow members to "check out" downloadable audiobooks.

If you do go the MP3 audiobook route, we highly recommend using a music program that has a bookmark feature. Otherwise, you could have an awfully difficult time navigating back to where you left off. Pocket Tunes Deluxe is one program that lets you bookmark your spot.

There's also the option of recording NPR and other spoken-word radio shows to your PC, then listening to them on your PDA. The program that makes this possible is Replay Radio, a $29.95 utility that can record, in ready-to-roll MP3 format, any streaming audio from the Internet. (The Web site describes it as "a VCR for Internet radio"—a pretty good analogy.) Thus, you could head over to the Web site for a show like "This American Life" (www.thislife.org), one of Rick's favorites, and record any or all of the archived broadcasts. Admittedly, you have to do this in real time, meaning it's a fairly slow process, but the reward for your effort is a library of top-notch listening material. And the shows themselves don't cost a thing. You pay only for Replay Radio. Highly, highly recommended.

Finally, there are podcasts—another great way to listen to spoken-word content on your PDA. See "Podcasts on Your Palm" for more details.

Getting Around in Pocket Tunes

PocketTunes is quite easy to use. The software automatically detects any audio files stored on your memory card—just tap the Songs button to see a complete list, then tap the song you want to play. In the meantime, let's identify the controls in the RealPlayer interface:

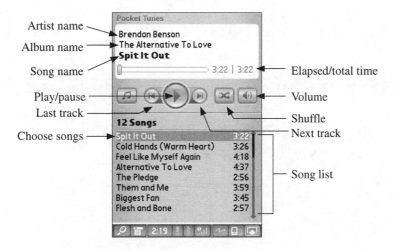

When you tap the shuffle button, which randomizes the playback order for the selected songs, you'll see it "light up" to indicate that feature is activated. Tap anywhere in the now-playing window (where the song, album, and artist are listed) and you'll see detailed data (derived from the song's ID3 tag) about the currently selected song:

14

NOTE   *The interface, and playback options contained therein, might be different depending on what skin you've selected. See the next section for info on finding, installing, and choosing skins.*

Choosing a Skin

One of the cool things about Pocket Tunes is its support for *skins*, which change the look and layout of the interface. There are dozens of skins to choose from, most of them free. Here's a sampling:

Downloading skins is easy: Just head to the Pocket Tunes site (www.pocket-tunes.com/skins) and browse the selections. When you find one you like, click the Download PDB button (saves time over getting the Zipped version, which must be extracted before you can install it on your Palm) and save the file to your hard drive. Then find the file and install it like you would any other Palm program: drag it into the Palm Install Tool (or just double-click it) and then HotSync.

After that, start Pocket Tunes, and then tap Menu | Tools | Choose Skin. You'll see this screen:

Choose Skin

| Apollo |
| Big Fingers |
| Built-In Skin |
| Geometry Fire |
| palmOne Skin |
| Pod_skin |

[OK] [Delete] [Copy] [Cancel]

Tap the skin you want and then tap OK. Presto-change-o!

Building a Playlist

Pocket Tunes makes it easy to create playlists, which can be handy when you want to listen to, say, a certain artist or kind of music. Suppose, for instance, you've got some classical tunes mixed in with your rock and roll. You probably don't want to listen to both during the same session, so you can build one playlist called "classical" and another called "rock." Then, just pick the one you want to hear, and Pocket Tunes will play only the tracks contained in that playlist.

There's no physical organization or division that occurs when you create playlists. Therefore, songs can overlap on more than one playlist, while other songs needn't ever be on a playlist at all. They're a convenience, a way to play specific chunks of music based on whatever grouping you desire.

The step-by-step process of making a playlist in Pocket Tunes is provided in the User Guide; no need to repeat it here.

Listening to Live Internet Radio

Another very cool Pocket Tunes feature is support for streaming audio—radio stations broadcast over the Internet. At this very moment, Rick is listening to NPR, live, on his Palm TX. It's a thing of beauty.

To do this, you need a smartphone like the Palm Treo or a Wi-Fi-equipped PDA like the LifeDrive or Palm TX. In other words, you need an Internet connection. Get yourself online, then follow the steps listed next.

14

1. Start your handheld's Web browser.

2. Go to Live365.com or Shoutcast.com, two sites that are home to hundreds of Pocket Tunes-compatible Internet radio stations.

3. Browse the list of sites or search for something specific. (Rick searched for "NPR" at Shoutcast and found a couple dozen stations.)

4. Tap "Tune in" (or whatever the appropriate button is). The browser will ask where you want to save the playlist (a tiny file Pocket Tunes uses to access the station). Choose Device or Card, and then tap Yes to download.

5. On the next screen, tap "Save and open." Be prepared to wait several seconds while the station downloads and tunes in.

6. Return to Pocket Tunes to control playback and volume.

7. Now that you've "saved" a station, you can tune into it again without having to go through all the same steps. In Pocket Tunes, tap Choose Songs, and then tap the category menu in the top-right corner of the screen. Choose Internet Audio and you'll see a list of previously played stations.

Playing Music Eats Batteries

Playing music on your PDA will use up the battery quite a bit faster than, say, looking up a few phone numbers. If you plan to listen a lot while you're on the road, be sure to pack a portable charger (see Chapter 16). Likewise, enable your music software's power-save feature (usually found in its Options or Preferences menu), which will turn off the screen after a designated period of time (usually anywhere from 30 seconds to three minutes). The music keeps playing, but the screen no longer gobbles up precious battery life.

If you're listening to streaming audio as described in the previous section, it'll really tax the battery, as you're maintaining a live Internet connection in addition to playing music.

14

Podcasts on Your PDA

A podcast is nothing more than an audio recording, usually of the spoken-word variety. These range from interesting and informative shows like *60 Minutes* and NPR's *All Songs Considered,* to homebrew recordings from individuals or businesses. Because most podcasts are produced in MP3 format, they can play on your Palm using just about any audio player.

We could easily fill another book on the subject of podcasts—how to create them, where to find them, and so on. For our purposes, however, we'll have to settle for teaching you how to get them on your PDA.

For this we recommend using Yahoo Music Engine, a free music-management program that also opens the door to Yahoo's music store and subscription service. Here's how to get started:

1. Visit the Yahoo Music Web site (music.yahoo.com/musicengine) and download Yahoo Music Engine. Install it on your PC.

2. Visit the Yahoo Music Engine Plugins site (plugins.yme.music.yahoo.com). Find the podcast plug-in and follow the instructions to download and install it.

3. Run Yahoo Music Engine. In the lefthand toolbar you should see a Yahoo Podcasts option. Click it. Read the accompanying Getting Started guide to learn more about using podcasts with Yahoo Music Engine.

4. Subscribe to one or more podcasts. The latest episodes will start downloading immediately.

5. Insert your Palm's memory card into your PC's card reader.

The Best Podcasts

At last count, there were approximately eight million-bajillion podcasts on the Internet. Wondering which ones are worth your time? As you know by now, we have an opinion on just about everything. Here's our list of the best podcast picks:

- **60 Minutes**   The long-running TV newsmagazine is now available in podcast form! You don't get all the segments from the show, but you do get one per week. Great stuff, though there are times when you wish you could see what the reporter is describing.

- **Battlestar Galactica**   If you're a fan of this awesome sci-fi series, you owe it to yourself to check out show-runner Ronald D. Moore's podcast. In it he gives you behind-the-scenes info and insights about each episode.

- **NPR: All Songs Considered**   This is one of many available NPR podcasts, and definitely one of the best. Host Bob Boilen plays lengthy snippets of music from new and newsworthy artists and bands. In fact, it was because of this show that Rick discovered Brendan Benson, who quickly became one of his all-time favorite artists.

- **The Ricky Gervais Show**   Although it's one of the few podcasts that actually costs money (you can purchase it from Audible or iTunes), this hilarious podcast from Ricky Gervais, who's known and loved as the creator and star of the British version of *The Office* (one of the funniest TV shows *ever*, by the way), is worth the dough.

6. In Yahoo Music Engine, click My Podcasts, then select the podcast you want to copy to your device. Drag it to the appropriate drive letter in the lefthand toolbar (whichever one corresponds to your memory card) and drop it there. Repeat the process to copy additional podcasts.

7. Put the card back into your Palm and enjoy some podcast goodness!

More advanced users can create a podcast playlist within Yahoo Music Engine, then configure the program to sync that playlist with your memory card—thus automating the copying of newly downloaded podcasts.

14

Audio on the Go

To really enjoy listening to music and other audio on your PDA, you'll need a few accessories. For starters, pack a good pair of headphones. Your PDA might have come with a pair, but trust us when we say: you can do better.

You may also want to consider a set of external speakers. Your PDA may be small, but the music it contains can be made much bigger. Heck, you can even plug it into a home stereo and really pump up the volume.

Finally, for folks who spend a lot of time in the car, there are ways to free your music from the bonds of your PDA; by which we mean pipe the sound through your car's speakers.

See Chapter 16 for information on these and other handy accessories.

Making Music on Your PDA

When you tire of listening to music and instead want to be in the band, it's time for some music software. And believe it or not, you can indeed use your PDA for a large number of music applications. Most models have a built-in speaker, and the display is perfectly suited for music notation. If you're a musician, be sure to check out some of these applications.

Metronome and Drumming Software

Even PDAs that have the most basic sound capabilities (meaning they can't even play MP3s) can perform simple tasks like keeping time. In fact, this would have come in handy a long time ago, when Dave used to carry a guitar around wherever he went. Having a metronome or mini-drum machine in a box as small as a PDA would have been really cool.

■ **PerfectBeat Metronome**   This is your standard metronome, with an attractive interface, a slider for choosing a tempo, and other useful features.

■ **Pocket Beat**   This app simulates a drum kit right on your PDA. It can remember two distinct tempos and you can switch between them easily by using onscreen controls or the Scroll button. Pocket Beat can also play straight or shuffle beats, and it can vary between 40 and 196 beats per minute. The best part, though, is that you can tap out your own meter on the screen—Pocket Beat memorizes the tempo and plays it accordingly.

Portable Music Lessons

Budding musicians can carry around the following applications to bone up on notes, keyboard positions, and fingering:

■ **Mozart**   Just learning to read music? Mozart makes a game of it, challenging you to guess the presented notes on a piano keyboard or guitar fret. It includes a sight-reading mode, two levels of difficulty, and various other features.

■ **McChords**   If you're learning piano, McChords is an essential portable tool for working through chord fingerings. It shows you which keys to press to form the majority of chords you need to master basic piano playing.

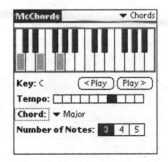

■ **PChord**   This program, shown next, is indispensable for anyone trying to get the hang of the guitar. In fact, PChord also supports mandolin, banjo, violin, and other stringed instruments. Choose a chord and PChord displays a variety of ways to finger it. The program includes every chord we could think of, including obscure (minor 9th and stacked fourths) chords you might play only once in a great while. As such, it's a good memory jogger even for experienced players. Similar programs to try include Guitar Power, FretTrainer, and CDB FretBoard Trainer.

14

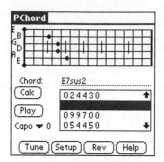

Getting in Tune

Tuning—bleh. We hate tuning guitars. If only there were some automated way ...

Well, of course there is. Every guitarist on earth probably owns a $30 electronic tuner, but did you know you can also use your PDA for tuning? We found a bunch of tuners. One good example is a program called Guitar Tuner Lt. Dave has used it himself on several occasions. It comes with standard and alternative tunings. Tap the appropriate onscreen string and the tone plays for several seconds. Or, tap the Auto button to hear each string's tone in turn.

Music Annotation and Recording

Perhaps you've experimented with (or frequently use) desktop applications that enable you to compose and play music. Those programs generally let you drag notes onto musical staffs or play an onscreen keyboard to construct musical compositions. Well, you can do the same thing on your PDA—the screen is just a bit smaller, and you don't have multiple voices to hear your multi-timbral creations. Here are a few applications you can try:

- **Magic Piano** This program enables you to play an onscreen keyboard while the notes you strike get added to a staff. You can then play back your creation. Most amazing of all, Magic Piano uses digitally sampled piano sounds, so your notes sound just like the real thing. Pretty impressive for a program that costs a mere 12 bucks. (Note: It requires Palm OS 5 or later.)

■ **MusicPal**   MusicPal is a MIDI program (if you have to ask what MIDI is, this probably isn't the software for you) that enables you to compose and listen to music, and then convert your MusicPal files to PC-compatible MIDI files. It's packed with music-composition features, making it the ideal companion for mobile Mozarts.

Other Music Programs

Listening to and composing music are by no means the end of your PDA's music capabilities. Just do a quick search of "MP3" or "music" on Handango or PalmGear, and you'll find dozens upon dozens of nifty programs. For example:

■ **2PlayMe**   Want to wake up to the sound of your favorite song? 2PlayMe is an MP3 alarm clock that works with AeroPlayer, Pocket Tunes, and RealPlayer.

■ **LightWav**   Another alarm-oriented program, LightWav lets you replace the standard Palm OS application alarms with MP3, WMA, WAV, Ogg Vorbis, or MIDI sound files. If you have a Treo smartphone, you can also use those files as ringtones and sms/mms/ voicemail sounds.

■ **Music Gadgets**   It's 12, 12, 12 music tools in one package! Music Gadgets includes a metronome, tuner, stopwatch, piano keyboard, time calculator, and seven other handy items for musicians. Not a bad deal for $14.95.

14

■ **Music Teacher** A must-have for music teachers, this program lets you organize all aspects of your home- or conservatory-based roster of students. It includes a daily schedule, order tracking, income/expense management, and the option to export records in CSV format for desktop use.

Movies and TV Shows

It wasn't all that long ago that watching a TV show or feature-length movie on a PDA would have been considered a peculiar kind of insanity, like eating lima beans or starting a political discussion with Dave. These days, though, there's no reason not to use your PDA to fire up *The Matrix* or an episode of *The Simpsons* on a long flight, or even a short train ride. You might need some extra software to make this happen. You'll definitely need some spare time and a little bit of tech-savvy.

NOTE   *We'll be the first to admit that watching video on your Palm can be a bit of a letdown. The screen is small, the images may be a bit jerky, and the audio sometimes gets out of sync with the video. Plus, it can be time-consuming and a hassle just to get the video on your device. We're not trying to discourage you, just give you a reality check.*

Watching DVDs

Believe it or not, you can watch a DVD right on your Palm. Well, actually, a ripped, converted, and copied DVD. How is this possible? In a nutshell:

■ You buy a special utility designed to copy the DVD to your PC in a Palm-viewable format.

■ You copy the newly created video file to a memory card.

■ You watch the video using a special viewer.

Let's get started. The first thing you need is a "DVD ripper," a PC utility that extracts video from a DVD and turns it into a file that can be viewed on your Palm (with the aforementioned special viewer). We know of three programs (all available from Handango.com) that can accomplish this task:

■ **Palm Media Studio** This one conveniently comes with a freeware media player, TCPMP, for your Palm (though you can always download it elsewhere if you decide to use another ripper).

■ **Pocket DVD Wizard, Palm Edition** A nice choice because it can create files that work not only with Palms, but also with iPods, Sony PSPs, and other devices.

■ **Pocket-DVD Studio for Palm** We like the way this one lets you preview the size of the ripped video as it will appear on your PDA.

All three are priced around $30, and there are trial versions of each, so you can decide which interface and feature set you like best. We think they're all pretty good.

With all three programs, you basically just stick a DVD into your PC's DVD drive and follow the instructions to copy the video to your PC. This can take a while—anywhere from about 45 minutes to a couple hours for a feature-length movie—so be prepared to wait. When the conversion is done, you'll be left with a video file that you'll need to copy to your Palm's memory card. The best way to do this is by inserting the card into your PC's media reader and dragging the file to it. Trying to copy it via HotSync would take *forever*.

The last step is to install a media player on your Palm, one that supports the newly created video file. (Palm's Media applet isn't suitable for these, alas.) We recommend the Core Pocket Media Player, also known as TCPMP. This freeware program isn't much to look at it, and it's not particularly easy to use, but it supports a wide variety of video formats—and the price is right.

14

How to ...   Copy Video Files with Palm Desktop

The current version of Palm Desktop comes with a built-in movie converter, though it doesn't support DVDs. But it can convert a wide variety of video formats (including AVI, MPEG-1, MPEG-4, and WMV) for viewing in the Palm's Media applet. Just click the Media icon on the left side of the screen, and then the Add Media button. Now navigate to the folder on your hard drive that contains the video file you want to convert. Depending on the size and nature of the file, this can take a long time—hours, even. When you're done, just drag the video to your memory card and HotSync.

That's all there is to it! Now, if you want to watch video from other sources, see the sidebar, "Copy Video Files with Palm Desktop."

NOTE   *Watching movies on your PDA is a battery-draining activity. That's because, like games, movies flex all your PDA's muscles at once: processor, screen, audio system, and so on. Therefore, plan ahead. If you're going on a long trip and want to watch a video or two, make sure you've packed the AC adapter or one of the travel chargers discussed in Chapter 16.*

TV Shows

One of the best ways to get video content onto your PDA is to record TV shows on your PC. You can accomplish this by installing a TV capture card (such as the Hauppauge WinTV-PVR-350) or a video card with TV-capture capabilities (such as the ATI All-in-Wonder). Both solutions come with the software you need to record TV shows to your computer's hard drive. Just connect a cable or satellite box and you're good to go.

The recorded shows usually end up as AVI or MPEG files (and usually you can choose the format you want—MPEG-1 is best for stuff that's going to end up on your PDA). Both formats are compatible with Palm Desktop, so once you have a show recorded, it's a simple matter to convert it.

Storage Space

You think music files take up a lot of space? Ha! A single two-hour movie can easily consume an entire 512MB memory card (see Figure 14-2). Needless to say, you'll want to invest in at least a few high-capacity cards if you plan to take video on the road.

Just how much video can you fit on, say, a 256MB memory card? Unfortunately, it's impossible to say owing to the huge number of variables involved. The bit rate, resolution, audio quality, and size of the original file all factor into the equation, as do the selected bit rate, resolution, and audio quality of the file you're creating. Unfortunately, Palm Desktop doesn't tell you how large the resulting file will be. You have no choice but to run the conversion process

Our Favorite TV Shows for the Road

What do we like to watch on our PDAs when we're on the road during those massive book tours? Assuming we ever wrote a book that was successful enough to warrant a tour, here's a glimpse into what we'd be watching.

Rick: I know you enjoy watching C-Span, "Yu-Gi-Oh," and reality shows about teenybopper pop stars, but I'm more partial to TV that's, you know, entertaining. And recording stuff on my PC is ideal for catching up on shows that I don't usually have time to watch, or that I normally wouldn't take time out to watch (*anything* is fair game when there's a flight delay at the airport). So on my PDA you'll usually find episodes of "Law & Order," "Third Watch" (quite possibly the most underrated show ever), "South Park," and "Smallville" (what can I say, I have a thing for Kristin Kreuk).

Dave: I wish I was your personal therapist; I could afford a new houseboat just dealing with your insecurities alone. Your wildly inaccurate accusations notwithstanding, I tend to watch old, familiar comedies on my PDA: "Seinfeld," "Everybody Loves Raymond," and "Friends" reruns, to be precise. I want to preserve the good stuff—new episodes of "Battlestar Galactica" and "Lost," for instance—for my big TV at home, where I can watch it with my family. But I hear that you like to keep your Powerpuff Girls viewing private, so it's understandable that you'd save those for the PDA (which, as we all know, you've named after your favorite Powerpuff character, Blossom).

14

FIGURE 14-2   A high-capacity memory card (or two) is all but mandatory if you want to take a lot of video on the road.

File Formats Explained

AVI? MPEG? MOV? What the heck are these things? Put simply, they're the most common and popular formats for video files. Palm Desktop and most of the aforementioned DVD rippers supports these and other formats, including:

- ■ AVI
- ■ DivX
- ■ MPEG-1
- ■ MPEG-4
- ■ QuickTime (MOV)
- ■ WMV

It's not really important to understand the technical differences between these file types, only to recognize them as the kinds of files you need to corral if you plan to use a converter.

and then check the size of the resulting file. If it's too big to fit on your memory card, well, you're out of luck. Experimentation is the key.

Other Movie Software

If you're a serious movie buff, you'll want to use your PDA for more than just watching your favorite films. Head over to Handango or PalmGear and do a search for "movie," and you'll find these and other gems:

- ■ **Leonard Maltin 2005 Movie Guide**   Perhaps you've seen the bulky paperback version of this handy guide—it wouldn't exactly fit in your pocket! The Palm OS version includes details and capsule reviews of more than 20,000 flicks, and you get a year's worth of updates to the database as new films are added. You can create and manage a film library and even keep track of movies you've rented (let's see a paperback book do that!). In short, this thing has more features than we have room to list, and is a must for anyone who's serious about movies.

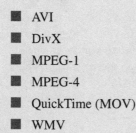

■ **Movie Mentor**   Tired of standing in the aisles of your local video store and scratching your head while trying to figure out what to rent? Movie Mentor to the rescue! This program includes a database of the "top" 2,500 movies, with updates added whenever you HotSync (so you always have the latest listings). Everything is categorized, so you can easily hone in on the genre you want and see a list of the top-rated choices.

Video	▼ All
☐5* Lord of the Rings: The Fello...'01	
☐5* Schindler's List '93	
☐5* Ran '85	
☐5* Amadeus '84	
☐5* Almost Famous '00	
☐5* Pride and Prejudice '95	
☐5* Saving Private Ryan '98	
☐5* Pulp Fiction '94	
☐5* E.T. the Extra-Terrestrial '82	
☐5* Band of Brothers '01	
☐5* Crouching Tiger, Hidden Dr...'00	
▼ Other Lists	(Search)

■ **Movie Quotz**   Users of the SilverScreen application launcher (see Chapter 12) will get a kick out of Movie Quotz, a SilverScreen ticker tape that displays thousands of classic lines. There's also a quiz mode that makes for an interesting trivia game.

■ **Palm Movie Maker**   If your handheld or smartphone has a built-in camera, you can use this nifty program to create and even edit simple movies. Just make sure it's compatible with your model. It works with most camera-equipped devices, but not all. Lights! Camera! PDA!

Private Listening—in Style

It goes without saying that you're going to listen to music and videos with some sort of earbuds or headphones. Your Palm might be a marvel of modern engineering, but its tiny speakers can't compete with background noise in public. Nor would you want it to. After all, you certainly don't want anyone else to know you're watching "Sailor Moon."

If, like Dave, you find wired headphones to be inconvenient and somewhat old-fashioned, you might want to untether yourself with Bluetooth wireless headphones. Dave is a big fan of using Softick Audio Gateway (www.softick.com) to connect to a pair of Motorola HT820 headphones. The headphones are light, comfortable, and sound excellent. He uses them to listen to music on his Palm while exercising. See Chapter 16 for more information.

14

Where to Find It

Web Site	Address	What's There
Aerodrome Software	www.aerodrome.us	AeroPlayer
Applian Technologies	www.replay-radio.com	Replay Radio
The Core Pocket Media Player	tcpmp.corecodec.org	The Core Pocket Media Player
Electric Pocket	www.electricpocket.com	Busker MP3
Handango	www.handango.com	Most of the music and movie apps discussed in this chapter
MMPlayer	www.mmplayer.com	MMPlayer
NormSoft	www.normsoft.com	Pocket Tunes Deluxe
PalmGear	www.palmgear.com	Most of the music and movie apps discussed in this chapter
PQDVD.com	www.pqdvd.com	Pocket-DVD Studio

Chapter 15

Books, Photos, Paintings, and More

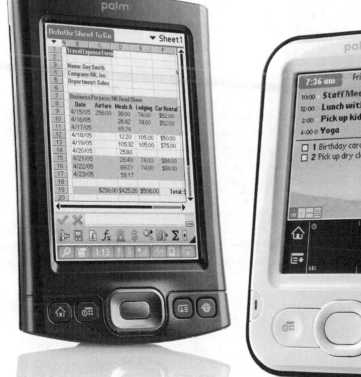

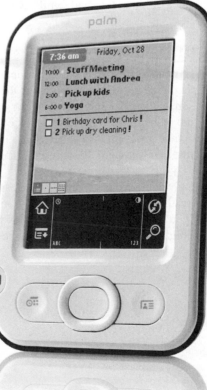

How to…

- Read e-books on your handheld
- Read in bed without disturbing your spouse
- Choose between public-domain and commercial titles
- Find and purchase e-books online
- Use eReader's advanced features
- View photos on your handheld
- Find third-party photo viewers
- Work with built-in cameras
- Create drawings, sketches, and paintings
- Capture screenshots

Whereas Dave enjoys zoning out to music or staring blankly at reruns of "The Simpsons," Rick prefers to use his handheld for more creative and personal pursuits: reading books, viewing photos of his friends and family, and even dabbling with a virtual paintbrush.

E-Books on the Go

If you're not reading electronic books, *e-books,* on your handheld, you're missing out.

Most people we mention this to balk at the idea of reading a whole book on a small, electronic screen—until they try it. Consider our friend James, who has carried a handheld for years but only recently tried reading a book on it. Now he's hooked.

"Since I take my Palm everywhere I go," he says, "I always have books with me and I'm able to whittle away at them." As a result, "I've read more this year (for pleasure) than ever before."

Indeed, given that your handheld is almost always at your side, it's only logical to stock it with some reading material. The next time you're stuck in line at the post office or your flight is delayed, you'll have a great way to pass the time. If you're a parent, you can even pack some illustrated children's books for times when the kids need a distraction, like during a long wait at a restaurant.

Prime Suspect.

Mr. Shears used to be married to Mrs. Shears and they lived together until two years ago. Then Mr. Shears left and didn't come back. This was why Mrs. Shears came over and did lots of cooking for us after Mother died, because she didn't have to cook for Mr. Shears anymore and she didn't have to stay at home and be his wife. And also Father said that she needed company and didn't want to be on her own.

And sometimes Mrs. Shears stayed overnight at our house and I liked it when she did because she made things

The e-books available today aren't just fringe titles from no-name authors. You can get the works of Dan Brown, Janet Evanovich, Carl Hiaasen, Stephen King, Anna Quindlen, and David Sedaris, to name but a few. Interested in Bill Clinton's autobiography, but not the heavy lifting that goes with it? The e-book edition of *My Life* weighs nothing.

It also consumes zero trees—and you needn't be an environmentalist to appreciate the practicality of that.

How to ...   **Read in Bed Without Disturbing Your Spouse**

Since the dawn of time, one seemingly insurmountable problem has plagued the human race: how to read in bed without disturbing one's spouse. Torches didn't work. They crackled too loudly and tended to set the bed on fire. Battery-operated book lights didn't work: they made books too heavy, leading to "carpal reader syndrome." But finally there's an answer—the handheld. Just load up a novel and turn off the bedside lamp. You'll have no trouble seeing the screen in the dark, and your spouse won't even know it's on. PDA or marriage saver? You be the judge.

15

Another e-book perk: instant delivery. You buy the books online and download them on the spot. No trip to the bookstore required, no week-long wait for Amazon to ship. Still not convinced? How about this? Thanks to your handheld's backlit screen, e-books are perfect for late-night reading in bed.

Now that you've seen some of the minor miracles handhelds can perform, it should come as little surprise to learn they're also great for e-books. In this chapter, you learn everything you need to know about using your handheld as a mobile library.

> **NOTE**   *We mostly discuss reading documents, not editing them. If you want to learn more about creating and editing documents on your handheld, see Chapter 11.*

To Buy or Not to Buy?

There are dozens of online sources for e-books, both free and commercial. The former are works considered public domain: either their copyrights have expired (as in the case of classic literature), or they've been written and released by authors not seeking compensation. There are literally thousands of titles available in the public domain, many of them already converted to the Doc format.

Commercial titles aren't unlike what you'd buy in a bookstore: they've simply been converted to an electronic format and authorized for sale online. Most commercial e-books are created using a proprietary format, meaning a special viewer is required. This is primarily to prevent unauthorized distribution. Unlike actual books, commercial e-books aren't meant to be loaned out or given to others (though there's usually a way around this—see "Share the Love" later in this chapter). When you buy one, you're effectively buying a license to read it on your handheld and only on your handheld.

Building a Library of E-Books

Most Palm OS handhelds come preloaded with the software you need to read e-books obtained from various online sources (which we'll discuss shortly). It's a program called eReader, though don't be surprised if your handheld came with Palm Reader instead. They're identical programs, only the name has changed.

> **NOTE**   *If your handheld didn't come with an e-book reader, you can download eReader free from eReader.com.*

eReader enables you to view the vast majority of handheld-compatible e-books that are out there—commercial and freeware titles alike. It also supports the Doc file format, which was developed years ago to enable Palm OS devices to view lengthy documents. (In case you're wondering, the reason Memo Pad didn't catch on as a basic e-book reader is that it has a maximum document size of about 500 words.) Many of the freeware books you'll find online will be in the Doc format, meaning you can load them right into eReader.

The Doc format developed for the Palm OS is not the same as the .doc format used for Microsoft Word files. Thus, you can't open Doc-format e-books in Word, nor can you open Word files in eReader. (You can, however, open Word files in programs like Documents to Go, but that's another chapter—namely, Chapter 11.)

Here are three of the top online destinations for e-books:

■ **eReader.com**   Formerly Palm Digital Media, this site (see Figure 15-1) is home to thousands of fiction and non-fiction titles. Most of them are discounted, and you can save even more by subscribing to the free eReader.com newsletter. Delivered weekly via e-mail, the newsletter contains a code that gives you 10 percent off each book you buy. Oh, and in case you haven't figured it out, eReader.com is also the company behind the eReader program.

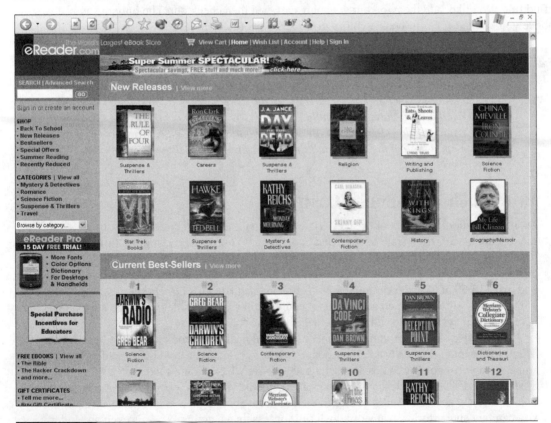

FIGURE 15-1   eReader.com is home to thousands of e-books—everything from Stephen King to *Star Trek* novels.

15

■ **Fictionwise**   Fictionwise started out selling short stories from relatively unknown authors, but has evolved into one of the Internet's largest e-book outlets. Not all titles are available for Palm handhelds (some books are exclusively for Pocket PCs), and among those that are, some require a program other than eReader. We'll talk more about that later.

■ **MemoWare**   If one site is synonymous with public-domain works of fiction and non-fiction, it's MemoWare. Here you can find thousands of texts divided into categories such as business, history, travel, biography, sci-fi, and Shakespeare. Whether you're looking for a collection of Mexican recipes, a Zane Grey western, a sappy love poem, or a classic work by Dickens, this is the place to start. However, as with Fictionwise, some of the titles here require different programs. (Anything available in Doc format is fair game for use with eReader.)

Buying and Reading Books from eReader.com

Shopping at eReader.com is not much different from shopping at Amazon.com. You browse to find titles you like, add them to your shopping cart, and then check out. The only difference is, once you've paid for your books, you're given a Zip file to download.

NOTE   *Not familiar with Zip files and how they work? Ay, caramba, read a computer magazine once in a while, would ya? Just kidding. A Zip file is a compressed file that contains one or more other files. Windows XP can access the contents of Zip files (which, in this case, are the e-books you purchased) directly; if you have an earlier version of Windows, you'll need a third-party program like WinZip (www.winzip.com). Just be aware that you can't install the downloaded Zip file on your handheld and expect to start reading. You have to open the Zip file and install the e-book file contained therein.*

How Much Do E-Books Cost?

Okay, let's talk turkey. E-books usually cost less than their printed counterparts, but the discounts vary from store to store and book to book. For instance, at press time, the hardcover edition of Thomas L. Friedman's controversial book, *The World is Flat: A Brief History of the Twenty-First Century*, was selling for $30 at retail stores, $18 at Amazon.com, and just $13.50 at eReader.com. On the other hand, Dan Brown's *Deception Point* was only a few bucks below the paperback price. Of course, when you consider what you save on gas, taxes, shipping charges, and all that, the deals look sweeter still.

Fictionwise employs a somewhat unconventional method of book sales. You set up a *Micropay* account (basically a debit account) on the site and use a credit card to deposit some money. E-book purchases are then deducted from the account. Fictionwise often offers great rebate deals in which some, or even all, of a book's purchase price is refunded into your Micropay account. And if you're in the mood for some light and inexpensive reading, you can buy short stories, many of which sell for less than a dollar. (There's even an Under a Dollar link where you can find all the site's e-book bargains.)

This file contains the e-book itself (in an encrypted .pdb format), along with the eReader program. Install the latter only if you don't already have it on your handheld. As for the e-book itself, just double-click the file to queue it in Install Tool for your next HotSync.

After you HotSync, start eReader, and then tap Menu | Open. Select the book you want to open by tapping it, and then tap the Open button. At this point, you'll need to "unlock" the book, which is done by entering the name on the credit card you used to buy the book, and the credit card number itself.

Don't worry—this information is completely secure and cannot be accessed by anyone (yourself included) once entered. The good news is that after you unlock one book, you don't have to repeat the process for subsequent e-book purchases.

Reading Books   Once you have a book open in eReader, there are four (yes, four!) ways to "turn pages"—that is, to flip from one screen of text to the next, just like turning pages in a book:

■ Press the down side of the Navigator (or your handheld's Scroll Down button, if it has one).

■ Tap anywhere in the bottom half of the screen.

These actions also work in reverse—you can flip to the previous page by pressing the Scroll Up button or tapping anywhere in the top half of the screen.

eReader automatically bookmarks your page, so if you switch to another program (or turn off the handheld) while in the middle of, say, Chapter 16, you'll return to that exact page the next time you run eReader. You can also add your own bookmarks by tapping Menu | Go | Add Bookmark.

SHORTCUT *If your handheld has a Navigator, press the button in the center to quickly add a bookmark. (Press it again if you want to remove it.) You can also tap the bookmark icon on the eReader toolbar, as discussed in the next section.*

In fact, let's take a look at the eReader toolbar and check out some of those cryptic icons (which you can add or remove by tapping Menu | Options | Toolbar Preferences):

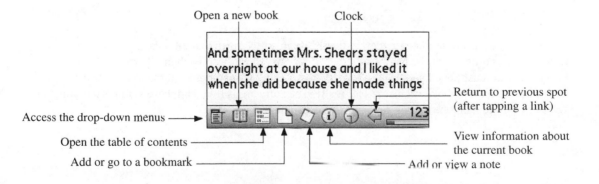

In addition to adding bookmarks to book pages, eReader enables you to add free-form notes, not unlike writing in the margins of a book page. To insert a note, tap Menu | Go | Add Note (or tap the Add Note icon in the toolbar). You can even export your notes to a memo, just by tapping Menu | Book | Export Notes.

eReader has many other handy features. You can beam books to other handheld users (keeping in mind that you'll also have to fork over your credit card number if you want them to be able to open your book), change the font size, and use Auto Scroll—a feature that makes the text scroll slowly up like a Teleprompter, so you don't have to keep flipping pages. Most of these features are self-explanatory, so spend some time exploring eReader's menus.

Sharing the Love   One common question asked by e-book fans is how to share their books with PDA-carrying friends and family members. This depends on the method of copy protection implemented by the e-book seller. We think eReader.com's method is both fair and logical: you can give the e-book .pdb file to anyone you like, but for them to actually open the book, they'll need your credit card number. That should discourage you from giving the book to strangers, but does allow for sharing with people you trust—family members, close friends, and so on.

Should You Upgrade to eReader Pro?   For a mere $9.95, you can upgrade to eReader Pro. Is it worth it? At press time, eReader.com was bundling the program with Webster's New World Vest Pocket Dictionary and five pre-selected books, which by themselves more than cover the cost of the upgrade. As for eReader Pro itself, its main attraction is support for more fonts. If you want to pack more text onscreen by using a really tiny font or want to make text easier on the eyes with a large font, eReader Pro is definitely a worthwhile upgrade.

Other Sources for Contemporary E-Books

eReader.com and Fictionwise may be the largest sources for commercial e-books, but other Web sites also offer contemporary works. Check out:

- **eBooks.com**   www.ebooks.com
- **eBookMall**   www.ebookmall.com
- **PerfectBound**   www.perfectbound.com
- **MobiPocket**   www.mobipocket.com

MobiPocket is not unlike eReader, in that it's both software and an e-book-selling Web site. Its selection is quite good, with a much larger library of reference titles than other e-book stores. However, you must install and use the MobiPocket Reader to read books purchased from the MobiPocket store. Is that a problem? Not really. The software is free, and there's no reason you can't have more than one e-book reader on your handheld.

Indeed, we recommend trying MobiPocket, as it has some unique features not found in eReader. For instance, it allows you to subscribe to any of 500 eNews channels, which are updated whenever you HotSync. This is similar to AvantGo, a program we've discussed in several other chapters, but AvantGo doesn't do e-books—it's just a news reader.

Making Room for the Books

Be forewarned: e-books can be large documents—another reason to consider adding a memory card to your handheld. Bill Clinton's autobiographical *My Life,* for instance, nabs a whopping 7.1MB of storage. Of course, that's the exception. Most e-books fall well under the 1MB mark. But if you don't want to sacrifice a big chunk of your handheld's internal RAM to e-books, load them onto a memory card instead.

Our Favorite E-Books

Rick: I have turned into an e-book zealot in recent years, recommending MemoWare and eReader.com to friends, family, and any strangers who will sit still for five seconds. Among the great titles I've read on my handheld are *Angela's Ashes, Battlefield Earth, House of Sand and Fog, Shadow Divers, The Kite Runner, Life is So Good,* and *The Corrections.* I also enjoyed rereading *The Most Dangerous Game,* a story I remembered fondly from high school. I got that one free from MemoWare.

Dave: I have to commend Rick on the progress he's made. When I met him a scant eight years ago, he hadn't yet learned to master the written word. Since then, I've seen him get his equivalency diploma, start on "chapter books," and even sign his name in ink instead of crayon. Bravo, Rick! Well done! As for me, I find the best for the buck is the magazine *Fantasy & Science Fiction*—eReader.com has a huge collection of them available. I'm rarely disappointed by any of those tales, and there's a month's worth of bedtime reading in each collection.

15

The PDA Photo Wallet

Still cramming pictures of your spouse, kids, pets, and Naomi Watts into your already overstuffed wallet? Sucker. You can fit an almost endless supply of photos into your handheld and it won't add one bit of extra bulge to your pocket. (By the way, sorry for that "sucker" remark—Dave's idea.)

Assuming you have a PDA with a color screen (and preferably one with a resolution of 320 × 320 pixels or higher), you can carry and view what amounts to a digital photo album. Great, but how do you get photos into your PDA? Glad you asked.

Loading Photos into Your PDA

Digital photos traditionally come from two places: your digital camera and your computer's hard drive (usually after you've copied them there from your camera). Where handhelds are concerned, you have several options for loading photos:

- You can take the memory card out of your digital camera (assuming it's a Secure Digital, or SD, card) and insert it into your handheld's SD slot.

- You can use Windows to drag and drop photos from your hard drive to a memory card (assuming you have a card reader in, or connected to, your PC), and then plug the card into your handheld.

- You can use Palm Desktop to browse the photos on your hard drive and select them for installation via HotSync.

> **NOTE** *Obviously, if you have a model like the Zire 71 or Treo 650, both of which have built-in digital cameras, you have the added option of snapping photos directly. But you can also load photos snapped elsewhere using one or more of the aforementioned methods.*

These three options assume that you already have a program on your handheld designed to view digital photos. Most current Palm models come with an app called Media (shown in Figure 15-2), though a few include the older Photos app. This probably comes as no surprise, but there are also numerous third-party applications available for users who don't already have Photos, Media, or a similar built-in viewer, or who just want more robust features than these apps provide.

> **NOTE** *As mentioned in Chapter 14, Media can be used for more than just photos. It's also a basic movie-viewer.*

This is one of those areas where we, as book authors, run screaming from the room. That's because different handhelds come not only with different photo-viewing apps, but also with different versions of Palm Desktop, which have different methods of managing photos. To try to cover everything here would require Herculean feats of writer-legerdemain that, frankly, Dave isn't up to. But fear not. We're going to give you the crucial skills and information you need to turn your handheld—whatever the model—into one killer photo album.

FIGURE 15-2   Most of the latest Palm handhelds come with either Photos or Media, both of which enable you to view digital photos stored in memory or on a memory card.

If Your Handheld Has a Photo Viewer, Start Here

As noted previously, most of the latest Palm handhelds come with the Media applet for viewing digital pix. If your model has one of these apps, this is the section for you. We're going to show you the basics of getting photos onto your device—and it all starts with Palm Desktop.

Even if you've configured your handheld to sync with Microsoft Outlook, you can (and must) use Palm Desktop for this particular activity. Either that, or a third-party program that has its own conduit. See the next section for details.

That said, this is where things can get a bit confusing, because there are numerous slightly different versions of Palm Desktop floating around (Palm often tweaks the program to fit the capabilities of a specific model). Thus, you might find a tool called Palm Photos, or you might find one called Media (see Figure 15-3). Both accomplish roughly the same thing in roughly the same way, but have a slightly different feature set. Media, for instance, includes the enviable option to automatically resize photos to fit the handheld's screen, which not only saves memory, but also makes synchronization go faster (because the photos are smaller) and often results in a better viewing experience (because the photos are optimized for the small screen).

Regardless of which version of Palm Desktop you have, the basic process for adding photos is the same:

1. Start Palm Desktop.

2. In the toolbar on the left, click the Media icon (or the Palm Photos icon, if that's what your version has).

15

FIGURE 15-3 The Media tool within Palm Desktop enables you to manage digital photos and HotSync them to your handheld.

3. You'll see a thumbnail view of some sample photos. Click the Add Photos icon (or Add Media icon), and then navigate to the folder on your hard drive that contains your photos.

4. Click the photo you want to add, and then click OK.

You can select multiple photos at a time by holding down your keyboard's CTRL key while clicking. Also, when the Add Photos (or Add Media) dialog box is open, click Windows' View Menu icon (top-right corner, usually) and select Thumbnails, which gives you a handy preview of your photos before you add them. It's also possible to drag and drop photos from Windows Explorer to the Palm Photos/Media window. Finally, you can skip Palm Desktop altogether by dragging and dropping photos to the Quick Install tool—though any subsequent organization will have to be done on the handheld, and you'll lose the option to automatically resize photos.

Now all that's left is to HotSync! When that's done, you'll be able to view your newly added photos in your device's Media (or Photos) app. Of course, obviously there are some variables to consider before you HotSync. For instance, do you want to organize your photos into albums (which is just another term for categories, which we've discussed at length in other chapters)? Do you want to load them to a memory card instead of your handheld's internal RAM (usually a good idea)? And what about basic edits like cropping and rotating?

Organizing Your Photos   Palm Desktop enables you to organize your photos into albums (or, to be more accurate, categories). The "Palm Photos" version of Palm Desktop includes several pre-defined albums: Family, Friends, Vacation, and so on. The "Media" version of Palm Desktop comes with no albums, but in both versions you can easily add, edit, and remove them. Just click Tools | New Album or Tools | Edit Albums and go from there—it's just like working with categories in the core Palm OS apps.

Edit Albums on Device	☒
Broida Family	OK
	New...
	Delete...
	Rename...
	Help

To assign a photo to an album, just drag its thumbnail from the main window down to the corresponding album icon. You can also drag and drop photos between albums.

You can tell that a photo has been assigned to an album by the little check mark that appears in the top-left corner of its thumbnail.

It's worth noting that the Media tool in Palm Desktop includes two separate album areas: Device and Expansion. The former represents your handheld's internal memory; the latter, its memory card. Thus, you can set up albums on a memory card and move photos directly to them from within Palm Desktop. Palm Photos doesn't have this option; in fact, photos stored on cards can't be organized; one reason to consider a third-party alternative.

15

Editing Your Photos   Now that you've pulled some photos into Palm Desktop, you might want to make some minor edits to them. Palm Desktop's built-in tools (accessible by right-clicking any photo and then clicking Edit Media) enable you to crop, rotate, and "enhance" your photos (the latter meaning to automatically adjust a photo's brightness and contrast). There's also an automatic red-eye removal tool and support for adding text and freehand drawings to your photos.

These tools aren't complicated, and the best way to learn them is by experimentation. If you make a change you don't like, just click Cancel and the photo will revert to its original appearance. Furthermore, keep in mind that any changes you make won't affect the original photo stored on your hard drive, only the copy that was pulled into Palm Desktop.

TIP   *Although Palm Photos doesn't have Media's auto-resize feature, you can use the crop tool to grab the portion of a photo that's most important—say, the faces—and create a smaller file in the process. Remember that you're going to be viewing your photos on a relatively small screen, so cropping can be very valuable.*

Putting Photos on Memory Cards   There are two basic ways to load photos onto a memory card (by which we mean a card you use primarily with your PDA, not one you use with your camera): with Palm Desktop and without Palm Desktop. The latter method requires the following steps.

1. First, you need a Secure Digital memory-card reader for your PC. Some newer systems have readers built in; if yours doesn't, you can easily add one. So-called 6-in-1 media readers (which also support other kinds of memory cards) that plug into a USB port sell for around $20, though if you shop carefully you can probably pick one up for half that.

2. Using Windows Explorer, check to see if there's a DCIM folder on the memory card. If there isn't one, create it. Without one, the PDA's built-in photo viewer won't know where to look for the photos.

3. Again using Windows Explorer, drag and drop the photos from your hard drive to the DCIM folder on the memory card.

The method for putting photos on a memory card by way of Palm Desktop varies depending on which version of Palm Desktop you have, so follow the instructions outlined in the manual and/or built-in help files.

If Your Handheld Doesn't Have a Photo Viewer, or You Want Something Better, Start Here

Long before Palm started equipping its handhelds with photo-viewing software, third-party vendors had developed some mighty fine applications of their own. Therefore, if your handheld didn't come with a viewer, or if you want a program that offers more features than Photos and Media (which are pretty rudimentary), you've come to the right section. Let's take a look at three of the best photo apps available for the Palm OS:

- **AcidImage**   Because it supports the most popular digital-image formats—BMP, GIF, JPEG, and TIFF—AcidImage doesn't require a conversion program. You simply copy photos to your handheld or memory card using the standard HotSync process, or pop in a memory card from your digital camera. AcidImage is probably the most feature-rich program of its kind, which helps to explain its relatively high price tag ($29.95).

15

■ **Resco Photo Viewer** Resco also supports the "big four" file formats, and has what we consider the most attractive and intuitive interface of any photo viewer. It also comes with a wizard-driven album-generation utility for Windows, thus simplifying the process of moving photos from your PC to your handheld. Better still, Resco is the bargain to beat, with a price of just $24.95. Or get the Lite version for $14.95.

■ **SplashPhoto** Though it supports only JPEG photos, SplashPhoto is still a very appealing product. It's the only one of these three to offer both Windows and Macintosh desktop utilities (used to organize and even edit your photos), and it offers the very cool feature of playing background music with your slideshows (which, admittedly, Resco can do as well). SplashPhoto also enables you to send photos as e-mail attachments. It sells for $29.95.

Trial versions of all three programs are available for download, so be sure to try before you buy. We've spotlighted only a handful of their features, many of which overlap with other programs.

NOTE

If you own a Tungsten T3, you'll want to download and install Palm's DIA patch to take advantage of full-screen image viewing. (Indeed, you'll probably want this patch for other applications, too.) Visit Palm's support page to find the patch.

Working with PDAs that Take Photos

The Zire 71, Zire 72, Treo 650, and Treo 700p are among the Palm-made handhelds that sport built-in digital cameras. (Several discontinued Sony Clié models do as well.) Unfortunately, because each model has a somewhat different picture-taking application, we can't provide detailed instructions for each (and anyway, that's what your instruction manual is for). But we can teach you a few digital-photography basics and help you shoot better pictures with your PDA or smartphone.

TIP

Let's get started with one important tip: Make sure you hold your device extremely steady while snapping a photo, and continue to do so for a full second or two after you hear the shutter-release sound. Until you actually see the captured image on the screen, any movement of the device can result in a seriously blurred picture.

How to ...   **Adjust White Balance**

The camera-equipped Zire and Treo models have a four-position control called "white balance" hidden in the Advanced button on the Options screen. Your old 35mm film camera didn't have anything like it. So what the heck is white balance? In a nutshell, different light sources have different color temperatures, meaning that a scene will appear to have a different color tone depending upon how it is illuminated.

You can get a sense of this yourself. Candlelight appears more yellowish than sunlight, for instance. And other sources—like tungsten lights—can cast strange, greenish glows around a room. But in general, our brains automatically adjust for different color sources and make the color correction for us. We usually don't even notice.

Your handheld's white balance control works like the human brain. It adjusts the exposure so your pictures have the same color cast no matter what light source you use. When properly balanced, your camera won't apply strange color casts to your pictures—whether shooting indoors, outdoors, in fluorescent lighting, or in candlelight.

Most of the time, your PDA is fine if you leave it set on auto. If you notice that your camera is taking pictures with a weird color cast—everything is coming out greenish or bluish, for instance—try one of the preset white balance settings and see if that improves your shots.

15

Notes on Camera Resolution

The Zire 71 and Treo 650 both have VGA-quality cameras, meaning they shoot pictures at
640 × 480-pixel resolution. That's pretty low, about the equivalent of 0.3 megapixels. As you
might know from shopping for standalone digital cameras, the bare minimum these days is
3 megapixels, and plenty of cameras offer a lot more than that.

So, what good are 0.3-megapixel photos? For starters, they're absolutely fine for viewing on
your handheld's 320 × 320-pixel screen. Snap photos of the kids, the dog, a new line of products
your company is selling, whatever—they'll look just dandy on your PDA. You can also transfer
the photos back to your PC for use in Web pages (which don't benefit from ultra-high-resolution
images) and to attach to e-mail messages.

As for the Zire 72 and Treo 700p, they can capture 1.2- and 1.3-megapixel images,
respectively, at which point printing becomes viable. We wouldn't output the photos on anything
larger than 4 × 6-inch paper—and don't expect film-quality results—but in a pinch these models
are great little snapshot cameras ... er, PDAs.

Where to Save the Photos

Although the photos taken by your PDA result in fairly small files, you should give strong
consideration to storing them on a memory card. That saves precious internal memory for things
like programs and data, while at the same time making it easier to copy photos to a PC (should
you care to use a method other than Palm Desktop). On most models, all you have to do is start
the picture-taking program and tap Options. Then, tap the "Save to" option and choose Card
instead of Handheld.

The only downside to this option, at least with some models, is that photos saved to a
memory card don't appear in Palm Desktop after you HotSync (as do photos saved to internal
memory). Instead, they're saved to a subfolder inside your My Documents folder, accessible by
clicking the Card Photos icon in Palm Desktop.

Painting on Your PDA

You're probably wondering why you'd want to paint on a canvas (that is, screen) that's so small
it fits in your pocket. Well, in the world of computers, the answer is often "because you can."
Programmers have never let something as silly as a technical limitation get in the way of doing
something, and so there are full-featured paint and illustration programs available for the Palm
OS.

Actually, it can be downright handy to sketch things out on your handheld. You can draw a
simple map, visually outline a process, or even throw together a simple flowchart. You can also
just doodle, using your PDA as a high-tech Etch-a-Sketch for those boring times when you're
waiting for the train or pretending to take notes in a meeting. Perhaps most important, you can
draw right on pictures you've stored on your PDA, effectively annotating images and adding
captions.

Although painting on your PDA can be fun and productive, you need to remember these limitations:

■ Palm models vary in screen resolution from 160 × 160 pixels all the way up to 320 × 480. The more pixels you have, the better, but even the largest screens don't give you a lot of room in which to draw. If you plan to transfer your drawings to a PC, you'll find that they're quite small. So, great as they might look on your PDA, your images probably aren't well suited to, say, a PowerPoint presentation.

■ Few paint programs support printing directly from the PDA, and not all of them let you transfer completed art back to the PC. That means, in some cases, what you draw on the screen pretty much stays on the screen. If you *can* print your work of art, it'll probably come out looking just as rough and jagged as it looked onscreen. The exception is a vector-based program like Leonardo (see the next section), which isn't affected by resolution in the same way that traditional "bitmap" images are.

Choosing a Paint Program

There are a ton of painting and drawing applications available for the Palm OS. Heck, a lot of models come with a doodle-pad already installed—Note Pad (see Chapter 8). But you'll probably want something a bit more robust than that, meaning you should search the archives at Handango or PalmGear for paint and/or illustration programs. You'll be amazed by what you find. In the meantime, here are a couple of our favorites:

■ **Leonardo**   An amazingly robust drawing and note-taking program, Leonardo provides a wealth of vector-based illustration tools. Yep, that's right, it's almost like having a CAD program in your pocket. It costs $24.95 and includes a desktop companion application for printing and exporting your drawings.

■ **TealPaint**   Perhaps the most full-featured paint program for the Palm OS, TealPaint ($19.95 or $24.95 for the Plus version) seems to do it all. The program has a complete set of painting tools, including lines, shapes, fill tools, an eraser, and a variety of brushes. It's also an animation tool. You can use TealPaint to create animations by playing in sequence all the images in a particular database. To make a simple bouncing ball, for instance,

15

make a series of images in which the ball moves a bit in each successive image. Then tap on the Anim button and tap the first picture in your series. What better way for animators to practice their craft—or kids to have fun messing around with flipbook-style animation?

Capturing PDA Screenshots

Perhaps while thumbing through this book, you've wondered what it would be like to have lunch with Dave and Rick. (Answer: Like keeping a pair of 6-year-olds entertained at a shoe store.) You might also have wondered how we were able to capture screenshots from our PDAs for publication in this book. As it turns out, it's pretty easy to create screenshots thanks to a third-party utility: the aptly named ScreenShot.

ScreenShot is a marvel. It can capture virtual Graffiti areas (if your model has one), capture instant or delayed screenshots, and be activated via Graffiti strokes or hard buttons. Plus, you can export screenshots to a memory card or your PC in BMP, GIF, or JPEG format.

A note of thanks: We are thoroughly indebted to the developers at LinkeSoft for providing us with this utility, which is not only a breeze to use but also an indispensable tool for writing a book like this. Of course, it's not just for us; you can get your own copy for a mere $16.90.

TIP *Visit the LinkeSoft Web site to download the conduit you'll need for transferring screenshots from your handheld to your PC.*

If you want something a little more, um, free, check out ZGrab. It's not particularly user-friendly, but it works.

Where to Find It

Web Site	Address	What's There
eReader.com	www.ereader.com	eReader and commercial e-books
Fictionwise	www.fictionwise.com	Commercial e-books
MemoWare	www.memoware.com	Public-domain e-books
MobiPocket	www.mobipocket.com	MobiPocket and commercial e-books
PalmGear	www.palmgear.com	Tons of Palm OS programs
Red Mercury	www.red-mercury.com	Acid Image
Resco Mobile Development	www.resco-net.com	Resco Photo Viewer
SplashData	www.splashdata.com	SplashPhoto
TealPoint Software	www.tealpoint.com	TealPaint (and other cool apps)
WireJunkie	www.wirejunkie.com	Leonardo

15

Chapter 16

Accessories and Upgrades

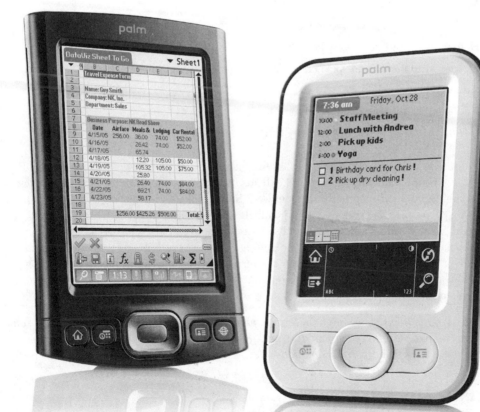

How to...

- Choose a case
- Choose a stylus
- Choose a keyboard
- Choose a cradle
- Do cool things with your cradled Palm
- Protect your screen from dust and scratches
- Navigate the world with a GPS receiver
- Recharge your handheld's battery while on the road
- Replace your handheld's dead battery
- Magnify your handheld's screen
- Mount your PDA in your car
- Use a hands-free kit with your Treo
- Help a lost PDA find its way home
- Choose headphones and speakers
- Add wireless capabilities
- Add a "skin" to your PDA
- Use the world's coolest SD memory card

There's more to PDAs than just software. We're talking gadgets, gear, accessories—the stuff that makes your handheld your own and extends its capabilities beyond what mere software can accomplish. Take the Proporta Retractable USB Sync Cable, an invaluable travel companion that lets you synchronize and recharge your handheld by plugging it into any USB port. Or the Palm Universal Wireless keyboard, which puts a full set of keys beneath your fingers for desktop-like data entry. Maybe you need help getting from point A to point B, in which case a GPS receiver like the TomTom Navigator 5 can turn your PDA into a full-blown navigation system. In this chapter, we look at these and other accessories and upgrades. For starters, let's tackle cases—a subjective category if ever there was one.

NOTE   *Most of the items we spotlight in this chapter are for Palm-branded handhelds, but some are compatible with other models. Check your manufacturer's Web site for leads to product-specific accessories and upgrades.*

Pick a Case, Any Case

As a new PDA owner, one of the first things you need to determine is how you plan to convey the device. In your pocket? Briefcase? Purse? Clipped to your belt? Backpack? Dashboard? Your answer will help determine the kind of case you should buy.

There are cases for every PDA and every occasion, and picking one can be a tough call indeed. Do you opt for practical or stylish? (The two are often mutually exclusive.) Do you look for lots of extras like card slots and pen holders, or try to keep it as slim as possible? Do you shell out big bucks for a titanium shell that can withstand being run over by a car? (This happens quite a bit, believe it or not.)

NOTE *Some PDAs have "built-in" (or clip-on) screen covers that negate, or at least reduce, the need for a protective case (though you might still want one to hold a pen, paper, business cards, and so forth).*

Because there are so many varieties out there, and because everyone's case needs are different, we're going to start by steering you to the case manufacturers themselves, then offer a few general tips and suggestions.

Company	URL	What They Offer
Arkon Resources	www.arkon.com	Car mounts
E&B Company	www.ebcases.com	The Slipper and other cases
InnoPocket	www.innopocket.com	Metal cases and other accessories
JAVOedge	www.javoedge.com	JAVO ClearCase and other accessories
Palm	www.palm.com	Various cases and accessories
ProClip	www.proclipusa.com	Car mounts
Proporta	www.proporta.com	Various cases and accessories
Saunders RhinoSkin	www.saunders-usa.com/rhinoskin	Metal and leather cases

Here are some things to keep in mind as you shop for a case:

- **Style**   If you're an executive-minded person, you might have purchased a Palm Tungsten E2 and want a case to match. That means leather. If you're planning to tote the PDA in a suit pocket, look for something that doesn't add much bulk, like E&B's Slipper or Palm's Slim Leather Case (see Figure 16-1).

- **Portability**   In the summer, when the tight clothes come out and the jackets get stowed, pockets are hard to come by. That's when something like a belt-clip case can come in mighty handy.

- **Screen protection**   When your PDA is bouncing around in a pocket, purse, or briefcase, the last thing you want is for some piece of flotsam to gouge or scratch the screen. That's one of the main reasons for getting a case in the first place.

- **Drop protection**   Gravity—it strikes without warning (especially if you're a klutz like Rick), and it can fatally wound a PDA in a matter of milliseconds. A case made of neoprene or metal, like InnoPocket's Metal Deluxe, can save the day if your PDA gets knocked or dropped to the floor.

16

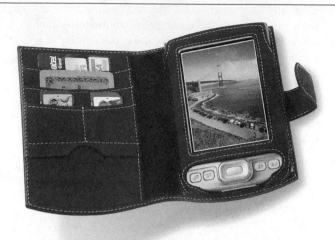

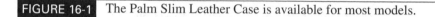

FIGURE 16-1   The Palm Slim Leather Case is available for most models.

- **Moron protection**   We've heard more than a few stories of people driving over their PDAs (not *again,* Dave!). Why they're being left in the driveway in the first place is beyond us, but at least there are aluminum and metal cases that can handle such punishment. Okay, maybe they won't survive being run over, but they can help you weather everyday hazards (like shark attacks and mortar fire).

- **Velcro**   Some cases rely on Velcro to keep your PDA secured. While we look upon this as a necessary evil (who wants a big square of the stuff stuck to the back of their device?), we do try to avoid such cases when possible.

TIP   *Want to keep pocket bulk to a bare minimum? Skip the case altogether, and instead slap on a screen protector (see "Protect Your Screen" later in this chapter). This keeps the screen safe while still allowing your PDA to ride in your pocket.*

The Stylus Decision

Many PDA users are perfectly happy with the stylus that came in the box, until they get a look at some of the alternatives. Indeed, while those bundled plastic pens do get the job done, they're not as comfortable or versatile as they could be. For instance, wouldn't a thicker or heavier writing implement feel better in your hand? And wouldn't it be nice if it doubled as an ink pen? These are just some of the options available to the discriminating PDA user.

As with cases, we wouldn't presume to pick a stylus for you. That's a matter of personal preference. So, here's a look at some of the stylus makers and their offerings.

Company	URL	Product(s)
Cross	www.cross.com	Various executive-minded sizes and styles, many with multifunction designs
Palm	www.palm.com	Lots of stylus choices
PDA Panache	www.pdapanache.com	Wide assortment of sizes and styles
StylusCentral	www.styluscentral.com	Wide assortment of sizes and styles

There are basically two kinds of styluses: those that are too large to fit in your PDA's stylus silo, and those that aren't. The former we'd classify as "executive" styluses: they seem right at home in a suit pocket or briefcase. The Cross DigitalWriter falls into this category—it's big, comfy, and has that classy business look. Replacement styluses, on the other hand, supplant the stock pen. We're partial to some of the latest offerings from Palm, which are designed to fit securely in the stylus silo and double as ballpoint pens.

TIP *If your PDA should happen to crash, the last thing you want is to have to hunt down a toothpick or paper clip to press its Reset button. Thus, look for a stylus that hides a reset pin. Most of them do; it's usually accessible simply by unscrewing one end of the barrel.*

16

Keyboards

If you typically enter a lot of data into your PDA—memos, e-mail messages, business documents, novels—you've probably longed to replace your stylus with a keyboard. After all, most of us can type a lot faster than we can write by hand. Fortunately, there are several keyboards available for

PDAs, most of them priced under $100, and all of them able to fold up neatly (and compactly) when not in use. Here's the scoop on our favorite 'boards:

- **Stowaway Infrared Wireless Keyboard**   The beauty of this keyboard is that because it relies on an adjustable infrared (IR) arm to establish a wireless link with your PDA, it's compatible with just about every Palm OS model on the planet. It lacks dedicated number keys, which can be a bummer, but it's a darn good deal at $69.99.

- **Stowaway Universal Bluetooth Keyboard**   This pricey ($149.99) keyboard relies on Bluetooth instead of IR to communicate with your PDA. Like its Infrared sibling, the UBK folds up beautifully and provides a full-size set of keys, but lacks dedicated number keys. We're hard-pressed to see the advantage of spending an extra $80 on this model over the IWK.

- **Universal Wireless Keyboard**   If you ask us, Palm's keyboard is the best option out there. It's compatible with most handhelds (it communicates via IR), it includes dedicated number keys, and it's priced at a reasonable $69.99.

Shop online and you can save big on Palm's Universal Wireless Keyboard. We checked prices at PriceGrabber.com (our favorite price-comparison site) and found it selling below $50 from a number of vendors, including Amazon!

Cradles

As we discussed way back in Chapter 1, one of the best accessories you can buy for your Palm is a cradle. In the old days, most handhelds came with one, but now all you get is a cable. For anyone who spends a fair amount of time at a desk, a cradle is a must. It gives your Palm a place to rest, keeps it upright so you can see the screen, and keeps the battery charging.

Alas, Palm charges $50 for the Palm Cradle Kit and Palm Mini Cradle—pretty steep, if you ask us. That's why we went looking for inexpensive alternatives. Here's what we found:

- **Alpinetop Palm USB Sync and Charge Cradle** The name really says it all, no? This simple cradle is the deal to beat, as it charges your Palm via USB or the included AC adapter and sells for just $9.99.

- **Brando TX USB Cradle** Also compatible with the Tungsten T5, this simple cradle requires no external power. The USB port supplies juice to your Palm. The only downside is that your Palm doesn't charge unless your PC is on. Also, it lacks a dedicated HotSync button, which we consider essential. Guess that's two downsides. But we still think this is a nice solution and a decent buy at $22.

■ **Brando Palm Music Dock**   Compatible with the LifeDrive, Tungsten E2, Tungsten T5, and TX, the Music Dock features built-in speakers so you can listen to your tunes without headphones. Alas, it has no audio-out jack for connecting to larger, powered speakers (one area where the Palm Cradle Kit has the advantage). But it's a nice-looking, full-featured cradle, and reasonably priced at that ($32).

■ **eBay**   We found lots of no-brand cradles on eBay, and even picked one up for our TX. It lacks a HotSync button (no big deal because we usually HotSync via Wi-Fi), but the price was right: about $10 shipped to our door. Your mileage may vary, but eBay is definitely worth checking out.

Things Your Palm Can Do In Its Cradle

Now that your Palm is sitting upright in a cradle the way the universe intended, put it to some good use. First, make sure the "On while charging" option (also called "Stay on in cradle" on

some models) is selected: Head to Prefs and tap Power to find and modify this setting.
Now, decide what you'd like your Palm to show you while it's sitting around. Some ideas:

- **A Photo Slideshow** Run the Media applet and start a slideshow. It's like turning your Palm into one of those pricey digital photo frames.

- **A Screensaver** Your Palm's screen doesn't really need "saving," at least in the traditional burn-in sense, but screensavers can be fun. Head to Handy Entertainment (www.handyent.com) and check out their beautifully animated Palm screensavers.

- **Your Calendar** Tap Calendar and head to the Agenda view. Now you'll see everything at a glance.

Protecting Your Screen

Keeping your screen pristine is the first rule of PDA ownership. Why? One word: scratches. A scratch in the Graffiti area can result in inaccurate handwriting recognition. A scratch on the main screen can impair its visibility. Fortunately, it's relatively simple to forestall such disasters.

What causes scratches? If your PDA is flopping around unprotected in a purse or briefcase, any loose item—keys, paper clips, a pen, or pencil—can create a scratch. That's why we highly recommend a case (see the first section of this chapter). More commonly, however, little specks of grit and other airborne flotsam accumulate on your screen, and when you run your stylus over one of them—scratch city.

CAUTION *Dave is a big fan of tapping on his screen with his big grubby fingers. They leave behind oil and smudges, which are more likely to trap dust and grit. Rick, who is much daintier, says that if you must use a finger, at least use your fingernail.*

We recommend that you buy a lens-cleaning cloth, the kind used to wipe dust from eyeglasses and camera lenses. Every day, just give your screen a little buff and polish to keep it free of dust and grit. Or, consider one of the following products.

16

TIP *Many of the latest Palm handhelds come with a screen protector! If you haven't looked through the promotional materials in your box, take a look. You may find a Palm Universal Screen Protector in there. Cut it to fit your model and you won't have to spend extra on one of the options discussed in the following sections.*

ClearTouch

Our new favorite screen protector is the BoxWave ClearTouch. This plastic overlay covers your screen from top to bottom, thus ensuring that your stylus causes no damage. It also cuts down on glare and helps keep dust away. Better still, unlike other screen protectors we've tried, which are disposable and must be replaced every month or so, ClearTouch is designed to be removed, cleaned, and reapplied. It leaves behind no gummy residue (do we sound like a floor-wax commercial or what?), and it seems to have endless lasting power. We've had one on a PDA for about a year, and it shows little sign of wear.

NOTE *JAVOedge, which makes some generally cool PDA accessories, offers a screen protector that's similar to ClearTouch. Same goes for ScreenGuardz. They're worth checking out if, say, BoxWave doesn't have a ClearTouch for your particular model.*

PDA Screen Protectors

We're not sure this deal will still be around by the time you read this, but it's worth checking out. At a Web site called FreeScreenProtectors.com, you can order an entire box of CompanionLink PDA Screen Protectors and pay only for shipping. That's right—just enter the coupon code "FREESP" when placing your order, and the sheets are free. Sounds too good to be true, but we placed an order and received our box within about three days. Shipping cost: about six bucks. Woo-hoo—free stuff! There's just one catch. The site doesn't offer screen protectors for the latest Palm models, so this deal is good only if you have an older PDA you're trying to keep alive.

How to ... Protect Your Graffiti Area with Scotch Tape

The Graffiti area is where most stylus contact occurs, and therefore it's where scratches are most likely to result. If you want simple, inexpensive protection for models like the Tungsten E2 and Z22, buy yourself a roll of 3M's Scotch Magic Tape 811. It's exactly the right height for most Graffiti areas, and one roll will last you a lifetime. Plus, its slightly rough surface makes for less-slippery handwriting—always a plus. Just cut a piece to cover the input area and replace it every month or so. You'll never see a single scratch.

Of course, you absolutely would *not* want to do this on a model with a virtual Graffiti area, like the Tungsten TX.

Navigating the World with a GPS Receiver

Dave is a huge fan of the Global Positioning System, the network of orbiting satellites used to pinpoint one's exact position on the planet. That's because he tends to get lost in his own driveway. Still, GPS is undeniably valuable if you're driving on unfamiliar roads or trying to find your way to, say, a new client's office. If you're interested in turning your PDA into a GPS (as shown in Figure 16-2), check out the products and companies in Table 16-1.

 The TomTom Navigator 5 is our favorite GPS solution for PDAs. It combines excellent navigation software with a Bluetooth GPS receiver.

16

Company	URL	Product
DeLorme	www.delorme.com	Blue Logger GPS Receiver, a Bluetooth GPS receiver that works with any Bluetooth-equipped PDA and comes with street-level navigation software (Street Atlas USA 2006). It's the bargain to beat at $149.95.
Garmin	www.garmin.com	Garmin offers several Palm OS handhelds with built-in GPS capabilities. We think they're overpriced and underpowered, but you can't beat the convenience.
Palm	www.palm.com	Palm Navigator Smartphone Edition, a $299.99 kit (based on TomTom's Navigator) designed expressly for the Treo.
TomTom	www.tomtom.com	TomTom Navigator 5 Bluetooth, which combines a Bluetooth GPS receiver with our favorite navigation software. It's priced at $299.95.

TABLE 16-1   Products that Will Change Your PDA into a GPS

If you're really a fan of GPS, check out the Garmin iQue 3600, the first Palm OS handheld with a built-in GPS receiver. It's one of our all-time favorite PDAs, though it's now a few years old and looking rather long in the tooth (and it's definitely overpriced). There are newer models in the iQue series, but we find them under-powered and don't like them as much. And may we also humbly recommend *How to Do Everything with GPS,* a book that covers all manner of GPS technology, including everything you need to know about turning PDAs into sophisticated, practical GPS systems?

TIP   *Adding a GPS receiver to your PDA can improve your golf game! No, we're not making this up. There are several Palm OS programs that can leverage GPS to help you determine your exact distance to the green, or even right to the pin. One of the best is IntelliGolf (www.intelligolf.com), which also happens to be a killer scorecard program.*

What Is Bluetooth and Why Does It Matter for GPS?

Bluetooth, in case you've forgotten, is a short-range wireless technology that has become popular in personal devices like PDAs, cell phones, and—you guessed it—GPS receivers. Why choose a wireless GPS receiver over one that plugs right into your PDA? First, because it's wireless, silly! No one wants wires strewn about their car. And by cutting the cord, you gain the freedom to position your PDA almost anywhere. Second, a Bluetooth GPS receiver is compatible with any Bluetooth-equipped PDA, so it can work with multiple models and stay with you when you upgrade. If you buy a plug-in (that is, wired) GPS, it might not be compatible with other PDAs you currently own or those you purchase down the road.

Things You'll Need for PDA GPS

So you've picked out a GPS receiver and software. Unfortunately, that's not quite the end of the story. If you plan to use your PDA as an in-car navigation system, you'll need a few accessories to round out the equation. Specifically:

- **A car mount**   Using any GPS system while driving can be dangerous, as it necessarily requires you to take your eyes off the road for seconds at a time. Adding a PDA to the mix is that much more perilous, as you either have to put it on the seat next to you, hold it in your lap, or prop it up somehow below the stereo—all extremely unsafe locations. Hence the need for a dashboard or windshield mount, which can position your PDA at or near eye level. We're partial to the ProClip, which offers custom-fit dashboard mounting for all kinds of cars and PDAs. You should also check out the kits offered by Arkon Resources (www.arkon.com), which include universal, powered, and even GPS mounts in a variety of configurations. And speaking of powered ...

- **Power for your PDA**   PDAs are traditionally used in short bursts—a few minutes here and there. GPS navigation requires a PDA to operate for extended periods, and with battery-draining Bluetooth running, too. As a result, you might have to recharge after just a few hours. That means buying and bringing along some kind of external charger. One nifty option is BoxWave's Car Charger for miniSync, which adds a cigarette-lighter adapter to the miniSync product (a retractable USB sync/charge cable available for most PDA models). Also, some of the aforementioned Arkon mounts include a cigarette-lighter adapter for powering your PDA, effectively killing two birds with one stone (not that we condone bird-killing or, for that matter, any other kind of killing).

- **Power for your GPS receiver**   Most Bluetooth GPS receivers use surprisingly little power, meaning they can last for quite a while on a single charge. That said, if your receiver didn't come with a car charger, you might want to investigate buying one from the vendor. The last thing you want is to get within a few miles of your destination and suddenly run out of GPS juice.

16

■ **A memory card**   The more map data you choose to load onto your PDA, the more storage space you'll need. Even a single state's worth of data consumes more RAM than most PDAs have to spare internally, so you'll need a memory card (unless, of course, you have a LifeDrive). As we've discussed in other chapters, 1GB SD cards are now available for peanuts, and that should be ample space for carrying several states' worth of maps.

Magnifying Your PDA Screen

Having a hard time reading the tiny text on your handheld's screen? You can, of course, switch to a larger font in the core Palm OS apps (such as Contacts, Memo Pad, etc.). Just tap Menu | Options | Font when running any of them. But that doesn't help you in other applications. If you need more serious magnification, check out Magnifico Plus, a clip-on lens that promises 2X magnification and compatibility with most PDAs. It's $49.99.

Recharging Your Batteries While Traveling

A PDA with a rechargeable battery is a mixed blessing. Sure, you don't have to keep a pocketful of fresh Duracells on hand, but what happens if you're on the road and the PDA runs out of juice? Fortunately, there are plenty of portable-power solutions that can save the day.

For starters, check the Palm Web site. You'll find a variety of travel-charging solutions, including vehicle and airplane adapters. Just make sure that the accessory in question is compatible with your particular model.

In Chapter 9, you learned a bit about USB chargers—cables that draw power from a computer's USB port to gradually recharge your handheld. We're partial to the BoxWave miniSync, which is available for a wide variety of handheld models and couldn't be more compact. Normally it measures just a few inches from end to end, but when you pull the plugs, they extend on thin cords to nearly three feet. When you're done charging, the spring-reloaded spindle retracts the cords. Pretty cool, and it doubles as a HotSync cable.

One Portable Charger Does It All

One of the coolest travel-charging solutions we've seen yet is the Triple Power Source Emergency Charger from Proporta. Compatible with many Palm models, it includes three parts: a USB HotSync/charge cable, a cigarette-lighter charge cable, and an adapter for charging from an ordinary 9-volt battery. We especially like the latter, as you can pick up a 9-volt cell just about anywhere in the world.

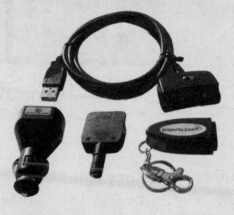

Finally, don't forget car chargers. You can top off your handheld while tooling around town, or supply extra power if you're using your PDA for GPS navigation or some other in-car application. The Expansys Car Charger is one option; the company offers chargers for many PDA makes and models.

Replacing a Dead Battery

It's a sad fact of life (as many iPod owners have discovered) that rechargeable batteries will eventually lose some, if not all, of their ability to hold a charge. If this happens to you, all is not lost—it's possible to replace the battery, even though it's sealed up tight inside your Palm.

A Google search can steer you to dealers that sell replacement PDA batteries. We like the selection at iPods99.com (which, as you might have guessed, also sells iPod batteries). For around $25, we scored a new LifeDrive battery (see Figure 16-3), one that promised to last 40 percent longer between charges than the original.

Just two catches to consider: Replacing the battery will require you to open your Palm's case, which can be tricky, and there might be some soldering involved in installing the new battery. Second, doing this will void your warranty, though we wouldn't let that stop us from contacting Palm if something went wrong with our PDA. The new battery can just be our little secret.

16

FIGURE 16-3 A dead or flagging Palm battery doesn't mean it's time to start shopping for a new handheld. In fact, you can replace the battery with one that lasts longer between charges.

If You Buy Only One Accessory...

Rick: Just *one* accessory? Can't do it—I gotta pick two, but they go together, so I think I'm within my sidebar-title-violation rights. My new favorite accessory is the ProClip, a car-mount that's custom-designed for my 1998 Chevy Cavalier and 2006 Palm TX. The ProClip kinda wedges itself into slim gaps in the dash, then provides a pivoting holder for the Palm. It keeps it almost at eye level, which is perfect for my other favorite accessory, the TomTom Navigator 5 Bluetooth. This GPS kit includes killer navigation software and a Bluetooth GPS receiver that seems to last forever before needing recharging. Definitely the best accessory a Palm user can own, but a car mount to go with it is a must.

Dave: I used to be an accessory nut like Rick. I'd carry all sorts of silly PDA gadgets and accessories, like keyboards, hand-crank battery chargers, GPS attachments, extra memory cards, and wireless modems. I'm not making this up. I really had a hand-crank battery charger. But eventually, I realized that they just bogged me down. More recently, Bluetooth has changed my life. These days I carry three things, and only three things: my Palm TX, a Motorola Razr mobile phone (with Bluetooth), and a Bluetooth earpiece from Logitech. Working in concert with each other, I can place phone calls from my TX and talk without ever touching my phone, check e-mail, and even surf the Web. Oh, I also have a 1GB SD card in my Tungsten filled with music, and occasionally use the Motorola HT820 Bluetooth headphones while I work out at the gym. But that's all. Really.

Hands-Free Car Kits

Dialing while driving is inherently dangerous, as is steering with one hand while the other mashes a phone against your ear. Thanks to the Treo's Bluetooth capabilities, however, you can take advantage of hands-free kits for safety and comfort. You might even save yourself the cost of a ticket, as many cities now prohibit talking on handsets while driving.

> **NOTE**   *These kits will work with any Bluetooth-enabled phones, not just Treos.*

We checked out a couple cool kits: the $99 Parrot EasyDrive (parrot.biz) and $129 Mvox MV900 (mvox.com), and came away with mixed feelings about both.

The Parrot EasyDrive

The EasyDrive consists of a trumpet-shaped speaker that plugs into your cigarette lighter and a microphone/controller that's tethered to it. There are no batteries, which is nice, but you have to find a place to mount the controller using double-sided tape. Rick had a hard time finding a suitable spot in his compact Cavalier—and the tape wouldn't stick to the dashboard.

Furthermore, the EasyDrive can be tricky to use, its name notwithstanding. There's no screen that shows mode or status; the system relies on voice-driven menus that you navigate using a large dial. Thus, setting up features like voice recognition can be cumbersome. Fortunately, once you've gotten everything configured to your liking, you'll rarely need to delve into those menus again.

The real problem we had with the EasyDrive was audio quality. Callers said we sounded tinny and far away, and at our end it was hard to get the volume up to a sufficient level (though this could have had something to do with the Treo's inherently poor volume).

Car noise can be a factor as well. When Rick tried the EasyDrive in a much quieter Ford Explorer, things improved considerably. Thus, we'd recommend the EasyDrive, but only for drivers with relatively quiet cars.

16

MVOX MV900

The feature-packed Mvox MV900 is about the size of a deck of cards and can clip to your overhead visor—a much more convenient placement. It relies on a rechargeable battery, which provides 4 hours of talk time and 200 hours of standby, according to the company.

During our informal tests, callers said we sounded reasonably good, though not great. At our end, volume was more than sufficient—almost too loud, in fact, resulting in some distortion. Regrettably, the volume controls are terrible. A jog dial adjusts the level, but there are no markings to indicate which direction is volume-up and which is volume-down. Plus, when you make a change, the MV900 beeps and the speaker momentarily cuts out.

The MV900's features include voice commands, voice dialing, and Caller ID (in which the unit rapidly announces the phone number of the incoming call). As an added bonus, the device is designed to double as a speakerphone. Sure, the Treo already has that capability, but you get much better volume from the MV900. You can even connect the little gizmo to your PC and use it as a speakerphone with Skype and other voice-over-IP services.

Except for its volume problems, the MV900 worked well, even in Rick's noisy car. It's a product we can wholeheartedly recommend.

Recovering Lost Handhelds

No one ever means to lose anything, but it happens. The only thing worse than losing your PDA would be realizing that whoever found it probably wouldn't know how to go about returning it to you. Sure, an address label pasted to the back might do the trick, but we have a better solution: StuffBak.com.

For as little as $1.95, you can buy a specially coded StuffBak label to paste on the back of your handheld. The finder need only call a toll-free number or visit the StuffBak Web site to arrange for its return, which requires little effort and includes a reward. You pay a $14.95 transaction fee, plus shipping charges and any cash reward you care to offer. (StuffBak's own reward is a pack of its labels, valued at $20.) If you believe people are generally honest, this is an inexpensive and potentially painless way to help a lost handheld find its way home.

Portable Speakers

Hey, quit being so stingy with your audio! Maybe everyone in the group would enjoy listening to your movies or MP3 tunes. Fortunately, with a simple pair of portable speakers, you can share the love ... uh, that is, the audio ... wherever you and your PDA go.

By definition, most portable speakers are pretty small, and therefore they have pretty small sound. On the other hand, they deliver bigger, better audio than what you get from the PDA's built-in speaker (if your PDA even *has* a built-in speaker), and they're usually pretty inexpensive—most models cost less than $50. A couple of portable speakers we like:

■ **Altec Lansing inMotion iM7**   Though designed with iPods in mind, these cylindrical speakers have an input for connecting just about any music-playing device, your Palm included. (You will, however, need a stereo patch cable, available for a few bucks at any Radio Shack.) The iM7 sounds fantastic and can run off batteries or AC power. Just be prepared for a little sticker shock: the speakers cost $249.95.

16

■ **Sonic Impact SI-5 Gen2**   We haven't had a chance to test these ourselves, but most of the reviews we've read have been very positive. They're thin, they look cool, and they have their own little stands. And they're a bargain at $29.99 (www.amazon.com).

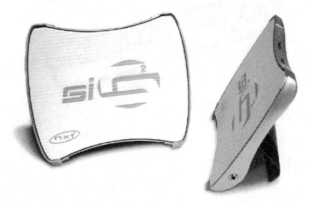

■ **Sony SRS-T77**   Sony's portable speaker system looks like a holdover from the mid-80s, but it cranks out decent sound and folds up into a pretty compact package when not in use. The retail price is around $90, but we found them selling online for below $50.

■ **Soundbug**   This is more of a novelty than anything else, but it's too cool not to mention. The Soundbug is not a portable speaker per se, but rather a portable gizmo that turns other objects into speakers. It's like a speaker driver coupled with a suction cup, and when you attach the cup to, say, a window, desk, or China plate, the vibrations turn that item into a speaker. No joke, it really works. Okay, but how *well* does it work? Quite a bit better than you'd expect, and it's fun to experiment with different surfaces. You can even link a second Soundbug to your first one to create a stereo effect using two surfaces. That said, we probably wouldn't pay the $40 list price for one of these—but you can pick one up on eBay for about $10.

Better Headphones

Most earbud headphones (technically, earphones) that come with PDAs (and, for that matter, MP3 players) are decent enough, but that doesn't mean you shouldn't consider alternatives. For example, Rick finds most earbuds extremely uncomfortable after awhile, and Dave won't step onto an airplane without headphones that block out that deafening engine noise.

As you've probably guessed, most PDA headphone jacks are of the standard 3.5mm variety (one notable exception being the Treo, which uses smaller 2.5mm jacks), meaning you can plug in just about any pair of headphones on the planet (even that huge pair you bought in the 70s, though you'll need an adapter for the plug). We wouldn't presume to pick headphones for you, not with so many varieties and price levels out there. But we will recommend a couple products we find interesting:

- **JAVOeBuds**   The problem with most headphones is their long, easily tangled cords. The JAVOeBuds keep the cord wound in a spring-loaded spindle—just pull the two ends when you want to listen to your tunes, and then pull them again to retract the cord. Pretty cool, except that the hard-plastic earbuds can get a little uncomfortable. But you can't beat the $18.95 price tag.

16

■ **Shure E3c**   Hugely popular among professional musicians, the Shure E3cs are in-ear earphones. Yep, they fit right inside the ear canal, which isn't nearly so uncomfortable as it sounds thanks to their soft rubber sleeves. The bad news is they're a bit light on the bass (though they sound generally excellent overall). The good news is that they block out a ton of ambient noise, making them ideal for airplanes. (Other so-called noise-canceling headphones rely on electronic circuitry to accomplish this, and with highly varying results.) The E3cs have a list price of $179 (ouch!), though you can find them for less by shopping online. You can also opt for the generally similar E2c, which sells for $99.

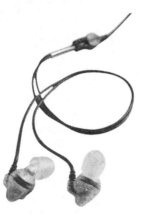

Bluetooth Headphones

Wouldn't it be cool if you could start your tunes playing, stick your Palm in your pocket, and listen to headphones, all without a pesky wire running between your hip and head? You can, thanks to Softick Audio Gateway (www.softick.com), a $20 utility that leverages your Palm's Bluetooth capabilities (see Chapter 10) to stream audio (including music, audiobooks, and whatever) to Bluetooth headphones.

Ah, but which Bluetooth headphones should you get? Dave has tested and thoroughly enjoyed the Motorola HT820, a comfy pair of over-the-ear "neckphones" that you can pick up online for around $90.

How to ... **Split Headphone Audio Three Ways**

Suppose you're on a flight with two of your best friends and you all want to listen to that primo mix of MP3 tunes you've loaded on your PDA, but there's only one headphone jack. What *do* you do? You buy yourself a Boostaroo, that's what. This little gizmo turns one headphone jack into three, while at the same time amplifying the audio so the split signal stays loud enough for all to enjoy. It's a little pricey at $29.95, but it comes with a 90-day money-back guarantee, so you can always return it if you don't like it. And at press time you could get it at ThinkGeek.com for $21.99. Rick and Dave are *always* looking to save you money, folks.

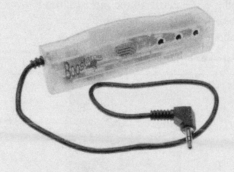

Alas, we weren't able to try out any other Bluetooth headphones, but just about any model should work. Here are the ones that Softick lists as tested and compatible:

■ Plantronics Pulsar 590A

■ Bluetake i-Phone BT420EX Bluetooth Hi-Fi Sports Headphone

■ Logitech iPAQ Bluetooth Stereo Headphones

■ Samsung SBH-100 Stereo Headset

■ TEN naviPlay

We also recommend checking out the Creative CB2530. Although they're not on Softick's list, they should work; but make sure that the store you buy them from has a fair return policy just in case they don't.

16

And, Finally, Wi-Fi

We love Wi-Fi (short for Wireless Fidelity, and also known by its technical moniker, 802.11), the awesome wireless technology that's making high-speed Internet access available in all sorts of places—libraries, Starbucks, Dave's home office ... Unfortunately, not all Palm OS PDAs have built-in Wi-Fi capabilities. The LifeDrive and TX are the only current models that do. Why, Palm, why?!

The good news, sort of, is that you can add Wi-Fi capabilities to certain PDA models with an expansion card. The Palm Wi-Fi Card (see Figure 16-4), for instance, works with the Tungsten E2, T3, T5, and Zire 72. Just pop it into the SD slot and you're ready for wireless Internet access (provided you're within range of a Wi-Fi hotspot, of course—see the upcoming Did You Know box: "Free Wi-Fi Is at the Corner Café"). The card sells for $99, making it a pretty pricey accessory.

The problem with this card, of course, is that it occupies the SD slot, meaning you can't use a memory card while using the Wi-Fi card. All the more reason to give strong consideration to a model like the LifeDrive or TX.

You can find out more about Wi-Fi in Chapter 10.

 FIGURE 16-4   With the Palm Wi-Fi Card, you can wirelessly access the Internet on your PDA. Too bad it's compatible with only a few models.

Free Wi-Fi Is at the Corner Café

At the Panera Bread in Farmington Hills, Michigan, the coffee's fresh, the bagels rule, and the high-speed wireless Internet access is free.

It's called Wi-Fi, though it's also known by its geeky technical name, 802.11. If you have a Wi-Fi-equipped PDA (or notebook PC, for that matter), you can stop in for a scone and enjoy speedy e-mail and Web access at the same time.

We may move in.

Panera Bread (and subsidiary Saint Louis Bread Co.) first began offering free Wi-Fi in 2003, starting with 70 stores and adding another 60 by year's end. The company ultimately plans to make these Wi-Fi "hotspots" available at all locations.

Contrast this with Starbucks, Borders bookstores, and Kinko's, all of which have added their own hotspots—but charge for the privilege. It costs $10 for a one-day pass or $29.99 per month for an annual subscription.

Needless to say, we'll be getting our baked goods and Google at Panera Bread.

There's something very liberating about sitting in a public place with your own PDA or computer and surfing the Web without wires. It's a fast connection, much faster than with a dial-up modem. It's also surprisingly uncomplicated—usually you just fire up your Web browser and presto, you're online. And did we mention it's free?

Mark our words: soon, Wi-Fi will be everywhere. You can already find hotspots in many airports, hotels, and libraries. Even Denny's and IHOP are getting in on the act. But except for libraries, most places still charge for access.

Big mistake. As Panera Bread has proven, Wi-Fi can and should be free. And we show our support by giving them our bagel and coffee business. That's a win-win proposition.

"Skin" Your Palm

Like the Rolling Stones? How about the Detroit Pistons? SpongeBob? If you want to show your true fan colors, check out the PDA and smartphone "skins" at Skinit.com. We could tell you more, but in this case a picture is worth a thousand words—so have a look at Figure 16-5.

The skins are priced at around $15 each and can be removed without leaving behind any gummy residue. You can also upload your own images and have them made into custom skins. Pretty cool, if you ask us.

16

You can dress up your PDA or smartphone with one of dozens of nifty "skins" from Skinit.com

The World's Coolest SD Memory Card

Throughout this book we've urged you (more like harangued, really) to buy a memory card for your Palm. You just gotta have one to store music, movies, maps, and all that other memory-hogging stuff that makes your handheld so cool and capable. So, which card should you buy? Should you snap up the cheapest deal from eCost.com (our favorite source for cheap cards)? Allow us to make the case for another product.

On the surface, it looks like an ordinary Secure Digital (SD) memory card. But this one, the SanDisk Ultra II SD Plus (sandisk.com), has a built-in USB connector. That means it can pull double duty as a USB flash drive—and a tiny one at that. It's ideal for connecting to PCs that don't have an SD reader. Plus, files transfer a lot faster over USB, so it's more practical than typical SD cards.

The Ultra II SD Plus is available in 512MB, 1GB, and 2GB capacities, and is priced at $54.99, $79.99 (the sweet spot), and $134.99, respectively.

Marvel of modern engineering, people!

Where to Find It

Web Site	Address	What's There
Altec Lansing	www.alteclansing.com	inMotion iM7 speakers
Arkon Resources	www.arkon.com	Car mounts
Boostaroo	www.boostaroo.com	Boostaroo
BoxWave	www.boxwave.com	ClearTouch, miniSync
DeLorme	www.delorme.com	Blue Logger GPS
Expansys	www.expansys.com	Expansys Car Charger and other accessories
JAVOedge	www.javoedge.com	JAVOeBuds, JAVOClearCase, and other accessories
MaxiAids	www.maxiaids.com	MagnificoPlus
Mvox	www.mvox.com	MV900 hands-free kit
Palm	www.palm.com	Various accessories
Panera Bread	www.panera.com	Panera Bread locations
Parrot	www.parrot.biz	Parrot EasyDrive hands-free kit
Proporta	www.proporta.com	Triple Power Source Emergency Charger and other accessories
Shure	www.shure.com	E3c earphones
Skinit.com	www.skinit.com	PDA and smartphone "skins"
Softick	www.softick.com	Softick Audio Gateway
Sony	www.sonystyle.com	Sony SRS-T77 speakers
StuffBak.com	www.stuffbak.com	StuffBak labels
Think Outside	www.thinkoutside.com	Stowaway keyboards
TomTom	www.tomtom.com	TomTom Navigator 2004

16

Chapter 17

Problems and Solutions

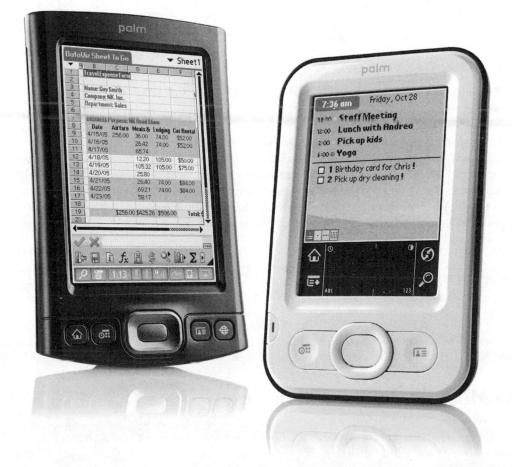

How to...

- Reset your PDA
- Avoid battery-related problems
- Prevent and fix scratched screens
- Fix a screen that no longer responds properly
- Fix alarms that don't "wake up" your PDA
- Deal with a handheld that suddenly won't HotSync
- Solve common HotSync problems
- Manage two PDAs on one PC
- HotSync one PDA on two PCs
- Upgrade from an old PDA to a new one
- Migrate from a Pocket PC to a Palm
- Troubleshoot audio hiss
- Replace a dead battery
- Obtain warranty repairs
- Obtain non-warranty or accident-related repairs
- Find answers to problems on the Web

No computer is perfect. Windows is about as far from the mark as you can get, Macs have problems of their own, and even PDAs suffer the occasional meltdown. Usually it's minor: an alarm that fails to "wake up" the unit or an oddball program that causes the occasional crash. But sometimes something downright scary happens, like a sudden and inexplicable lockup that wipes the PDA's entire memory. In this chapter, we help you troubleshoot some of the most common PDA maladies and, hopefully, prevent the worst of them.

> NOTE *Many common problems are addressed on Palm's Web site (and the sites of other PDA and accessory manufacturers). We're not going to rehash them here, but we are going to suggest that you check out those sites if you've got a problem we haven't addressed. Chances are good that you'll find a solution.*

We also look at managing multiple PDAs on one PC, and at moving from an old PDA to a new one—both common practices these days. But first, let's deal with the all-important matter of when, how, and why to reset your PDA.

Curing Most Problems with a Reset

Just as rebooting a computer will often resolve a glitch or lockup, resetting your handheld is the solution to many a problem. And it's usually the first thing you should do if your device crashes—or just acts a little strangely.

Just What Is a "Crash," Anyway?

When a computer crashes, that generally means it has plowed into a brick wall and can no longer function. Fortunately, whereas a car in the same situation would need weeks of bump-and-paint work, a computer can usually return to normal by being rebooted. In the case of PDAs, a "reset" is the same as a "reboot."

When a PDA crashes, one common error message is "Fatal Exception." Don't be alarmed; this isn't nearly as morbid as it sounds. It simply means that the device has encountered a glitch that proved fatal to its operation. Very often an onscreen Reset button will appear with this error, a tap of which performs a "soft reset" (as we describe in the next section). Sometimes, however, the crash is so severe that even this button doesn't work. (You know because you tap it and nothing happens.) In a case like that, you have to perform a manual reset.

Different Ways to Reset a PDA

On the back of every PDA, there's a little hole labeled RESET. (On some models, like the Treo, the hole may be tucked inside the battery compartment or another unusual spot.) Hidden inside this hole is a button that effectively reboots the unit. When that happens, you see the operating system startup screen, followed a few seconds later by the Prefs screen. That's how a successful reset goes. About 99 percent of the time, everything will be as you left it—your data, your applications, everything.

Technically speaking, there are three kinds of resets: soft, warm, and hard. (Mind out of the gutter, please.)

- ■ **Soft** This is the most commonly used reset. Only in rare instances do you need to perform anything other than a soft reset, which is akin to pressing the Reset button to reboot your computer. You simply press the Reset button, and then wait a few seconds while your PDA resets itself. No data is lost.

- ■ **Warm** This action, performed by holding the Scroll Up button while pressing the Reset button, goes an extra step by bypassing any system patches or hacks you might have installed. Use this only if your PDA fails to respond to a soft reset, meaning it's still locked up, crashing, or stuck in a "boot loop" (the manufacturer logo is flashing or the screen is displaying garbage). No data is lost, but certain capabilities and settings might be temporarily disabled. You might have to re-enable or reinstall any system patches you've installed. The warm reset can be useful for retrieving data from your PDA before the sometimes-inevitable hard reset.

- ■ **Hard** With any luck, you'll never have to do this. A hard reset wipes everything out of your PDA's memory, essentially returning it to factory condition. In the exceedingly rare case that your device is seriously hosed (meaning it won't reset or even turn off), this should at least get you back to square one. If it doesn't, your handheld is toast and will need to be replaced. The good news is this: even after a hard reset, all it takes is a HotSync to restore all your programs and data. Some third-party applications may have to be reinstalled manually (or, more likely, you'll have to re-enter the registration codes for those programs), but most will just reappear on your handheld. It's like magic!

17

How to ...   Perform Warm and Hard Resets

There's a bit of a trick to doing a warm or hard reset successfully. With your PDA on or off (it doesn't matter), hold down the Scroll Up button (for a warm reset) or the Power button (for a hard reset), then press and release the Reset button on the back of the unit. Now, here's the trick: *wait until the Palm logo appears onscreen* before releasing the Scroll Up or Power button. If you release both buttons simultaneously, before the logo appears, all you get is a soft reset.

How Am I Supposed to Press that Tiny Reset Button?

Perhaps you've eyed that teeny little reset hole and wondered how to press the button hidden within. With a few PDA models, the hole is large enough that you can press the button with the tip of the stylus. In most cases, however, you'll need to find something thin enough to fit inside the hole.

Surprise! Your stylus might be hiding a reset tip. Just unscrew the top (or, in some cases, the bottom) of the barrel to find it. If your handheld came with a plastic stylus, one that has no top or bottom to unscrew, you'll have to find a paper clip or toothpick.

TIP   *Attach a small paper clip to one of the business cards in your wallet. Chances are you'll never know it's there, and you'll always have a reset tip handy if you need it.*

Seven Great Tips and Tricks

These handy little secrets will help you go from novice user to PDA pro.

1. **Find the Latest Freeware**   At PalmGear.com, scroll down to near the bottom of the main page and look for the Freeware link in Software Categories. Presto! Nothin' but freebies.

2. **Help for HotSyncs**   Can't HotSync all of a sudden? Try a soft reset of your handheld. More often than not, this solves the problem.

3. **HotSync with the Web**   Did you know you can synchronize your handheld with Yahoo Address Book, then access your calendar, contacts, and memos from any Web-enabled computer? Just set up a My Yahoo account (www.yahoo.com), go to the calendar (calendar.yahoo.com), and find the Sync link (usually located near the top-right corner of the page). From there, you'll have the option to download Intellisync for Yahoo, the utility that makes this Web synchronization possible. It's free, as is the account you'll need to set up with Yahoo. One word of warning: Intellisync for Yahoo can be a little tricky, so be sure to read the provided

instructions carefully. You could wind up synchronizing with the Web but unable to HotSync with your PC.

4. **Multiple-Personality Buttons**   Your handheld's application buttons needn't be limited to launching one application each. Utilities like QLaunch and SmartLauncher let you program the buttons to launch multiple programs with multiple presses.

5. **Happy Holidays**   Want to add all the holidays to your Date Book? Just download 2006 USA Holidays 1.1 (www.freewarepalm.com). It contains 36 U.S. and religious holidays. While you're at it, get the 2007 through 2010 calendars, too. Just import the file(s) into Palm Desktop, and then HotSync.

6. **Louder Alarms**   If you've set the alarm volume to "High" in Prefs but your alarms still aren't loud enough, try switching to a different alarm sound. In Date Book, tap Menu | Options | Preferences. Tap the arrow next to Alarm Sound, and then choose a tune. You'll hear it played immediately. Find the one that's loudest, and then tap OK.

7. **Graffiti at a Glance**   On most models, if you swipe the stylus from the bottom of the screen to the top, a handy Graffiti reference chart will appear.

Avoiding Battery Problems

Batteries are the lifeblood of any PDA. When they die, they take your data with them, effectively returning your handheld to factory condition. (The exceptions to this rule are the Tungsten E2, T5, TX, and the latest Treos, which employ *non-volatile* RAM that doesn't require a constant supply of power.) That's why it's vital to keep a close eye on the battery gauge shown at the top of the Applications screen (see Figure 17-1), and to take heed when the device notifies you that your batteries are low.

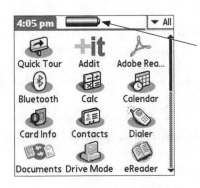

The battery gauge tells you how much juice your PDA has left

17

FIGURE 17-1   All Palm OS devices equipped with Palm OS 3.0 and later have this handy— and reasonably accurate—battery gauge at the top of the screen.

Of course, if you HotSync regularly, a wiped handheld isn't the end of the world. Once you've recharged (or replaced) the batteries, a HotSync is all it takes to restore virtually everything. Still, there's no reason to let things reach that point. The following are some tips to help you avoid most battery-related incidents:

- **Avoid the drain game** Suppose you head off to Bermuda for a two-week getaway (you lucky vacationer, you), leaving your work—and your PDA—behind. When you return, don't be surprised to find the unit dead as a doornail. That's because it draws a trace amount of power from the batteries, even when off, to keep the memory alive. (Again, there's an exception to this rule: If your Palm has non-volatile RAM, then it sips almost no power while off.) If the batteries were fairly low to begin with, the long period of inactivity might just polish them off. The obvious solution is to keep your PDA with you as much as possible. (It's great for games, e-books, and other leisure activities, remember?) Alternatively, if you know you're going to be away from it for a while, just leave it connected to your powered cable or cradle.

- **HotSync regularly** Most PDAs are recharged by the same cradle/cable that HotSyncs them with their PCs. If you HotSync daily (always a smart idea, battery charging notwithstanding), that should keep your PDA's battery "topped off." Just get in the habit of dropping your device into the cradle for a few minutes each day and you'll rarely encounter a power problem.

- **Keep an emergency charger on hand** If you travel a lot or just can't get in the habit of topping off your PDA, you should invest in a good travel charger. See Chapter 16 for some of our favorite products.

Fixing Scratched Screens

Scratches happen. They happen most often when your stylus hits a piece of dust or grit or your PDA rides unprotected in a pocket or purse. That's why it's important to keep your screen as clean as possible (we recommend a daily wipe with a lint-free, antistatic cloth). Better still, take a few preventative steps:

- **Tape** A piece of Scotch Magic Tape 811 placed over the Graffiti input area (where most scratches occur) not only makes existing scratches less tangible while you're writing, but also prevents future scratches and provides a tackier writing surface. Note: We don't recommend this option for the Tungsten TX and other PDAs that have virtual Graffiti areas.

- **Screen protectors** As discussed in Chapter 16, products like the BoxWave ClearTouch are plastic overlays that protect the entire screen. They won't remove scratches, but they will prevent them and, like the tape, make them less pronounced.

■ **Screen cleaners**   Available at most office-supply stores, these wash-and-dry systems may remind you of those wet-nap packets you get in those greasy-spoon restaurants Dave likes to eat in. One packet contains a wet cloth you use to wash and wipe the screen. The other has a dry cloth used for drying and buffing. These won't repair scratches, but they will remove all the dust and grit that can lead to them, leaving your screen looking pristine.

Fixing a Screen that No Longer Responds Properly

As noted in Chapter 2's discussion of the Touchscreen (a.k.a. Digitizer) option, it's not uncommon to experience some "drift" in the screen's response to your stylus taps. For example, you have to tap just a bit to the left or right of your desired target for the tap to be recognized. This occurs over time, when the accuracy of the digitizer (the hardware that makes the screen respond to your input) degrades.

Unless the digitizer has gotten so off-kilter that you can no longer operate your PDA, the solution is to hit the Prefs icon, and then choose Touchscreen (or Digitizer) from the list of choices. Here you can reset the digitizer, effectively making your handheld good as new. If you can't even manage to tap Prefs, you can do a soft reset (as described earlier in the "Different Ways to Reset a PDA" section in this chapter). That gets you to the Prefs screen, where you should at least be able to select the Touchscreen option.

> TIP
>
> *You can use the Navigator to select the Prefs icon and then to select Touchscreen. Just press the four-way pad until the desired option is highlighted, and then press the center button to select it.*

How to ... **Cure "Mad Digitizer Syndrome"**

What happens when the digitizer gets so out of whack that your PDA essentially becomes inoperable? This problem, which some have dubbed "Mad Digitizer Syndrome," tends to plague older models, though it can strike even if your handheld is only a year or two old. One very effective way to cure MDS is with a utility called AutoDigi5 for OS 5 (or AutoDigi2 for older models), which automatically recalibrates the digitizer after a reset or after a certain amount of time has elapsed. You can buy the $36 program (ouch! But cheaper than a new PDA) at PalmGear (www.palmgear.com).

Fixing a PDA that Won't "Wake Up" for Alarms

It's easy to fall out of love with your PDA when an alarm you set fails to go off (meaning the unit doesn't "wake up" and beep). There are several reasons this can happen, from low batteries to a corrupted alarm database to a conflict with third-party software. The first is easy to resolve by making sure your PDA is adequately charged. For the other two problems, try a soft reset, which very often does the trick.

If you use a third-party program that has anything to do with alarms (such as BugMe or ToDo Plus), it's very possible that this is causing the snafu. To troubleshoot it, try doing a warm reset (hold the Scroll Up button while pressing the Reset button). This will disable any third-party applications that tie into the operating system. Set an alarm in Date Book and see if it works. If so, then another program is very likely to blame. A process of elimination should help you determine which one. In any case, you might have to discontinue using that program if it keeps fouling up your alarms.

If none of these options work, it's possible that your PDA is damaged. Contact the manufacturer for service.

Avoiding the Dreaded Display Memory Error

A new variation on the age-old not-enough-memory error can happen if you are using high-resolution background pictures (sometimes called wallpaper) on your Palm. Those pictures might be pretty, but they eat up precious memory needed by other programs, such as AvantGo, Web browsers, and games. If you get a display memory error, the easiest (and often only) fix is to turn off your Palm's wallpaper. See Chapter 2 for a wallpaper refresher.

Solving Beaming Problems

Having trouble beaming? Chances are that the problem is caused by one of three factors. First, make sure the two handhelds aren't too close together. People often make the mistake of holding their devices right next to each other, which can give the infrared transceivers trouble. Keep the units at least a foot or two apart (their range is about five feet).

Second, make sure the Beam Receive option is checked in the Prefs | General (or Power) screen. Even though you might not have unchecked it yourself, sometimes it just seems to happen.

If neither of these suggestions solves the problem, try moving to a darker area. Beaming doesn't always work if you're in a brightly lit room or outdoors on a sunny day.

If all else fails, you might want to perform a soft reset on one or both PDAs; that should clear up whatever problem was keeping your devices from chatting with each other.

The Last Chapter

Dave: Well, this is the last chapter ... and it's almost complete. It was a blast to write this book, but I have to admit that I'm kind of burnt out on all this tech-writing stuff. I think I'll take my half of the advance (a cool half-million or so) and move to Bermuda. There, I'll build a cottage on the beach and let my army of trained monkey butlers bring me cool drinks all day long. I'll pass the time staring at the waves as they gently break onto the sandy, white beach, and occasionally dabble at writing a best-selling novel on my Palm with a Bluetooth keyboard. My MP3 player will be loaded up with Kristin Hersh music and my cats will be napping in my lap. Yep, that's what I'm going to do ...

Rick: Always with the monkey butlers. As for me, now that the yoke of another book has been lifted, I'll be returning to the soup kitchen where I volunteer three times a week, though not before I finish the urban-beautification program I spearheaded and the fundraiser for Greenpeace. Just have to decide which charities will be getting my royalty checks this year—always a tough choice. Honestly, there's no better reward for months of hard work than good old philanthropy. Oh, but, uh, your plan sounds really good, too ...

Dealing with a Handheld that No Longer HotSyncs

It worked fine yesterday, but today your handheld just refuses to HotSync. We hear your pain—this drives us up the wall, too. We wish we could blame Windows, because it's just the kind of nonsense we've come to expect from it, but this is usually due to a PDA software, hardware, or cradle problem.

Best bet? Start with a soft reset. Use the end of a paper clip (or unscrew the barrel of your metal stylus to find a hidden tip) to press the Reset button on the back of your handheld. In many cases, this will solve the problem outright, and you can get back to playing Bejeweled. If it doesn't, consider reinstalling Palm Desktop. This action won't affect your data, but it will provide a "fresh" version of HotSync Manager, which often solves HotSync problems. (Don't worry, reinstalling Palm Desktop will *not* overwrite your data.) If you're not comfortable with that step or it doesn't work, consult your manufacturer's Web site for other remedies.

TIP

This bears repeating: a soft reset cures the vast majority of HotSync problems, and a warm reset can solve most of the rest of them. Try both before you e-mail Dave for help (though he's glad to troubleshoot all glitches, really!).

17

In the meantime, let's take a look at some common HotSync obstacles and how to overcome them:

- ■ **Not enough memory**   If you're trying to install new software but your PDA doesn't have enough memory available, the HotSync will fail (at least, the installation part will). You'll have to free up some memory or route the new program(s) to a memory card, as discussed in Chapter 16.

- ■ **Check the connections**   Make sure your PDA is properly seated in its HotSync cradle, or that the HotSync cable is securely connected. Sometimes even the slightest shift in the connection can cause HotSync failure.

- ■ **Check your USB ports**   On a Windows PC, USB is guaranteed to work only with Windows 98 or later. If you still have Windows 95, get with the program and upgrade if you expect to reliably use USB devices like a PDA HotSync cradle/cable. Whatever your operating system, make sure your cradle/cable is plugged directly into one of your computer's USB ports, not a USB hub. The latter are handy for adding more ports to a crowded system, but they can cause HotSync problems.

- ■ **Check Palm Desktop**   If any records are "open" (meaning you're still in a data-entry window) when you try to HotSync, or the HotSync Manager options screen is open, the process will fail. Close these windows and then HotSync.

- ■ **Make sure HotSync Manager is running**   See the little blue/red HotSync icon in the Windows System Tray (lower-right corner of the screen)? (You might have to click the little Show Hidden Icons arrow to see it.) If not, that means HotSync Manager isn't running, and you can't HotSync without it. Click Start | All Programs | Palm | HotSync Manager to start the program.

Managing Multiple Palms or PCs

The Palm OS allows you to HotSync the same PDA to more than one PC, or to HotSync several devices to the same PC. However, there are some potential complications to consider. For instance, you should make sure you have the same version of Palm Desktop installed on both PCs. Or, if you're synchronizing multiple devices to the same PC, you need to make sure you're using the latest version of Palm Desktop. Read on to learn more.

Two PDAs on a Single PC

If you have two PDAs and only one computer, you're not alone. In fact, it's a pretty common scenario: many married couples have their own handhelds and want to HotSync to the household computer. No problem—Palm Desktop can easily handle multiple users and maintain separate, non-overlapping sets of data.

Let's assume you've just purchased a second PDA. Once it's all charged up, you're ready to HotSync it for the first time. As long as you're using two PDAs in the same family—like a pair of Tungsten E2s—you can use one HotSync cable for both handhelds. However, you can't always mix and match. A Palm TX, for instance, won't work with a Zire 71 cradle. However, it is possible to have multiple cradles connected to the same PC. You could have one plugged into a serial port and another into a USB port, for instance, or two cradles plugged into two USB ports.

Now, this is the really important thing to note: You must be sure to install and use only the newest version of Palm Desktop. In other words, suppose you have a Zire 71, and the new PDA in the family is a Treo 700p. The latter won't work properly with the version of Palm Desktop that came with the Zire, but the Zire will work with Palm Desktop for the Treo. That's because PalmSource always engineers Palm Desktop (and HotSync Manager) to be backward-compatible with older models.

TIP   *The most reliable way to get things working is to install the Palm Desktop that came with the older PDA (if you haven't already), HotSync, install the version for the new PDA, and then HotSync that.*

Assuming you're good to go, connect the second PDA to its cradle/cable and perform a HotSync. Your PC will ask if you want to create an account for the new device. Click Yes. Make sure you give the second PDA a different user name than the first one!

Now fire up Palm Desktop and click the User box in the top-right corner of the screen. You'll see a drop-down list containing your username and the name you just gave to the new PDA. Incidentally, this is how you switch between users within Palm Desktop. Just be sure that when you're entering new data for your device, your username is the one that's showing!

We should note that Outlook, unlike Palm Desktop, will share a single database with all users unless each user has his or her own Windows login account.

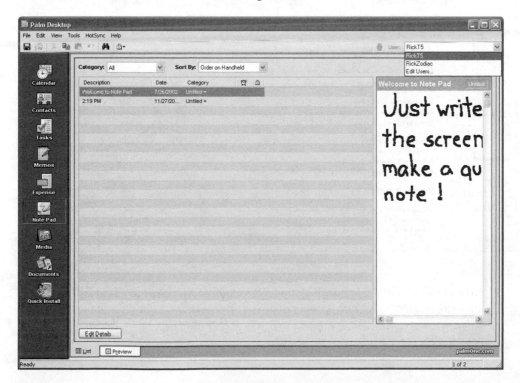

How to ... Find the Latest Versions of Palm OS Software

The more software you install on your PDA, the harder it becomes to keep everything up to date. Developers add new features, fix bugs, and make other changes to programs—but how are you supposed to know when a new version of any given program is available? Simple: Head on over to VersionTracker (www.versiontracker.com/palmos), which lists software updates as they're released. The site is free, but with a paid subscription to VersionTracker Plus ($24.95 per year) you can get custom update listings, meaning the site will show you updates for only the programs you own. VersionTracker is also a handy site for learning about new products, as it catalogs all Palm OS software, not just updates.

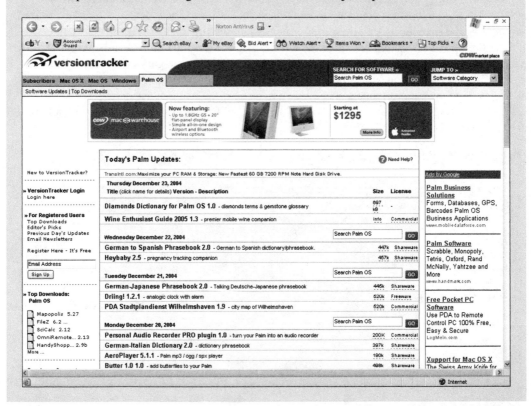

NOTE *Palm Desktop doesn't support Windows XP's multiple users feature. That means if you log onto your PC using one account and your spouse uses another, you have to install Palm Desktop twice—the first time when you're logged in as you, the second time when your spouse is logged in as your spouse.*

One PDA, Two PCs

Your PDA can keep two different PCs straight just as easily as one PC can keep a pair of PDAs straight. When you HotSync, the handheld updates the second PC with whatever data it previously got from the first PC, and vice versa. This is a great way to keep your office PC and home computer in sync, or even a PC and a Mac—the PDA can serve as a nonpartisan conduit for keeping all the data in agreement.

> **TIP** *Make sure that you have the same version of the Palm Desktop on both PCs. If you're using a PC and a Mac, you can't do that, but you should keep up with the latest release of the Mac Palm Desktop.*

Of course, the most efficient way to use a dual-PC system is to acquire a second HotSync cradle. You can buy an additional one for about $30, or you can get a HotSync cable instead, which is a little more streamlined for traveling. See Chapter 16 for information on USB HotSync cables that also charge your battery.

Migrate From Pocket PC to Palm

So, you've decided to abandon the Windows Mobile Pocket PC camp in favor of a Palm PDA. Good decision. There's just one problem. How will you migrate your data from the old handheld to the new one? Actually, if you're planning to stick with Outlook as your desktop PIM, the transition should be relatively quick and painless. But if you need to ditch Outlook and switch to Palm Desktop, the PIM that comes with all Palm OS handhelds, plan on a few extra steps to relocate your data.

Option One: Stick with Outlook

Ideally, you should retain Microsoft Outlook, which you undoubtedly used with your Pocket PC (it comes with all models), as your desktop PIM. It's vastly superior to Palm Desktop in terms of contact management, calendar management, and the like. What's more, it syncs easily with Palm PDAs thanks to conduits included with most models.

To install these conduits (and other necessary Palm software), insert the software CD that came with your new Palm. When presented with the option to sync with Palm Desktop or Outlook, choose the latter. Eventually the installer will instruct you to perform your first HotSync. When that's done, you'll see that all your data has been copied from Outlook to your PDA. Future HotSyncs will keep both sides synchronized.

> **TIP** *Even if you choose to sync your Palm with Outlook, you might need to run Palm Desktop (which gets installed regardless) for access to specific features. For instance, Outlook doesn't enable you to copy photos to your device—that function requires Palm Desktop.*

17

Option 2: Switch to Palm Desktop

If circumstances dictate that you sync your Palm with Palm Desktop instead of with Outlook (perhaps your company is reclaiming your Pocket PC, and Outlook along with it), have no fear—you can transfer everything in just a few steps. Here's the breakdown: Pocket PC to Outlook, Outlook to Palm PDA, and, finally, Palm PDA to Palm Desktop.

Because you'll be relying on Outlook as the go-between in the Pocket PC-to-Palm migration, synchronize your Pocket PC one last time to make sure that Outlook contains the most current data.

> **TIP** *Before going any further, you should also make a backup of your Outlook data. Scan your hard drive for the file called Outlook.pst, then copy it to another folder (such as My Documents) or some kind of external storage device.*

Close Outlook, then insert the software CD that came with your Palm PDA. Follow the installation instructions, making sure to select the "Synchronize with Outlook" option when it appears. (Note that in newer versions of the installer, the option reads, "Sync with both Microsoft Outlook and Palm Desktop." See the Tip in the previous section for an explanation of why.) Don't worry—this is a temporary move. A few steps from now we'll get you syncing with Palm Desktop as promised.

Eventually the installer will instruct you to perform your first HotSync. Doing so will copy all the data from Outlook to your Palm PDA. Don't stop there, however—make sure to complete the installation of the Palm software before continuing.

Once you've verified that all your Outlook records now reside in your Palm PDA, it's time to change the latter's sync setup. Reinsert the Palm software CD and select the option to reinstall the software. This time through, choose "Synchronize with Palm Desktop."

> **NOTE** *With some newer Palm models, reinserting the software CD will present you with a list of "discovery" options, including "Change your synchronization method." If you see this option, click it and follow the instructions. It'll switch the HotSync conduits from Outlook to Palm Desktop in just a few seconds. And no reboot is required!*

After this second installation (or conduit switch, if your model supports that option), all that remains is to HotSync your Palm again. When it's done, all the data originally stored in Outlook will now reside in Palm Desktop. Now you can uninstall Outlook, if necessary, and sync normally between your Palm PDA and Palm Desktop.

Troubleshooting Audio Hiss

Take one Palm book author, add a Palm TX, throw in a 4GB memory card stocked with MP3s, and you've got yourself one happy camper. Or so Rick thought, until he plugged his favorite headphones into his handheld. Before the music even started playing, he heard a very distinct hiss. And although it was diminished somewhat when the music kicked in, it was still very noticeable during quieter parts of certain songs. The horror!

This is a known problem on some Palm handhelds, though at press time Palm hadn't addressed it directly. It seems that some models have the problem and some don't—or at least don't have it to such a severe degree. What can you do if hiss is ruining your listening experience? There are a few options:

- **Try different headphones** Rick's beloved Shure e3c in-ear headphones produce the most hiss; unsurprising given that they lodge right next to the eardrum. But switching to more traditional earbuds resulted in considerably less hiss (though less comfort, too). Try a few different pairs if possible. Also, try headphones that have an inline volume control.

- **Exercise your warranty** Because anecdotal evidence suggests that not all Palms exhibit the hiss problem, you can try getting your unit replaced under warranty. Of course, if it's less than 30 days old, you might be able to return it to wherever you bought it.

Replacing a Dead Battery

After a couple years, your Palm's battery will probably start to fail. It might die outright, or it might not last as long between charges. Either way, you're probably thinking this means it's time for a new PDA. Wrong! You can actually replace the battery, though you need to be handy with a few tools. See Chapter 16 for more information on buying and installing a new battery.

Upgrades

If you're like Dave, you're probably a little obsessed with having the latest and greatest of everything: gotta have the latest Palm, the latest version of the OS, and the fanciest wetsuit. This section helps you manage the increasingly common step of migrating from an old PDA to a new one.

Upgrading from an Old Handheld to a New One

To those of you still living with a Palm V, we salute you. But when you finally decide you're ready for a nicer screen, more memory, and a bunch of cool accessories that won't work with your old model, we'll be here for you. Specifically, we're here to help you make the move from an older handheld to a new one—an increasingly common task these days, now that the devices have been around for so many years.

Unlike upgrading to a new PC (which requires an obnoxious amount of effort), upgrading to a new PDA is shockingly easy. The following list describes the process in a nutshell.

TIP *Before you perform step 1, take the time to "clean out" the old handheld by deleting applications and data you're no longer using. This is especially true if you're running any hacks. They won't get along with Palm OS 5, so disable them and then delete them. Pitch the old hack manager as well. The end goal here is to avoid transporting old, unnecessary, and potentially incompatible stuff from the old device to the new one.*

17

1. Do one last HotSync of your old PDA.

2. Unplug the old cradle (making sure to turn off the PC first if it's a serial cradle).

3. Install the Palm Desktop software that came with your new handheld. It should detect the presence of the older version and proceed accordingly. Don't worry—all your data will be preserved!

4. HotSync your new handheld. When you do, a box appears listing your username from your old model. Click it, and then choose OK. This will restore all your data.

Most of your third-party applications will be reinstalled along with your data, but a few might not. Thus, you might have to manually reinstall some programs. At the same time, you might have to re-enter registration codes for any software you've paid to unlock. Don't be surprised to find that some older programs aren't compatible with your new model. C'est la vie! There are probably newer versions that work faster, look nicer, and so on.

TIP · *If you plan to continue using the old PDA on the same machine (or perhaps pass it down to a family member), make sure to hard-reset the device and choose a new username (upon the first HotSync) to avoid HotSync conflicts.*

Upgrading the OS

Sorry, Charlie. (You're not Charlie? What are you doing with Charlie's book!) It's impossible to upgrade the OS in most Palm OS handhelds. However, your device manufacturer may issue "patches" (software updates) designed to fix problems or add features, so check its Web site periodically.

Where to Find It

Web Site	Address	What's There
PalmGear	www.palmgear.com	Loads of Palm OS programs
Palm	www.palm.com/support	Support and extended warranty programs for Palm-branded PDAs

Index